I0759338

OLLY

Race, Class, and Gender in the Invention of a Rustic Modernity

Patricia Reinheimer

OLLY

Race, Class, and Gender in the Invention of a Rustic Modernity

Patricia Reinheimer

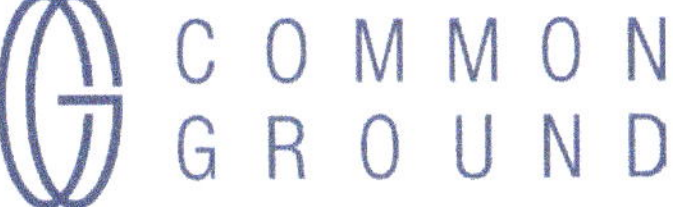

First published in 2020
as part of the Communication and Media Studies Book Imprint
http://doi.org/ 10.18848/978-1-86335-209-3/CGP (Full Book)

Common Ground Research Networks
2001 South First Street, Suite 202
University of Illinois Research Park
Champaign, IL
61820

Library of Congress Cataloging-in-Publication Data
Names: Reinheimer, Patrícia, author.
Title: Olly : race, class and gender in the invention of a rustic modernity
 / Patricia Reinheimer.
Description: Champaign, IL : Common Ground, 2020. | Includes
 bibliographical references. | Summary: "This is a story about a weaver,
 Olly Reinheimer. Through the trajectory of her life and work, we can see
 that freedom and subalternization are not necessarily opposites. In the
 1960s, her name became synonymous with art and fashion. She mixed
 various other techniques, such as sewing, painting, embroidery, and
 etching. She also worked in dimensions beyond clothing, such as the
 production of handmade paper. Her production in fabrics circulated
 mainly in Rio de Janeiro, São Paulo, Belo Horizonte and Curitiba (and
 some Latin American countries) and was presented in museums and
 galleries dedicated to exhibiting Modern Art. Until the end of the
 1970s, the things produced by this artist were associated implicitly and
 explicitly with modernity, tropical nature, feminine sensuality, and
 being Brazilian. Although her work was briefly popular, she quickly
 slipped into oblivion after her death and therefore little is known
 about her today. Thus, this work presents her artistic trajectory and
 outlines her role in developing a decorative style particular to
 domestic spaces inhabited by a new intellectual middle class in the
 1960s and 1970s in Brazil. Moreover, her story also avails itself to a
 feminist reading about the role of textile production and decorative
 arts in the process of institutionalizing design in Brazil"-- Provided
 by publisher.
Identifiers: LCCN 2020017221 (print) | LCCN 2020017222 (ebook) | ISBN
 9780949313362 (hardcover) | ISBN 9781863352086 (paperback) | ISBN
 9781863352093 (pdf)
Subjects: LCSH: Olly, 1914-1986. | Textile artists--Brazil--Biography. |
 Women artists--Brazil--Biography. | Art and
 society--Brazil--History--20th century.
Classification: LCC NK8898.R46 R45 2020 (print) | LCC NK8898.R46 (ebook)
 | DDC 746.092 [B]--dc23
LC record available at https://lccn.loc.gov/2020017221
LC ebook record available at https://lccn.loc.gov/2020017222

T ABLE OF C ONTENTS

Dedication

In 2013, Erika Hasenberg published a children's book with stories she invented. The title "Raconta ancora"[1] was a tribute to the family children. The first story was invented for her nephew, René Reinheimer, in the 1940s. When she gave me a copy, the last time we were together in 2014, she proudly said, "he always asked me to tell him the same story over and over". The book turned out to be a tribute to the children in her life including me, as I asked her so many times to tell me the family story again and again. I dedicate this work to her (in memoriam) who told and lived part of the stories here described.

I also dedicate it to my parents, Ivone and René, heirs of Olly and Werner's artistic and social abilities.

And above all, to Olly and Werner, who carefully archived themselves allowing me to reencounter and unfold them.

---

[1] It means "tell me once more time" in Italian.

Let us consider first of all, the radical and necessary heterogeneity of an inheritance, the difference without opposition that has to mark it [...] an inheritance is never gathered together, it is never one with it itself. Its presumed unity, if there is one, can consist only in the injunction to reaffirm by choosing. "One must" means one must filter, sift, criticize, one must sort out several different possibles that inhabit the same injunction. And inhabit in a contradictory fashion around a secret. If the readability of a legacy were given, natural, transparent, univocal, if it did not call for and at the same time defy interpretation, we would never have anything to inherit from it.
(Jacques Derrida, *Specters of Marx*, 1994)

How much time does a person's biography have?
(Virginia Woolf, *Orlando: A Biography*, 2014)

ACKNOWLEDGEMENTS

This book is the result of the research "Olly and Werner Reinheimer: fashion, art and politics: From the personal archive to the national patrimony", approved in two different Brazilian development institutions and its edicts, CNPq Universal research funds in 2013 and Faperj's Young Scientist of Our State in 2015. I thank those foments, without which it would not have been possible to organize the collection and carry out much of what I present here. And also thank, Maria Lúcia Bueno's partnership, especially in the project's beginning.

Luiza Macier, Michelle Kauffmann and Marcia Bibiani's receptivity was essential and also Maria do Carmo Rainho's opinion regarding the submission of the collection to MOW-Brazil (MEMORY OF THE WORLD OF BRAZIL) was a contribution to the understanding of archiving processes.

I must also mention the Berlin Jewish Museum and the Pforzheim Hotel that opened their doors to me, allowing me to record interviews in their interiors in 2014. Michaela Metz was essential for mediating the contact with these institutions, as well as making possible some the interviews in Germany.

In my institution, the Universidade Federal Rural do Rio de Janeiro (UFRRJ), I would especially like to thank my Department and the Postgraduate Program (PPGCS) colleagues for the approval of leaves of absence that were fundamental for the accomplishment of the fieldwork outside Brazil and for the writing of the book. Even with all thematic, disciplinary and personal differences sharing the professional life with these colleagues, and especially with the colleagues in the field of anthropology, makes the wear and tear of academic life and current productivity requirements a little less cumbersome.

I am grateful to Angela Heider and Monika Schmidt and to Luiz Edmundo Moraes for mediating my contact with them, all of which great historians who helped me with the German dimension of the research. Thanks also to Fábio Koifmann for the innumerable searches of people and information in his files and for indicating Olly and Werner Reinheimer's archive to be part of the Casa de Stephan Zweig's digital format archive.

I would also like to thank the research groups "Todas as Artes, Todos os Nomes", NIEM (Interdisciplinary Group for Migration Studies) and CULTIS (Research Group on Culture, Identity and Subjectivity), the Sociology and Anthropology Art Discussion Group at the Brazilian Antropology Association (ABA) and the Discussion Group on collections at the National Association of Post-Graduate Programs in Social Sciences (ANPOCS), the discussion and research group of the Universidade Federal do Rio de Janeiro (IFCS), and also to Andrea Roca and Nuno Porto for the seminar organized at the Escola de Altos Estudos Brasileiros. In all these spaces I had the possibility to present parts of the work and listen to suggestions and criticisms that added density and pointed out ways that enriched the process and, hopefully, the final work. I owe them all sincere thanks.

A special thanks goes to Ana Paula Alves Ribeiro who participated body and soul in several stages and in various ways, from the most professional to the lending of a friendly shoulder in the hours of despair. And also, for her precious indications: João Xavi, Luiz Guilherme Guerreiro and Rafael Mazza who produced beautiful images that will one day become a film.

Also, to Miriam de Oliveira Santos and Nathanael Araújo for the careful readings and precious suggestions for the final text. Ilana Goldstein contributed particularly to the second chapter, sharing her still unsystematic impressions on the idea of "indigenous art" today. And Ana Paula Simioni who generously shared sold-out publications so that I could have access to essential material for the construction of the last chapter.

To Paola Terranova for having made available the Franco Terranova collection, lending books and documents, even before the end of the organization and systematization of the material.

To Nedra Westwater, both for the interview in her home, as for sending the excerpts where she recounts meetings with Olly and Werner in her still unpublished memoir.

To Betty White and Stephen Strauss. From everything we have built over the years, the most exciting thing was to discover them living in Toronto just as I was attending a congress in the city. The dinner we were able to share, exchanging memories, and the set of letters sent by Olly and Werner throughout the 1970s that was handed to me, was undoubtedly one of the magical moments of this research.

Gustavo Silva Saldanha and Maria Cristina Volpi for having indicated the incredible organizers of the collection, Juliana Taboada, Regina Verly, Carolina Morgado and Jessica Serbeto Baldez de Souza who were responsible for a Herculean task which they conducted with extreme competence.

Several other people were also essential in this process for many reasons and I can not fail to mention them. In alphabetical other they are: Alexandra Tsallis, Ana Cristina Maciel (and Marcelo), Angela Mega, Brigitte Brändle, Carlos Acselrad, Clementina Duarte, Daniel Bitter, Edith Karla Waitzfelder, Erika Hasenberg, Felipe Reinheimer, Freddy Van Camp, Frederico Morais, Gerhard Brändle, George Seligmann, Genevieve Boghici, Giralda Seyferth, Heiner Pflug, Heinz Seligmann, Helena Lewin, Hélion Póvoa Neto, Heloisa Helena Santos, Hetty Goldberg, Hilda de Azevedo Soares, Ira Seligmann, Jannyne França de Souza, Jerônimo Morais, Joana Bahia, João Dalla Rosa Júnior, Jonas Bergamin, José Gabriel Correia, Juliana Carapeba, Liane Monteiro, Luiz Guilherme Vergara, Manfred Jöchle, Márcio Acselrad, Maria Aparecida Silva, Mela Pflug, Miriam Juvino, Neila Tavares, Noemi Acselrad, Noni Ostrower, Pamela Silva, Raissa Xavier Pinto, Regina Schmecken, Rene Renato Reinheimer, Ricardo Szpilman, Roney Cytrynowics, Rossela Terranova, Sabine Krussen, Sara Andrade, Stefan Rinke, Thorsten Schmitz, and Wagner Seixas Melo.

Many other people participated in a variety of ways, friends who waited patiently, sometimes impatiently, for my return to a "normal" life. They endured lost commemorations and excuses that certainly seemed insufficient in view of the importance of the events.

To my mother I owe the affectionate support, but also financial participation. Without it, most of what I could develop would not have happened. My father and siblings accompanied interested and shared many memories. This is no small matter.

If returning to artistic doing was one of the ways to revive the past in my body, sharing in the classroom the reading of theorists who contributed to the analysis of materials and practices was the other side of that process. Therefore, a special thanks goes to the students who have been inexhaustible source of inspiration and knowledge with their questions, insights and criticisms.

Many things that are here I wrote with my heart and not with my fingers. But not with less seriousness and analytical investment. I hope I have succeeded in balancing academic objectivity with my passion for the subject and the grandparents. And I also hope the final product, besides content, offers a pleasant reading.

About Socks, Skeins, and Embroidery

"It was still dark when she awoke, as if she heard the sun behind the edges of the night. And then she sat down at the loom. Clear line, to start the day. Delicate dash colored as the light, which she passed between the outstretched wires, while in the brightness of the morning the horizon was drawn." Thus begins "The Weaver Girl", a tale by Marina Colasanti (2004). It is the story of a woman who wove everything she needed, food, clothes. She ended up weaving the time of loneliness. To overcome, she wove a husband. But the man, perceiving the power of the loom, wanted palaces, gaudy clothes, white horses.

She thus saw herself weaving, without rest, to his convenient whims. But without realizing it, she also wove her sadness, the lack of simplicity, of well-being alone. She waited the night, and while he slept, she sat by the loom and began to undo little by little everything she had built. It is about weavers' stories that this book's narrative deals. More specifically about a weaver entangled in another universe of meanings. However, while Colasanti uses the weaving metaphor to speak about female liberty from marriage conventions, Olly's trajectory shows that freedom and subalternization are not necessarily opposites and that the extravagant display of the right to ambiguity is one of the ways in which privileged groups weave new social positions.

In the 1960s, a style in art and fashion began to emerge in Brazil. Olly Reinheimer blended other techniques into weaving such as sewing, painting, embroidery and engraving. In addition to clothing, she also wove fibers from bark, vegetables and even old straw hats when she produced handmade paper. Her production circulated in Museums and Modern Art Galleries in Rio de Janeiro, São Paulo, Belo Horizonte and Curitiba, and also in some Latin American countries. Until the end of the 1970s the things produced by this artist were more and more explicitly or implicitly associated to modernity, tropical nature, feminine sensuality and Brazilianness.

Although her work was highlighted, she quickly slipped into oblivion after her death and therefore little is known about her today. Thus, presenting her trajectory is as important as developing analyzes about the social context in which she participated.

I recover then the course of her social life before entering the artistic field and I also sketch two ways of interpreting the context of her professional trajectory: the role of collecting in the constitution of a decoration style of domestic spaces that structured a middle-class subjectivity in the 1960s and 1970s in Brazil and I offer a feminist reading on the role of *textile production* and decorative arts in the process of design institutionalization in Brazil.

In order to carry out the analysis I take advantage of the definition of *textile production* formulated by the museologist Teresa Cristina Toledo de Paula (2006). This production does not refer to anything wholly or partly produced in fabric or fibers, but it is restricted to objects whose support base is a flexible product resulting from the interweaving of yarns. This definition is broader than fabrics and may incorporate other objects such as weaving made from straw, for example, but restricted enough not to contain things made predominantly from other materials, such as feathers or wood.

The beginning of this investigation is related to the apartment in which Olly lived with her husband a great part of her life. It was photographed for magazines on decoration and mentioned by several interviewees. It shelters today the collection used here for the investigation. Through the reactions among the next generations' relatives, it was possible to follow some transformations in this domestic space that contributed to perceive the conquest, throughout time, of a professional recognition that was mirrored in the house, but to which the organization of this domestic space also contributed to build. Olly and Werner's home made it possible to observe perspectives on gender relations complementary to those apparent in the public space, but also complementary to the valuation of private collecting as a social technology of subjectivities construction and also of a white middle class identity that used objects produced by specific ethnic groups. The things collected were used as reference in Olly's textile production.

This book is the result of a project that aimed to research and organize the documents collection (Figures 1 and 2) of this German Jewish immigrant couple who arrived in Brazil in the mid-1930s. There are two stories that met only after they crossed the Atlantic. They are two people with distinct trajectories, but who were married for 47 years.

There is no intention to deal with both Olly and Werner. If Werner's[2] left-wing political militancy may seem to some social scientists to be more relevant, it was Olly's contribution to art, design, and fashion in Brazil that had the greatest implications for social life's dimensions. Her public life allowed me to follow her movements and ensure a significantly higher amount of information on her, thus constituting her as the chosen axis for the analysis of the organized collection.

---

[2] Since there is more than one Werner in the family, I reserve to Werner Reinheimer the exclusive use of the first name. When I refer to the other one, I will always use the surname Hasenberg. See kinship table in figure 5.

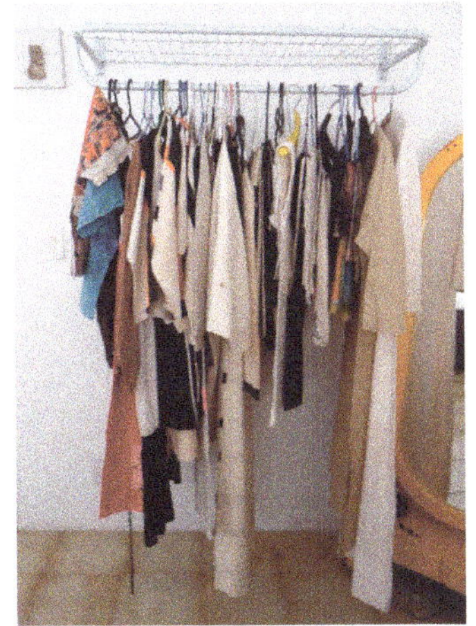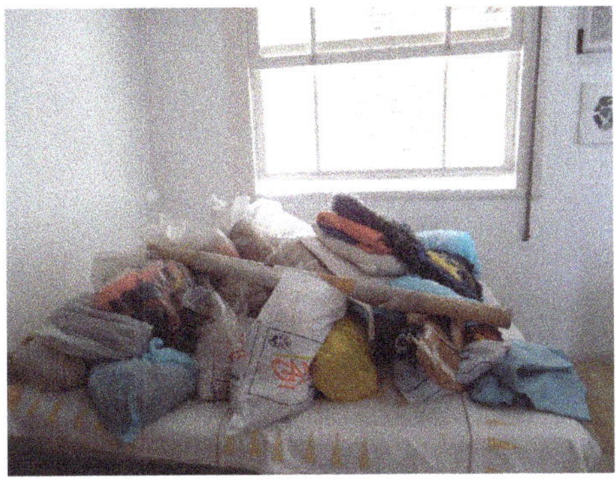

Figure 1: *Olly and Werner Reinheimer's Archive* before organization, 2013.

The readings and discussions on politics, imperialism and colonialism that Werner undertook provided the basis for my understanding of the artist's work. Both Olly and Werner showed a close relationship between politics and art, anthropology and art, art and fashion. But my first interest was to understand and analyze the artist, mobilizing the trajectory and interests of Werner when necessary.

Still, I am speaking of two people in a relationship of nearly fifty years. Therefore, they have mutually constituted one another as they have aged together and continually participated in one another's becoming. This dimension of processual and mutual constitution of the world (Ingold 2011) has different intensities depending on the form, temporality and strength of the relationship. Olly and Werner's marriage had difficulties like any other, but it was also a relationship with mutual influences on their world conceptions and actions. For this reason, to take into account, even superficially, Werner's trajectory and actions helps to understand some of Olly's interests.

Olly was born at the dawn of the twentieth century, daughter of a single mother. She built her financial and social autonomy in a foreign country that became her own. Although she achieved social recognition for both her work and her personality, after her death her name and production were gradually forgotten. Writing this story sheds light on yet another woman who was obscured. I try to minimize the difficulty in finding subsidies to broaden the knowledge about the professionalization of female artists. I offer here data about her life and work. I intend to build another link in the chain that strengthens the recognition of women artists' trajectories and/or a history of women in the field of arts.

But the feminist social and political struggle should not be fought only in the present time of action. It is also about remaining as a symbol of women who helped in the past to build the present, as an example for new generations. Therefore, the gender issue itself must be thought of in its relation to invisibility and recognition in time and space, important dimensions of this struggle.

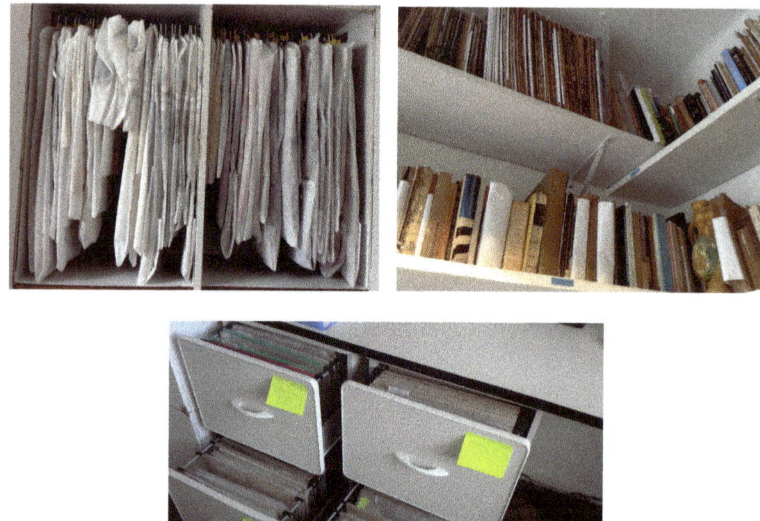

Figure 2: *Olly and Werner Reinheimer's Archive* after the organization, 2018.

One of the advantages of working with an artist around whom a critical fortune has not been built steadily over time is the greater freedom in choosing the perspective through which to analyze her trajectory and production. Thus, instead of investing in the attempt to inscribe her in an art history, the intention is to use her trajectory to understand some processes of constitution of values that conformed the beginnings of a cultural field, that coincided also with the beginning of the institutionalization of design as a profession and the discussion about fashion in Brazil.

Consecrated authors/artists have around themselves a socially constructed image by those who comment on them. Depending on specific weights and positions of their commentators, the comments condition the meanings of their works and the appropriations they suffer over time. These appropriations create representations, usually posthumous, that become recognized within the field, even if they are not always in line with the original propositions of the social actors to which they relate. Taking a character who is marginal to the consecrated "artistic field" (Bourdieu, 1968) and still relatively unknown in the incipient "fashion world" (Sousa, 2012) offers me the freedom of choice as to the approach. This autonomy is at the same time the opposite side of the security offered by interpretations recognized by respected researchers.

I have prioritized to present the historical processes which constituted a certain social entanglement that made it possible to perceive things under a new gaze. The new perspectives renewed classifications which in turn constructed new narratives, social categories and things. This approach was done in opposition to an art history whose emphasis falls upon objects. Olly and Werner were part of this mesh and were woven by it, just as they helped to weave it. This means assuming a certain "methodological philistinism" (Gell, 2005), that is, assuming an attitude of indifference towards the aesthetic value of art works. Olly's work is then observed as an emergent property of the relations between the various elements of the social systems in which it circulated. This is not to say that I have no admiration for her production, but I try not to use my personal feeling to criticize or endorse the value judgments made by her peers.

I try not to take things in an essentialised way or as a result of some *Weltanschaung*, the spirit of time. But I do try to understand the conditions of possibility for the emergence of certain values from a set of people and things that were knots in a social fabric. What the anthropologist Tim Ingold called "fluxes of the medium", the ever-moving, ever-growing world of movement and becoming, woven from the vital lines of its human and non-human components that stitch their way into the tangle of relationships in which they are entangled (Ingold, 2011).

How did Olly and Werner *happen*, what paths did they get through, what marks did they leave? Part of what was used to produce this interpretation is due to my childhood and adolescence memory as the granddaughter of this couple and "heir" of some of their artistic sensibilities, political postures and things. Therefore, it is not a matter of making a certain kind of objective science, since defamiliarization would be impossible to some extent. On the contrary, to understand those people was in part reminiscent of my experiences with clay, paint, glue, paper, cloth, pencil and scissors. It was not a matter of inventing an interpretation, but of taking into account the intimate relationships with the tools, materials, and references used by Olly, Werner, and some of the various other people who crossed their path to understand how they moved over time, what they created and how they impacted their world.

Anthropologists Luiz Fernando Dias Duarte and Edilaine Gomes discuss the work with their own families using Marilyn Strathern's argument. She defends as the fundamental criterion of anthropological research the search for the knowledge of the original sense of the experiences in their difference with the sense that "we" ourselves give them (2008: 27). Knowing Olly and Werner in their context is not the same as talking about my grandparents, although having shared life with them has offered me a privileged place from which to observe them.

As I was drawing on the studio table, helping to collect soil to make paint, picking seeds, or producing the string and wool yarns for Olly's weavings, I was an active witness to her energy and creative improvisation (Ingold, 2007). Unable to sit down to watch television or have a conversation without a basket of threads and needles and a cloth in her hands, it seemed that it was the practice that produced energy and vigor in that white-haired, jovial-looking lady. In the apartment in which they lived in the last decades of their lives, the colored fabrics drying around several rooms sometimes gave way to the threads that were spread on the spinning wheel or used in her enormous loom. Other times, these vivid colors were exchanged for the neutral tones of paints made of earth or craft paper. The latter occupied the physical space that earlier belonged to the threads and fabrics, the sound of the blender replaced the classic music in the phonograph, almost always chosen by Werner. Whatever the activity, Olly's round body was constantly moving back and forth between the rooms of the apartment.

How could I overcome the loss of these grandparents? According to philosopher and anthropologist Vinciane Despret, we are practically the only culture that thinks that "when people die, they are dead" (2010), sliding the meaning between the first and second part of the sentence. However, the dead actively resist oblivion.

To carry out this project with a multi-location team, I opened an account on a cloud data storage system with an email on behalf of Olly Reinheimer. To get more space, I sent invitations to my address book and received back a single reply:

"Who are you?"

I explained what it was all about. The answer had come from someone who had met Olly in the 1980s. When I met this person, he joked, "I thought iGod[3] had finally been invented to communicate with the beyond". This anecdote speaks of the power of things, including technologies, in transforming realities, confusing times, and shuffling spaces.

Olly and Werner are present in the numerous objects distributed throughout their home and around the world. Everyone who had been in their apartment in Rio de Janeiro inquired about the forest they had grown in the living room. That's how they invented their return. They screamed from inside the drawers, from the cracks in the

---

[3] The reference here is to communication gadgets such as iPad, iPhone, iCloud etc.

clubs and from the pages of the books. They broke furniture and invoked ghosts. And it is in response to this claim that I present this work.

The stimulus to concretize this research project and reconstitution of their trajectories is due in large part to these things and their effects on me and other people (who have been present in the lives of the protagonists of this story or who have had contact, with their legacy). After Olly's death, the artist's studio in the couple's apartment in Ipanema was kept almost unchanged, although Werner, who continued to reside there, had sold many of the art works and collections she had accumulated. After Werner's death, the son and the grandchildren maintained the same conduct toward the house and the things that told the couple's story.

Both of them died in this apartment. The last time I hugged Olly, her body was still warm, lying in the room where I wrote parts of this book. Paraphrasing Duarte and Gomes, the apartment "veiled their bodies" (2008: 182). This dwelling was at once a place of artistic creation and death, two opposing forces in temporal terms, beginning and end, but similar in their relation to sacredness. The couple's domicile appears as a family temple in which objects are relics (Heinich, 2009) that should not be desecrated. Temple of creation and finitude, the apartment is an entity, sign and meaning.

On the couple's centennial anniversary three descendant generations met there and commented on what had changed in terms of structure and objects[4], as well as the relationships they had with these things, past stories and present wishes. The objects' evocation power, their insistence on the occupation of space, and recollection of times and affections led to this investigation.

If we assume the indistinction between objects and people proposed by sociologist Nathalie Heinich (2009) and think the notion of personhood as a function and not an essence, objects and their bodies fulfill this function through their capacity to motivate the presence of those who one day possessed them. Bodies then refers to both the objects and the people that are recollected. What existences are then inscribed in these bodies?

What bodies are those inscribed in the present? What circumstances got them there? Which relationships mediated those circumstances? From Germany to Brazil, Brazil to Peru, Italy, Greece, Spain, the USA and back to Germany and Brazil. So many paths could be counted. I suggest here an "archeology of domestic relics" (Perrot, 2011), trying to understand through the material culture the trajectories of these two social actors, but also the meanings of these objects through their trajectories. This approach demands us to remember that the archaeological work

---

[4] Aware of the debate on the meanings of "object" and "thing" (Ingold, 2010, Brown, 2001, Latour, 2000), I use the two terms here in the sense given to them by Ingold and Brown. I do not take the notion of object as something to be inflated with agency from the intentionality of its producer, but from social life traversing all things perceived by following the lines along which social webs are built and trajectories of people and things happen. The term object is then used as a synonym for thing, in an attempt to escape the tiresome repetition in reading the text.

always depends on the traces preserved and therefore it is always marked by blind spots.

Possessing these things is an affirmation of membership, not to the event but to the prestige generated by the event. This "origin narrative" raised by things is in fact a genealogy, as suggested by sociologist Thorstein Veblen, as well as anything that shows that wealth has been in the family[5] for generations. The function of the heirlooms (which means both inheritances and looms) is to weave, through narratives, a meaning of blood relations at the expense of history and causality (Stewart, 1993).

The first people interviewed exclaimed, "I still have a towel Olly made for my mother. We gave it to my son and daughter-in-law!", "That banana tree still exists?", "Do you still have the pre-Columbian pieces?". If the stories of these objects refer to Olly and Werner's trajectory, their individual trajectories are connected to diverse collectivities, historical and social contexts; they speak of collective values; morals and behaviors. It is these boundaries between individual and collective memories that we take most advantage of, but that is also where we need to be vigilant and understand how our stories are part of the stories of others.

The relationship between individual and collective memories are variable according to the scale of what is remembered. The reconstructions of our memories often go through demarcated lines outlined by the memories of others. New memories enrich the previous picture being appropriated as part of our original memories. We then have difficulty distinguishing our memories from others incorporated through stories, photos, documents, etc.

The objects through which we tell stories are also enriched by the interpretations of other people. Erika Hasenberg, Olly's sister, told me their mother had a box where she kept her memories. Like her, we all have our "chests". At the age of 86, Erika transformed hers into a book called "The Chests" (Hasenberg, 2012), where she tells her life story. Through the objects we keep in our chests we recount stories and reinvent ourselves. Thus, this research recounts and reinvents not only Olly and Werner, but all of those who participated in this process of recollection and invention of the couple as well as themselves. It also reinscribes me in my family's framework as well as in my professional field.

Even people who have accurate information about dates and addresses and who therefore seem reliable in terms of the fidelity of their memories reinterpret stories according to new experiences. Some interviewees recalled the past from diaries maintained over the years. Due to their writing in the heat of the moment, diaries are quite reliable in terms of dates, places and names, although the interpretation of events may vary.

---

[5] I use the notion of family as defined by Duarte and Gomes, that is, "a cut in a network of relational memberships so defined from a particular ego or domestic unit" (2008: 161) that here is always Olly and/or Werner.

Having made an initial investigation into Olly's trajectory in 1998 and returning to it in 2014 I experienced some situations in which the stories were recounted in modified versions. Sometimes interviewees brought as part of their lived memory something that had been added by me in the course of the 1998 research project. I present here the versions that seem most reliable after crossing data. The collection of documents, videos and audios is a rich source, and from it, other versions can certainly be told.

The more personal the memories, the more unstable they are. In this sense, archives are important sources of speech production and stabilization. *Olly and Werner Reinheimer's Archive* was initially solely Olly's *project*[6]. In a manuscript, she explicitly speaks about "my archive" as the place where one could find certain information. This file can be interpreted as yet another attempt to legitimize her artistic work and give visibility to her image, giving meaning to her trajectory and materializing her investment. Werner also accumulated a few things, but although they were all in a box (letters, photographs, and documents), unlike Olly's case, it did not seem to have the sense of a systematized memory implicit in the term archive.

However, if the act of making the art work is not enough to guarantee its historicization, neither is the "archival gesture" (Lopes, 2017). It is necessary that this gesture goes from the private to the public dimension. The organization of this collection in the form of a public archive, the aim of the project of which this book is a result, is a moment of rearrangement and memory control, enclosing it in a *lieu de memoire* (Pollak, 1992, Nora, 1993).

It is a requirement of CONARQ - National Council of Archives (acronym in Portuguese) to systematize the trajectory of the organizers of the archive as a way of justifying its relevance. It is in this game of selection and organization of the remnants of the past in a systematic account that turns the archive into a place of memory. Organizing this archive engenders itself Olly and Werner's story, crystallizing it, governing it, controlling it in a laboratory where memory is built. In this sense we can think of memory as a space of disputes where symbols are reified, and parts of the past are strategically arranged to elaborate a synthesis. This place of memory is a way of inserting Olly and Werner's individual trajectories into a larger plot. In this place we cross data, visualize memory through photos and artistic creations and fabricate abstract, standardizing relationships, but also contribute so that it does not get lost in time, offering subsidies for revision by other people and new approaches.

Regarding temporality, testimonies and documentary research challenge contiguities. Just as people tell their memories in a pendular movement that goes back and forth between past and present the investigation in documents transits between

---

[6] When I use the word *project* in italics, it concerns the individualization process whose stability and continuity depends on the symbolic and political efficacy of social actors in establishing a convincing, coherent and rewarding definition of reality (Velho, 2003). In the case here developed, this *project* was related, among other things, to the process of building a professional identity, a *career*.

noncontiguous spaces – *"the Italian orange I first tried in Germany (1930s). In fact, I just bought it last week (in Italy, 2014), although it is off season"*[7]. The organization of these memories in systematic reports is then a cut and paste of information obtained from comings and goings to different places and times and, in this sense, an arbitrariness that leaves aside some possible poetic associations. But it is this pendular movement that defies the senses (and the physics), which reinvents the meanings of the teller and the story told.

Memory is in part articulated by individuals in relation to their membership and life experiences. When we decide to investigate the past, we set in motion people and groups with different investments, interests, tastes, and desires. In the organization of *Olly and Werner Reinheimer's Archive*, their trajectories were composed of the memories of people scattered throughout the world and with quite distinct stories, although all of them have more or less close ties with experiences of migration and artistic manifestations.

These people spent time with the couple 30, 40 and even 80 years ago, with all the gaps and reconstructions that it entails. Throughout the life cycles of the couple, two Great Wars took place or, according to historian Eric Hobsbawm, 31 years of world conflict, between the Austrian declaration of war to Serbia, July 28th 1914, and the unconditional surrender of Japan, August 14th 1945 and a socialist revolution that destroyed much of the history of German citizens. Today, German archives are largely composed of documents kept by individuals. This period also deeply transformed Russia. Both, Germany and Russia, were the Blank and Reinheimer families' countries of origin.

Olly is the pseudonym of Olga Helene Blank and the name through which she was recognized in the Brazilian artistic world in the 1960s and 1970s. To speak of her trajectory is also to speak of the subjective transformation implicit in her name changing. Without abandoning her past, Olga invented a new future. The notion of *retrospective notoriety* coined by anthropologist Mariza Corrêa (2005) can help to understand how an acquired renown can shed new light on one character's past and overshadow another. In the case analyzed here, the artist's recognition contributes to illuminate contrasts and similarities with the actions of other characters of the cultural field of the period, indicating how some representations happened because of the tracks followed by these people. But this notoriety also helped overshadow her husband's trajectory, which, however, is essential to understanding some of the artist's choices.

Werner had an important role in accompanying her in this invention. Accustomed as we are to finding stories in which women give up their dreams to accompany their husbands, we see them both walking side by side, one supporting the other. But in the second half of the 20th century Olly was the main protagonist of a plot that Werner

---

[7] Excerpt of Erika Hasenberg's testimony talking about Germany in the 1930s and Italy in 2014. The words were not exactly those, but the idea of the pendulum in time and space were there.

would have lived differently had it not been for his wife's professional success. This does not make him a coadjuvant, but a fundamental ally for the mutual reconstruction of their subjectivities. The critique of the erasure of women when talking about the trajectory of male personalities makes it urgent to show the collective process of social life. This also includes talking about Werner's social universe and its importance for Olly to have *happened* the way she did.

The trajectories of Olga Helene Blank and Werner Siegfried Reinheimer began in Russia and Germany before they were born. Their births and deaths followed the brief twentieth century (Hobsbawm, 2005) almost to perfection, from 1914, when the first Great War was declared, to 1991, with the reunification of Germany and the dissolution of the Soviet Union. The difference in the quantity and quality of information available about each one of them and of their families is due in part to the fact that Olly has become an artist, which means that at least the professional part of her career is well documented, and her memory cultivated through the objects she has produced and an extended circle of relationships which nourishes itself in part from that memory. This difference regards also her sister's interest about the family history and her ability to retell in vivid detail this story in video, letters and e-mails; and also testimonies written by the artist during the last year of her life, when she was physically weak and unable to work.

From Werner Reinheimer, on the contrary, discretion was required. His active political participation in the first two decades of his life in a country that was heading for a Nazi system, forced him to take refuge in Brazil. When he arrived there, this country was living under a dictatorship that lasted until 1945 and, after a brief interregnum, entered another one, in 1964. His left-wing political positioning, as well as his nationality and ethnic identity demanded discretion. Werner also left us no testimony of himself except some letters exchanged with his friends after Brazil's redemocratization and the fall of the Berlin Wall, that is, written in the last years of his life. Nor did I find any member of his family who could clarify about his past. What we have of this family branch is then a knowledge based on documents, some assumptions, testimonials given by his son, a few friends and testimonies given to the historian Gerhard Brändle that resulted in the publication of books and an exhibition on the political group in which Werner was a part.

Werner left few articles he wrote about his arrival in Brazil and specific contexts. He also left markings in a book (Brändle, 1985) on the Jews of his city. His family is mentioned there. He underlined several passages. The marked information was like a way through which I followed the story that he literally underlined.

Perhaps the greatest sadness during the research was to arrive at the city where he was born only to find out that the family of a former colleague of political activism in the 1930s would not allow me to interview his dear friend (figures 3 and 4). I was prevented from having access to the only person capable of speaking about Werner's formation and youth and his personal history which he certainly told during the various trips he made to Germany in the 1960s and 1980s (in which he stayed in this family's house).

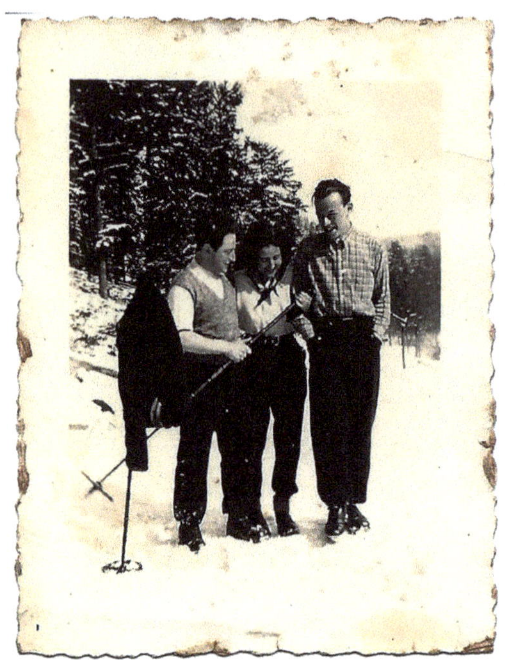

Figure 3: Werner, Klara and Karl Schroth, Germany, 1930s.

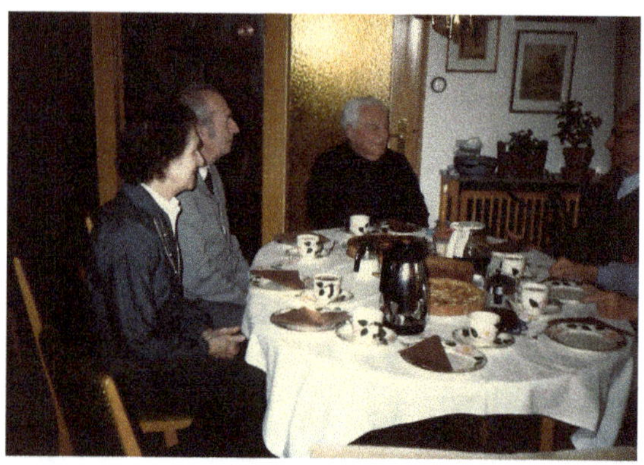

Figure 4: Werner, Klara and Karl Schroth and Bob Zental in Germany (1980s).

I can only try to interpret this family posture, since there was no explanation. As can be seen from the collection, Klara and her husband, Karl Schroth communicated with Werner until 1992, upon his death. It was an intense relationship maintained over 60 years. I was questioned why I contacted the family through a local historian who recovered the history of the political group in which the Karl Schroth and Werner participated. The Schroth's family annoyance led me to imagine that perhaps some interpretation or action around that story may have displeased the members of that family. But that's just a guess.

Some authors have already drawn attention to the role of women in the systematization of family trajectories (Duarte and Gomes, 2008). So far, I have shown how women in all families have taken the lead in systematizing, controlling and disseminating family memories. Throughout the book it will appear the names of incredible women who have helped in some way to enrich this research: Erika and Monica Hasenberg, Noni Ostrower, Edith and Monica Waitzfelder, Paola Terranova and even those who have controlled and prevented access to family histories such as the Schroth's.

Perhaps part of the imbalance of information regarding the Reinheimer couple is related to the presence of so many women in Olly's family, as opposed to the absence in Werner's. Erika's memory is founded on a constant storage and systematization of information ranging from photos and letters exchanged by her ancestors to written and lifelong journals and also on family investigations intended to pass this story on to her daughter (figure 5).

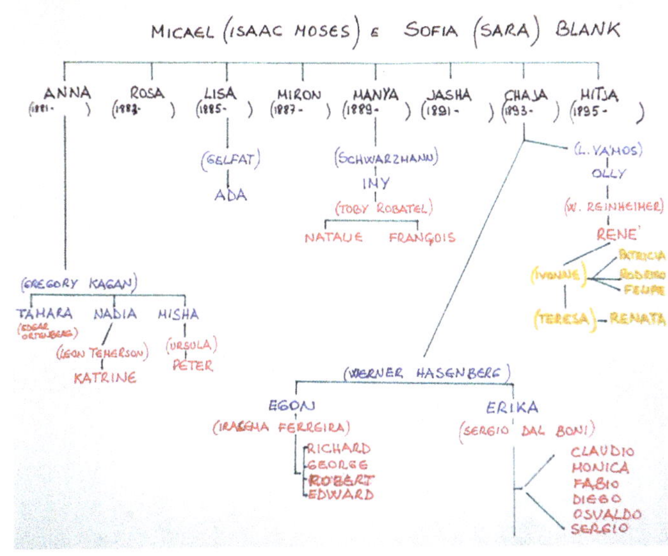

Figure 5: Family tree of the Blank-Hasenberg family by Erika Hasenberg (MI-39).

In the week we spent together in 2014, Erika told me that motivated by the interest of her daughter Monica she listened to her mother's stories as I was listening to hers. Aware of her role as a guardian, Erika declared to be "the last historical memory of the family and the only one who cared about it (sic)". This was in part a result of the accumulated apprenticeship of feminist movements about the importance of self-construction as a way of giving women another place, a context different from that in which Virginia Woolf (2004) wrote. In this story, retold at the beginning of the 21st century, the disproportion of information is in favor to Olly.

The option to treat the couple Olly and Werner as a heuristic unit, although with very different material about each other, refers to believing that besides having spent two thirds of their lives together, the social, ethnic and nationality backgrounds of the two were similar, as was the experience of escape and refuge. This makes aspects of one's life a way to understand dimensions of the other one's trajectory. In addition, I believe that Werner, with his militancy and political ideology, contributed to some of Olly's work's subjects. It may have also facilitated Olly's insertion into a group of left-wing intellectuals who were defining a new order of representations and hierarchies in the period when she was devoted to art.

Some social actors who participated in their web of relations were closer to Werner, but certainly also impacted on Olly's work. Many books in the couple's collection point to interpretations about Olly's performance. Some of those books were certainly Werner's. Thus, although this analysis focuses mainly on Olly's artistic production and her contribution to understanding the formation of new professional fields in Brazil, Werner is always present in between the lines.

The couple's relevance lies in the fact that their trajectories have accompanied intense political climates since the First World War until the reunification of Germany. Between both events, Olga and/or Werner became involved in political militancy groups against German anti-Semitism; they arrived in Brazil during a period of dictatorship in which the administrative elite of the state was sympathetic to Nazism; they approached socialist and communist politicians; witnessed the impact of the Second World War; she entered the artistic field and contributed to the construction and legitimation of a cultural field in which the medium and the message were Brazilian popular and indigenous production and contributed to transformation of representations on middle class women in their professionalization. They lived the civil-military dictatorship in Brazil. He witnessed the return to democracy, the dissolution of the Soviet Union and the reunification of Germany.

They saw that century's dawn and sunset marked by the impact of a Russian Revolution that naturalized the idea of a world defined "by the opposition between "capitalism" and "socialism" as mutually exclusive alternatives, one identified with organized economies based on the USSR model, the other with all the rest" (Hobsbawm, 2005: 14). They also witnessed the legitimacy of the idea of a country formed by ethnic and cultural diversity, interpreted on the one hand as reinforcing the ideology of miscegenation as constitutive of Brazilian identity, on the other, as a way of recognizing the contribution of various minority groups in the formation of a multi-ethnic Brazilian national state. They witnessed too the beginning of a feminist movement in Brazil. Many of the events that took place in this century are indicated in the documents of the couple's archive.

I selected and established relationships between the documents and the statements of those who knew the couple, trying to keep within the factual limits. I tried to verify the statements and authenticate the facts. When it was not possible, I tried to clarify in the text whether it is an inference or an assumption. Perhaps more than in any other of my research projects, it was an intellectual craft (Wright Mills, 1959). Separating, classifying, discovering connections, scanning, photographing, mapping the documents, contacting people, insisting to interviewing them, not always successfully, were some of the activities that this project demanded, and it was with them, along with my memory of the past, that it was possible to construct the interpretations presented here.

When the objects are private property, they are part of situational illusions (Lopes, 2017) and exist within a greatness' regime of affections that makes them participate and inserts them in the daily plot of time, relativizing the moment of creation in face of the new meanings constantly incorporated. This relative erasure of the inaugural moment of the object can be seen by analogy with the natural wear and tear that light and weather conditions impose on things exposed to conviviality. In the preparation of this collection for donation to a preservation institution, the ideal stowing conditions seek to keep the object intact, freezing it in time. However, this crystallization is also the insertion in a new temporal register, in which the senses that are imprinted there are no longer those of the individualized, affective conviviality of family and friends, but of history and its relation to other events, of a collective illusion (Lopes, 2017). An example is the sending of Olly's works' photos to be incorporated into a research on art and fashion of the 1960s and 1970s by the clothing committee of the International Council of Museums (ICOM). It is with consecrated stories already crystallized from specific biases that Olly's work is being constituted as part of a "fashion history in Brazil".

The collection's organization is part of a broader process of building memory places. To a certain extent it is contrary to the relationship I had with the apartment where the couple lived in the last decades of their lives. The organization of this collection was like removing the family memory from the apartment and systematizing it so that the documents could tell a story in other physical and symbolic places. The apartment was previously permeated by the physical and symbolic presence of the couple. It then emptied itself of the elements in which this memory was anchored and it was filled with new objects, new experiences and new stories linked or not to the couple.

Those changes also brought about a change in the affective configuration of the apartment. The fact that every room in the house was no longer *inhabited* by the Olly-Werner couple turned it into a real estate, like any other, also frequented by researchers, archivists and librarians (coincidently, or not, it has been a project done almost strictly by women). The aura of colors, odors, textures, languages, flavors, souvenirs was gradually being concentrated in one of the rooms, where the collection is now. It came to symbolize childhood memories that were previously scattered throughout the apartment, witness to the family life. At the same time, the exchange of messages with people who participated in their life previewed a past to be unveiled.

SOUVENIRS AND COLLECTIONS: INTERIORITY AND EXTERIORITY NARRATED THROUGH THINGS

My interpretations are linked to production in the areas of sociology of art and anthropology of things, from the perspective of the domestic space. I observed how the construction process of a new middle-class *sensibility* was closely related to a renewed perception about the productions of several social groups and the institutionalization of design as a field of professional action. I am interest in perceiving how artistic manifestations contribute for the transformation of social values. The dimension of consumption appeared as an important form of constitution of external universes. The acquisition of things observed along with pronouncements and writings related to the processes of disclosure and supply allowed me to make assumptions on the construction of new forms of perception, categories and social actors.

One of the main axes of this work was a certain sociology of values (Heinich, 2004) that considers aesthetics as one of the possible modalities of qualification of works and/or their authors. In this type of analysis, morality, *sensibility*, economic rationality or the sense of justice are also ways of judging which, however, do not have the same relevance in terms of the proper artistic qualities of a work. In this sense, the positioning of some actors in relation to the figuration-abstraction debate, for example, is the evaluation regarding these multiple dimensions and the attempt to legitimize the aesthetic evaluation as the only one accepted in terms of artistic producers and production[8].

It was in abstract art that the idea of artistic autonomy, based on a discourse that did not take into account the practice of sensitive perception of artistic phenomena (Cf. Campbell, 2010), reached its peak. This form of expression had "the value of a practical demonstration" of the modernist proposals (Schapiro, 1937). The apparent lack of relation to empirical reality made even more conceivable the idea that aesthetic thought and feelings were prior to the represented world. The aesthetic qualities of artistic artifacts came to be measured against new criteria, expressive of an emerging *sensibility* that considered gift in a laicized form as an innate ability of the creator to produce authentic things.

The artistic modernity instituted in Brazil after this debate presented the aesthetic record as being the one that instituted the rupture as a norm. *Freedom* from tradition was then on an obligation of innovation. In the sociology of art, several authors have

---

[8] This relationship between the production of artistic artifacts/actions and their meanings is no longer the same in contemporary art.

already analyzed the notion of *freedom* from different points of reference. Heinich, for example, speaks of the rupture as a new canon by instituting a regime of singularity as opposed to a regime of communality (1991, 1993, 2005). The ideas underlying abstract art penetrated deeply into all artistic theories, even those of its adversaries. The language of absolutes and pure sources, whether of feeling, reason, intuition or the subconscious, appeared even in schools that rejected abstraction. The "objective" painters strove to be "objectively pure", cherishing the "essence" and completeness of their objects, supposedly without a point of view. Surrealists, for example, sought to derive their images from a purely theoretical thought, freed from the perversions of reason and everyday experience (Schapiro, 1937).

One of the main characteristics of this historical period was its a-historicism. The very history of the period was presented as internal, a process immanent to artists. The idea of talent as something innate was potentialized by experiences with "madmen" and children. In Brazil, the psychiatrist Osório César started along this path, but it was Nise da Silveira, another psychiatrist, in partnership with art critic Mário Pedrosa, who paved the way for the values of artistic modernity from the aesthetic experiences among the "insane". In the same period, the Museum of Modern Art of Rio de Janeiro (MAM-RJ[9]) exhibited the results of classes artist Carlos Scliar gave children in Brazil and the USA. Paradoxically, artistic modernism thought art would modify the very reality from which it was detached.

Sociologists Vera Zolberg and Joni Maya Cherbo (1997) analyze this process using the notion of *outsiders*. Groups usually considered external to artistic worlds producing things classified as art. This movement contributed to an opening in artistic hierarchies, but also generated what these authors called *uncertainties*. If these uncertainties as to what would be considered art and how to construct an artistic career in this context can be perceived as the negative dimension of the changes in this universe, *estrangement* is its corollary. Women entering a predominantly male professional field, a urinal considered art when before only oil paintings and bronze and marble sculptures were, are just a few of the boundaries that artistic modernity allowed to break. Admiration, amazement, perplexity at something that is not known or not expected were institutionalized reactions in the Brazilian artistic world after the figuration x abstraction debate. This debate was to a great extent led by art critic Mário Pedrosa, between 1945 and 1960 (cf. Reinheimer, 2014).

Estrangement is in anthropology a presupposition of distancing oneself from the investigated subject so as to perceive it no longer from the norms and values with which the researcher identifies herself. Strangeness is therefore a strategy to see from other perspectives and to produce reflections that situate both what is being observed as well as the observer on a new ground. In anthropology, the conscious attempt to produce a social and psychological distancing is *par excellence* the way for relativizing similarities and differences, generating a state of openness for the

---

[9] Acronym in Portuguese.

production of a knowledge less based on pre-assumptions, in concepts formed in other contexts and applied to what is observed without taking into account the situational particularities.

Among anthropologists there is a certain enchantment for this suspension of values that strangeness should entail. If in its beginnings as a scientific discipline the "others" surveyed by anthropologists were always geographically distant and culturally and socially very different, just after the discipline's institutionalization, the similar ones, or *familiars* (Velho, 1987) were perhaps the main reason for understanding what was at the heart of anthropological knowledge. To strange something is perhaps the best way to discover new things and rediscover oneself[10].

The similarity in the emotional reaction that the encounter with an object of inquiry and/or admiration may cause may also be what justifies renowned art critics and historians such as Hal Foster (2014), Terry Smith (2012) and Hans Belting (2006) to seek understanding in the idea of an "ethnographic turn" in art. This turn is related to an hermeneutic opening that led to postmodernity, or to what has been called "contemporary art". Pretension of universality begun to be questioned as a vision that did not care about what lay beyond the edges of the European world. Fragmentation of experience, the dilution of frontiers once taken as insurmountable, and the difficulty of sustaining any idea of totality are dimensions of what has been called *freedom* in contemporary art.

In my point of view, this artistic *freedom* for which modernity has opened its doors has not been satisfactorily investigated in Brazil. It is often naturalized in sociological and historical investigations on artistic manifestations and their constitutive processes. The idea of contemporary art emerged as a corollary of the expansion of the idea of art to new and varied contexts. The multiplicity of proposals resulting therefrom makes any form of totalization of the very idea of contemporary art seem reductionist. Is every art produced contemporaneously really contemporary? Or is contemporary art a style? For sociologist Nathalie Heinich (1993), contemporary art puts into operation an act that reiterates the artistic values enshrined at the beginning of the twentieth century, that is, transgressing borders and bringing the borders themselves to light, making them visible.

One of the ways of expanding artistic boundaries in Brazil was related to the valorization of peripheral manifestations in ethnic, class, age, gender and rationality terms. The things and people I came across during this research gave me a glimpse of this process. Between the 1950's and 1970's, objects by popular, indigenous, children, and also the "insane" (the latter one barely present in the empirical material) appeared

---

[10] Perhaps that's why important anthropologists and social scientists (Ingold, 2007, 2011, Gell, 2005; Heinich, 1991, 1993, 1998, 2004, 2005, 2009; Bourdieu, 1968, 1996, 1998, 2004; Clifford, 1988, 2003) among many others) have made efforts to overcome the narrowness of seeing only art's elitist dimension and tried to understand how it can also be one of the ways in which to wonder, question and/or reconstruct values.

as signs of this hermeneutical opening in the art produced, exposed and commercialized in Brazil.

My interest, however, was not to work strictly with artistic objects, final products of complex social processes. In an attempt to escape a retrospective analysis (Ingold, 2011), I turned my attention to the formulations of theorists who sought to think the materiality of the world and its materials. Initially, the idea of material culture (Miller, 2009) seemed appropriate, since it seemed to encompass all the things that the couple in question had been given and which were being organized by the project. Little by little, the concept of the materiality of culture and the notion of object (Latour and Woolgar, 1997 and Latour 2000) have gradually been replaced by things and the social lives that emanate from it (Ingold, 2000, 2007, 2011). The processes of production also seemed less important than thinking the people who crossed Olly's path from the perspective of consumption.

Things and consumption are not recent subjects in the social sciences and can be referred to classical authors such as Max Weber, Karl Marx, Georg Simmel, Thorstein Veblen, Franz Boas, Bronislaw Malinowski and Marcel Mauss. However, current visibility began to gain momentum in the 1990s. This visibility is related to issues that anthropologist Johannes Fabian called the "object turn" (2010). For him, this movement was as important as the "literary turn", because it placed museums again at the center of the anthropological debate. Such a "turn" included rethinking practices of memory selection and forgetting, policies of time (Fabian, 1983), each with its own peculiar forms of display (Dias, 1994), sets of relationships and activities around evaluation, collection and exhibition of cultures and histories in museums (Pearce, 1994; Clifford, 2006) and forms of collecting and accumulation (Lopes, 2017). These investigations sought to unravel the polysemic qualities of things and the role of institutions in the processes of attribution of meaning in expository narratives and archival systematizations.

In these new reflections, consumer ideas, narratives and things appeared as complex and socially constructed, expanding the frontiers of inquiry beyond the limits imposed by the economist's perception of an autonomous and sovereign subject. The consumer used to be considered the final stage of the production process and, consequently, secondary. This reductionism made the analysis of consumption restricted to *use value* to the detriment of the social values present in consumer practices (Miller, 1987). These analyzes promoted a moral reading of the practices of consumption (Miller, 2001) perceiving it negatively as loss of identity (in mass consumption) and as a superficial materialism that would be absent in other societies.

In this investigation, consumption was related to sets of things that until then were classified by common sense as crafts or ethnographic objects, but were then reclassified as "folk art", "black art", "indigenous art" etc. inaugurating new fields of artistic practices and discourses. The quantity and the modes of exposure of each of these sets of things instigated me to seek authors who analyzed the idea of collections, souvenirs, and the narratives that constitute them and are constituted by them. Susan Stewart (1993) uses the notions of *souvenirs* and *collections* as metaphors for the construction of interiorities and exteriorities, that is, forms of delineation of the *self* and the world that define and delimit each other.

The author differentiates the two practices. According to her, the *souvenir* contracts, diminishes the world and expands the personal, the *self*. The *collection*, on the other hand, expands the process of commodification through which the narrative of the *self* operates within contemporary consumption society. In the collection labor is transformed in exchange, nature into market. Significantly, the *collection* marks the space of meaning for all narratives, the place where history is transformed into space, into property.

Souvenirs are, for Stewart, a reduction of experience to the dimension of the body. They reduce the public, the monumental, the three-dimensional to the private representation, often two-dimensional, that can be contained or carried by the body. Photography as a *souvenir* is analogous to the flower compressed between the pages of a book, the freezing of an instant and the reduction of dimensions to which corresponds an increase of meanings produced by the narrative. The silence of the photograph, its promise of visual intimacy at the cost of other senses (its possible bright surface that reflects us but prevents our penetration into what's represented) makes the narrative, the story told, even more acute. Over time, the narrative of the photograph becomes nostalgic. Over time all relatives without markings become anonymous, all journeys become the same (Stewart, 1993) (Figure 6).

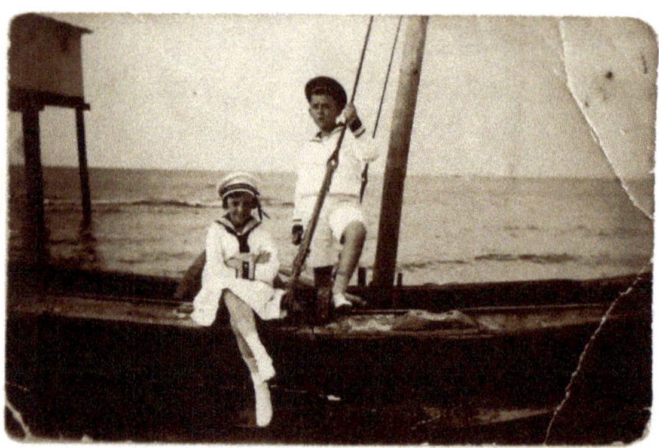

Figure 6: On the back of the photo it reads: "Tamara and Mischa Kaegan?" (PH-1116). The question mark is on the photo and suggests the kids were no longer recognizable and their names were written much later than the photograph was taken.

The creation of such objects depends on fictions and abstractions of the bourgeois *self* in the exchange economy. In capitalism, history presents itself as a commodity. Through narrative, *souvenir* replaces the context of consumption with a context of origin, representing not the lived experience of the producer, but the secondhand experience of its owner, that is, of its acquisition. They are *souvenirs* of a time that no longer exists. And so, a style of decoration of the entire domestic spaces is transformed from production to consumption, the culture as *commodity*, the culture of tourism (Stewart, 1993).

It is a narrative of origin, at the same time of interiority and authenticity, whose object representing it marks the appropriate distance, in time and space, as a specimen, a trophy. The object must at the same time be marked as exotic and strange, but it has to be the result of the direct and immediate experience of its possessor. It is then placed at an intimate distance, space transformed into interiority, into personal space, just as time is transformed into interiority in the case of antiquity. This intimacy with the exotic object is also dangerous (like the magical objects of fairy tales a giant's hair is at the same time what can save the hero, but also kill him). The exotic *souvenir* is then also a sign of survival.

Werner, for example, became, in Brazil, an "other" in relation to Europe, even if he kept himself to death an "other" for Brazilians (his accent was so strong, people joked he spoke German in every language, including Portuguese). The *souvenirs* of his trips to Europe in the 1960s and 1980s are a way of rebuilding his childhood, while at the same time remembering that he was no longer strictly European. Survival, then, is not of the objects, but of their possessor in contexts of unfamiliarity. The otherness of these *souvenirs* speaks of the alterity capacity of the possessor: it is the possessor, not the *souvenir*, that is the curiosity. The danger of the *souvenir* lies in its unfamiliarity, in our difficulty in subjecting it to interpretation. There is always the possibility of meaning getting out of control, causing the object to take control and awaken its ability to destroy.

Most exotic *souvenirs*, however, must be understood from the metaphor of domestication: the *souvenir* retains its capacity for meaning only in a general sense, losing its specificity and eventually pointing to another abstract that describes its possessor. Thus, the object satisfies a nostalgic desire for use value while offering an exoticization of the *self*.

Unlike the *souvenirs* that are exemplary, the collections offer examples, metaphor and not metonymy. According to Stewart, the collection does not call attention to the past, but puts the past in the service of itself. While the *souvenir* lends authenticity to the past, the past lends authenticity to the collection. The collection replaces history by classification, instituting an order beyond temporality. In the collection time is not restored to an origin but made simultaneous or synchronous to the world of the collector. While the souvenir may retain traces of its use value, the collection is the complete aesthetization of this value (Stewart, 1993: 151).

Aesthetization is an art form as a game, reframing objects from the context of their collector. "But unlike many other art forms, the collection is not representational", it presents a hermetic world. "To have a representative collection is to have at the same time the minimum and the complete number necessary for an autonomous world that is both unique and complete, which has annihilated repetition and gained authority" (Stewart, 1993: 152). This world is not, like the *souvenir*, a world of nostalgia, but of anticipation. While the *souvenir* deals with remembrance, with the invention of memory, the collection points to oblivion: to begin again in a way that a finite number of elements create, by combination, a trance, a contemplation.

The substitution of the narrative of production by the narrative of collection, or the narrative of history by the narrative of the collector herself is one of the resources by which the collection is dispossessed of its context and inserted in the context of the classification itself and its collector. For Stewart, "while the *souvenir*'s space is the body (the talisman), the periphery (memory), or the contradiction of the private display (contemplation), the collection's space is a complex play of exhibition and concealment, organization and infinite chaos" (Stewart 1993: 157). In order to be constituted then, the collection must destroy work and history.

All collected objects then become *objects of luxury*, abstracted from their use value and materiality within a magical cycle of self-reference exchange. In consumer society, the collection combines the manufactured and unique object of pre-industrial aesthetics with the post-industrial mode of acquisition: the *ready-made*. This comprehensive formulation of the accumulation process could be used to think about the sets of things Olly accumulated.

However, theories that attempt to account for phenomena universally lose sight of the specificities of the daily practices of social actors. In interpreting the trajectory of people who have accumulated things over time, I came across the difficulty of tracing limits of what would be those things: collections or souvenirs? The only reference to any set made by Olly was in relation to the documents as an *archive* and a generic mention of her collections in a column on her last exhibition which presented sets of stones, shells, glass shards, leaves, and so on (figure 7).

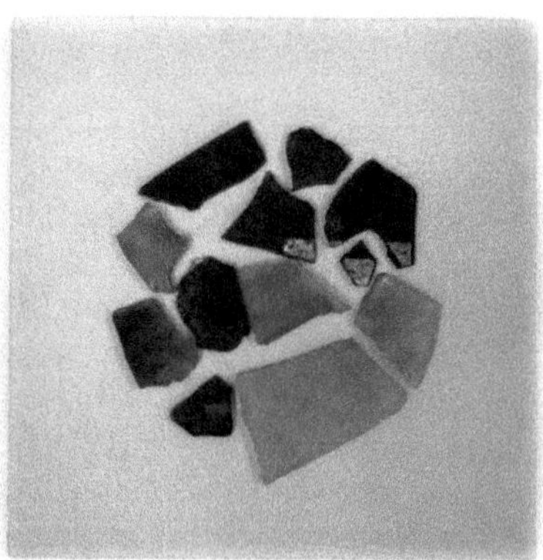

Figure 7: "*Blindex mandala (MAM after the fire)*" was presented at Olly's last exhibition between 1981 and 1983. The exhibition was entitled "Origins: colors, forms and textures".

A set of paraca fabrics was sent to be sold in New York in the 1990s. From that I can deduce that the couple was aware of the exchange value these things could achieve. Even so, there was no symbolic investment in the production of this value, linking things to the trajectory of its collectors, as we will see, for example, with the collections of Franco Terranova. So, if we take Stewart's conceptual formulations to think Olly and Werner's things over, it is possible to think of these accumulations sometimes from ideas tied to *souvenirs*, others to collections. While he was collecting his past, she was collecting her future by inserting herself into the classification that constituted the present. Still, the boundaries between who collected what are not totally clear.

It is also possible to note how the recovery of the couple's trajectory had an impact on the very trajectory of Olly and Werner's heirs. Thus, ethnographic objects, archaeological things, art, jewelry, clothing, among other artifacts, gained new meanings as they entered the domain of *souvenirs*, collecting and/or inheritance. Collection and souvenir, as inheritance or not, and the inheritance of collections or sets of things have transformed the status of objects and people, reorganizing the perceptions that subjects have of themselves and the webs of their existences. Ontogenesis, genealogy, and nationality appeared in this perspective as scales of membership to which these things continually shuffled as they shuffled past, present, and future, fostering alliances, exchanges, and tensions, and connecting generations along the lines that weave the social fabric.

I try to understand the creative processes, circulations and uses of these things in motion and in the process of transformation and resignification emphasizing the value created by exchange or accumulation rather than by labor, and also consumption, rather than production. I try to understand how the social subjects who are the central axis of this research have relied on things to affirm, evoke, subscribe or revise conventional meanings, manipulating cultural senses. It was possible then to think of inheritance, collecting and artistic creation as means of attributing meanings that go beyond the established forms of categorization of the social world, challenging theories that try to comprise the classifications triggered by the actors to include things and people in the same cosmology. All of them being responsible for weaving the social mesh along which they gain existence and meaning.

Investigating transformations over time, with visual and discursive references, contributed to the perception of the changes in taste and the influence that the classification struggles had in the institution of new forms of self-presentation that went through the objects exchanged and consumed: names and things.

Although I have been dealing with Olly and Werner, this is an eminently feminine story. However, it is also important to note the positions occupied by men in these contexts of space negotiation. Therefore, I cannot minimize the importance of her meeting with Werner. But SHE is the axis of the analyses. Olly's trajectory pointed to the importance of women in the process of industrialization of the mid-twentieth century and to the construction of a supposed modernity of white-collar women. This representation of modern women went through the process of adding value to female professionalization by exposing domestic work, not to question it, but to assert women's capacity to accumulate both domestic and professional responsibilities. In the properly artistic dimension, it was the construction of a supposed universal *sensibility* that was, in fact, the production of conventions around representations of subalternized groups as a form of fabrication of subjectivities and class identity. Race, class, and gender appear as inseparable dimensions of this process.

A FLOWER INSIDE A BOOK

Arlette Farge (2009) worked with the judicial archive of eighteenth-century France. She used statements on things that people would not speak about if they were not compelled by the need to stand in the face of coercive power. They are small narrated misdemeanors that provoke a real effect that no printed text do, however original. Rather than coming across a *speech on* or an *account about*, she reports having the naive sense that the file captures what really happened to those people. The fragments of the experience seem covered with clarity and credibility in the archived documents.

Personal archives also spark such an impression. They talk about the life of the accumulator through documents and correspondence sent also by third parties, giving the impression of randomness, of chance. And so, they evoke the impression of allowing the querent to cross the opacity of knowledge and access the essence of things and beings, which justifies its denomination: source. However, as the author recalls, "the archive presumes an archivist; a hand that collects and classifies "(Farge, 2009: 11).

However, a dive into the archive always gives the sensation of the miracle of overcoming death by offering details of a forgotten or unknown past. After the discovery, past the physical pleasure of the vestige, "comes the mixed doubt to the impotence of not knowing what to make of it" (Farge, 2009: 18). The 'proof' of the past, the overcoming of death is not in the 'documents', but in the sensitive testimonies: in a flower stored inside a book or in tortuous traces of stretches underlined in its pages, in small old photo albums that seem to save very particular meanings to the time and space to which they are referred. One does not expect flowers in archives, but when you've met the owner, finding flowers is remembering the pleasure of smelling, naming and walking among the flower beds, making anecdotes about their names and the stories that certain species raise.

It is as difficult interpreting their meanings as it is exciting to encounter those small pieces of testimonies. After all, scientific relevance is not in the granddaughter's affection, but in objective questions posed by anthropological, historical, archivistical, feminist, and the recent fashion investigation fields. How could I equalize, without erasing, the emotion of 'reunion' with the objectivity of scientific inquiry? Arlete Farge called attention to Michel Foucault's discontent in the face of archives. According to the author, Foucault would be aware that analysis cannot say everything about them, but emotions do not satisfy historians (and social scientists) (Farge, 2009: 36[11]).

However, it is in the details that the accumulators of documents lose control over their image. There, they show more than selected documents that relate to an accurate dimension of their lives. How then resolve the tension between presenting all the details, especially those that thrill, and question the set of documents that forms the file? One of the ways to try to solve this is to always remember that the file does not show the people as a whole. Although the sets of documents can be bulky and varied thematically, the file is just the cut of the dimensions that its owner has chosen to save, to be discovered.

Olly's sets of documents concern her professional life. All the letters, passages and photos relating to her personal life were added posthumously, either because her documents mingled with Werner's after her death, or because the way of the research to organize the collection led me to find material dispersed throughout the apartment and the world. Therefore, unlike archivalists' conception of 'organicity,'[12] *Olly and Werner Reinheimer's Archives* were constituted both by the accumulation of documents by their original owners and by the addition, by an anthropologist and granddaugther, of other documents which seemed to contribute to the understanding of the trajectory of these two characters, the context in which they lived and their webs of relationship.

Other archives were consulted to compose part of the picture that was outlined here on the trajectory of both families, Reinheimer and Blank, in Germany. Thanks to the power relations Jews and immigrants were submitted in Germany in the first half of the twentieth century, I could find traces of the possible trajectories of these families. I assumed that Olly and Werner, as children or youngsters, accompanied their parents and close relatives in the address changes that were registered in the municipal archives of Berlin and Pforzheim.

However, in addition to the interest in the trajectory of these Jewish immigrants to Brazil and the possibilities for reflection on the personal archive[13] as an object of investigation, *Olly and Werner Reinheimer's Archives* also offers the chance to take the documents as testimonies of the trajectory of a female-artist in an eminently masculine universe of the mid-twentieth century. Although we know that the 1960s

---

[11] Farge refers to Foucault's article, La vie des hommes infâmes. Cahier du Chemin, n. 29, Jan. 15, 1977, p.13.

[12] The term is used in archivology assuming a certain "naturalness" in the process of accumulating and classifying documents in a file, resulting from actions and activities that generate documents to be classified. The category obliterates the cuts and power relations that suppose the organization of any file.

[13] It is a personal private archive, that is, "papers related to family, civil, professional life and the political and/or intellectual, scientific, artistic production of statesmen, politicians, artists, literati, scientists, etc". (Bellotto, 1991, apud Heymann, 1997). To refer to the set of assorted documents and things accumulated by the couple, I will alternatively use the expressions "personal files", considering that, because they have been accumulated by private individuals, the documents are private (even publicly available) and "Olly and Werner Reinheimer's Archive".

and 1970s were especially important for the white middle-class feminist movement, we should consider the conditions of possibility of a woman who was not married or was the mistress of an occupant of socially relevant positions in a world conducted and controlled by men. To systematize, digitize and make available the collection of this couple is a way of making known the trajectory of this woman, whose contribution, although not mentioned in the institutional Brazilian art history, contributes to the understanding of important dimensions of the formation of a cultural field and the institutionalization of design in Rio de Janeiro.

Misogyny invisibilized the female characters as a way of attributing also to men the share of power and strength that was the part of women in the trajectories of important male characters. Although much of the activities marked as feminine are essential for the conduction of exceptional trajectories, they are usually taken for granted when stories of important characters in artistic, economic, political, and so on fields are told. All glories are meant for men.

Werner's participation is important, but his "superlative" condition as a human being, as his friend Alaíde Pereira Nunes stated, is not sufficient to justify his presence in the research and the presence of the documents he accumulated in the couple's collection. Why treat this collection as a couple archive? Why not take the biographical approach to deal with Olly as a research character and her documents as a collection? Or in another perspective, why not take the Reinheimer-Blank family as an object of investigation? Because it is not a research on family, but it does not fit into a biography either. That is why I treat the couple as a heuristic unit, in which Werner helps to illuminate the dimensions of Olly's trajectory, but SHE is the protagonist.

Olly is torn from the anonymity of the multitude of women who have contributed to the organization of society's dimensions without gaining recognition for it. Many of these women were secretaries, agents, administrators of a personality allowed to be an 'artist', with all the idiosyncrasies that the term denotes, because dimensions such as organization and administration (time, money, family, etc.) were excluded. Olly was secretary, agent and administrator of herself and of others, as suggested in interviews. Her name was not enough to compose the universe that structures the artistic field as systematized in the Brazilian art history. But the organization of this archive redeems her as a socially relevant character insofar as it sheds light on so many other women who contributed not only to the configuration of the artistic and cultural field, but of all the other fields/social worlds that compose the Brazilian society of the mid-twentieth century, preserving its proportions and particularities.

Doing research involves spending a few years looking at the same subject. This necessarily results in identification with its object of study. However, as Farge points out, there are a thousand ways of doing this and one has to make sure that you do not get to the point of:

> "Not recognition of differences, exceptions or contradictions to better highlight the beauty of the initial hypothesis one has long dreamed of

establishing solidly. This blinding symbiosis with the chosen object is, to a certain extent, inevitable, comfortable, and often indiscernible to the one who practices it. Inevitable, because there is no historian who can reasonably say that his choices have not been oriented, little or very, by a dialectic of reflection or contrast with oneself. It would be a lie. Comfortable, because identifying yourself, in any way, brings relief. Dangerous, however, because this play of mirrors blocks the imagination, immobilizes intelligence and curiosity, remaining confined in strict and suffocating ways. To identify oneself is to anesthetize the document and the understanding one can have of it "(Farge, 2009: 72).

It was therefore important to produce a distancing and question my research subjects, not my grandparents, and their trajectories to better understand them. Was Olly an exceptional artist? Yes and no. Everyone who was interviewed in 1998 and between 2014 and 2018 seemed to think so, as they had many positive comments about her generous, cheerful and jovial personality and her innovative and creative work. Yes, because Olly, as an artist, was the most incredible grandmother one could ever want. This cannot be left out in any work, not even an academic one, because if we indisputably agree there is no neutrality, objectivity can only be acquired by methodological systematicity and also by showing the reader the place where one talks about the subject/character researched.

She was also exceptional to Werner, who kept most of her things after her death. On the one hand, because of her ability to accumulate and produce, but on the other, for the value he attributed to what she had accumulated and produced. It was thanks to this admiration that so many things resisted to be organized and investigated. Peter Stallybrass (2008) mentions a series of reports real and fictional of people who got rid of the things left by the death of their loved ones. These people found it easier to deal with emptiness than with the ghostly presence of the dead's things. Werner lived with his wife's things for seven years after her death. Neither the son of the couple nor the grandchildren who lived in their apartment were able to dispose of the memories materialized in the numerous objects.

And no, she was not exceptional. She did not obtain recognition by the field, although, in the reverse economy, the recognition can always happen in the future. In part, this is the expectation of her granddaughter, although the research has been conducted trying to avoid the laudatory tone to her work and her person and with a systematicity that allows the material to shed light on significant social and cultural issues. That does not mean I have no admiration for Olly's work. I find her production absolutely incredible! Let it be clear!

Therefore, what I intend here is not a kind of struggle against the absence of a character whose role can contribute to the understanding of the institutionalization of this cultural field, but the construction of a new *social illusion* of which Olly and Werner can be part. The illusion is not the opposite of truth, nor the synonym of error, but it is itself part of the desire. As Freud put it:

"An illusion is not the same as a mistake, and it is not necessarily a mistake either. Aristotle's view that insects develop from remains was a mistake, and likewise the opinion of an earlier generation of physicians that *tabes dorsalis* was the consequence of sexual excesses. It would be abusive to think these mistakes as illusions. On the other hand, it was an illusion of Columbus to think that he had discovered a new sea route to the Indies. The part of his desire in this error is quite evident. It is characteristic of the illusion that it derives from human desires" (Freud, 2010, 84-5 apud Souza, 2018).

George Perrec (2004) and Vitor Giudice (1999) have created tales that are fictions about building social illusions in the form of collections and works of art. What these two authors point out is that while sciences are obsessed with the idea of "truth", the social world is constituted from a series of inaccuracies, errors, manipulations, and interests that have enduring effects of "truth". Both stories could be considered fakes or exemplary actions in the world of contemporary art. In each case, they would mobilize a series of actors with particular professional actions to confirm, reject, question, condemn and/or absolve their protagonists. Both are like games with their own rules, actors, materials and results with influences in their own universes. In this sense illusions have practical value, utility.

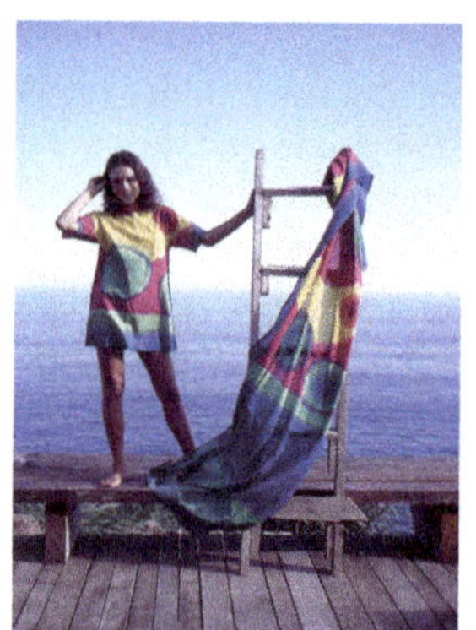
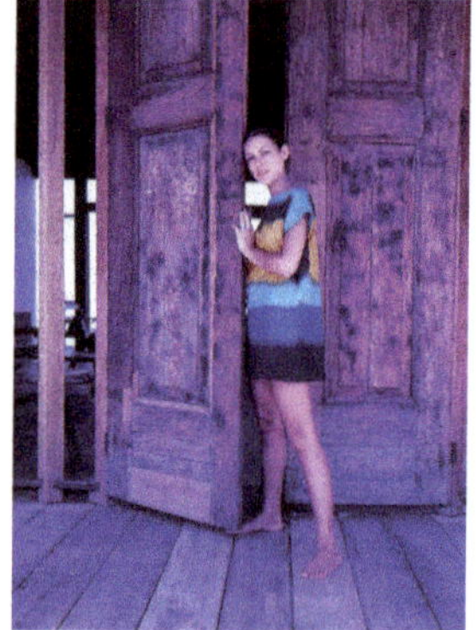

Figure 8: Model photographed in a house designed by the architect Zanini Caldas

It is also in this sense that the debates about the authorship of William Shakespeare's works do not have significant consequences in the effects that this author exerts in the human imaginary (Souza, 2018: 30). The Latin origin of the term illusion is related to gambling. Moving from *situational illusion* to a *social illusion* is to insert a certain subject into the social game, which may include history, art, sociology, anthropology, archivology. It is to construct that hermeneutic space of which Nathalie Heinich (1991) speaks, where a new creator is inserted, or a new sphere of social interest is constituted. There is no denying that I would like Olly to become part of the *social illusion* that constituted the Brazilian cultural field.

However, the relevance of this project of systematization of the Archive is not in the exceptionality of the artist or the political activist, but in the analytical doors that a personal archive can open for future researchers. If their biographies are less relevant than the ones of so many other artists and militants, the accumulated collection seems to outweigh them in importance, encompassing places, events, characters, and spheres of action with which they were directly and indirectly related. It is not, then, the crowning of a consecrated public performance, although some future redemption and history recognition is expected.

As Farge argues, what can be found of most importance in an archive is not a treasure, discovered by the cleverest or most curious, but the gap, the emptiness. *Olly and Werner Reinheimer's Archive* is also made of gaps, despite the diversity of forms of speech and their polyphony. And it is this lack that nurtures its relevance. It is the emptiness that makes its research an immense source of knowledge. It is the infinite possibility of translating this void into questions that makes the organization, digitization and availability of this collection for consultation a possibility of expanding the forms of knowledge and knowledge production.

But questioning the archive is stripping of passion the relationship with the documents and the people represented in them. This movement of detachment began with the documents' organization and systematization. Classifying them is at the same time restricting the senses that they may have as personal objects so that each one who has access to the collection can attribute to the documents its own meanings. However, the very process of organization and systematization went beyond the limits of an objective rationality, mixing the close relationship with the couple over nineteen years and seven more with Werner.

Investigating a personal file, in the case in question of two subjects, means being careful not to treat them as average individuals, but to try to show how the original accumulators of the archive organized their space and constituted their agency with what was socially available to them. To what extent can we question collective phenomena from their trajectories? More than talking about an individual creation, Olly's "*ouvre*", from an elevating perspective of the uniqueness of her production, I am interested in showing the collective aspect of building a cultural field that was also woven with the threads of the two actors' discussed here. The presentation of these trajectories reveals a complex web of people, institutions and materialities, which are not subject to the status of an encompassing society (in the Durkheimian sense).

The Book's Structure

To tell this story, I divided my interpretation into five chapters. Instead of presenting three different instances – context, trajectory and production – I chose to structure the research from three other perspectives: the domestic space, the collections and the textile production. Context, trajectory, and production will then always appear sewn into these three conceptual dimensions. The option for this structure was an attempt not to use the analytical procedure of presenting separately dimensions that are inseparable and overdetermining. Historical, political, economic, social, cultural, and material conditions, that is, context, were mentioned in relation to spheres of action, participation and production where their pertinence and adequacy were important for understanding the meaning of the conceptual interpretations proposed here.

The methodological option of not dividing Olly's performance into periods is also to think of her performance less in relation to significant events than to a transverse axis that differentially crosses her production, and which lends it diachronic unity. A chronological presentation of her production and performance can be unveiled from the chronology included in the annexes. In the second and fifth chapters I present the couple's initial and final trajectory, while in the first, third and fourth chapters, I develop more reflexively the significant points of their production of themselves and of a cultural field in Brazil, articulating them with contextual data to allow some conclusions and generalizations.

In the first chapter I present my readers to the couple's apartment. I try to draw attention to the rooms and objects of decoration. I make a brief historical survey of how the concept of domestic space and its relationship with consumption and the production of self arose in anthropology. I show how the historical construction of this idea itself produces a symbology of this space that is generalized and elitist, contributing to the division of the world between moral versus technical spaces. I start the book with this chapter in order to take seriously Ingold's (2011) proposal to use space, its occupation and construction as forms of intervention in social life.

The constitution of the domestic space as an object of study in anthropology is the result of an increasingly broad interest in the role of women in the constitution of social practices and meanings. The neighborhood of Ipanema, in Rio de Janeiro, is the setting for this chapter where Olly and Werner lived, and also where, since the end of the 19th century, many immigrants' lives have been concentrated. The decorating magazines that presented the couple's apartment since the early 1960s are a means of observing the transformation of the artist's status in her marriage and the constitution of a new form of organization of the domestic space.

I try to show how it was constituted what I am calling a new *style* of decoration of the domestic space based on the mixture of modern elements with the material production of Brazilian rural and ethnic cultures. This new *style* contrasted objects that were the result of total control over the materials with materials that kept the memory of their "natural" condition as part of the objects produced: polished metals, perfectly sanded and smooth woods with the knots and shafts of the wood, or the imperfections of the incorporated leather.

This *style* was linked to the formation of a new middle-class that was distinguished by a *sensibility* expressed in the domestic space as an arena of consumption and sociability. The decoration of the house represented, at the same time, a class *habitus* and the engagement in a new modernity. To compose the picture of this system of values and representations, I present the neighborhood where the apartment was located. The domestic space is then inserted into a classification system in which the social space is delimited by the residents and bystanders of Ipanema.

In the second chapter, I partially recover the trajectory of the two families until Olly and Werner met, their marriage, and Olly's first attempts at artistic experimentation in the 1950s. Given the lack of an earlier systematization of these trajectories, this work supposed a long and meticulous process of data collation, search of information of various orders and contact with a series of people scattered throughout the world, to what the Internet was an indispensable tool.

The notions of *project* and *conditions of possibility* (Velho, 1987) guided me in the investigation to show how there are complex relations between the representations built on the social world and the biographical trajectories and practices of consumption expressed in the private space. The couple's file presentifies their deaths, making them survive on the trail of objects. But this archive also offers a certain biographical illusion, seeming to tell the story of one or two, totalities.

Still in this second chapter I summarize the work on German and Jewish immigration to Brazil, especially Rio de Janeiro, mentioning the importance of the debates about race in the constitution of the Brazilian national state and, therefore, also in the migratory process. I also present the neighborhood where the couple's apartment was located, as well as the migrant trajectory of these two families and their ethnic identity. Those are important dimensions for understanding the context in which Olly's *career* developed and the reach she obtained while producing and after her death.

The chapter is chronologically organized, presenting both trajectories as a sequence of dates, places, and events that Werner, Olly, and their families passed through. The intertwining of these actors with the web of relationships that assigns a complexity to their trajectory will be approached, mainly, from the third part of that chapter onwards. It is in these subsequent chapters that the relational dimension of these trajectories is observed, as well as Olly's production presented from the perspective of a socially constructed individuality that expresses shared and non-shared values and symbolic systems.

In the third chapter, I returned to some extent to the couple's apartment to understand how the objects collected by Olly had an impact on her production and also constituted a social technology for the construction of subjectivity and membership. For that, I also investigated other physical and symbolic spaces following Franco Terranova's collections of *ex-votos* and *carrancas*[14].

In this chapter I also link the transformation of the sense and organization of the domestic space to the verticalization of the neighborhoods in the South Zone of Rio

---

[14] Ex-votos are votive offerings to a saint or divinity in the fulfillment of a vow, or in gratitude or devotion. Carrancas are "figureheads" attached to river crafts to which it was attributed power to protect the boatmen from the river's evil spirits.

de Janeiro. The radical alteration of the landscape, which rapidly lost its houses and villages and gained skyscrapers, created a sense of the conviviality of distinct temporalities at the same time that it stimulated nostalgia for an idealized past. Consumption became a privileged form of self-construction both in the body and in the spaces in which it circulated. Clothing and home decor were thus two of the ways in which values were built to recognize the membership of groups of actors.

It is in this context that folklore emerged as popular culture, actively participating in the present through some names that came to be recognized as popular artists and their works as "popular art" or "afro-Brazilian art". Contrary to folklore that was based on the anonymity of the productions, "popular art" or " afro-Brazilian art" was the recognition of the aesthetic qualities of the work of some producers, with clay and wood as privileged materials. This process took place in the context of the intensification of the consumer society and the massive entry of household appliances, which altered the dynamics as well as the appearance of the domestic space. The consumption of popular production was then a way of valuing manufacturing as a symbol of a circuit in which production, circulation, and fruition were integrated, contrasting with the logic of the market linked to industrial goods. Brazilian modern art museums were the locus of action of a set of actors that connected fashion, design and art from this axiology that linked goods from popular culture to industrial products, valuing both in a complementary way.

"Art" and "culture" appear as consumer goods exhibited in the living rooms of a white middle-class that was also constituted by their ability to "discover" the aesthetic values of the production of people membership to groups that had not participated in the universe of Brazilian "High culture". Petite Galerie owned by Franco Terranova inaugurates the possibility of Cariocas[15] buying art in installments, like any other consumer good. Just as art entered a consumer market, peasants, Indians, or generic pre-Columbian peoples were transformed into fashion. I mention here the essential role that Brazilian design had at the moment when it was institutionalized.

In chapter four, I try to understand Olly Reinheimer's trajectory, the impact of immigration and her ethnicity on the *career* she has built, articulating this trajectory with the social context and the specific meaning of textile production. As in the previous chapter, the text here gains a more thematic than chronological dimension. I try to articulate the artistic modernity to class, ethnic, generation and gender reconversions that had to be made in the construction of this *career*, showing the role art teaching had in the construction of some of this modernity canons. In this process we also see how the clothes are *artified*, that is, the magic of the artistic field is put into operation to transform the clothes into objects of art.

The participation of the State in such an enterprise aligned a naturalized idea of culture with an industrial dimension. It can be perceived in Itamaraty's[16] sponsorship

---

[15] People born in Rio de Janeiro.
[16] Brazilian Ministry of Foreign Affairs

of various exhibitions. Olly's entry into the art scene in Rio de Janeiro, with participation in other Brazilian states such as São Paulo, Bahia, and Minas Gerais, among others, gave visibility to her practices in such a way that seemed to put Werner's trajectory in the background. However, through his library it was possible to gain access to a system of thought that provided political and social support, while at the same time providing visual references to Olly's work. The "decorative art" appears as the feminine dimension of design, potentializing the meanings of fabric while inserting it, at the same time, in the universe of the artistic and industrial world. Olly was only one of the many women who contributed to a sweetening of Brazilian industrial capitalism and to the reification of gender representations for middle-class white women.

In chapter five I deal with the closure of Olly and Werner's life trajectory and research for now. To do so, I divide it into four parts. In the first, I talk about the last years of Olly and Werner's life, and the impact that the end of the Brazilian dictatorship, the dissolution of USSR, the fall of the Berlin wall and the contact with a German historian interested in Werner's trajectory had in terms of the archivistic impulse. In the second, I elaborate on the central theme of Olly's career, a renewed relation between "modernism" and "primitivism", no longer as a state project, but as a form of construction of association by a new middle-class constituted in great measure by first or second-generation of white immigrants[17]. The encouragement of the use of indigenous, popular, children, and afro-Brazilian references inserted the production of these groups into an emerging racialized consumer market through the paradoxical character of appropriating the productions of these groups as a way to create value for the commodities produced by and for this white elite.

Impacted by European modernist movements, the social actors investigated here reinforced the values of authenticity without a critique of the asymmetric relations produced and sustained by a colonialism that was maintained through a grammar that found in the artistic universe its most elaborate form. The immigrants' desire to escape the condition of foreigners renewed the idea of the opposition to the "natives", situationally valued as positive or negative. The things produced by these groups were collected as a way of marking identities and fabricating images of the past and producing a future. People and groups have invented themselves from the possession and use of these things.

The notion of *freedom* emerged as a way of constituting the representation of the artist as one who went against social conventions and not someone who created from what society offered. Forged as a way of escaping totalitarian systems, this category was re-signified to obliterate the ways in which canons such as authenticity,

---

[17] I do not detain myself on the trajectories of these other immigrants who were part of the web of relations of the couple, because in addition to the differences in reasons for immigrating, social status and reception in Brazil, what unites these immigrants is both being part of the same web and also the fact that in one way or another they were all involved with local/folk/popular cultural production.

singularity, and rupture became demands of the social world. In other contexts, creating could be understood as shaping the world, at the same time shaping our own humanity, engaging conscious bodies and discovering the meaning of things in the process of use; blend into the world to perceive it in different ways (Ingold, 2011). I try to show in this process of conformation of a certain Brazilian national modernity the challenge to the polarization between "novelty and convention, or between the innovative dynamics of the present time and the traditionalism of the past, which has long been a powerful subliminal tendency in discourses on modernity" (Ingold and Hallam, 2007).

The idea of creativity is instituted in this period, from which the artist must present herself in opposition to the conventions, obliterating this norm, itself, as conventional. The way of working the materials – leather, wood and fibers – was one of the ways to institutionalize this notion of creativity as a break with conventions.

In this concluding chapter I also point to the tense relationship between anthropology and art history, arguing for the complementarity and opposition that prevail in its perspectives. I reflect on the personal archive as an object of study, my inevitable involvement with the subject, and how to use it for, instead of against, research. I also try to analyze the resistance to death in the preservation of things. At times I allow myself to abandon the attempts at objectivity and openly declare the love and admiration of the granddaughter for these grandparents. In this statement, I expose part of the research process and some field experiences that have narrowed the gap between generational, temporal and ethnic memberships between us. I also talk a little about the tension that was to write about the trajectory of Jews who fled from Nazism but who had lives marked by joys and recognition. The holocaust still weighs on the survivors, three generations later, so happiness and joy need justifying.

A NOTE ON THE USE OF SOURCES

Ethnographic sources are often handwritten, typed texts, newspaper columns taken out of context and pasted on blank sheets or reproductions of articles on the internet. In general, this material has never been paginated or was decontextualized, losing the original pagination of the vehicle where it was published. Thus, pages are indicated only when this applies. To facilitate the distinction between the ways I use my sources, I assumed the italics format with quotation marks for the ethnographic sources (interviews, magazine articles, material from *Olly and Werner Reinheimer's Archive*), and quotation marks without italics when the texts are used as an analytical tool or for adding information and interpretation. The analysis categories, in turn, were placed in italics without quotes.

CHAPTER 1

Entering Olly and Werner's Universe

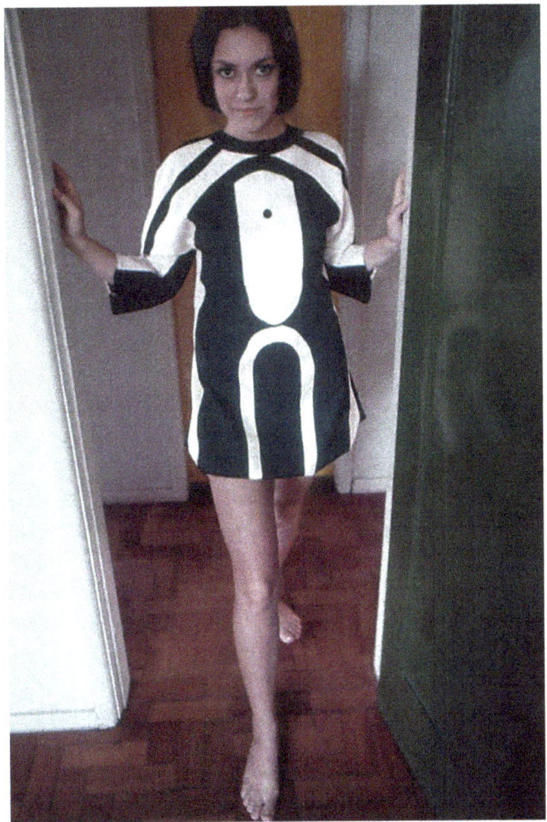

Figure 9: Model entering Olly's studio,
behind we see Olly's bedroom door, 1970s (DIA-772).

1.1 DOMESTIC SPACE IN ANTHROPOLOGY

In the beginnings of modern anthropology, classic authors used homes of their informants as context for observing the constitution of the family relationships, practices and identities of its members. Nevertheless, domestic environment, understood as a social space in which relationships are developed, as well as an ideological dimension that constitutes these same relations, was a late subject in the discipline.

Along the discipline institutionalization process, anthropological investigation privileged the public domain, even if it were in the domestic universes that the researchers had the first contacts with their research subjects. The basic instruction was that one should live with the "natives" and these were often their main informants. Thus, observing the details of the house became central to field work. These spaces, however, have been treated as scenarios for expressing the forms of appropriation of the wider world, as well as representation of this world in the private sphere.

The existence of a common project in the construction of housing contributed to the creation of a strong relationship between this entity and the community formed by its inhabitants. It is no wonder that Lewis Henry Morgan, responsible for important work on kinship systems, inaugurated, in 1881, the perspective of the domicile as representative of the social complex to which its inhabitants belong. Under the title "Houses and house-life of the american aborígenes", Morgan sought to prove his theory that mankind would have evolved through stages of progress by analyzing the structures of the houses of various North American groups.

Bronislaw Malinowski is also a historical reference in the anthropology of the domicile for having published the work "The Family Among the Australian Aborigenes", in 1913. In this work he associated family with a physical space in the attempt to put an end in the debate on the inexistence of family structures in some human societies. In the quest to "prove" that family is a universal institution, Malinowski made the mistake of treating it as a concrete entity and not as an ideological construct with moral implications (Collier, Rosaldo and Yanagisako, 1997). However, the association between household and the domestic space instigated several researches both to confirm and to reject the proposition, among other purposes.

However, it was the work of sociologist Pierre Bourdieu (1970) that claimed housing as more than just a setting where social relations could be observed. Linked to structuralism, the author emphasized the relevance of housing in the study of social organization. With emphasis on practice, contingency, and strategy, by strict opposition to structure he showed how a series of symbolic oppositions constitute the axis around which people structure their beliefs in the world. The dwelling then appeared as central in the structuring of what he called *habitus*. In the house, the social structure would be present in an externalized order and not only in the minds of the inhabitants. In his theory *habitus* is the incorporation of culture through a practice based on things, themselves structurally ordered.

The villages' general design and their houses' interior would thus mirror variations of the structuring binary oppositions of those societies. Oppositions such as nature/culture, male/female, death/life, dark/light, east/west, left/right were considered universal. However, implicitly these symbolic structures were considered common to exotic cultures, suggesting that industrial societies no longer relied on symbolism.

From the perspective of British anthropology, Mary Douglas (2002), for example, dealt less with these polarities and focused more on behavior that expressed ritual zones and symbolic frontiers, as well as limited important social values to be preserved. In her book "Purity and Danger", practices considered hitherto mundane were interpreted as border markers. The house rituals were thus perceived from a symbolic analysis of culture. Space as a social construction made housing a way of observing social organizations thought in relation to cultural, economic and political practices and values.

French anthropologist Claude Lévi-Strauss (1982) elaborated on the notion of "house society" (Société à Maison) relating the moral person to its domain of material and immaterial goods perpetuated in the transmission of names and titles. The author's work is important, because his notoriety amplified the potential of the home as a unit of analysis. Criticisms directed at his work advanced the analysis of the dwellings.

In the early twentieth century, with the advance of colonization and the disappearance of what were considered to be "authentic" societies, as well as the progressive reduction of research funds, anthropologists began to turn to groups that represented a certain "Primitiveness" within their own societies. This is how the rural communities ceased to be of interest only to historians and sociologists and began to be investigated from ethnographic perspectives.

For some, the social reproduction of the peasantry was treated on the basis of the property indivisibility composed of the whole house, gardens and orchards. This was considered the main nucleus of the peasant patrimony, not necessarily represented by the whole land owned by the family (Bourdieu, 1962; Shanin, 1971; Segalen, 1980).

None of these works, however, took into account the emotional and ideological connotations that were so important in the process of building the idea of home in the modern West. Thus, the shift from an analysis of housing to investigations of the concept of "home", or of domestic space (Carsten, 1999), emerged in the late twentieth century reflecting an epistemological shift in the discipline. The postmodern critiques of primitive/civilized polarity implicit in anthropological analyzes showed that in these interpretations Westerners seemed to have been devoid of symbolic motivation throughout the civilizing process. However, while the symbolic dimension was not considered appropriate for the anthropology of urban communities, it flourished in the investigations of rural communities perceived as primitive isolates in modern society (Carsten, 2017).

In Brazil, anthropologist Beatriz Heredia (1979), for example, analyzed the internal organization of peasant production units in Pernambuco, Northeast of Brazil. She showed a sexual division of labor and classifications that associated spaces and people. Inside the dwelling, the kitchen was identified as a female domain. Women, in addition to working at home and on the farm, tended the animals and the cultivation near the dwelling. Children were socialized in these spaces, according to sex, following models of masculinity and femininity.

The segregation of the sexes became the center of interest of several feminist anthropologists who began to seek patriarchal domination at all levels. The feminist perspective cemented the transition from the traditional idea of the house in anthropology to the concept of *home* while searching in the symbolic dimension a confluence between space, gender and power. Influenced by the criticism of postmodern anthropology, it became a project to show the relevance of the symbolic analysis of contemporary *homes*. Thus, mundane practices such as washing, cooking, decorating, and arranging the rooms of the *home* have become symbolic, household rituals with significant categories.

These investigations also had an impact on the interest in the so-called "material culture"[18]. Anthropologist Daniel Miller (2002), for example, captured the power of consumer practices and replaced the idea of alienation that Marxist rhetoric relates to impotence through the empowering notion of appropriation. The author shows the mass production of objects incorporated in domestic use are transformed into personal universes of meaning. In such studies, the concept of identity generally designates the subject of appropriation or creation. Consumption appears in anthropological investigations, no longer as a (de)moralizing dimension on a causal chain, of which production would be the noblest dimension. Consumption is the potency of its positivity (Foucault, 2003). It is in this sense that Miller seeks to identify the sociological implications of consumption in contemporary life, noting the relationship between the cultural dimension and the creation of subjectivity.

Feminists, in turn, sought to find in social history the process of forming the modern emotional *home* centered on feminine domesticity as the core of societies where men hold power. How would this domain have emerged as a female prison that segregates women from public spheres? The process can best be described from England, since the ideological sense of domestic space was shaped throughout the process of colonization, industrialization, and urbanization. According to anthropologist Anne McClintock (2010) the formation of these ideological universes, the home and the public sphere, was a movement concomitant with British imperialism and the invention of industrial progress from a cult of domesticity in which race, class and gender maintained intimate, reciprocal and contradictory relations.

For this author, domesticity is a space as much as *a social relation of power*, with a historical genealogy that "involves processes of social metamorphosis and political

---

[18] Ingold (2002) criticizes the term "material culture" arguing that it is an attempt to overlap the domains of culture and materiality by delegating form to culture and its substance to nature, even if the object is made of plastic, for example. His claim is directed to the fact that little attention is paid to materials and their properties, and the emphasis falls almost entirely on questions of meaning and form that is, about culture as opposed to materiality. I use the term aware that form and substance need to be taken into account in the analysis of things.

subjection of which gender is the permanent dimension, but not the only one" (2010: 63). The construction of a domesticity cult was at the same time a process of racialization of the domestic space and of domestication of the colonial space. The author shows how gender and class domination join evolutionist scientism as civilizational justifications for colonialism with tactics of sexual control in the process of South African conquest. In this process, the temporal and spatial distinction between primitive nature and civilized culture produces representations of domestication of landscapes that are reinforced through propaganda.

Internally to English cities, the construction of domesticity as a generalized ideological dimension was linked to the rise of the bourgeoisie and its desire to differentiate from both working and aristocratic classes. Dialectical relations between the absorption and control of various "others" as women, workers and blacks show the intimate connection between the domesticity cult and the valuation of female idleness as the frontier of membership to a particular, "respectable" social class. It was created in the nineteenth century a contrast between the image of the working woman, who became the equivalent of non-white men in their vices and moral failings, and the middle-class woman. In the construction of these values, the fetish of the merchandise was associated with the cult of cleanliness as a way of sanitizing domestic space. The soap, in particular, became the industrialized product responsible for a social magic of producing a "clean" and "brilliant" home, which erased in the advertisements the feminine work they entailed, while at the same time racially purifying subaltern classes.

However, the construction of the idea of a specific domain of the family was also associated with professions such as urbanism, architecture and design. When large numbers of rural workers moved to cities seeking jobs in factories, the middle class created a spatial and mental segregation, rebuilding their lifestyle in the suburbs outside the sprawling cities. These new (sub)urban neighborhoods thus emerged as an interpretation of domination based on city/countryside opposition, in addition to work/home, in which the first terms were male spaces *par excellence*.

This spatial separation resulted in distinct gender and class spheres, with their associated behaviors and values. The city was the space of economic rationality, marked by profit and efficiency, while *home* was the space of affection and morals. This distinction deepened in the early twentieth century, when interior designers and city planners expressed these values in urbanization and home decoration projects. The urbanization of cities, for example, sought to discipline the working classes, considered dirty and disorderly. Cleanliness and organization were *home* values supposed to be created and maintained explicitly by women. The work of producing *home*, however, should not be perceived, hence the cult of female idleness and the jettison of women from the spaces of power. This was done under the guise of protection by segregating them in areas away from the presence of dangerous classes. In Europe, and also in Brazil, the suburb initially had this connotation of family area in opposition to the city centers, properly urban regions. However, if this organization was an idea of isolating bourgeois women under the guise of security, these same women conformed to this separation, seduced by a certain "ideology of devotion to the family" (Tiburi, 2018). The middle-classes thus constructed a whole universe of consumption and lifestyles around these ideas that presupposed also spatial separation of gender (Friedan, 1971).

At the end of the twentieth century and especially at the beginning of the twenty-first century, the domains of *home* and work and the gender separations within *home* are no longer as marked. Neither the notions of public and private in the era of social networks. However, the oppositions that are based on those notions are still relevant in today's society. *Home* lends meanings to several other social spaces, especially when apart from them, as for immigrants and refugees. For them, it may mean the home or the country they left behind. Building a new and better home can mean establishing oneself in the host country or returning to the country of origin, which is not possible, most of the time.

Refugees who had to flee their homes have lost not only their material possessions, but their privacy, their neighborhood environment and their compatriots, their families and their jobs. Nostalgia, or homesickness, in this case, is a disease that has no cure when one does not have a home to go back to (Carsten, 2017). To some extent, this was Olly and Werner's case, as I shall describe in the next chapter.

Home escapes simple definitions. It implies in deeply connected but different cultural and personal senses. Depending on how much you earn, you can have access to different types of homes, with different amenities, that will give its inhabitants varied experiences. In the first place, its meaning also depends on the biography of the person: for a child, a teenager or an elderly home can mean very different things. The surrounding neighborhood also has an influence on the way we feel and the meanings we attribute to our home: living in the Southern area of Rio de Janeiro, as the couple lived, allows an experience of urbanity completely different from what one has when living in the Northern or Western areas. Social life is also constituted by the various cycles of homes reinvention caused either by internal motivations like marriage, new jobs, search for experiences or external catastrophes, wars, political persecutions.

It is one of the central concepts of modern Western culture, because its meaning is the result of a historical development of the progressive separation of two domains, production and consumption, respectively related to work and domestic space. It also represents two conceptions of distinct rationalities, the public domain of profit and the private domain of morality. However, deeply embedded in Western culture and social organizations, this ideal is not based on spatial, emotional, and social oppositions of work and domestic space. As well as race, gender, and class are not distinct realms of experience like Lego pieces (McClintock, 2010). Public and private, home and work, production and consumption exist only through the relationships they maintain with each other, even if in contradictory and conflicting ways.

Ideally, home and work were constructed throughout the nineteenth century, mainly in opposition to one another, even though they are interdependent and mutually constitutive categories. The home is thus a historical condition, dependent on this development. The initial approaches that took the house as a mirror of social organization are today criticized for the fixity of their analyzes. Adopting the notion of *domestic space* was a way of reinforcing the home as a process to be unraveled through historical comparison.

Affirming the processual character, it emphasizes the procedures of construction, wear and tear, maintenance, organization and reorganization, decoration and redecoration to which the environment is permanently subject, as well as the social processes that take place there. Instead of the objectivity of finished things, the poetry of things happening. It is a matter of looking at forces and resistances that align with one another to give life to forms (Ingold, 2002).

An important criticism to the structuralist approach to housing was that they reflected other domains but could also themselves be an instrument in solving dilemmas as well as being constitutive of social relations (Miller, 2001). These critiques were part of the reformulation in the theoretical-methodological approaches of the discipline when the participation of things in the social phenomena was revised and resized, giving origin to what some investigators conceive as an ethnology of the subjectivity that showed that the personal identities are deeply linked to cultural dimension, without being reduced to them.

Rethinking anthropology's epistemology, Ingold seeks to bring this discipline closer to archeology, art, and architecture by thinking about them as forms of knowledge and intervention in the world. For him, while anthropology, with its exigency of objectivity would have purged the life of its narratives, in art, in drawing and architecture the author finds the reestablishment of an inverse path that replaces the world as a historical form of life, *inhabited* in its full meaning.

His intention is to show life on the move, with an emphasis on the process and not on the final product. To do so, he reviews a number of analytical categories used by the discipline. One of them is the recapitulation of the analyzes of some Marxist authors on the idea of production, including Marx himself, to argue that the verb to produce should be understood as an intransitive one, as well as to inhabit, grow, wait, plan, build and do. This would restore the existential primacy of production without putting intentionality as a necessary condition.

Ingold rejects the idea of productive work as a way of transcribing preexisting ideal forms onto an amorphous material substrate (Ingold, 2011: 35). Therefore, his choice to use the verb to *dwell* as a way of expressing the way, alone or together, that human beings produce their own lives. To inhabit a world is not only to occupy certain structures, but to work with materials, bringing form to existence "within the currents of activities in which they are involved and in the specific relational contexts of their practical commitments to their surroundings" (Ingold, 2011: 35).

Ingold's interest in processes, as opposed to products, regards production as part of the conditions for the updating of potential identities not as attributes received but as a result of productive achievements. The notion of consumption, then, is not considered as an opposing dimension to labor as a generalized activity with symbolic and economic connotations historically constituted in the post-industrial world. Like production, consumption appears, in its formulation, as a dimension fixed in objects and pre-conceived images from the transitivity of means and ends.

However, just as Ingold conceives production as a movement that describes a path without fixed places and pre-established identities, the choice for consumption as a perspective of interpretation of the trajectories and things of the couple Olly and Werner has a political dimension in which gender relations are the point of departure and arrival. Production for Ingold is related to the ontology of being. In the interpretation proposed here, consumption is also constitutive of the subjects in question, with emotion and affection being explicitly activated in the description and interpretation of the investigated material. If Ingold uses the idea of production to speak of a sentient body, bathed in light, submerged in sound, and snatched from feeling, I use consumption to describe this immersion in the emotion and affection awakened throughout the investigation of things as close as a "Cosmology" in which some familiar people were built and helped me build myself.

As some authors (Fabian, 1983, Santos, 1988, Short, 1999) have already mentioned, modernity privileged the metaphor of time, but little was developed over space, considered as the locus of rigidity in socio-anthropological analyzes. Evolutionism was an exemplary set of attempts to show how things unfolded over time. Domestic space is, in this sense, a key place to understand how family relations, gender, and class identities are negotiated. However, it is not a space separate from the movements that produced it, but a dynamic and open space. An *inhabited* – not *occupied* – space, a dense knot of intertwined vital lines (Ingold, 2011). It is in this domestic space, in constant transformation, that we live important parts of our constitution as a social position, health, physical and emotional well-being, an essential condition for our socialization in the world.

***

In 1929, Virginia Woolf explained the difficulty women had in finding a place for themselves within what was essentially their work space, the domestic domain. In "A Room of One's Own", the author speaks of the importance of a place that guarantees privacy and financial resources to give women the minimum to obtain their autonomy from men. In anthropology, as in literature, home appears as a space where genders are in conflict. But more than scenery, the dwelling intervenes in the practices there developed (Miller, 2001). Its analysis should take into account the architectural structure, the people who spend time in it, as well as its surroundings, that is, the physical and social space in which it is found, and also the ideal on which people base themselves to found their private home and its transformations over time. As it is not possible, in the scope of this book, to address all these dimensions, I have tried to emphasize those pertinent to the symbolic universe constructed by the people who were related to the Reinheimer couple, as well as their participation in the constitution of this universe.

The apartment where Olly and Werner resided from the beginning of the 1950s on was to a certain extent what led to the research here presented. Full of cabinets, drawers, and innumerable other places to store things, every piece of furniture opened presented itself as a world of documents, fabrics, molds, wood forms, ceramics, acrylics, metal, threads, wool, reels, needles, looms, silk screens, blank canvases, painted canvases, drawings, engravings, pencils, pens, erasers, slide projectors, paints, glass, cameras, boxes and many other things that seemed to have no end. The couple remained present through the multiplicity of things that, even without classification or interpretation, were not to be discarded.

This apartment was for most of my life referred to by the various family members as "Grandma's house". As in the Anglophone languages that differentiate *house* from *home*, in Portuguese, we also have two terms to refer to the domestic space. The term apartment in Brazil is generally used to refer to the architectural structure of a home in a vertical community located in urban space, which may or may not have the affective connotations related to the domestic space. Rosales (2015) presents the debate about the terms house and home arguing that Birdwell-Phesant and Lawrence-Zuniga (1999) attribute to the former the sense of a physical structure or shelter, while to the second would be reserved the idea of origin, context of membership. *Home* would then be an idea of place and not simply of space and would imply emotional connections and meanings.

In Portuguese, this clear distinction is not simple, since the term casa/house condenses both meanings, and can be used to refer to a property to be bought or sold, to the home, the neighborhood or the country of origin. If I am in a car along with friends coming out of any town to return to where we live, home is this last city. If we are, the same group, on a tour and we leave from a historical site to the hotel where we are staying, home can be this hotel. Thus, I chose to use the term house, apartment and domestic space as interchangeable variants of this social space where different subjectivities, relationships, values and behaviors were related in one way or another to Olly and Werner, but also contributed to the construction of these values and relationships.

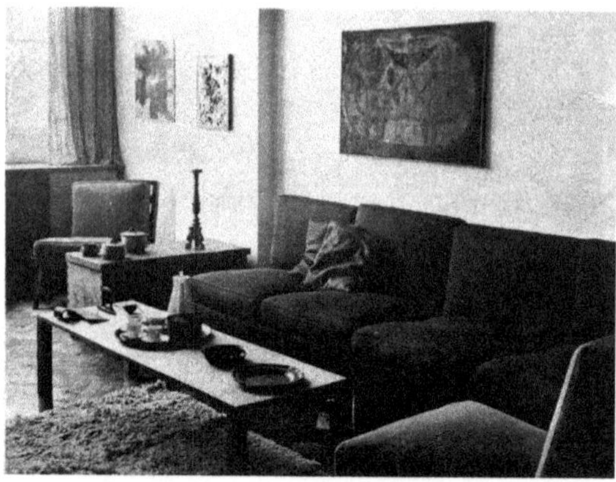

Figure 10: Article in the magazine Interior e Decoração (Interior and Decoration), 1966, on the apartment's decoration. In this photo, we see the entrance hall wall opposite the previous photo and at the bottom, to the right, the entrance door (MROW-G-80).

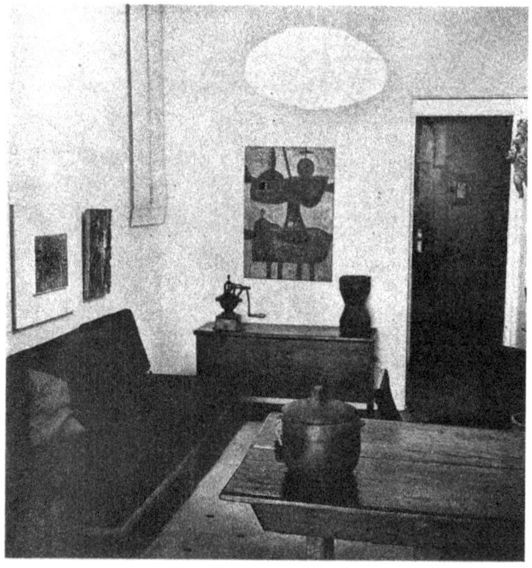

Figure 11: Article in the magazine Interior e Decoração (Interior and Decoration), 1966, on the apartment's decoration. In this photo, we see the entrance hall and on the right, the entrance door (MROW-G-80).

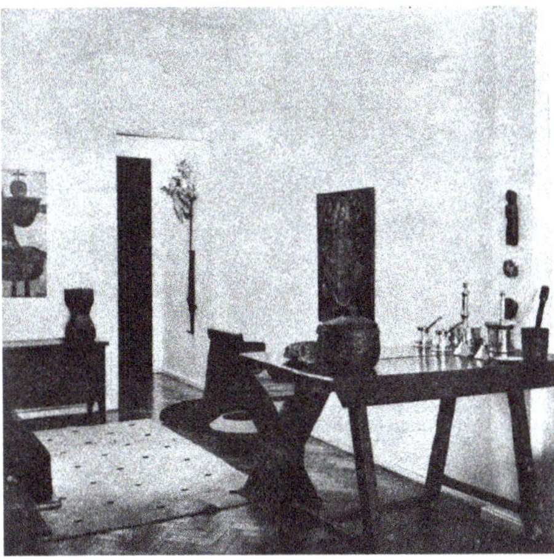

Figure 12: Article in the magazine Interior e Decoração (Interior and Decoration), 1966, on the apartment's decoration. Living room, adjoining the entrance hall (MROW-G-80).

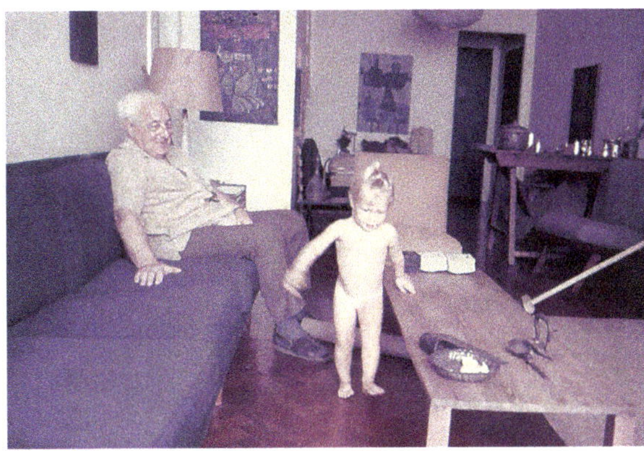

Figure 13: Werner and Patricia in the living room,
in the background, the hall and the front door, 1968 (DIA-693).

As English anthropologist, Janet Carsten, (1999) argues the construction of meaning is not necessarily conscious but is related and sustained by practice. The sense dissolves if it is not constantly actualized and reenacted. Its recurring practice in anthropological vocabulary is called "ritual". For the Reinheimer family, "grandma's house" was a place of origin, affection and creativity. It was also a feminine space. It took a few years, after Olly's death, for the apartment to be renamed "grandpa's house". It was also a work space, a place for intellectual debate and, above all, new experiences. For children as well as for adults, one would experience textures, combinations of colors, flavors, odors, sounds and ways of being in the world. And it is in this place I invite the reader to enter.

1.2. NEGOTIATING A WAY OF LIFE

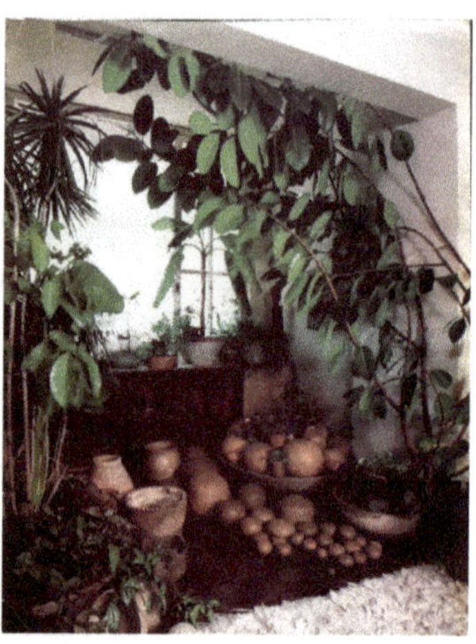

Figure 14: Casa & Decoração Magazine (Home and Decoration), 1978. Garden in the couple's appartment living room. (MROW-G-83-11d).

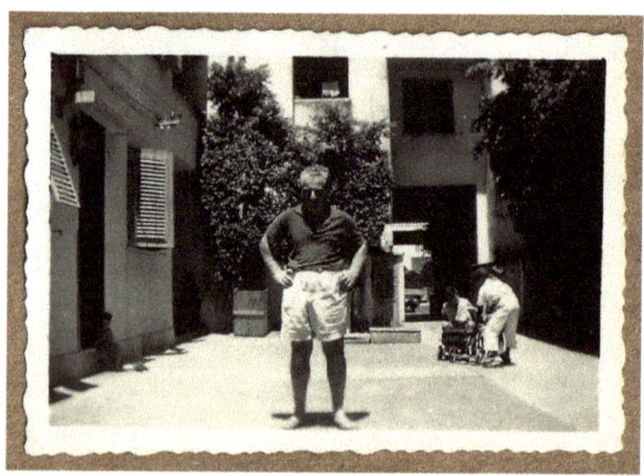

Figure 15: Werner in Ipanema's Bar 20, 1940s (PH-862).

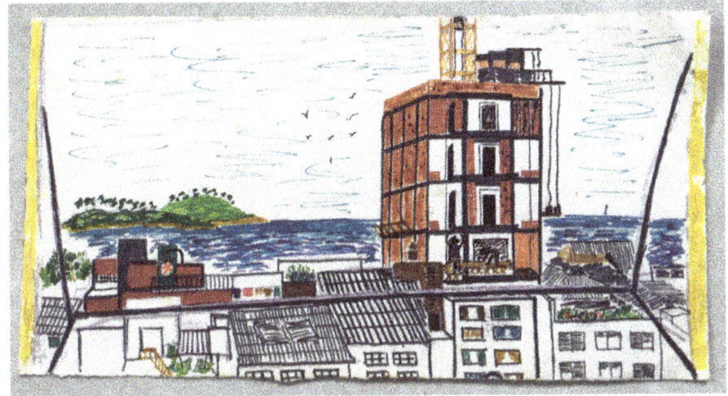

Figure 16: From Werner's room we see the first eight-story building under construction. On both sides and in front of it, all others still have 4 or 5 floors. Drawing not signed, *Olly and Werner Reinheimer's Archive*

As soon as they got married in 1939, they moved to Ipanema (Figure 15 and 17). In the 1950s, they moved again to the apartment where they would live for the rest of their lives, and where the collection is currently located (Figures 9 to 14, 16, 18 to 33).

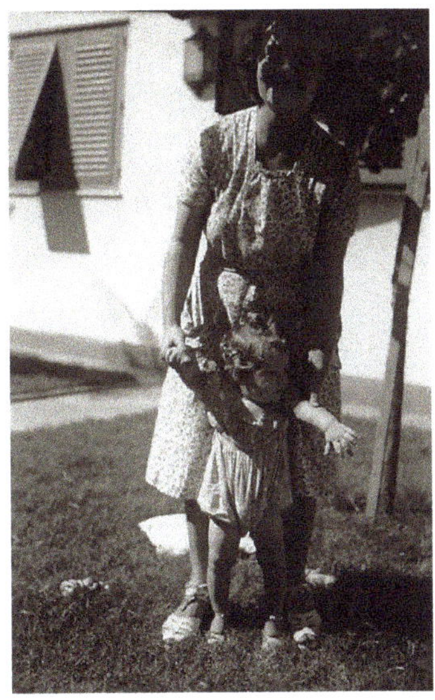

Figure 17: Olly and Rene in Ipanema's Bar 20, 1941 (PH-820).

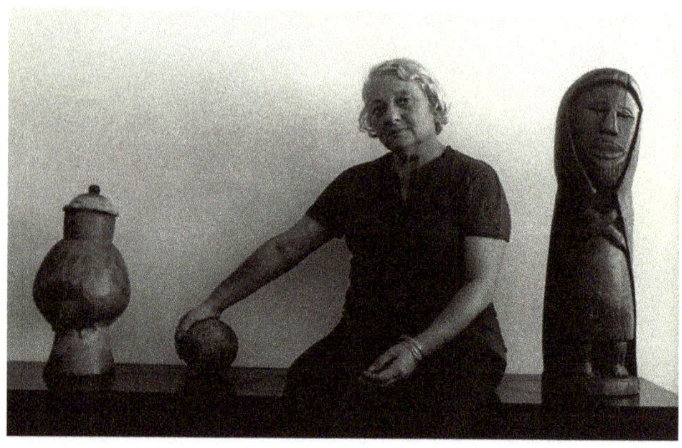

Figure 18: Olly sitting on the black lacquer furniture, with her hand in a cannon ball, between a sculpture by Agnaldo (about this artist see chapter 2) and a clay filter.

Figure 19:

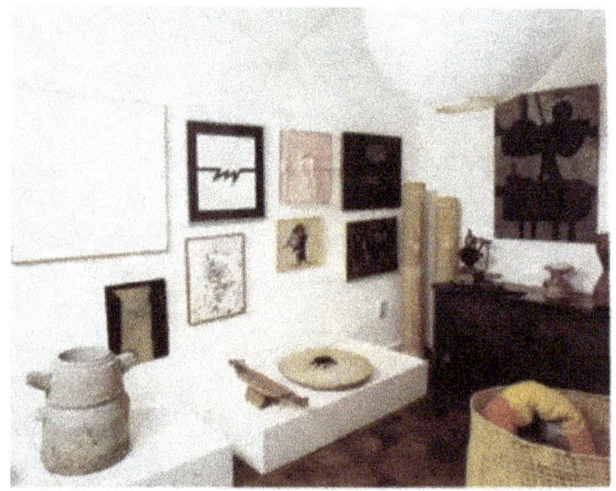

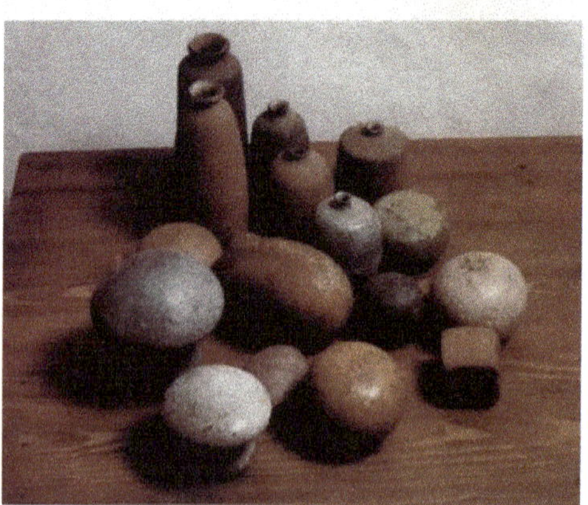

Upper picture,
Entrance hall. Paintings by Ana Maria Maiolino, Roberto Magalhães, Franz Krajcberg, Juan Le Parc, Gamarra, Ivan Serpa and a blank painting on the wall. A bench and an indigenous basket with a mobile sculpture by Olly (a colored snake), a ceramic piece (probably by Celeida Tostes) and an unknown cement piece. On top of the chest, a wooden pestle, a manual coffee grinder and an African piece.

Bottom photo, decorative ceramic objects, late 1970s (unknown authorship). The photos belong to the publication Casa & Decoração (Home and Decoration), 1978 (MROW-G-83).

It is a back unit in a building two blocks from the beach, that is, it faced the beach when there were no tall buildings. In the collection, a drawing of the view from Werner's bedroom window shows the beginning of the change in the pattern of buildings on Ipanema waterfront (unfortunately, there is no reference to the author) (Figure 16).

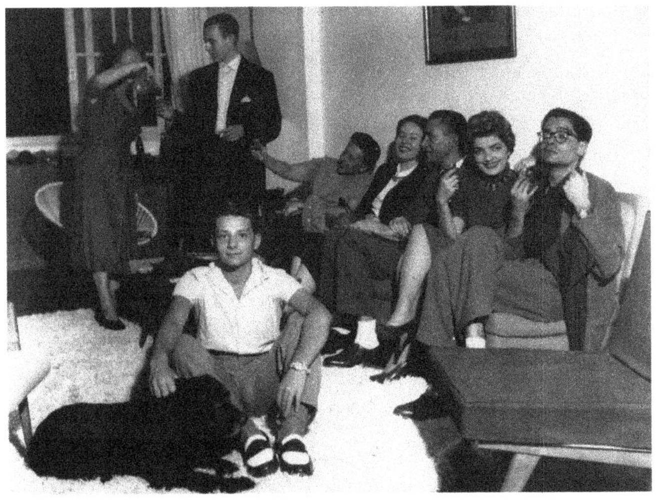

Figure 20: Olly's apartment living room. She serves drinks to someone in the space where decades later will be a garden. Photo from the mid-1950s (PH-032).

One enters through a large room, illuminated by a 6 x 19 feet window. From the end of the 1970s onwards, 19 square feet in front of this window were occupied by circular asbestos vases up to six feet in diameter large. The area was transformed into a garden with various plants (Figure 14 and 23). Among them, there was a banana tree and a fig tree whose branches, over time, bowed to accompany the ceiling. Scattered on the floor, near the pots, were Celeida Tostes'[19] ceramics shaped like balls in various sizes, other vases and an ancient ceramic stove. Still on the floor of the "garden", there were other pieces of ceramic in the shape of spools also in different sizes produced by Iberê Camargo.

The room was decorated with a large navy-blue square shaped sofa, mid-century designed chairs (Figures 10, 11 and 13) and a low black lacquered cabinet, on top of which various objects with shapes, materials and sizes made up the decoration (Figure

---

[19] About this artist, see Aguiar, 2017.

18 and 23). A rustic[20] table was in a corner, also used to support decorative pieces, such as old mortars, bronze pylons and ceramic vases (Figures 12 and 13).

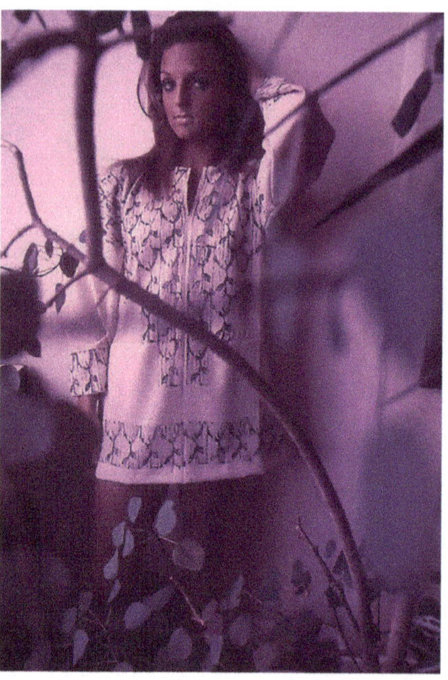

Figure 21: Model photographed in the apartment living room. 1970s.

Many pictures of models wearing Olly's clothes were taken in this apartment (Figure 21 and 30). Until the 1970s, the apartment had a wooden floor with a decoration significantly less marked by the mixture of styles and materials that represents what I am calling a "style of decoration of domestic spaces" founded by the practices of production and consumption that I will describe in the course of the book. In the late 1970s, the decoration was redone. The wooden floor was substituted by brown ceramic tiles. White wooden cubes of various shapes and sizes served as a support for decorative pieces in the entrance hall. Inside these cubes, things were stored. In the artist's last exhibition, they served as supports for the works (some examples can be seen in Figure 17-superior). On the walls there were paintings of various artists, most of whom contemporaries of the couple.

---

[20] The meaning I attach to this term will be developed throughout the book.

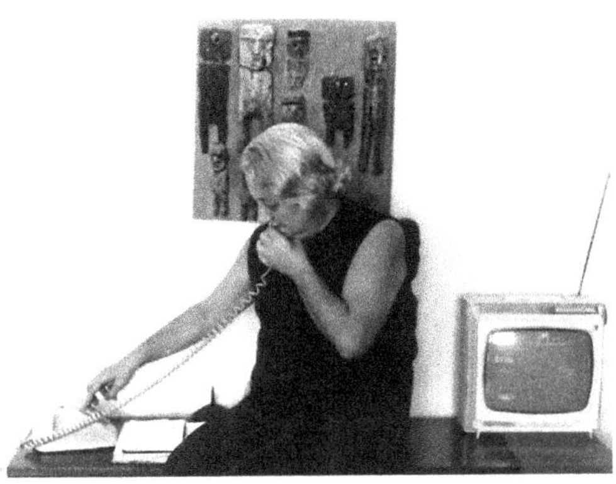

Figure 22: Werner's room. In the background, a picture with wooden ex-votes. The wood has been time-consumed, which makes the ex-votos seem almost archaeological pieces (PH-1291).

The rooms where each one slept were contiguous, while the room that leads to the inner part of the building was used initially as the son's bedroom and, as of the mid-1960s, as the artist's studio. Alison Clarke (2001) draws attention to the fact that the birth, death or change of a family member is always an important marker that instigates redecoration. His son's exit to graduate in engineering in Minas Gerais may have been the incentive for the first redecoration we can perceive through the photographs. However, although linked to key life cycles and events, the act of redecorating a home always requires a reversal, perpetuation, and/or reinvention of its material world. The physical act of "redecorating" requires negotiation with traditional and modern cultural, social and aesthetic knowledge, and requires also certain foresight and idealization.

In the first change visible through the photographs, we see how the room gained a wide sofa, unlike the small sofa that tightly accommodates four people in figure 20. This replacement seems significant if we think several interviewees described as an apartment open for visitors. The almost bare walls in figure 20 were decorated with different paintings as seen in figures 10 to 12 and 19. There is no way to be sure that the pieces from the rural areas of Rio de Janeiro and Minas Gerais already existed in the 1950's, but I suppose that these are the result of the couple's son's trip to the university in Minas Gerais, and his move to the interior of the state when he started working at one of Furnas's[21] power plants.

---

[21] Central Elétrica de Furnas S. A. was created for the energy supply of the Brazilian Southeast region. Its original mission was to implement an integrated generation and transmission system, by harnessing the potential of the Rio Grande in the Furnas rapids, near the city of Passos, interior of Minas Gerais State.

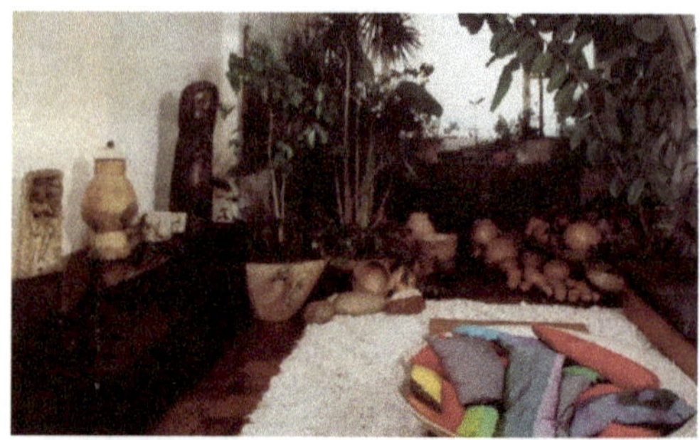

Figure 23: Living room, late 1970s (MROW-G-83).

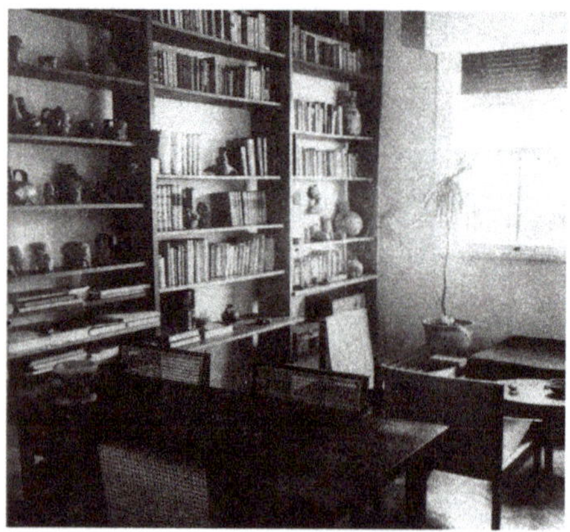 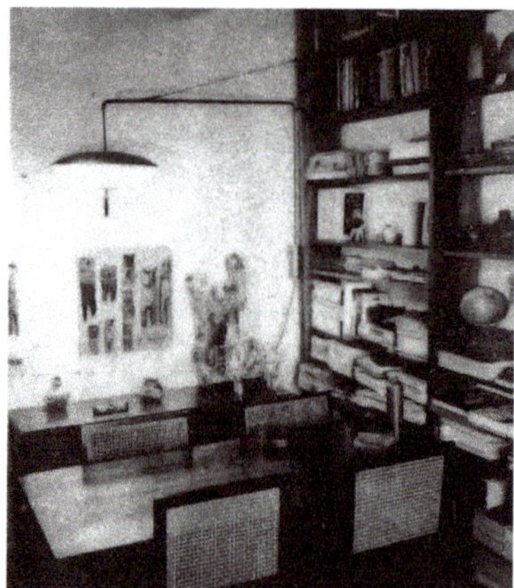

Figure 24 and 25: Werner's room (MROW-G-83).

In the late 1970s, the dining table, as well as the television and shelf with books and various pre-Columbian, indigenous, and African pieces were placed in Werner's room (Figures 22, 24 and 25). The pre-Columbian ceramics were purchased in the 1960s, most likely during two trips to Peru. In 1950, MAM-RJ organized a ceramics exhibition at the request of David Rockefeller, Nelson Rockefeller's brother, founder of NY's MoMA. Rockefeller's intention was to gather "folklore" pieces and pre-Columbian material culture. During this decade and the beginning of the next, various efforts were made to bring to Brazil exhibitions on pre-Columbian cultures, which finally resulted in the constitution of the Museum of Art and Archeology of the University of São Paulo.

Throughout the 1960s and 1970s, there seems to have been a dispute between the Paulista, Nacional and Goeldi museums (Paula, 2006) in the formation of pre-Columbian Andean tissue collections. These collections were one way of inserting the country into a South American antiquity, attributing Brazil a temporal depth that contradicted the idea of a "young nation". It was also a form of internal colonialism, in which the narrative of imperial progress was now converted into a spectacle of consumption (McClintock, 2010). Collecting these pieces was both a form of insertion in this "antiquity" through a circle of actors that valued this notion of South American historical and cultural depth, as well as a way of using collectionism as a technology of social innovation and production of subjectivity (Swann, 2001).

When in Peru, Olly visited archaeological sites and the local archaeological museum. Acquiring objects was probably one way of funding researches, as was common at the time. The anthropomorphic and zoomorphic ceramics vessels, funeral urns and pots, along with a collection of Paraca tissues she also purchased were later used as reference in her textile production. These references were materialized both in the stylization of animal figures – until then her work could be classified as abstract since the absence of identifiable forms – and the inclusion of vibrant colors in a palette previously made of neutral tones.

From the late 1970s on, there was in Werner's bedroom an armchair in wood and leather, designed by Márcio Mattar. Mattar's furniture used the imperfections of materials and the marks of manual labor as a style, affirming the relationship between craftsmanship and nature's own design. Thus, the wood's knots were left exposed and the wood was not perfectly sanded for its veins to stand out (see Figures 30, 38 and 86). Instead of painted, the furniture was blackened by the burning of a torch, so it would not lose its texture. The leather was also left with some imperfections and it was hand sewn. The armchair had a low wooden frame and a circular brown leather cushion, about six feet in diameter, which was thrown over the frame, so that the wooden feet hinted underneath the leather. As the leather cushion fell over the structure, one could see only the four feet made of thick pieces of black wood (Figure 38).

In a world marked by the attempt of domestication and control over nature, this chair and other similar furniture would be considered appropriate for rude people and farmers' houses. In the social context of transformation of taste that I am describing, it has been changed into a *style* that, together with indigenous and popular objects, formed a specific way of constructing and presenting oneself through the decoration of one's domestic space.

Knowing the provenance of some objects, their biography or part of it, contributed to interpret the role that the acquisition of one piece and not some other one would have in the context of Olly decoration of the apartment and construction of Olly's and Werner subjectivities. This was made possible thanks to the set of notes written by the artist on some of the objects present in the house (books and objects of decoration mainly) and also by family memory. Most of the furniture and some objects still remain in the family.

While the living room hosted larger meetings with people, usually participants from Olly's world, Werner's room served as a reception room for his friends, as well as family dining and television room. Almost every meeting mixed other languages besides Portuguese. According to interviewees, it did not feel as they were in Rio de Janeiro, both for the languages and the range of subjects discussed that went from international politics to modern art. Most of the interviewees referred mainly to the 1960s and 1970s, a period of authoritarianism in Brazil that turned several subjects into taboo.

Through photos and reports, we can get an idea of what these meetings were like. They could be dinner or afternoon meetings with tea or coffee. The crockery used was in ceramics with unusual colors and shapes: green square plates, black wooden base jugs and embedded ceramic pieces in burgundy and black, blue or dark green ceramic bowls.

Artist Marilia Rodrigues (1998) described these meetings as theatrical:

> *She (Olly) was a very refined woman. One of the things I remember very well is the refinement of the tables. She made the food herself. She cooked incredibly well and with a lot of refinement and a lot of visual beauty. Then she made, for example, a (10')22, she came with a gazpacho and at the right moment she poured that white cream in the center of an immense vessel. It was a feast, with applauses. It was a theater around that.*

The apparently "spontaneous" presence of outsiders was reported as frequent: one hour the house was empty, the next minute a small troupe came by surprise and the hostess prepared food and/or drinks to be served.

Design historian and anthropologist Alison Clarke (2001) identifies a transformation in the relationship with the home in England, after the 1990s, from the proliferation of a wide range of media aimed at its improvement. Decoration magazines, DIY crafts (Do It Yourself), TV shows geared toward tips on restoration in general and restoration of furniture and environments in particular indicate the aspiration to build the house as an inalienable environment and as an achievable commodity. Houses and gardens appear as aesthetic entities and their construction/decoration related to an expressive form associated with the consolidation and formation of a middle-class identity. Observing the relationship of some residents with their dwellings, the researcher also identified a disparity in the amount of investment placed in the decoration of domestic spaces compared to the evidence that they are rarely exposed to other looks, apart from that of their residents. This latest aspect is not the case represented by Olly and Werner's trajectory.

---

[22] Incomprehensible in the interview recording.

The couple's domestic space did not appear at any moment as an isolated and oppressive space, but I do not have enough information to affirm that it has never been so. However, after Olly's entry into the art scene, her apartment became a place of sociality appropriated by her as a way of building and expressing her aesthetic skills. This domain was one of the ways for the couple to establish relationships with the social world. The consumption of the things there exhibited was then a form of self-production, not a "reflection", of the construction and negotiation of styles and philosophies of life. The bookshelf full of pre-Columbian and Indigenous objects, as well as books and publications related to the couple's travels should therefore be understood in this context. I will talk about these collections in the next chapter.

Some colors predominated in the most stable things of the house, in the 1980s: blue, green and brown. The kitchen had dark green floors and white walls. The bathroom had beige floor and brown crockery. A cabinet with white marble shelves accommodated bathing towels and baskets from indigenous groups and folk crafts. These neutral shades were broken by Olly's colorful cushions, moving sculptures, and paintings, like those shown in Figures 14 and 19.

Figure 26: Olly and grandchildren's room. Fitting room for customers (MROW-G-80-22).

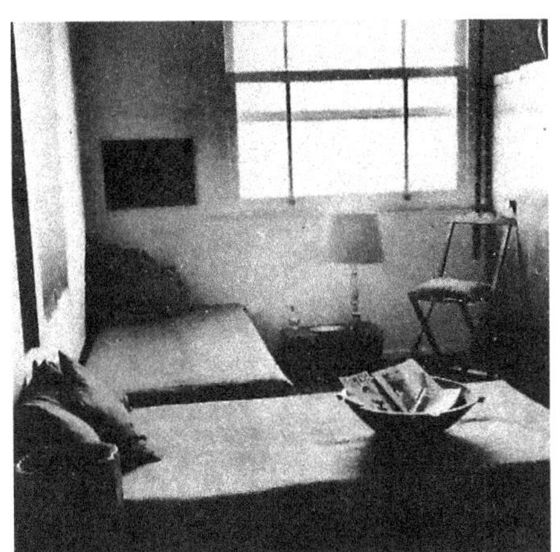

In Olly's room (Figure 26), there were two single beds, one for her, one for her grandchildren. This was the simplest room in the apartment. A large, simple white wardrobe kept the couple's personal belongings, as well as bedding and some other household things. This room also served as a dressing room and, there, her clients could try the artist's productions on. For some time, the third room (Figures 28, 29, 30 and 32) still kept the single bed that was once used by their son. In the late 1970s, this bed ceased to exist and was substituted by a 6 x 9 feet table topped with white Formica, whose "feet" were black lacquered wooden cubes. Inside these cubes there were work material: flaps and whole pieces of cloth, which came largely from the Bangu factory (now a shopping mall); wooden geometric shapes; material silk making; photographic equipment; slide projector; overhead projector; blocks of drawing paper; engraving gouges; paint supplies.

In this room, there was also a built-in closet where the yarns of crochet, knitting and loom were stored, and a white chest of drawers kept many documents which are now part of the current collection. On a shelf, 16 inches from the ceiling, various other materials and work equipment were stored. A spinning rock rested on the floor. On the wall there were large wooden squares, compass, scissors, and a wooden frame with spools kept the variously colored sewing threads that made up her palette. Paint chemistries were in a cabinet in the hallway (Figure 27).

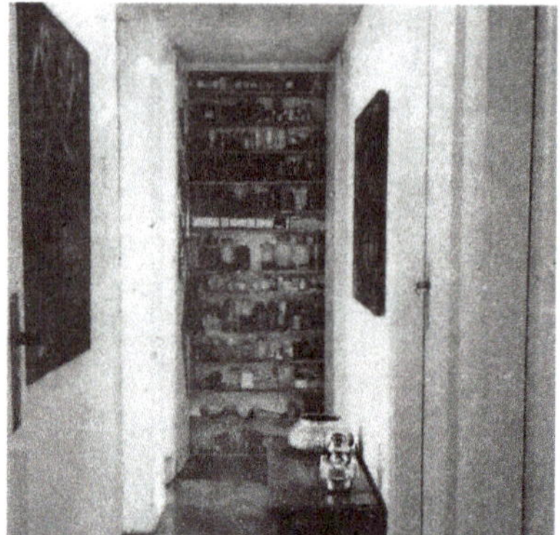

Figure 27: Hallway with cabinet and chemical for paints (MROW-G-80).

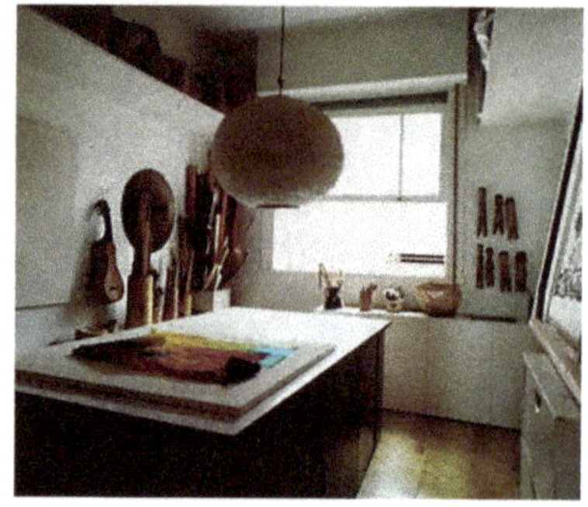

Figure 28: Artist's Studio (MROW-G-83).

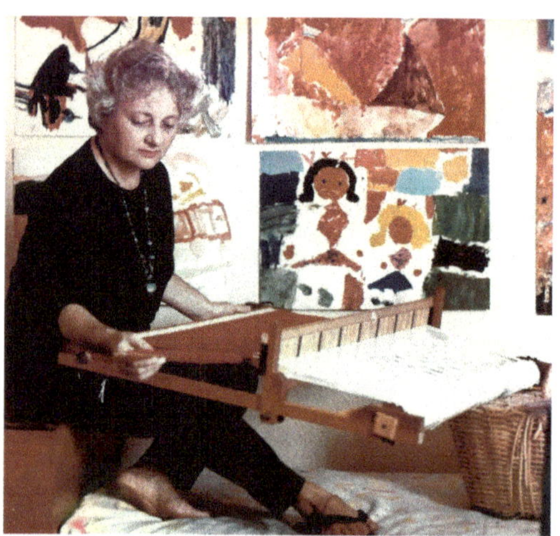

Figure 29: Olly Weaving (PH-1166).

Jean Baudrillard, whose contact in Paris was on Werner's phone book, spoke of the furniture configuration as an image of family and social structures:

"The typical bourgeois interior is of patriarchal order: set of dining room, sleeping room. The furniture, diverse in function but strongly integrated, gravitate around the cupboard or the central bed. There is a tendency to accumulate and occupy space, to its confinement" (2004: 21).

However, speaking from a structuralist perspective, the author did not take into account the diversity of ways of dealing with the values and representations of gender, class, and race in their particular historical contexts. At Olly and Werner's house nothing seemed typical. In the 1980s, life did not gravitate around the couple's bed—they did not even sleep together—nor of a cupboard that recalled the wife's domestic duties. The furniture was all aimed at presenting Olly's artistic production and consumption. Her *sensibility* was expressed through these objects and was constituted in contact with them. The dinners and snacks she prepared for friends who were invited or who surprised her to some extent also had this function as well as being reciprocal rituals. The receptions, especially dinners, unfolded in a web of endless retributions maintaining active ties and establishing new bonds. These meetings were also likely to circulate information about financings, subjects, buyers, among other things.

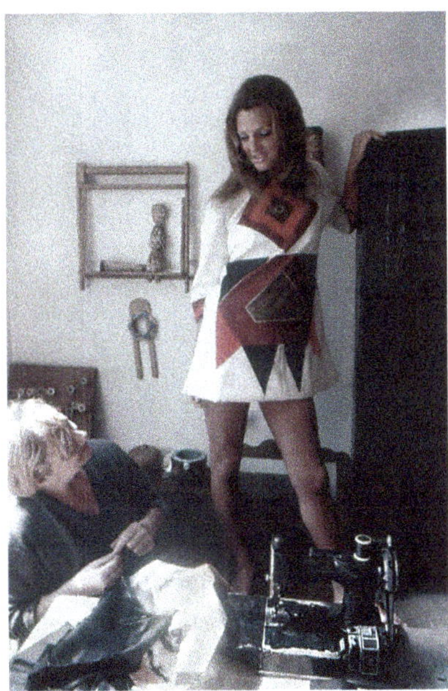

Figure 30: Artist's Studio with Olly and a model (PH-660).

The domestic space is to some extent a way for the family's construction and for symbolizing its integration of personal relations in a semi-closed web (Rosales, 2015).

Therefore, the organization of furniture and rooms in Olly's apartment represented a distinct morality from the typical carioca's middle-class. The apartment had no rooms closed to visitors. In Werner's room, the armchair, the dining table and the television made it a small living and dining room. In Olly's room customers and models circulated. Even the kitchen had its share in artistic production. When she started to focus on handmade paper, it was there that she cooked several things to separate the fibers and make the pulp that would be turned into sheets. With her typical humor, Olly mentioned this new passion in a letter to Canadian artist Betty White. According to Olly, Werner would stop at the kitchen door's threshold and ask, *is it food or paper?*, To which she replied in the letter, *it is almost always paper* (Olly, s.d.). In that same letter, she talks about her new experimentations: *Making paper is my new mania. All I see mentally becomes paper: among other things, straw hat, palm heart that is too hard to eat...* (idem)[23]

Even before paper production, the kitchen was the place for the manufacture of paints, dyeing cloths and where the largest loom stayed, 3 x 4 feet. Several people worked in this loom. Thus, more than a private space, the kitchen was also part of the artistic production and as such was not restricted to the transit of the inhabitants of the house. Perhaps only the servants' room, which had shelves covered with cloths to conceal more stored things, was not opened to outsiders' visiting.

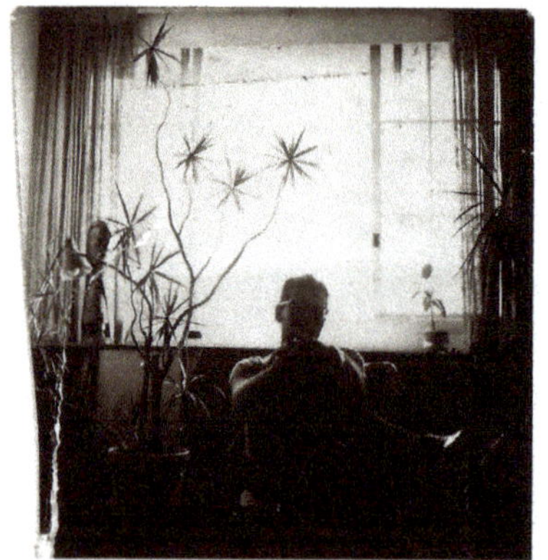

Figure 31: Living room, late 1950s (PH-922).

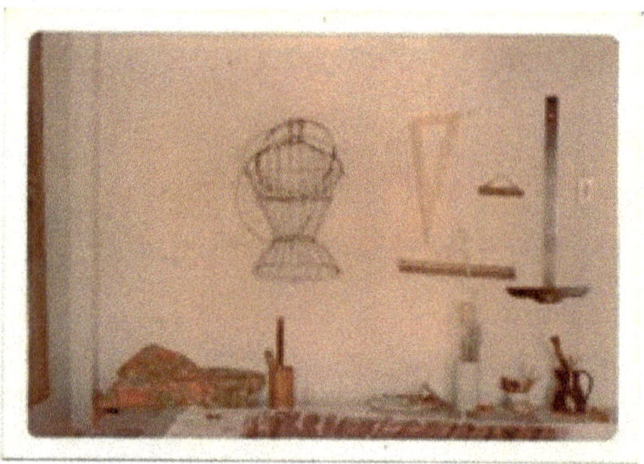

Figure 32: Artist's Studio (PH-792).

---

[23] Letter from Olly to Betty White and Stephen Strauss. s. d. CO-101.

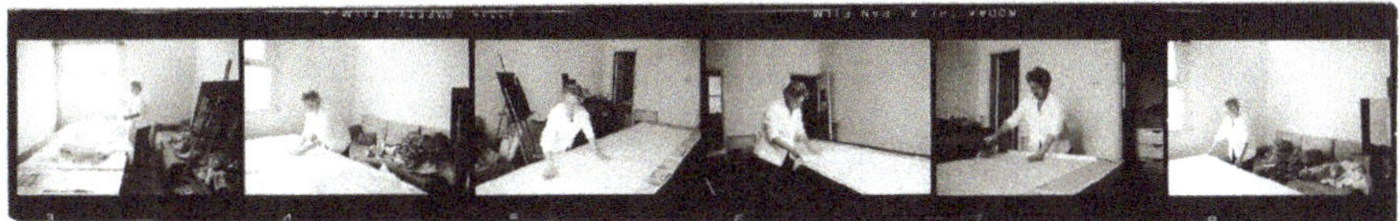

Figure 33: Olly painting in her studio (PH-992).

The apartment appears as a process and also as the materialization of a *project* (Velho, 2013). At the same time scenario where this *project* is acted out in the couple's several activities, the apartment itself was a supporting character in the construction of Olly's subjectivity and professional identity. In this sense, the interaction between people and things in the apartment results in the couple's actions, but their status is also legitimized against the background of the apartment which affects their actions. This same background is modified by the transformation of statuses, possibilities and contexts in which the couple is inserted.

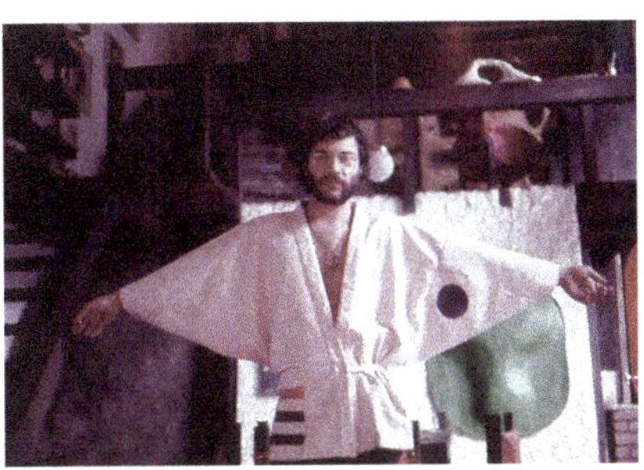

Figure 34: Márcio Mattar in his house, wearing a kimono made by Olly (DIA-769).

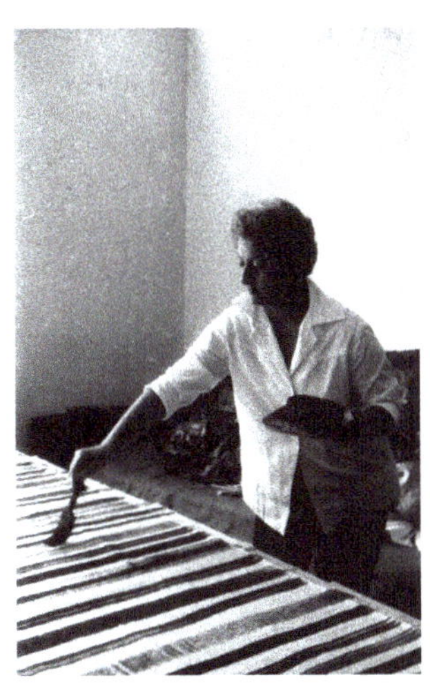

Figure 35: Olly in her studio (PH-992).

From the social point of view, the representation of this domestic space is associated with the formation and consolidation of a *middlelayer*[24] that asserted itself in its

---

[24] I use this concept as proposed by Gilberto Velho (1987), who sought to escape the ideology and social class ideas, investigating the urban middle-class lifestyle based on their projects and the tensions in the consumer society. The author sought to show that behind a fixed self that presented itself there was a plasticity that indicated a game between permanences and changes. Without abandoning economics as a

"instability", oscillating between heresies and conservatism (Vianna, Kuschnir and Castro, 2013) from the Southern Zone of Rio de Janeiro[25] throughout the 1950s and 1970s. The home as a private consumption arena gained momentum in this area along with real estate speculation and the increasing construction of tall buildings. The authoritarian regime that seized power in 1964 stimulated, specially for the sympathizers of left-wing ideologies, the use of private spaces to express their ideas. Private domains became then privileged spaces of subjectivities' construction. The decoration and practices inside and outside the apartment assumed importance in the constitution of a new class *habitus* that had nature, the sun and the popular as a paradigm of a youth that represented a new modernity, rustic but technological, sensual, critical and cheerful, but engaged in political and social issues. The women of this new middle class had in this process an important role as agents in the production of notions of femininity/masculinity, whiteness/blackness, work and class[26].

The decoration of the house is an inseparable practice of the past and future trajectories which are negotiated between families and their actions, projections and interiorizations. This was a stage for observation of how the privileges of class and color allowed that blacks, indigenous, peasants and others appeared in the objects produced and consumed, but not as subjects and consumers of artistic production. The process of transforming home is engaged in a social aspiration that goes beyond the accumulation and articulation of cultural capital (Bourdieu, 1979), but also implies ambitions and projections of ideal social relations. Though moved by feminist demands for a new social place for women, racial differences, diversity among women, and alliance politics often led to middle-class white women ignoring other subalternities, benefiting from other oppressions. This is how I see the transformations in the apartment as a social process, which includes gender, class and ethnicity, and not just an act of individual expressiveness.

---

dimension of social conflict and the importance of sets of values that are historically formed by certain groups and incorporated by others as universal truths, I also try to show a little of this social game in which many changes can be perceived as continuities, and vice versa. Therefore, I do not abandon completely the notion of social class, preferring this last one as a more comprehensible one for the English-speaking readers.

[25] This is the richest area in the District.

[26] In the nineteenth century, within what McClintock (2010) calls an anachronistic space created by colonial imperialism, the work of women, the colonized, and the working classes was denied and shifted from the historical time of modernity to prehistoric, atavistic, and irrational dimensions. In the second half of the twentieth century the work of middle-class white women was once again used to deny the impossibility of women from other ethnic and class groups to choose between caring for the family and working, caring for the family and caring for themselves.

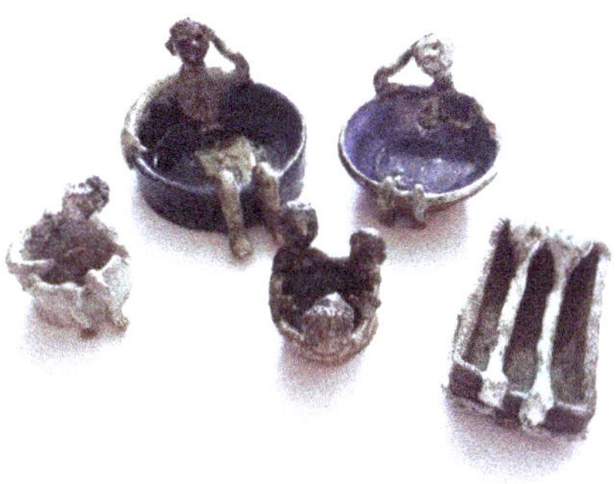

Figure 36: Brennand's ceramic ashtrays

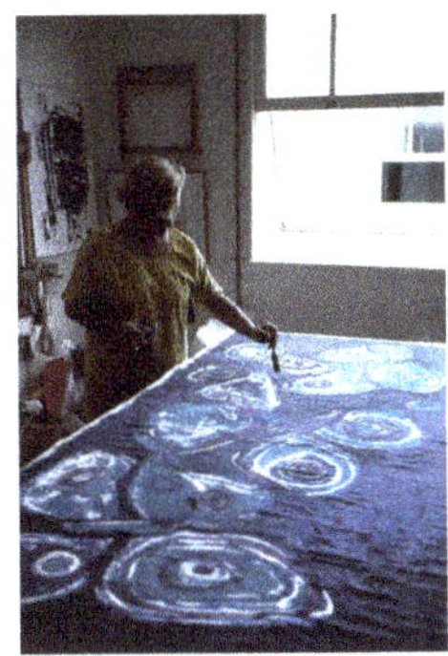

Figure 37: Olly in her studio (DIA-575).

I consider the apartment from four specific dimensions: decoration objects (furniture and utilities like ashtrays, plates, cutlery, etc.), non-utilitarian objects (paintings, sculptures, etc.), domestic spaces (different rooms) and the practical activities of the inhabitants.

The choice of furniture in Olly's apartment from the 1970s onwards apparently responded to two principles: furniture with simple lines and extensive use of leather and wood, with modern design (some possibly designed by Sérgio Rodrigues[27] and Joaquim Tenreiro[28]) and furniture exchanged or purchased from residents of the rural areas of Rio de Janeiro and Minas Gerais, mostly made of wood and marked by the passage of time. In this second category, one finds, for example, tables whose feet and tops are not cut at perfect angles and whose nodes and "defects" are incorporated into the furniture. In the same *style* it is possible to find in the photos of the collection a cabinet produced by Márcio Mattar (Figures 30, 38 and 86), designer jewelry and furniture as well as chairs produced by Olly's former daughter-in-law, Ivone R.

---

[27] Sérgio Rodrigues (1927-2014), was a furniture designer and architect, one of the designers of Forma important decoration store from São Paulo and Rio de Janeiro. In 1955, he opened Oca, his own furniture store in Ipanema. He created the first system of prefabricated modular architectural elements in Brazil for residential construction made in wood and exhibited the prototypes in MAM-RJ (Encyclopaedia Itaú Cultural http://enciclopedia.itaucultural.org.br/pessoa230381/sergio-rodrigues).

[28] Joaquim Albuquerque Tenreiro (Portugal 1906 - Brazil 1992) was a carpenter, furniture designer, painter and modern sculptor. He moved to Brazil at the age of two and between the 1940's and 1960's, he was dedicated to furniture design. Some of his furniture was upholstered with fabrics designed by Fayga Ostrower.

This furniture became reference for designers of the period. We can compare the taste for furniture style by carioca elites with other elites. The Portuguese elite from Goa, who left Mozambique at the time of its independence (Rosales, 2015) explicitly valued European designs, originals or copies. The appreciation of the memory inscribed in the work, both of the "natural wood" and human was one of the forms of constitution of a statute for this new Brazilian middle class. And it paved the way for new hermeneutics of modernity in Brazil. At the same time, and contradictorily, the group I am appreciating here appeared as an ambiguous accomplice appropriating the anachronistic space created by colonial imperialism, where the work of women, the colonized and the working classes was denied and displaced from the historical time of modernity to prehistoric time, atavism and irrationality to build a white patriarchal modernity in Brazil.

The admiration of European furniture was the counterpoint of the devaluation of Brazilian furniture (as in the case described by Rosales, 2015, the devaluation of "African objects"). None of these forms of appreciation is unanimous. Not all of the Brazilian elite considered European furniture better than Brazilian ones, and not everyone in this group I am calling the "new intellectual middle class" considered the objects of popular culture worthy of composing a new style of decoration of household spaces. For the ones that did value the furniture found in the rural areas, however, it seemed this kind of furniture had a secondary value in relation to furniture produced by designers and acquaintances, inspired by that "rustic style" (Márcio Mattar, Ivone R, for example).

This "new middle class" acquired importance in the face of the industrial consumer market that was beginning to flood urban centers. Along with the industrial transformations, the international movement for the constitution of the idea of a "primitive art" brought about transformations in the legal status of several native populations, reflecting the visibility and status of Brazilian local productions.

More than an emerging field of production, it was a new consumer market, since the valorization was not so much of the producers of these objects but of its consumption by this elite, to a great extent consisting of immigrants and first-generation descendants. The valued action was to find, conquer, collect, and eventually market such things. The valued work was not that of production, but of consumption as construction of oneself. It was thus the ability to see quality in certain things that made things and people who had such *sensibility* valuable.

It is the process of "giving visibility" to those objects, or in other words, the construction of these things as aesthetic values that it is important to unravel. For that, it is interesting to think about the possible analogy with the German intellectuals who constructed the idea of volk as a distinctive value for German national identity. It is also an intellectual elite, relatively lacking in political power, and largely opposed to the Brazilian authoritarian regime established in 1964. The construction of a cultural value of its own was thus one of the ways to attribute a different status whose base was also that of the popular as a source of authenticity, not so much for the Brazilian people or culture, but for this consumer elite who was also producer of artistic things.

Historian Vânia Carneiro de Carvalho (2008) talks about the organization of space and the domestic system, starting in 1870, in São Paulo. During this period, the urban houses underwent radical, physical, economic, social and cultural transformations. The author focused her observation on the relation between domestic objects and gender identities from the dynamics of daily life. She showed there were markedly feminine spaces in relation to others considered as masculine.

For her, there was an educational role in the decoration of the domestic environment in the late nineteenth century and in the practice of male collectivism as one of the matrices for the construction of domestic furniture as an alternative world to that of urban working places. The house would have been gradually transformed into small domestic museums with evocative emblems of culture, important tools for the training of children and adults.

According to the author, the modernity that was projected through the house during this period was the result of the simplification of European aristocratic residential models adapted to the bourgeois aspirations in nineteenth-century Brazilian elite. In it we can find defined spaces such as public, private and service areas, intermediated by internal and external transitional areas. These nineteenth-century houses are part of new consumer practices, transforming the simplicity of the colonial interior into a way of life generically called bourgeois.

The transition to a consumption-oriented way of life has meant the introduction of a new modeling force of social relations: luxury artifacts. This luxury presupposed the manifest imbalance in social hierarchy and inequality. Those excluded from the consumer society, the poor, indigenous groups, the insane, were thus the privileged others through whom these social identities and individual subjectivities were constituted.

Carvalho speaks of two distinct forms of gender construction through the relationship with the domestic space and the arrangement of objects within that space. In the masculine case, the body-object relationship was regulated by a principle of self-reference that related to the physical, intellectual and social interests, involving public exposure in the private space of the house. In the female case, the body-object relationship had a diffuse character that was extensively and nonspecifically expressed in the appropriation of the domestic space. These two formats were associated with equally distinct body patterns, senses, values, and actions. The gender perspective from the body-object relationship allowed the author to perceive the relevance of daily actions and body routines in the construction of generalized subjectivities. Generally, the production considered feminine was that which represented some kind of screen between the external and the internal world, curtains, lamps, pillows. Objects that softened the hardness of furniture or filtered the intensity of light.

In nineteenth century male iconography, a recurring theme was the domestic office as an image of intellectual work and a form of social prestige. If we take Werner's office-room in the late 1970s, we came across a room that was not marked as a predominantly male space. The furniture denounced the uses of that space. Thus, the dark wood shelf, occupying the left wall from floor to ceiling, exposed both collections of objects and books. A large part of the lower shelves (about 9 linear feet) housed a collection of the National Geographic[29] magazine, accumulated from the early 1960s to the early 1980s; on the wider shelves there were several art books; a set of shelves stored the albums with postcards and tourist books on mostly European Countries, but also Brazilian and Latin American cities where the couple traveled; many shelves exhibited the collection of pre-Columbian, indigenous, African, and Oriental objects; the books in Portuguese, German, English, and French were mostly on political science, anthropology, philosophy, economics, art, and literature, as well as a collection of Polish childrens' drawings magazines. All of those occupied the wall from top to bottom.

There it was exhibited the couple's "formation trips", either through the souvenirs that built the interiority of the immigrant who was not Brazilian, and neither no longer German, or through the collections that inserted Olly in a Brazilianess that both contributed to construct by participating in the web of relations in which they were immersed. But if in the nineteenth century it was possible to think of a body formed from the centripetal movement as opposed to another centrifugal one, in the second half of the twentieth century this opposition was no longer explicit. Not only Olly was a point outside the curve of the gender representations idealized for women of the Brazilian elite, but also Werner was an accomplice in this micro-revolution perceptible in the distribution of spaces within the house.

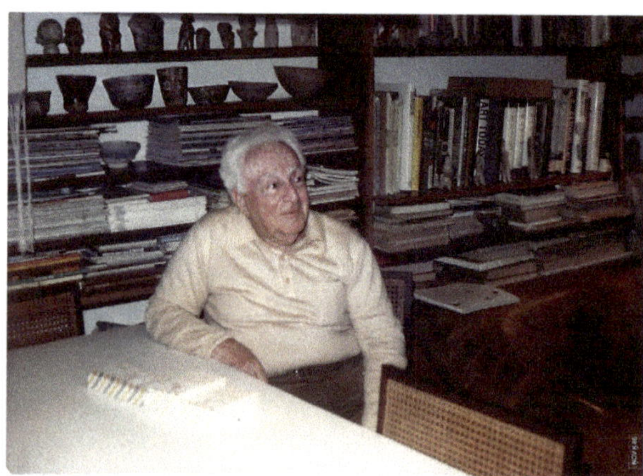

Figure 38: Werner in his bedroom-office-dining and TV room, 1980s. In the background one can see the bookshelf with the couple's books and pieces. To Werner's right, one sees the leather cushion that belonged to Márcio Mattar's armchair (PH-1221).

Werner's space was also the space of family and affection. His desk, where the typewriter was placed and his letters typewritten, was not typical of the large, dark, massive men's office desks. It was a modern design table, with simple lines and a white Formica top. The six chairs that surrounded the table followed these lines, being of dark wood, with braided straw seats and backs. The design could be by

[29] This collection was donated in the year 2000 to the library of the Geography Department of the Federal University of Rio de Janeiro (UFRJ).

Joaquim Tenreiro or Norman Westwater. The masculine space of the house was transpassed by the feminine. Perpendicular to the shelf full of books was this table that was both a dining table and where the family sat to watch television. From the late 1970s, the family nucleus gathered in Werner's room/office (Figures 22, 24, 25 and 38).

Pictures from previous years (Figure 39) indicate that Werner's room once looked more like a traditional male office. Yet it is possible to glimpse details that anticipate the following "style", denoting a change in the centrality that Olly had in the house (on the last shelf one can see a small African sculpture). In the early or mid-1970s, the relatively small size of the bookshelf required choosing those things representatives of intellectual reflection. Books, postcards, and travel albums that were evidence of the family's commitment to the bourgeois universe of values were only exposed in the eyes of visitors a few years later.

This collection of objects and publications can be perceived in its unity as constituents of the subjectivities of both Olly and Werner. Nevertheless, only with time and developments of their trajectories these collections were arranged as a showcase "of civility, good taste and refinement". Since these values are not an essence of these objects, it was not enough in another context to show them as a way to associate the couple's image with these notions. It was necessary that their life trajectories be built along paths that had these notions as a basis so the diverse objects that were part of this construction could be appreciated in this way. These values

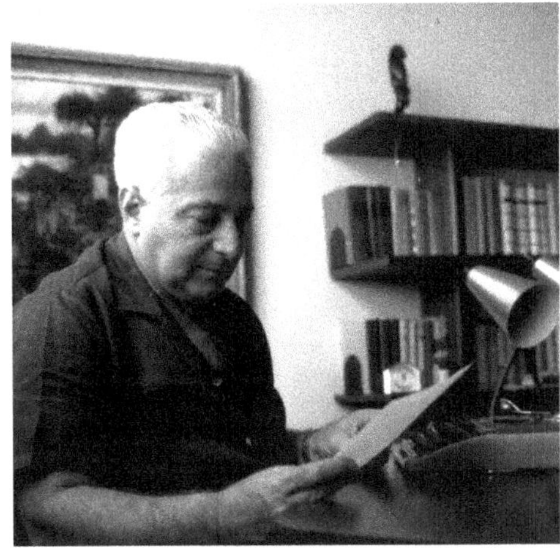

Figure 39: Werner in his bedroom-office, early or mid-1970s (DIA-1250).

then become part of their meanings when they are inserted into a system within which other objects, practices, and people expose them to the detriment of other senses.

In the nineteenth century, "colonial style" was revised to represent the luxury consumption of a Brazilian bourgeois elite, seeking in the inequality an affirmation of superiority. In the second half of the twentieth century, the recognition of the aesthetic qualities of the production of the ones excluded from consumer society – poor, indigenous, crazy – was a way to construct social identities and individual subjectivities based on a political superiority that believed in the ideal of social equality expressed at least in the recognition of that material production. The appropriation of the production of those peripheric groups was ambiguous and contradictory, the privileged other of this construction being not only the excluded, but also those who did not recognize them as subjects of human rights. This insight does not apply to all those who were part of the couple's web of relations, but it certainly formed the basis of Werner's political stances shared by Olly. Race, class, and gender were dimensions intertwined in these appropriations. But there was also the recognition of cultural practices distinct from those produced by western industry.

In Brazil, it was only after the first two decades of the twentieth century that we saw the diffusion of objects aimed at the decoration of residences. Nevertheless, in 1948, Monteiro Lobato denounced the eclectic models of the palacetes' decoration by the lack of a "Brazilian style". In the 1960s, it appeared the first magazines focused on domestic decorations. The observation of fashion and decoration magazines in Olly and Werner's collection allowed me to understand the attributes and meanings conveyed about Olly's artistic production, inserting them into forms of *sensibility* and patterns of taste. The descriptive categories used to present objects constitute a lexicon of cultural concepts related to the sensory experiences that evidence particular ways of organizing the world.

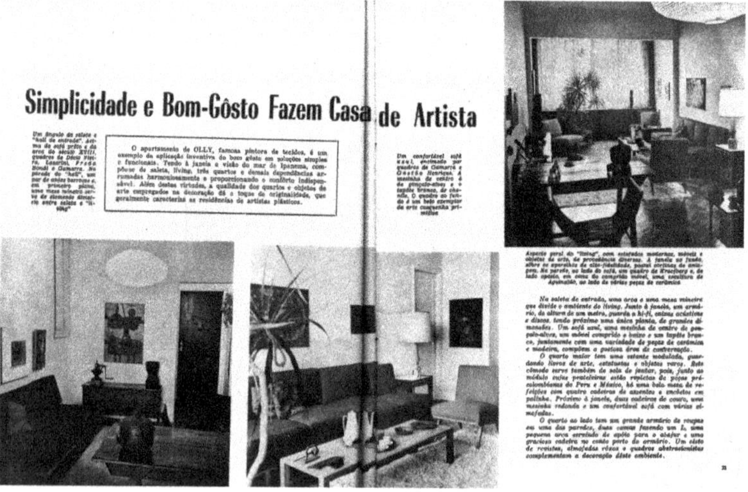

Figure 40: First issue of *Casa e Decoração* (Home and Decoration) magazine. Three-page article about Olly and Werner's apartment decoration, 1966 (MROW-G-80).

In these journals, I found values associated with home environments, arrangements and certain objects, as well as work routines indicating ways to map practices, attributes and meanings that helped me to understand some terms used such as *rustic, wild, modern*. These journals were an important means of disseminating models. Instead of disposable, like today, the magazines were saved for consultation. Interior photos, associated with known or unknown professionals served as a diffuser of new taste patterns, suggesting to potential consumers arrangements by associating values with specific sets of objects.

The things accumulated by the couple thus gain the meaning of a pre-industrial world, where manual labor was full of collective senses. It is not a question of associating rarity, antiquity and monetary value, as in the case of antiquities. In the case of pre-Columbian, indigenous and rural and popular pieces, the value is given by the cultural sense. As a system that draws on the relationships between objects, these values were embodied in design pieces, whose technology and rationality conveyed a sense of modernity lacking historical depth. In Europe, modernity had been built up over the centuries by intellectual reflection and political and technological development. Brazil continued with a profoundly unequal system and with an economy that privileged the importation of technology. One of the ways of adding historical value to the modernity of objects was to insert them into a system in which indigenous and popular cultural production was redefined from an aesthetic perspective.

This was not a strictly Brazilian movement. That's why it is possible to see in the exhibition of furniture and architecture of prefabricated houses references to oceanic "art" in French (Figure 41). In 1966, Agnaldo Manuel dos Santos, an afro-Brazilian sculptor produced what was classified at the time as "African art" or "afro-Brazilian art"[30]. It was an international movement the expansion of the artistic field to incorporate new categories recognized as art. It can be observed in Brazil from the performance of a group of intellectuals of which Olly and Werner were part.

This movement of artification of objects of preindustrial peoples happened not only in museums, galleries and books, but also in peoples' homes. The set of meanings incorporated in things is produced by the association of objects with the place they occupy in the decoration and by the association of these with the artist and her web of relations. At the same time as the artistic objects were the setting for Olly's performances, Werner's books placed production and performances in a political context of capitalism and colonialism's criticism. Although it is possible to sketch a critique of the instrumental use of the culture of non-Western peoples (pre-Columbian, "orientals" and Brazilian Indigenous groups) as an unauthorized appropriation for personal gain, belief in the apolitical dimension of modern and

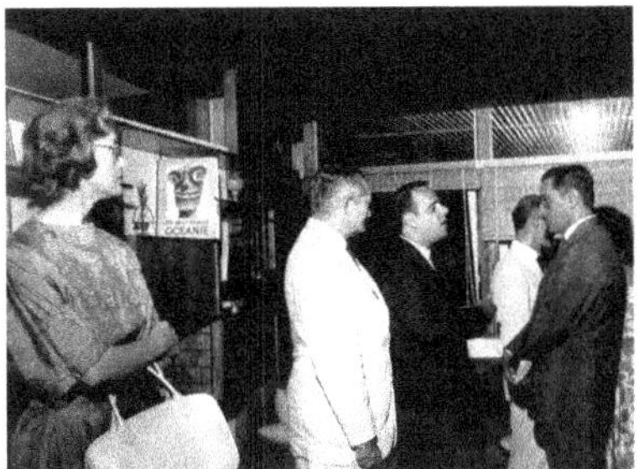

Figure 41: In 1960, Sérgio Rodrigues appears at the opening of the exhibition of Oca's projects of prefabricated houses. On the shelf we see a representative figure of a candomble orisha and a book on "Oceanic savage art." (MAM-Rio Collection)

---

[30] In chapter 3, I introduce the sculptor in more detail. See in figures 16 and 21 a sculpture by Agnaldo that belonged to Olly.

contemporary art collapses when we understand that the locus of producing visibility for Olly's work was not only museums and galleries but the apartment where critics, artists and art collectors apprehended the sense of her practice at the intersection of her performances with Werner's political rhetoric. The cloths and clothes then carried part of the value of these inalienable objects which were the exhibited collections and the souvenirs around the apartment.

In the 19th century the decorative ideals were brought by "foreign companies that saw in the country a way to expand their markets and by national groups inserted in the international economy that saw as a factor of progress and modernization the dissemination of European taste patterns" (Carvalho, 2008). In the mid-twentieth century, transformations in taste were implemented mainly by a European web of arts and design professionals (mainly furniture and architecture designers, but also graphic, clothing and jewelry designers) that came before or immediately after the Second World War and/or first- or second-generation descendants. Modernity in the second half of the twentieth century appeared as the production of a "decorative style" based on the idea of *rusticity*, the foundation of a Brazilian authenticity. The arrival of several foreigners fleeing the imminent war or its consequences introduced in Rio de Janeiro new ways of living and being in the world, new lifestyles, moral, aesthetic and economic values. War thus engendered objective and subjective conditions for the development of new forms of subjectivity.

Carvalho notes that in the nineteenth century there was an aversion of the wealthy segments of Sao Paulo society to local culture. This revulsion was related to a project of ascent of the Brazilian elites. It was up to the architects to translate the interests of the contracting families in terms of manipulating the symbolic universe of the social daily life of that family seeking to materialize the fantasies and desires at the time of the construction and decoration of the house. With the knowledge of the historical and architectural culture, this professional gave form to the not always explicitly expressed aspirations and desires of individuality, cosmopolitanism and refinement (2008: 158). By the mid twentieth century, this new middle class, mostly of immigrant origin, triggered what much of Brazilian society was neglecting to constitute a new social identity associated with the country that received it.

Thus, the meanings of tradition and ancestry emanating from Olly and Werner's living room furniture are not those referred to Germany or Europe, but to Brazil and Latin America.

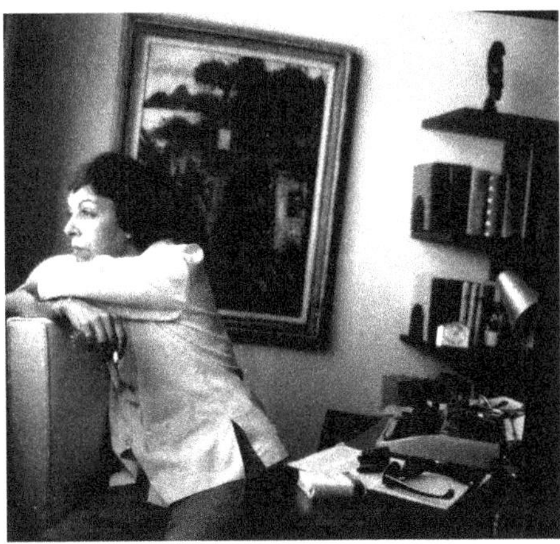

Figure 42: Writer Clarice Lispector in Werner's bedroom-office, c. 1974 (DIA-1248).

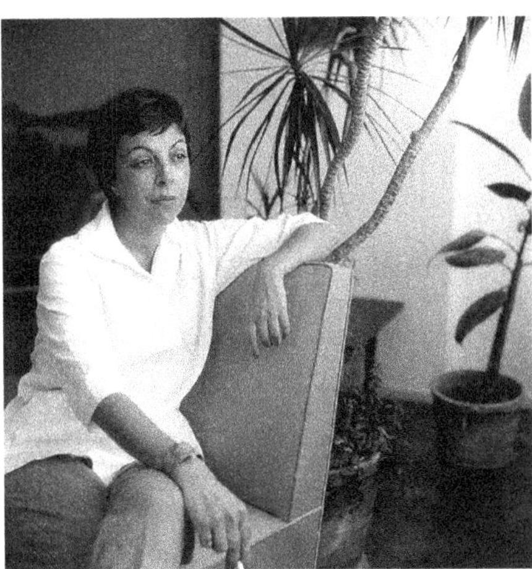

Figure 43: Writer Clarice Lispector in the living room of the couple's apartment, c. 1974 (DIA-874).

The house, as a place of social coexistence, worked in two formally differentiated registers. In a more public sense, some interviewees described the couple's home as an open space to the arrival of friends who were promptly invited to lunch, dinner, or snack. It is in this record that the couple's son recalls having watched, in the 1950s, a film about the Holocaust used during the Nuremberg trial. According to him, sanitarist Noel Nutels was present. In another opportunity he also recalls having heard musician Paulinho da Viola play the guitar, way before the singer and composer achieved social recognition.

Described by René and other interviewees, the informality inscribed in these daily practices reflects the existence of ties of greater or lesser proximity between these people. It also reinforces the idea that the apartment could not be rigidly conceived neither as a public nor a private space. Olly received her clients there where she also produced her fabrics and clothes. The photos of writer Clarice Lispector sitting in the living room and in Werner's office can be interpreted as part of this idea (Figures 42 and 43). She bought Olly's fabrics and made them a character in the tale "O morto no mar da Urca" (The dead man in the Urca Sea) (Lispector, 1974). The private dimension of Clarice's personal consumption is transformed into an event when recorded in the story and the photos mediate this transition from private to public dimension.

Both these photos and the statements of the interviewees denote the importance of the domestic space as a context of sociability, offering elements of social distinction that were legitimized by the practices of the couple. Practices and objects then materialized this legitimacy into a constant movement between the material and immaterial dimension of cultural life. While the idea of "refinement" denotes, in other contexts (Rosales, 2015: 213), social class, in the case of the couple this category was accompanied by the idea of "visual beauty" and "theatricality", which linked the hosts, as well as the guests, to the circuits of cultural production.

In 1966, the first issue of the magazine *Interior and Decoration* presented in its editorial the objective *to awaken and develop the taste*. It invested in aesthetics as a criterion of distinction based on interiority, regardless of economic value: price did not determine quality. That year, clearly the main reference for decoration was still Europe. Anglicisms and Frenchisms were added to the images and spelling of Portuguese, and most environments and objects resembled romanticism and rococo, with a lot of brocade and walls and furniture covered by floral prints. The environments presented referred to European and North American museums and films. It was still an American designer, George Nelson (1908-1986), who was offered as an example in the production of modern interiors by his use of space and straight lines. Nelson had been hired by Herman Miller, creator of the Herman Miller Research Corporation in 1960, to research the changes in office furniture usage during the twentieth century. This modernity represented by Nelson was widely influenced by Bauhaus, a movement that was appropriated by Playboy magazine for the constitution of decorative styles representative of a masculinity that affirmed the presence of men in urban apartments, independent of marriage (Preciado, 2010).

However, on the page following the editorial Olly's apartment was the reader's suggestion for its "simple" interior decoration. In the review, the "famous painter of textiles" presented "objects of art" that gave *the touch of originality that characterize the houses of fine artists*. Unlike ALL the other environments in the magazine, the apartment was pointed as an example of *simplicity and good taste*. The things exhibited in the rooms were referred in the text to the idea of origin and primitiveness: the old coffee grinder, the wood pestle marked by time, pre-Columbian pieces and plants made up the various environments presented in the account. A picture of "primitive Cusco art", "an ark and a mining table", "a mattress lined with rustic fabric", "an old chair" and "a coffee table made in Gonçalo-Alves wood"[31] were particularly named, 1966). The categories used to qualify objects denoted both the past and the opposition to the city. There were references to certain primitivism and Brazilian modernism of the 1920s that, through Mário de Andrade and Tarsila do Amaral, sought a Brazilian authenticity in the interior of Minas Gerais.

This anonymous "rustic man", who had produced and stored what was exchanged with or sold to Olly, and others, was the counterpoint of those named: Ivan Serpa, Franz Krajcberg, Roberto Magalhães, Carlos Scliar, Agnaldo Manuel dos Santos, Ivan Freitas, Celeida Tostes (among others). The modernity of the artists nominated was constructed in opposition to the old, rustic and anonymous, at the same time, the value of the *rustic man's production* was constituted by the participation in the same system of objects produced by these "modern artists". This is how the indigenous material culture gained some recognition in broader circles than the proper anthropological one, even if kept anonymous or always referred to collective memberships: Karajá[32], Bororo, Yanomami.

Rustic, ancient and *primitive*, terms that formed the presentation lexicon of the artist's house, had their senses transformed by the presence of the "abstractionist paintings", becoming signs of distinction, identity and ancestry. On the one hand, this was a period of enlargement of the anachronistic space (McClintock, 2010) produced by colonialism. On the other hand, the fetish of the archaic gained aesthetic contours in Brazil. Olly's alleged originality in the decoration of her apartment was then the result of a mixture of meanings implicit in objects that could belong to the semantic field of poverty, deprivation of culture or knowledge, places of scientific research and proper political action. But in the apartment, they were merged with objects and people who were building a sense of modernity and were thus capable of a magical conversion of meanings. Part of this magic is the transformation that naturalized the artist's form of decoration into an "originality" present in the totality of artists. But it is this same conversion that adds aesthetic value to the whole production of these peripheric groups that once more embody the narratives of modernity of this middle class.

Ten years later, in 1976, Casa Vogue featured the title "The Victory of Natural Wood" (Casa Vogue, 1976). A photo of Ivo Pitanguy's house, designed by Sérgio Bernardes, illustrated the mention of the tendency to value "rare" and "exotic"

---

[31] It is the Astronium fraxinifolium tree originary of the cerrado, that is, the vegetation of the interior where a certain Brazilian origin was forged by several authors from the end of the 19th century to the middle of the XX

[32] Carajá or Karajá are two ways of spelling the old denomination of the Iny people. I opted here for the karajá spelling because it was the one that prevailed at the time and in most of the documents related to the researched material. When in some document the name was spelled with c, I respected the spelling of the document.

objects. In this picture we can see gardens designed by Burle Marx[33]. Some articles in that volume were titled, "The sophistication of the primitive house"; "Back to the nature of American homes"; "Embu: the past lives in São Paulo"; "The return of natural wood".

In "The sophistication of the primitive house", ethnologists Villas Bôas brothers spoke of the indigenous dwellings using beautiful black and white photos. The house of an architect was presented with an apparent contradiction of terms in the headline "evolution to simplicity". The subject presented São Paulo's colonial architecture. The first article on "modern" furniture made with Brazilian wood, in a rustic style, began with an excerpt from the presentation of Zanine Caldas' exhibition at MASP. Modernity was not PVC, fiberglass or aluminum, but it was not their rejection either. These industrial materials were presented along raw materials and the memory of artisanal work. The neon picture gained new sense through the frame of the plants that flanked it (Figure 44).

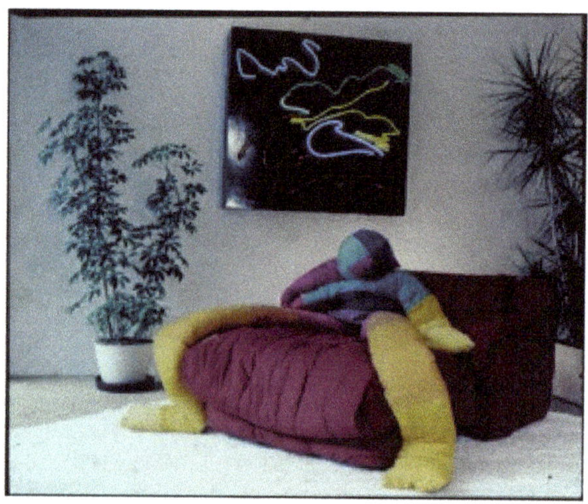

Figure 44: Olly's speech on clothes to wear and to hang on the wall eventually led her down the decorative path. From the 1970s onward, she began making pillow fabrics, mobile sculptures like the one on the photo and various objects for decoration. The Forma store, which had its headquarter in São Paulo and a branch office in Rio de Janeiro, was the venue for exhibitions and frequently had her products sold together with the furniture it commercialized.

In the context of this second magazine, a small call with two photos dispensed Olly's presentation (whose CV "would be too long") and her work was announced to decorators and architects. The style was settled. The *Casa & Decoração* magazine,

---

[33] Landscape designer of the period.

three years later, spoke in "typical" crafts to compose a *"very Brazilian habitat"*. Carvalho (2008) argues that the notion of *ambience* in a reference to the domestic space as a refuge from the external and impersonal world arose in Brazil in the nineteenth century. The idea of *habitat*, which makes the inner space of the house part of an external nature appears in decoration magazines for the first time in the 1960s.

Casa & Decoração's column discussed Paulo Terra's decorating style stating that if you "Tell me how you live, I'll tell you who you are". In the same magazine, the closing advertisement announced the Peroba Oil product as the care of a *living nature at home* (Casa & Decoração, 1979). This nature, presented as beautiful and noble, was the earthly paradise as opposed to civilization and European modernity. Nature and rusticity were a constituent part of a specific modernity, properly Brazilian. Colored cushions painted by Olly were laid out on top of a white rug of raw cotton and among unpainted pottery plants and vases. It was in the distance of Europe that the immigrants returned to their *human nature* and women to their *instincts* mediated by notions at first contradictory like simplicity and elegance, rusticity and modernity.

In 1980, handicraft items were already considered items collectable by the wider public: *If you like crafts, start saving your works, whether by theme, affinity or material. Because they can turn into collections.* (Home & Decoration, 1980) Each could become a collector of handicrafts and as such distinguish themselves, constitute their subjectivity from an apparently purposeless hobby. Individuality forging new ways of differentiating oneself through the constitution of groups that shared that specificity. It was the distinction between the types of handicrafts collected and the way of classifying them that made the collections at the same time differentiating their collectors, although they could all belong to a unique group of crafts collectors.

If we take the metaphor of the salad, used by Montaigne and appropriated by the anthropologist Hélio Menezes (2018) to think the idea of Afro-Brazilian art, although the collectors who were formed in that period had very different trajectories, objectives and kinds of collections, it is possible to use the idea of collection as a technology of self-construction to think of the similarities between them. According to anthropologist Anne McClintock, in the nineteenth century the imperial state watched deviant classes, races, and genders for an appropriate distribution of money, sexuality and property, and the idea of an anachronistic space "became central to the discourse of racial science and urban vigilance development of women and the working class "(2010: 73). In the 1960s and 1970s, in Brazil, the narrative of origin also through its collecting and exhibition was one of the forms of revisioning the women's place in the white and heterosexual middle class. The "primitives" were again fetishized through *spectacles of domestic consumption* and this space was once again racialized as a form of class, race, and gender domination.

Voting analysis can be thought of as a reference for reflecting on the issue of artistic styles not as individual choices, but as *adhesions* in a process that will compromise the individual, her/his family or group over time. Analyzing the political vote, anthropologists Beatriz Heredia and Moacir Palmeira questioned intentionality and individuality in the choice of political candidates: the "social perception the populations have of the processes and activities in which they are involved, as well as the social meanings that they invest in their actions, which have objective consequences for the results of these actions, suggests that voting is not necessarily an individual undertaking, that the question of intentionality may not be relevant, and that a choice is not necessarily at stake; that the importance of elections may not be limited to the indication of representatives or rulers and that seemingly natural sequences may not be a matter of logic, but of "socio-logic" (2006: 38).

In the same way, the meanings invested in the actions of producing and consuming certain books, objects, clothes have objective consequences for the results of these actions. Thus, the choice of certain "aesthetic parties" is not an individual enterprise, but a socio-logical one. The analogy with the idea of a specific "politics" of art, although not with the system of adhesion described by Heredia and Palmeira, is present in the discourse of art critic Mario Pedrosa when he assumed the direction of the Museum of Modern Art of São Paulo in 1960: he declared then that his *aesthetic militancy* had come to an end. The idea of an *aesthetic militancy* founded the notion of aesthetic party used here. I take the movements that succeeded between the 1950s and 1980s in Brazil as ideological systems more or less formalized with spokesmen, defenders, followers and often, specific training or support institutions.

To associate to a certain discourse or *aesthetic party*, in verbal or visual terms, was to associate with a set of actors that held positions of more or less influence. It contributed to the enlargement or reduction of power to nominate new artists, new styles, produce new exhibitions, issue opinions, define values and join a web of reciprocities. It also matters the public statement on the "side" chosen in the dispute. In the artistic field, the interaction between the actors happens from the definition of "styles", or lines of works that authorize names (to convert ordinary people into artists). To have at home abstract pictures and objects related to a certain artistic style, or style of decoration of domestic spaces amounted to a declaration of affiliation, of "adhesion". While voting is the expression of a connection with a particular candidate, regardless of platform and party, involving personal loyalties, adherence to an *aesthetic party* is adherence to a web of actors, institutions, things and values. The nodes of convergence of lines through which relationships develop are the collections and artistic objects, in the broadest sense possible, including contemporary manifestations as performances, for example.

The idea of accompanying an *aesthetic party* was pertinent in a given context. It was a kind of asymmetrical connivance with those with whom this artist had established reciprocal commitments, be it with her audience, gallery owners, art critics and other artists. This accompaniment was a reference for her daily actions and a legitimate instance (based on a reciprocal relation) to whom to turn in certain situations that could be indications for works, loans of works for decorations, exhibitions or even suggestion of buyers.

I am not saying that choosing a certain *aesthetic party* is relative only to "interests" in participating in a specific group of actors, but that participation in a particular group is decisive for the choice of the "aesthetic party". To understand this proposition not as opportunism, but as alliances we need to extend the meaning of the term interest beyond its strictly rational and economic sense. Sahlins draws attention to the broad meaning of the term: "the word" interest derives from an impersonal verbal construction in Latin, meaning "that which makes a difference". "Interest in something is [then] the difference it makes for someone" (2004: 310). Bourdieu, in turn, drew attention to the idea that ""interest" may be the effect of affinities linked to the identity (or homology) of positions in different fields" (Bourdieu, 2002). Elective affinities, which reinforce positions in the intellectual field, are what "makes the difference" in the choice of aesthetic parties, styles or intellectual projects.

Contrary to the "time of politics" (Heredia e Palmeira, 2006) among peasants, "aesthetic politics" in artistic worlds is a permanent activity, although in certain periods may be more evident as in Art Biennial periods. It is not limited to a specific period when "factions" are identified, and exist in open conflict. These "factions" are only tentatively and temporally delimited and defined, and conflict only in specific situations is opened. The same way as voting, the objective signs of adhesion to an *aesthetic party* are more than a matter of an individual decision. These signs are also spread throughout the house, in the participation of the family, especially spouses, and friends.

Adherence to a given *party* can be thought from the disputes between artistic "styles" – figurative, abstract, concrete, neoconcrete – but influences are not always declared. In Olly's work, the influence of Paraca fabrics is reinforced when she raised money for refugees from an earthquake in Lima, by her property of a collection of Paraca textiles, and also by the presence of pre-Columbian objects in her house. On the other hand, the Oriental influence (Japanese, Chinese, Thai) is almost invisible. If I hadn't found reference books on the subject and some Oriental stamps used in the fabrics, that influence could not be mentioned. The greater visibility of some influences to the detriment of others is part of a thematic, iconographic and axiological range that constitutes the *aesthetic party* to which Olly was affiliated.

The participation of a social actor in the artistic world is capable of increasing her/his authority within a family unit. Although the aesthetic choice is part of an individualistic ideology (Dumont, 1985), the one who belongs to this universe, depending on her/his recognition in the field, tends to automatically compromise her/his domestic group. At the same time as expressing the unity of the family, the artist gains legitimacy with this family support and this support also contributes to the recognition of the aesthetic party in question. In Olly's case, all the grandchildren work, or worked at some point, with some artistic expression. Her daughter-in-law became a recognized artist in the city where she lives, with such identification with her mother-in-law that many of the interviewees believed Olly was her mother. This is, in part, the internalization of canons, analyzed by Bourdieu (1996), which reinforces the idea of a hereditary transmissible gift. Olly's son, however, although he has dedicated himself to piano and singing in sporadic moments of his life, has never identified himself with the cultural production. The house can then be perceived as a political space where declarations and adhesions are produced through different practices. However, the artistic production of a social actor can be understood as a political investment, it is not limited to these choices.

Hardly a man would have his professional practice related to the decoration of his house. However, Olly's thinking about her home and the objects she collected and exhibited, both in her apartment and in her last exhibition – Origins (1981) – offers a rich perspective on collectivism associated with a new style of decorating domestic spaces and the possible meanings attached to it.

In Carvalho's research on patterns of decoration of domestic environments in São Paulo from the mid-nineteenth century to the beginning of the twentieth she argued that furniture, transmitted between generations, could be used for more than a century in the same family. The furniture and utensils eventually acquired strong personal and affective connotations. Therefore, forced migration can be understood as partly responsible for creating new lifestyles to replace the impossibility to carry family furniture along. The chests and safes, made to store objects during transport, were in the medieval European period the most significant furniture of the families. In Brazil, these furnishings predominated during the sixteenth and seventeenth centuries, as part of the unstable occupations of the territory. The sense of memory contention has been updated in the book published by Olly's sister (Hasenberg, 2012) where she tells the story of her multiple migrations – Germany, Brazil, Colombia, Venezuela, Cuba, Italy. Olly left behind chests, several furnishings and other objects that accumulated her memories. While she was alive and producing these furnishings helped the construction of her recognition in a cultural field [34] that herself contributed to constitute. After her death they were important allies in evoking her memories.

Alison Clarke (2001) argues that in England, after World War II, there was a greater identification of working classes with their households, rather than work, and a shift towards self-identification issues with consumption, a domain over which one had more control. The author shows that at the end of the 19th century (1881) some publications presented the house as widely instrumental in daily life and the decorations as expressive of practices of perpetuation of bourgeois social aspiration's values, material comfort and lineage. While collectivism was linked to male doing, craftsmanship was generally related to female domains. Articulated, both presented the house as a showcase, at the same time a refuge and a civilizing space.

Through Olly and Werner and their web of relations we see the process of building a new lifestyle expressed in the decoration of the domestic space. However, in addition, we also see how ideas were imported into Brazil from the experience of

---

[34] I follow Martins' definition of "cultural field" in its descriptive sense, of a space, "at the same time, abstract and physical, where cultural activities and their institutions concentrate" (Martins, 1987 apud Vilhena, 1997). In this sense, I move away from Bourdieu's concept to whom there is a principle of organization in this space that leads to a relative autonomy influenced by a set of forces and rules (Bourdieu, 1977). At the same time, I consider the abstract dimension of this cultural field the positive and negative cooperation that fundaments the notion of artistic worlds (Becker, 1982), as the reciprocity between the actors.

foreigners who mixed values and practices of their countries of origin with local possibilities and combined them to identify or differentiate themselves from the groups and classes that they found in the new Country. Thus collecting, decorating the domestic spaces and the value of textile production are some of the social technologies (Swann, 2001) for the construction of values and identification of groups that were articulated by these social actors who in this process reaffirmed and/or challenged representations of femininity/masculinity, ethnicity/nationality and class.

1.3. IPANEMA VANGUARD AND DAZZLE

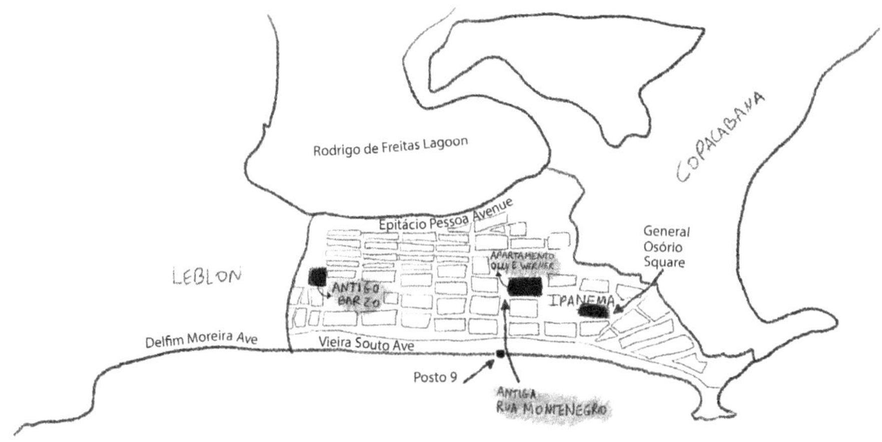

Bourdieu (2004) calls attention to the value of the private residence. For the author, this value is defined by reference to the social characteristics of the neighborhood where it is located and the social characteristics of the population of residents, as a club effect. It is possible to build social maps from these spaces based on the distinctions between goods, to which consumers have privileged access and the possibility of encounters at the same time fortuitous and predictable in the simple act of descending to buy bread, for example. But the frequenting of certain places and the presentation of oneself in the condition of artistic producer are also the prerogative of some neighborhoods. Participation in these spaces occurs mainly through the consumption of objects with the potential to institute "lifestyles" (Miller, 2007). Therefore, to better understand the meaning of the consumption of objects of decoration and production of the domestic space I will present the location of the couple's apartment and the moral meanings tied to that urban area.

The apartment is in Ipanema, a neighborhood which history is linked to the migratory waves of the first half of the 20th century. The neighborhood has received several groups of European immigrants since the first decade, with important reinforcements from the 1930s on. Until the beginning of that century, the sea was still considered a place for the dumping of waste and treatment of ill patients. It was only around 1910 that the sea bath has become a form of entertainment, largely by French influence (Corbin, 1989). Some personalities who lived in the neighborhood in the first decades of the century also contributed for the construction of the image that was forged in Ipanema in the 1950's to 1970's as a neighborhood of intellectuals and artists. Álvaro Alvim, João do Rio and Ernesto de Nazareth were some of them (Castro, 1999)[35].

Vieira Souto Avenue was named after the engineer responsible for the neighborhood's urbanization project at the end of the 19th century. The avenue was named in 1917, at the inauguration of the widening and central afforestation works. In 1910, there were 175 houses in the neighborhood which lands were sold with a financing of up to 10 years by a Company that closed its works in 1927. From that year onwards the area gradually increased its real estate value. In 1936, Revista Ilustrada published an article in which it mentioned that twenty years earlier Ipanema was an area with few houses, but that in the 1930s it had become a rival of Copacabana in terms of urbanization. The streetcar that had its end point in "Bar 20" was gradually replaced from 1927 on and completely stopped circulating in 1963 (Koifman, 2005). The neighborhood children moved to and from school (Erika Hasenberg, 2014) in this public transportation. It gave the neighborhood a community aspect where neighbors knew each other face-to-face.

While the Praça Onze[36] neighborhood agglomerated the Jews of Eastern Europe, the Germans tended to concentrate in Ipanema and Copacabana. However, they were not the only immigrants in these neighborhoods. French, Italians, and English continued to arrive, escaping the economic and political turmoil in Europe. They brought ideas from their countries 1910s and 1920s avant-garde, and the experience of being far from conventional models offered these immigrants a discourse of freedom in choosing new patterns of behavior. Simmel (2005) analyzed the foreigner's ambiguous place. They are not seen or do not feel like an insider, but at the same time they are part and interferes in the group. This offers a privileged status in the construction of singular individualities.

Olly and Werner's statuses, as well as of some other members of this middle class, was imprecise. McClintock's (2010) notion of "white black" used to analyze the imprecise use of the notion of race in the nineteenth century helps to understand the unstable position that Jews and immigrants had, and continue to have, in Brazil. Skin color is for these groups an imprecise marker of its hierarchical position, making other forms of affirmation of social position necessary. By taking seriously the interpretation of Jewish as an ethnic category, we can see how the structures of racial, ethnic, class, and gender power are related in ways that are often contradictory in the

---

[35] Important carioca born physitian, Journalist and musitian respectively.
[36] In Rio's downtown area.

process of forming a new white middle class that forged ways of presenting itself as national.

In the 1930s, it was still inexpensive to live in Ipanema, since the neighborhoods near the center were more valued. Until the 1920s, "the neighborhoods with the highest percentage of German citizens were Santa Tereza, Glória, Lagoa, Copacabana, Gávea, Engenho Velho, Rio Comprido, Tijuca and Andaraí" (Michahelles, 2003: 17). The low cost associated with the value conferred by Europeans to the seashore was probably what prompted some immigrants to choose Ipanema as the place to rebuild what they left behind. Thus, families such as Miriam Etz's (who arrived in 1937), the Seligmann couple, the Hasenberg's and Werner Reinheimer (all in 1935) and the Weitzfelder's (Joseph in 1933 and Edith in 1947) moved there. At the beginning of this survey, those who were still alive continued living there.

Olly and Werner's address, from the 1950s onward, was situated around Posto 9, one of the references that would elevate the neighborhood to a metonymic category of Rio de Janeiro and that city as representative of the country in the upcoming decades. Some of the social actors of this construction were the architects who had decoration shops in the neighborhood, also exhibiting local artists'[37] production. In 1955, Sérgio Rodrigues (1927-2014) opened Oca furniture store in General Osório square. Oca produced the award-winning "Poltrona mole" (soft armchair) designed by Rodrigues in 1957. Gea owned by Sérgio Camargo and his brother was transferred to Ipanema in 1959, also around the same square. A landscape artist, Camargo sold furniture, plants and promoted exhibitions by artists such as Heitor dos Prazeres and Iberê Camargo.

In the same area, other furniture design shops were Norman Westwater and Michel Arnould's Mobília Contemporânea (Contemporary Furniture), Emeric Macier, Chirstian Roule, and Sérgio Rodrigues's Meia-pataca. Franco Terranova's Petite Galerie may have been one of the neighborhood's most important cultural undertakings. In addition to being the longest in the market, Terranova innovated by running a gallery that was "a mixture of gallery, antiquities and furniture store" (Bueno, 2005: 389). The space eventually became a meeting place. All these cultural spots were located just outside General Ozório Square, two blocks from Olly and Werner's apartment, and all the characters were part of their circle of acquaintances and friends.

Ruy Castro (1999) described in his book what he called the "classic century" of Ipanema, that is, the first three quarters of the twentieth century, showing the construction of values of a counterculture that, according to him, became hegemonic in the 1950s until the 1970s. In this sense, it is possible to read his book as a summary

---

[37] Photographers who registered the boardwalk design in Copacabana are some of the examples of central characters for the construction of the image of Rio de Janeiro that would be known nationally and internationally from the 1980s onward. However, since these people did not appear as references neither in the interviews nor in the documents of the collection they will not be mentioned here.

of the emergence process of a new white middle-class mentality that proposed behaviors, values and an aesthetic having Ipanema at the same time as stage and a character in chronicles, prose, songs, plays, movies and television programs. This was the period of Bossa Nova, Cinema Novo, the beginning of television and international projection of Ipanema as a space for experimentation in behavior patterns.

The period covered by the book is one in which certain folklore about the neighborhood was produced through the "visibility" (Heinich, 2011) of some of its residents. During this period, Rio de Janeiro was a smaller representation of Brazil, mainly because it was inhabited by countless artists, cartoonists, chroniclers, poets, designers, architects, composers, journalists, photographers, playwrights, screenwriters, set designers, TV directors, models, fashion designers, filmmakers, musicians, writers and sportsmen. There, the apogee of the so-called counterculture was seen, a movement that gained strength mainly in the 1960s, questioning established values and using the mass media.

The behaviors characteristic of these characters was labeled "bohemia", "playfulness", "eccentricity", "freedom from conventions", and a certain "irresponsibility". If we think of the statute of creators, which includes not only the actual situation but also the imaginary role and its symbolic place, we see how this group of artists, intellectuals and political activists took on the modern representations of the cursed artist described by Nathalie Heinich (1998) based on Van Gogh's case. As in seventeenth-century France, proportions guarded, we see the emergence of what will become a series of new professions that are still little formalized and, therefore, based more on vocation than on learning. In the trail of Romanticism, human particularity and its achievements are emphasized, inaugurating or incorporating into the practical life of actors the value of singularity. Behavior considered deviant, transgressive was the way to express it.

The 25 years after the end of World War II was considered a "golden age" (Hobsbawm, 2005). The "winners" of this war experienced extraordinary economic growth and social transformation, that profoundly changed societies. In Brazil it was no different. In the 1950s, Brazilian cities daily life were transformed with the entrance of household appliances into middle-class homes and Brazilian automobiles on the streets. In 1955, Brazil produced its first national vehicle, the Romi-Iseta. Television introduced singers who thrilled crowds, reinforcing the idea of national unity, but what was considered modern was the American way of life and modernizing, in generic terms, meant incorporating this style in the decorations of domestic spaces: lots of plastic, vibrant colors and polished surfaces where civilization could see its own image reflected.

However, modernity and large cities were also the ideal social space for the diversification of individualities as a struggle for differentiation. Rapid and uninterrupted changes allowed comparisons between present and past times. Constructing new identities was less based on particular class, ethnic or gender conscience than one another's superimposition of impressions. This is what Simmel (2005) calls the intensification of "nervous life". It is the idea that the distribution of power depends on social situations overdetermined by race, class and gender in relationships that are often contradictory.

Part of the values coined during the 1960s and 1970s can also be perceived in new words that have been added to the dictionary and/or incorporated in the everyday discourse of Cariocas: dica (tip) (consolidated as an abbreviation for "indication"), pichar (whose meaning was to reprehend), for example were created or consolidated in the pages of *O Pasquim*[38] (Castro, 1999). A new graphical language included LP, books and magazine's covers (Senhor, published from March 1959 to January 1964, being perhaps the most paradigmatic one[39]) and the use of asterisks as substitution to the curses that became part of the journalism was another token of fidelity to everyday speech. The aura of futility that surrounded Ipanema's residents was in part what allowed the flourishing of an armed opposition to the military dictatorship established in Brazil from 1964 onward but also a pacifist group who expressed themselves through new artistic and cultural proposals.

The presence of German immigrants in Ipanema can be perceived in some neighborhood commercial ventures. Bar Lagoa, on Epitácio Pessoa Avenue, was founded in 1934 under the name Berlin Bar and belonged to a German couple. It featured a quartet who played Viennese waltzes. In 1942, with Hitler's decision to sink ships on the Brazilian coast, the bar was attacked by the Cariocas, like the Rhenania bar (1935-1995 on #80 Visconde de Pirajá). Both changed their names then. Berlin Bar became Lagoa Bar and Rhenania, became Jangadeiro. Thus, the values of the 1950s and 1970s were constituted by a mixture of distinct social groups, each with its tools of expression and its discursive space of production.

According to historian Andrea Cristina de Barros Queiroz (2012), the group of chroniclers who lived in Ipanema between 1950 and 1970 contributed to the construction of Rio's "ideal type": "characterized by its local, but at the same time, national dimension. That is, one could be born in Rio de Janeiro or be "Carioca" in spirit, what identified them as such was the feeling of membership to that particular "citizenship". This became so striking that the idea of a Carioca "state of mind" was perpetuated for decades. Millôr Fernandes, like others, consecrated the myth of Rio de Janeiro as a "marvelous city", by extolling the singularity of Ipanema as a representation of Rio de Janeiro and this as a representation of Brazil.

This construction took place in contrast to other neighborhoods and their temporalities. Hence the journalist Paulo Mendes Campos (1922-1991) used to say the city of Rio was born old, but it was rejuvenating. In space, Campos relates downtown to old age (convents, bureaucratic buildings), Flamengo and Botafogo represents the maturity, Copacabana the adolescence, and Ipanema and Leblon its

---

[38] *O Pasquim* was a tabloid published between 1969 and 1991. It was recognized for its role as representative of the counterculture as well as an opponent of the military regime.
[39] There was another magazine with the same name, but a different proposal, edited by the São Paulo group, in the mid 70s.

youth. The reformulation of these symbols and values included the valorization of youth as a sign of modernity. Past, present and future as systems of values, old/modern or progress/conservation and old age, maturity/youth as projections of these values in the city and its inhabitants. Hence the stores that began to appear in Ipanema in the 1960s, aimed at this audience, "young", "careless", "hedonist". It did not matter, therefore, how old one was, the resident of Ipanema was considered young.

During this period, between the 1960s and 1980s, Ipanema was a reference to a form of self-presentation that was largely done through clothes and accessories. Until 1961 there were no clothing stores in the neighborhood. One either went downtown, or bought fabrics at Casa Miro, Alberto, or Madame Faria stores to send to their seamstresses. Between the end of the 1960s and beginning of 1970s, following the urbanization of the country and the expansion of the consumer society it began to appear the so-called boutiques. Those were clothing stores directed to the feminine public concentrated in Copacabana and Ipanema.

On August 25th, 1961, it was inaugurated the first boutique in Ipanema, Mariazinha. After it, others came: Bibba (1966-1983), Aniki Bobó (1968-1980), Fragile (1969-1973), Blu-blu (1972-1987), Company (1972). These stores contributed to create attitudes and behaviors that would define the lifestyles of Ipanema's residents. However, despite the improvement of industrial clothing confection in the country, it was not until the 1980s that Brazilians began to dress mostly with ready-to-wear clothes. Until then, those made by seamstresses predominated (Bonadio, 2010).

Two art galleries that existed in Ipanema during this period and their founders were fundamental for the transformation of values. Jean Bogichi (1928-2015) who was born in Moldavia, a Bessarabian province in Rumania, came to Rio in 1947. In 1960 he founded Galeria Relevo. He organized the Opinion 65 and Opinion 66 shows[40], in 1965 and 1966 respectively. Together with Franco Terranova (1923-2013), in the Petite Galerie (1954-1988), both modernized the Brazilian art market. Terranova, an Italian from Naples, also arrived in Brazil in 1947 and settled in Rio in 1953. He began working with art in 1954, when he bought the Petite Galerie from the Italian artist Mario Agostinelli (1915-2000). In 1960, he joined José de Carvalho, owner of the Ducal stores and moved the gallery to General Osório Square, in a space designed by Sérgio Bernardes. At that time Petite Galerie was the first to make exclusive contracts with the artists. It was also the first to sell art in installments, as if they were house appliances. In 1971, he broke up the partnership and moved the gallery close by. In the space of General Osório square José de Carvalho founded Bolsa de Arte an art auction house.

Petite Galerie worked with artists such as Emeric Macier (1916-1990), Milton Dacosta (1915-1988), Maria Leontina (1917-1984), Jose Pancetti (1902-1958), Franz

---

[40] Important art shows around the 4th anniversary of Rio de Janeiro. Both happened at the Museum of Modern art.

Krajcberg (1921-2017) and Alfredo Volpi (1896-1988) and Ernesto Neto. In the same year, it exhibited for the first time a number of artists, such as Jac Leirner (1961) and Ernesto Neto's (1964). According to Terranova, *Petite Galerie did not have a line.* Terranova sympathized with the neoconcretes, but also exhibited folk art, such as carrancas of the São Francisco River and ex-votos. In 1980, Mario Pedrosa's birthday was celebrated in Jean Boghici's gallery. Art and politics walked together in this social space, physically and temporally delimited. Leftist activists called "dazzling" people who participated in the counterculture and had unconventional behaviors, such as listening to rock, reading the beat poets, keeping long hair and smoking marijuana instead of using guns as resistance.

Ipanema, since the 1930s, had already been a scene of intense political activity. In 1935, Luiz Carlos Prestes (1898-1990) and Olga Benário[41] (1908-1942) lived in Barão da Torre street. Nearby was the couple from the German Communist Party, Harry Berger and Machla Lenczycki. The neighborhood was chosen precisely because it contained many foreigners, mainly Germans.

After Prestes, Ipanema remained a stronghold of Communist Party militants. Some historical ones like Valério Konder (1911-1968), who was a senator for the party in 1946, had his mandate revoked along with the party's registry. Their children, Rodolfo and Leandro Konder later became militants. The architect Silo Costa Leite, along with all his family, had been affiliated to the Party since the 1930s. Adão Pereira Nunes was also a party deputy in 1946. Along with his wife, Alaíde Pereira Nunes, founders of the PDT (Democratic Workers Party), were close friends to Olly and Werner, as well as Leandro Konder and even Luiz Carlos Prestes had its share of contact with the couple.

Adão Pereira Nunes was responsible for the reparation processes that Werner moved in his name and that of his father against Germany. Both were approved in the 1960s when his father, Herman Reinheimer, had already died. Abigail Pereira Nunes, Adão and Alaíde's daughter, believes that Werner had joined the Party when he met her parents, in the 1950s. But Werner's son believes his membership happened shortly after Werner's arrival in Brazil, in the 1930s.

Other sympathizers of the Communist Party were Ferdy Carneiro, Albino Pinheiro (whose brother, Cláudio was a resident in the same building where Olly and Werner's apartment was), Mânlio Marat and João Saldanha, who together with Silo Costa Leite (and others) founded the Ipanema Band[42]. Still in the political dimension of the neighborhood, in the 1970s, the artist Marília Kranz (1937-2017) transformed her house into a VPR (Revolutionary Popular Vanguard) apparatus, welcoming people wounded in the dictatorship's worst years. Artist Anna Letycia Quadros (1929-2018), a former resident of the neighborhood, hid people from the civil-military

---

[41] He was an influential Communist militant who married Olga, a German Jewish communist activist who was extradited to Germany when pregnant and died in the gas chambers.

[42] A traditional carnival band parade that is part of the touristic atractions in carioca's carnival.

regime during the hardest years of repression. Werner Reinheimer helped some people flee the country.

Common interest groups in politics, art and culture had meeting places in bars, on the beach, as well as in intellectuals' houses such as Aníbal Machado, Lúcio Cardoso, Nelson Dantas, Rodrigo Melo Franco de Andrade, Mário Pedrosa, all neighborhood residents.

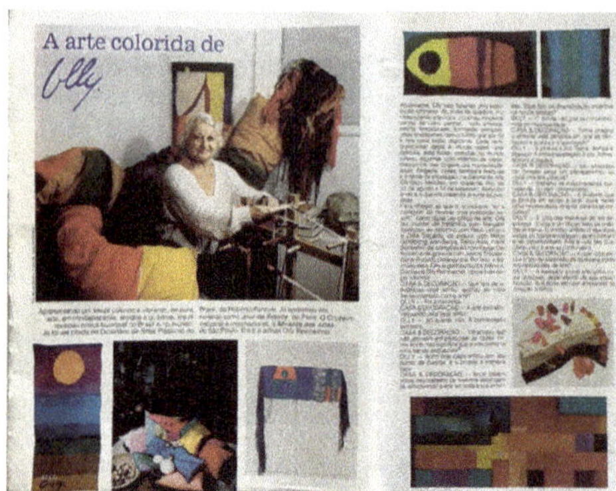

Figure 45: Article in *Casa & decoração* magazine (Home & decoration), 1981 (MROW-G-84).

Lourdes Mello, friend with Olly and Werner, spoke of these meetings: *"Ipanema is where Anibal Machado lived. People from all over Brazil came there, theater people, music people. I went many times with Olly. Rossini Perez, Scliar, Benjamin, Glauco Rodrigues, Ana Letícia, Fayga, Vera Tormento were all in the beginning of their careers"*

According to her, Olly's apartment was also a meeting point: *"Her house was a center. It brought together many groups, many people with different thoughts that manifested themselves in an aesthetic way. A vanguard movement. Olly's parties reveal her a lot. A modern person, of extremely good taste. She valued highly colors. This appreciation was seen at her home, where she hosted everybody from Fayga to someone who was just beginning. There was Frank Schaefer who had a more classic thought. But suddenly someone crazy came such as Roberto de Regina and Robertinho Delamonica. Many people who did not even continue the artistic practice passed by. It was almost an open-house. People would show up there. The house always had people".*

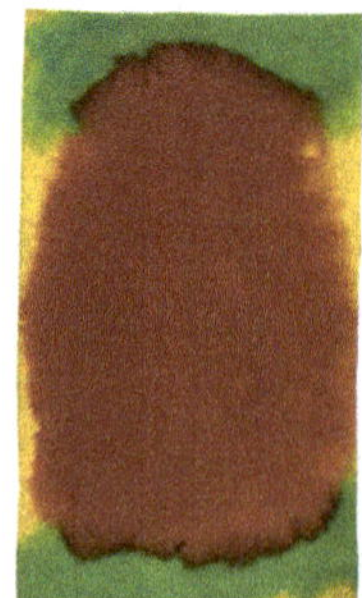

Figure 46: Illustration for the book "Uma porção de açúcar, duas de amor" (A portion of sugar, two of love). Recipes by Henda and illustrations by Olly, 1980 (PACA-0140).

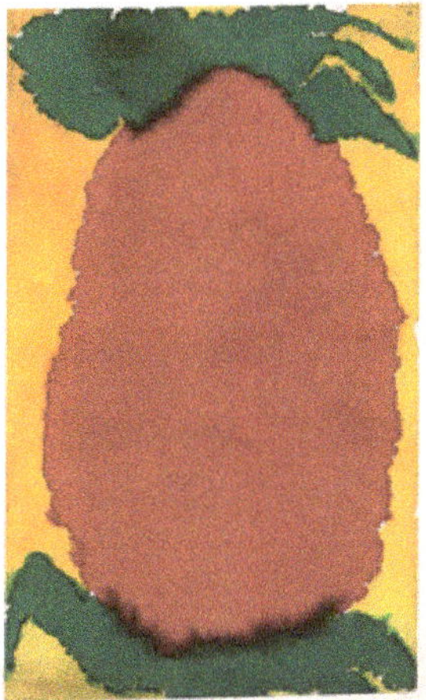

Figure 47: Illustration for the book "Uma porção de açúcar, duas de amor" (A portion of sugar, two of love). Recipes by Henda and illustrations by Olly, 1980 (PACA-0120).

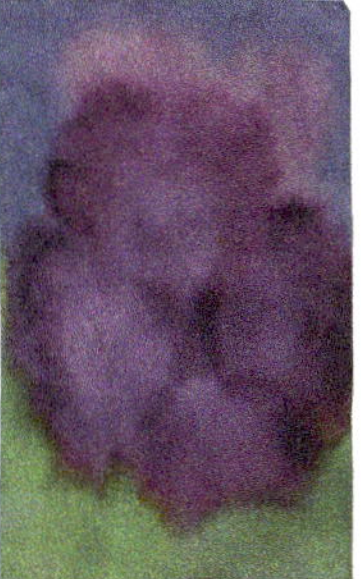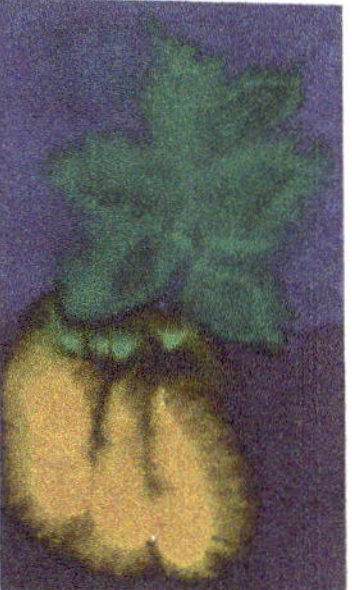

Figure 48: Illustration for the book "Uma porção de acúcar, duas de amor" (A portion of sugar, two of love). Recipes by Henda and illustrations by Olly, 1980 (PACA-0131).

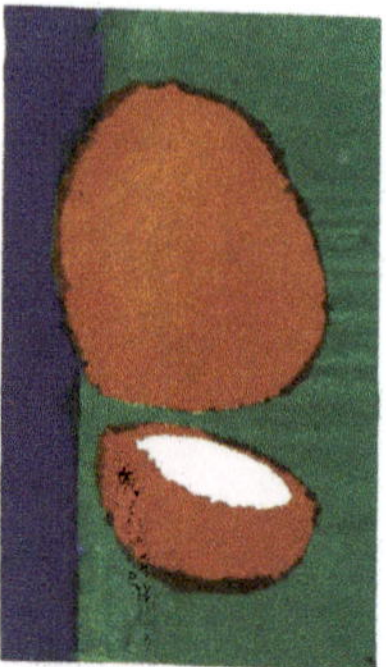

Figure 49: Illustration for the book "Uma porção de açúcar, duas de amor" (A portion of sugar, two of love). Recipes by Henda and illustrations by Olly, 1980 (PACA-0126).

Art critic Mario Pedrosa had been exiled from Brazil between 1937 and 1945. When he moved back to Brazil, he moved to Ipanema. There he helped found the Brazilian Socialist Party and received artists and intellectuals for heated discussions at his home in Visconde de Pirajá street. From these discussions, according to Gláucia Villas Bôas (2014), emerged the ideas that led to the deconstruction of the figurative representation that prevailed in Brazilian art at that time. Between 1953 and 1962, Nelson Dantas, a TV, theater and cinema actor and director, kept his house open on Saturday nights, to friends and friends of friends.

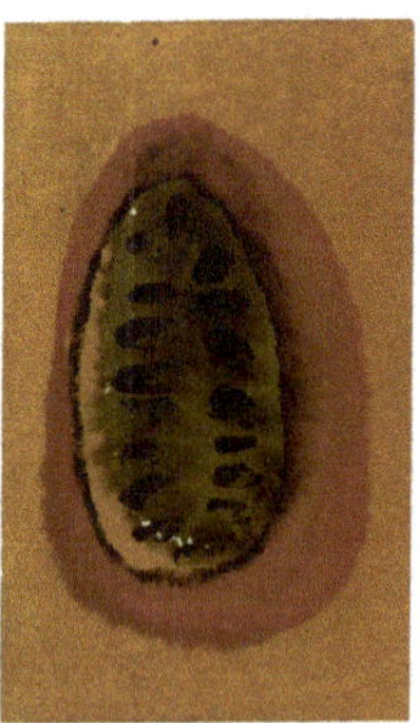

Figure 50: Illustration for the book "Uma porção de açúcar, duas de amor" (A portion of sugar, two of love). Recipes by Henda and illustrations by Olly, 1980 (PACA-0141).

After 1964, Plinio Doyle also started to open his house for debates. The beginning of the dictatorship required that people stayed in contact in their private spaces, since the public ones were more and more insecure. All of these, as well as the vernissages in the art galleries that were either in furniture stores or art galleries were important socialization spaces. These socializations were communication rituals where values related to behaviors, ideas, practices, objects and names were exchanged.

Consumption was thus essential in this process of constructing subjectivities. However, it was not a mechanical process in which people bought ready-to-use "social identities". This was made clear in this investigation. As Daniel Miller (2013) calls attention, there is an imaginary, experimental and reflexive component that takes place between the places of purchase, the things consumed and the forms or places of their exhibition. These people were building a sense of modernity different from the massively-sold American way of life.

Consumption as a form of communication, a system to exchange and control information (Douglas e Isherwood, 2013) turns things into – clothes, accessories, cars, furnishings, real estate, exhibitions, theater plays, cinema going, electronic equipment, among others – values communicators and boundaries setters. Access to them is not just a matter of economic possibility, but also a question of learning their utility, their *ethos*. Therefore, the choices reflect moral values and carry relevant meanings. They can either communicate something about someone, a group or a class, or build new subjectivities, values and life styles (Miller, 2013).

In the next chapters I present Olly and Werner's trajectories and elaborate about the strategies used for the construction of these values expressed specially in their apartment decoration and the wardrobe designed by Olly.

CHAPTER 2

From Gloomy Germany to Tropical Brazil

In this chapter, I present Olly and Werner's trajectories before they entered the social context that is properly the object of this book's analysis. To understand the collections that they accumulated and the meaning these things could have in the constitution of a new way of life in Brazil I present a little of the social course of these actors. I indicate the social origin of their families and the status of their migration to Brazil. These previous trajectories situate them in the context that will be analyzed later and how they were incorporated into that context and intervened in it.

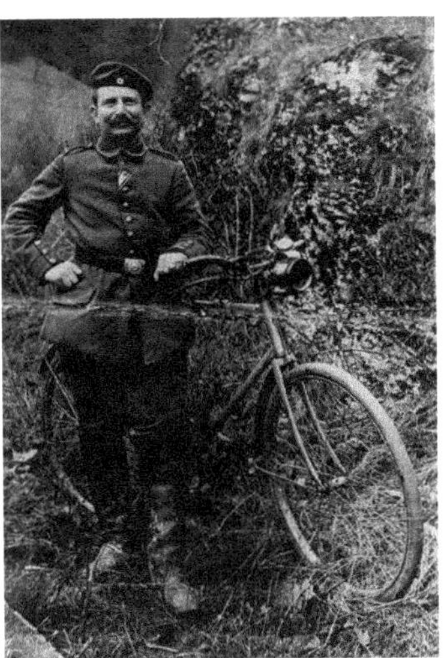

Figure 51: Hermann Reinheimer,
World War I, 1914-1918 (DIA-1287).

I opted here for a periodization that follows the historical determinations and the set of documents which are in the couple's collection, as well as the information transmitted by the conducted interviews. It is not a matter of dividing the trajectory of the couple in stiff periods, but of presenting it descriptively seeking to show data referring to the period from the end of the nineteenth century to the middle of the twentieth, specially things that were important for the construction of both subjectivities, for the reception they had in Brazil and for the process of individualization to which they were subjected after the Second World War.

The individualization model in Olly and Werner's case may be linked to the period of capitalist expansion, and to their immigration in the sense that family dispersion turned both to their minimum nucleus from which other relatives were removed either by dispersion in other countries, or by death as a result of the World War II and the Holocaust. In the second generation, that is, among the grandchildren, the differential ascension model is perceptible with all the implications for which anthropologist Gilberto Velho (1987) calls attention: trajectories of differential social ascension generating a continuous and progressive distance from the network of family and strengthening ties of friendship with professional colleagues and people whose social positions are distinct from those of their family of origin. This is how the "project" gains temporal depth, transcending the founding couple.

The concept of *project* appears as an important instrument for the discussion considering the idea of choice (constitutive of the modern individual, especially in urban space and even more important in the artistic field) and the limits imposed by social norms. The projects can only be elaborated within a *field of possibilities*, historically and culturally circumscribed. It is the subjects, paradigms and cultural priorities that exist in the context of Olly's production that I try to show in the following chapters, that is, within what *field of possibilities* she was proposing her subjects and the sense of reception they had. They are the meanings of the central or dominant concerns and problems that I try to indicate when dealing with the subject of collections and textile production.

The most conscious dimension of Olly's project maybe the physical manifestation expressed by the file she left. The file is part of what has been organized and digitalized to be made available for consultation. It is in the attitude of "filing oneself" that one sees a somewhat elaborate biographical construction. In this file she builds a life story where she shows some things and hides others, making it possible to perceive in the accumulated documentation a strategy for the realization of her career.

The collections are the result of *situational illusions* (Lopes, 2017), projections of individual attributes or projects of status' constitution and, in this sense, of legitimation of attributes not yet necessarily individually and socially recognized. When they get their own biographies and become singular, they become representative of *collective illusions* (Perrec, 2004, Giudice, 1999) gaining diverse meanings related to the memory of groups, States, historical periods, events, etc. Thus, collections are always constituted in the interaction, be it between the subject and the collected things, or between the social actors that identify collective meanings in the logics of organization that generalize the collections. Therefore, the need to investigate the biography of these actors as a way of understanding the stimuli and the intentionalities of this accumulation. In a second moment, the conceptual analysis associated with this archive and the understanding of the contexts in which it is inserted is a step towards its singularization and production of a *collective illusion*.

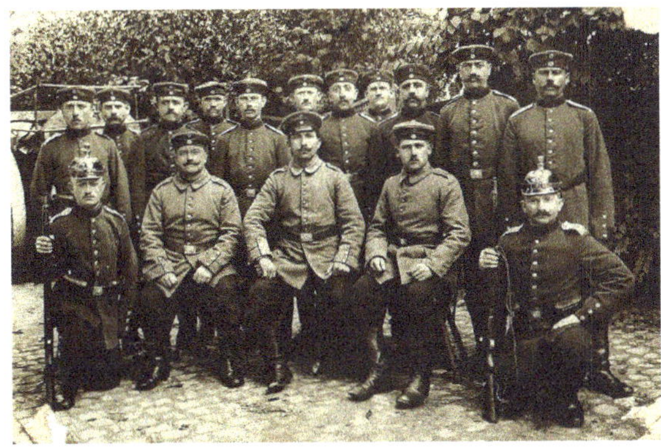

Figure 52: Hermann Reinheimer, kneeling on the far right. First World War (PH-974).

2.1. TWO TRAJECTORIES

2.1.1. Werner Siegfried Reinheimer

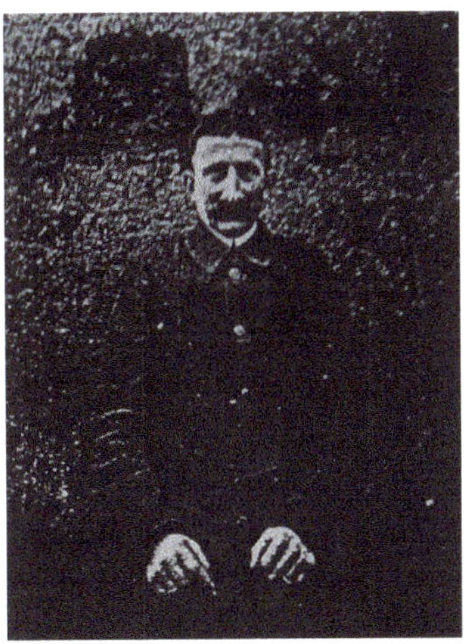

Figure 53: Abraham Reinheimer, Hermann's brother and Werner Reinheimer's uncle

Werner was Hermann and Mina Reinheimer's son. His father was born in Habitzheim, north of Heidelberg, in Hessen, on October 20th, 1878. His son would be born on this same day, when he was thirty-four. He had two brothers and a sister. One of his brothers was Abraham who was Married to Ida. Abraham was a member of the local synagogue group led by Rabbi Salomon Reinheimer. A local organization in Habitzheim published a series of books on that city's history of the Jews (Häzemer Dorf und Kultusvereins, 2010). The books mention several Reinheimer, not all of them were Werner's family. Most of them disappeared during World War II. The Jewish community of this town was quite traditional, and Hermann was not different.

Zwi (HIRSCH) Reinheimer oo Güthel (Gitel)
*1754(Handelsmann)   * 1774 +17.3.1846

Sohn

Moses 00 Bella Wolf   Salomon Reinheimer oo 18.12.1838 Sprinz (Sophie)Sommer   Lazarus (Lößer?)Reinheimer oo Ettel Sommer
*1793 +12.10.1873   *20.11.1803 + 18.10.187(9)   + 5.3.1898   *1814   (Schwester d.v.)

Sohn

Jakob (Abraham) Reinheimer (Haus Nr. 48) oo Jette Sommer
*13.10.1842 +11.1.1918   +24.8.1923

Sohn

Hermann Reinheimer (Metzger in Pforzheim) oo Mina Löwenstein (Weingarten)
*20.10.1878   *14.1.1874

Emigriert nach Brasilien

Sohn

Werner (Pforzheim)   oo Olga Helene Blank

20.10.1912 in Pforzheim *1992 (Rio de Janeiro)

Sohn

Rene Renato Reinheimer (Brasilien)

22.03.1940

Figure 54: Reinheimer's family tree made from data provided by the author and by German and American researchers from the Löwenstein and Reinheimer families, respectively. http://www.calzareth.com/tree/p93.htm#i2778

Mina Reinheimer, born Löwenstein, on January 14th, 1887, in Weingarten, was the daughter of Julchen (born Fuchs) and Leopold Löwenstein. Leopold was a butcher, a profession with ritual meaning among Jews. Mina had three sisters (Jenny, Sophia and Bertha), of whom I discovered nothing. Hermann Reinheimer and Mina Löwenstein were married on November 6th, 1911. Hermann was "master butcher" at Pforzheim, like his father-in-law in Weingarten.

Hermann and Mina were born when the past was still a strong reference for the present. This world would be completely transformed by the end of World War II. They witnessed the collapse of nineteenth-century (Western) civilization. That civilization believed in a capitalist economy,

> "Liberal in its legal and constitutional structure; bourgeois in its hegemonic class image characteristics; exultant with the advancement of science, knowledge and education, and also with the material and moral progress; and deeply convinced of the centrality of Europe, the cradle of the revolutions of science, the arts, politics and industry, whose economy had prevailed in most of the world, which its soldiers had conquered and subdued; a Europe whose

populations (including the vast and growing flow of European emigrants and their descendants) had grown to a third of the human race[43]; and whose major states constituted the system of world politics" (Hobsbawm, 2005: 16).

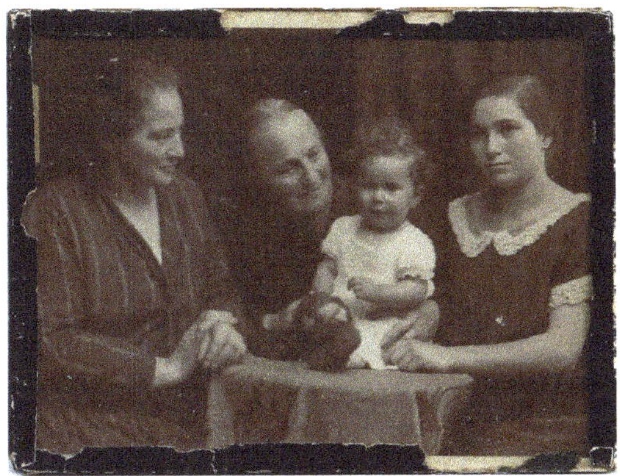

Figure 55: Mina, her parents (or parents in-law) and Werner Reinheimer

After "seven or eight millennia of human history that started in the Stone Age agricultural revolution" (Hobsbawm, 2005: 18) a largely agrarian and rural world would come to an end between the two World Wars. It was with this instability, two years before the Great War, that Werner was born.

Werner Siegfried Reinheimer, the couple's only child, was born on October 20th, 1912, in Pforzheim. The town was 37 miles from the border of France. He looked like a Viking baby, with red hair and very fair skin. Educated in orthodox Judaism, Werner was encouraged by his father to devote himself to reading and playing piano.

Germany lost 15.1% of its active male population in this war. According to Hobsbawm, "not much more than a third of the French soldiers left the war unscathed" and "a quarter of Oxford and Cambridge's students under the age of 25 who served in the British Army in 1914 were killed" (2005: 33-34). This was the first war of mass destruction, "hence the German term" materialschlacht "(battles of

---

[43] Modern anti-Semitism was occasioned by (and deepened) a confusion between notions of race, nationality, religion, and culture. Therefore, without detracting Eric Hobsbawm's work, it is necessary to mention the annoyance with the presence of the term race in his text, although it is referred to the totality of the human species and not to particular groups. If anthropology began by relying on this notion to construct its legitimacy as a scientific discipline, it was getting out of it and seeking to unravel the social situations in which it is still used to classify human groups that the discipline have achieved greater recognition and produced more relevant knowledge.

materials) to describe the western battles of 1914-18, since mass destruction required mass production (2005: 52).

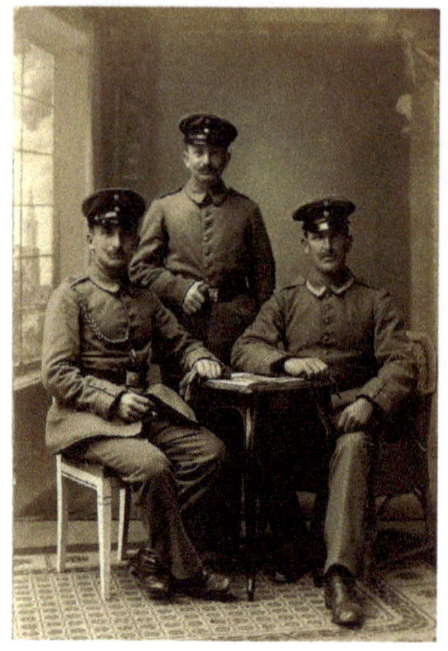

Figure 56: Hermann and two other soldiers in uniform, during the First World War

However, the photos of Hermann and his fellow soldiers during the war period show clean uniforms that hide this destruction. This was also a nationalist war in which propaganda sought to mobilize public opinion by claiming challenges to national values and requiring the population to invest also financially in the war. One fought for these values against the supposed barbarism of others. Photography was an important part of this strategy. Unfortunately, there are no records of who was the author of Hermann's photos, but it is known that photographers were hired to go to battlefields to register the "peaceful environment" of the war.

Gisèle Freund (1995) argues that, in order to conquer the masses for the enterprise, the photographs of the American Civil War obliterated the horrors. Soldiers were presented in idyllic situations with generous smiles and poses that emphasized their authority. Deaths and destruction were carefully erased by the large majority of photographers who used this technology. Both the photos that were sent to the Reinheimer family and those that were the Hasenberg family's attest to this barbarism's cleaning also in World War I. Hermann survived.

The end of the first Great War marked in Germany the end of the Empire and the beginning of the period known as the Weimar Republic. In May 1919 appeared in Pforzheim the "National Association of German Citizens of Jewish Faith" claiming the protection of civil rights and social equality for the Jewish people. The constitution of this association makes more sense when we learn that in that year, posters scattered around the city said, *Meet the real enemy! We are being deceived by the Jews!*

From the beginning of the twentieth century a new phenomenon required a new category of classification. Anti-Semitism came to refer to prejudice that was not based on the traditional religious argument but was structured in political and "racial" considerations (Motta, 1998). The emergence of this association was related to this new phenomenon and to the process of formation of a democratic State, where several minorities began to claim the recognition of their status and social rights. But the association was also linked to modern Judaism that sought to integrate the Jewish community with civil society demanding equality of conditions.

However, in 1920, the expected future was still far from anticipating what in 1933 would be the economic boycott of Jewish enterprises, with the motto *Jews Out!*

Do not Buy from Jews! spread on posters around Pforzheim (Brändle[44], s/d). In retrospect, we could say that, instead of setting the stage for a future of equality, that association marked the threshold between the past of prejudice and persecution against the Jewish religion and the complex anti-Semitic contemporary manifestations.

Werner studied at a local public school where he was the striker of the Rugby team. His sports teacher, Prof. Dr. Herbert Kraft, was an active Nazi as of 1929 (after 1933, he became Interior Minister in Baden and later Minister of Education in Alsace). This professor made an anti-Semitic remark directed to Werner's classmate Hans Pollak. This remark caused a reaction in Werner that resulted in his expulsion from school. This prevented him from doing the Abitur, an exam that marks the ending of the German secondary school and allows the student to join universities and technical schools. Werner then turned to the jewelry trade, a market in which, along with the making of watches, the Jewish community of Pforzheim stood out in the first decades of the twentieth century.

After 1917, the October Revolution offered the world an economy that seemed capable to overcome capitalist economic growth. Soviet communism proclaimed itself an alternative system superior to capitalism and thus "destined by history to triumph over it" (Hobsbawm, 2005: 63). The German revolution "confirmed the hopes of the Russian Bolsheviks" when in Bavaria in 1918 a short-lived socialist republic was proclaimed. In the spring of 1919, a brief Soviet republic settled in Munich (idem, p.75). The October Revolution had won sympathies. Almost all international socialist movements emerged from the war radicalized and strengthened. According to Hobsbawm, "for this generation, especially those who, although young, lived the rising years, revolution was the event of their lives; the days of capitalism were inevitably counted" (2005: 79).

About ten years later, the Great Depression produced a global effect from which several political upheavals emerged "over a period measured in months or in a single year, from Japan to Ireland, from Sweden to New Zealand, from Argentina to Egypt" (Hobsbawm, 2005: 111). In the period 1929-1930, three options competed for "intellectual-political hegemony. Marxist communism was one. A capitalism deprived of its belief in the optimization of free markets and reformed by a sort of unofficial marriage or permanent connection with the moderate Social-Democracy of non-communist labor movements, was the second. The third option was fascism" (Hobsbawm, 2005: 111-112).

---

[44] Gerhard Brändle is a German historian, born in Pforzheim and specialized in the history of this city's Jews and resistance against the Nazis. Various information exchanged with him relates to *mimeos*, e-mails and face-to-face conversations, in addition to his publications. Brändle began builting his knowledge in the 1980s also through direct contact with the local group of Socialist-Laborer-Party, of which Werner Reinheimer was a part. Werner participated actively in the interviews that gave rise to the historian's first book on the subject.

It was not possible to precise when Werner joined the "Kameraden" movement, but in 1930, at the beginning of the Great Depression, he was probably already a member of this Jewish youth movement along with colleagues Kurt Baruch, William Blum, Paul Strimpel and Hans Pollak. Free Jewish-Yiddish Youth movement (FDJJ) was one of three currents in which Kameraden was divided in 1932. A militant of this current states in testimony to the Leo Baeck Institute that this movement could be described as a romantic "cultural revolution", oriented against the bourgeois values of the turn of the century, mainly individualism and capitalism. After the Great War the movement gained momentum against collectivist aspirations. The very participation of Jewish youth in this movement was an expression of Jewish assimilation. The movement was restricted to the adolescents and youngsters of the Jewish middle-class, usually from large cities (Eckstein, 1981).

One of the reasons for the youth's interest in such a movement was their displeasure of the Synagogue reforms that had been taking place since the nineteenth century. However, after the political radicalization during the Great Depression the response to anti-Semitism, nationalism and anti-intellectualism was the formation of three groups among the young German Jews, dividing the Kameraden. A part followed with the leader Hermann Gerson to form the Hazorea kibbutz in Israel; one part maintained the fiction of an apolitical movement, supposedly ideologically neutral; and another, socialist bias, rejected Jewish teachings for considering the idea of the Bund threatening to the Jews for their potential segregation, which would bring the Jewish people back into the ghetto. The latter was the FDJJ, which considered Jewish assimilation both inescapable and desired, although recognizing the particularities that this membership gave them in terms of formation. It is in this context that I understand the excerpt from Werner Reinheimer's text, taken from a "Kameraden" pamphlet.

> *"When you reach a certain maturity then it is time to leave, without regret that this does not bind you to the circle in which one day you were formed or formed others. Then you go to a party or any other place taking something of the community with you: the ability to form a certain type of human being"* (Reinheimer, 1931 Apud Eckstein, 1981: 234)

For that group, anti-Semitism was the result of economic causes and could only be eliminated with their solution. The road was socialism, not Jewish nationalism. Their nation was Germany. The choice for socialism was due to the perception of control that the Communist Party tried to maintain over all the organizations in which it was represented. However, several members had a communist inclination. Werner was one of them.

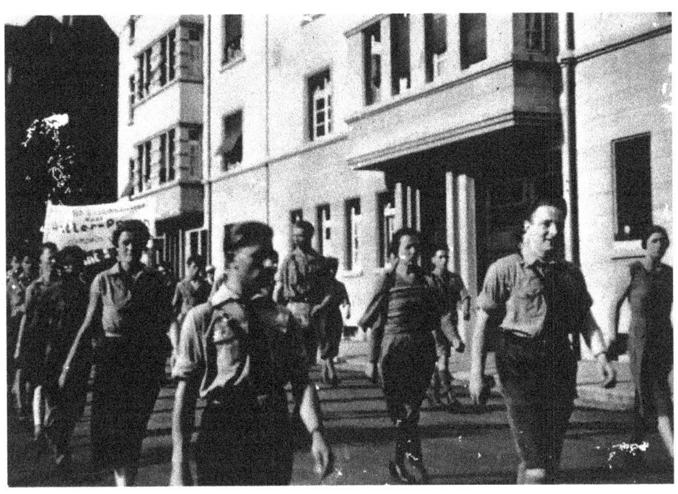

Figure 57: Werner in the foreground, in the middle,
in the SAP parade, 1933 (PH-977).

Werner's posture towards Zionism, as well as his engagement with the Jewish community, has changed over the course of his life. Bernardo Sorj (2008) makes a sociopolitical synthesis of Judaism in modern times pointing out its landmarks. According to this author, modern Judaism corresponds historically to the period from the Enlightenment and the French Revolution to the Holocaust and the creation of the State of Israel. This reformulation nourished the secular universalism of the Enlightenment and the idea of national citizenship of the French Revolution attempting to overcome the persecution of Jews during the Middle Ages. In this sense, all aspects of modern Judaism were strategies for Jews to be accepted as equals by the surrounding circles, integrated into modern social and political life.

Zionism was founded in the great ideological movements of its age - liberalism, socialism and nationalism. Despite its diversity, it was composed of two great currents: one religious and one nationalist. However, Zionism, that is, the attribution of a territorial base and a state to the Jewish people, implied the denial of much of the Jewish tradition. Thus, "at the individual level (modern Judaism) was experienced as a crisis of identity between tradition and modernity, between loyalty to the primary ties and to society as a whole, between the private and the public, between feeling and reason" (Sorj, 2008: 5) [45].

---

[45] In Brazil, the Zionist movement in the early decades of the twentieth century became known as "progressive Judaism" and manifested itself in Rio de Janeiro through institutions such as the Sholem Aleichem Association and its summer camp Kinderland, to which Olly and Werner's son and grandchildren attended.

Werner ended up not being part of the FDJJ because in 1931 the leadership of the "Kameraden" movement supported the construction of warships. Support for the war movement defined its breakup, along with other members of the radical anti-militarist group. Werner then joined the Socialist Youth Movement (SAJ), an arm of the Social-Democratic-Party. In 1931 most of the members of the SAJ joined the Socialist Laborer Party (SAP), founded in 1931, with antimilitarist orientation. The group was also attended by Karl Schroth, Werner's close friend throughout his life.

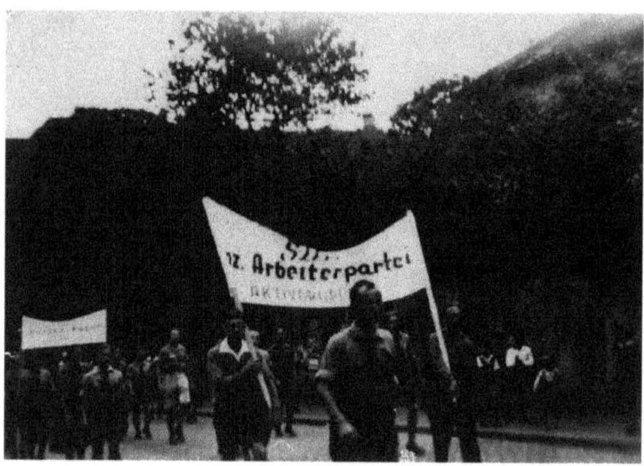

Figure 58: SAP march, 1933 (PH-978).

Duarte and Gomes analyze the subject of physical strength and the advantages and risks involved in its use through adult life as a reference to the "permanent threat of the inappropriate use of this force as a bellicose disposition" (2012: 202). In Werner's case, mentions of his athletic body as well as reaction to his gym's teacher anti-Semitic remark may be a way of asserting masculinity as a compensation for his pacifist disposition in German party politics, and for his escape from Germany before the war begun. His physical disposition for sports and athleticism is again mentioned in the 1980s, when the German historian Gerhard Brändle interviewed him about the political movement of which he was a part. The fact is mentioned in the book published on the subject and again in 2014 when I interviewed the historian in Pforzheim. The subject was again taken up by his son in his testimony in 2015. It is thus part of a value system that marks a certain masculinity that has crossed generations, as a way of affirming him also in relation to his wife's strong personality and professional success.

Werner's non-alignment with Zionism did not alienate him from political activities of resistance to Nazism or the Jewish community. Werner Reinheimer used his commercial activity in the representation of Pforzheim's jewels to distribute the informative leaflets that he produced with Karl Schroth warning about the activities of National Socialist Party. Those leaflets shared the news about what was happening in Germany to other cities. Written on Bible paper and rolled to fit in the motorcycle hoops they were distributed throughout the Badens and other cities in southwest Germany as part of his militancy in the SAJ.

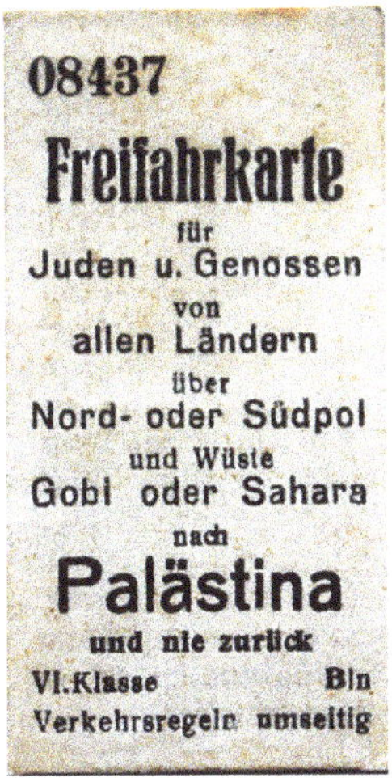

Figure 59: Round trip to Palestine, the North Pole or the Sahara Desert. Tiket simulation for Jews and foreigners from all countries. Image submitted by Gerhard Brändle.

The Socialist Labor Party (SAP) was created in 1931 through left-wing members of the Social-Democratic-Party. Its goal was to unite the trade unions, the communists and social-democrats against the Nazi-party. In 1933 SAP was declared illegal but continued its activities clandestinely. Werner then adopted the pseudonym Uli.

Arrested by the Gestapo, he was accused of being responsible for the party's finances and the printing of illegal pamphlets but was released shortly thereafter. In 1934, he spoke publicly at a SAP's meeting and presented the theater-group *"Die Roten Trommler"* (The Red Drummers) in several places. The play was written by him and Karl Schroth. A Gestapo officer heard verses such as *"we emigrated to Burma and founded a new company, founded a new bank, because that's what we know, thank God"*. This put him in the line of fire as a political opponent of the regime. Werner begun receiving death threats and "one-way tickets to Palestine!" (figure 59).

The jewelry trade had also become almost impossible. The difficulty of selling was just one of the problems. The hotels in the cities he visited were progressively refusing Jewish guests. In 1935, at the age of 23, Werner took advantage of business contacts and SAP's mail service in Paris to emigrate to Brazil. Asked about the possible motive for Brazil's choice, Brändle regretted not having asked Werner this question, but he listed some hypotheses, including that perhaps this was the fate of the next ship to leave. By this, Brändle hinted that the refugee's destination country from Nazi persecution could be the result of the most diverse situations, the least likely being a strictly rational choice.

Werner's parents stayed in Pforzheim until 1939. The sadness of the farewell and the uncertainty of a reunion are narrated by him in a text written in 1983:

"October 1935, farewell at the Nagoldstrasse, very bitter, but it had to be. The revolt against the Nazis, who enslaved my homeland, the absolute certainty that the new strategic roads (Reichsautobahnstrassen) were proof that war would arrive in a short time.

Farewell at the Nagoldstrasse, the voice was not mine, but that of a man who had to control himself.

My father accompanied me to Kehl (the border town) and I went alone to Paris, where I stayed for a few days with friends, who were already worried. In Bordeaux I waited for the ship of Chargeur Réunis "Massilia" Company and we left Europe facing the cold and fascinating sea to far South America. I have to confess, that all my knowledge about Brazil, came from the writer Karl May[46] and were completely false, and perhaps for that reason my enthusiasm" (Reinheimer, 1983).

About Hermann's brothers, who were killed by the Nazis, I did not retrieve any other information. The Nazis killed people and erased much of their stories. To immigrate was to begin again, *"to build a new existence"* (Reinheimer, 1983). What remained of Werner's family were photographs and official documents: identity cards, death certificates, testaments. In this new beginning the photograph had a triple role. In addition to taking from the past what was possible, according to Heinz[47], a German who arrived in Brazil in 1935, bringing a Leica was an important economic resource. As soon as they arrived, the sale of the camera guaranteed some sustenance. After the establishment in the new homeland, the accumulation of photographs was evidence of the reconstruction of the affective and professional life. To keep the past, to allow the present, and to invent the future, made photography a treasure to be cultivated and, most of the time, scattered throughout the residence.

In addition to the official Reinheimer photos and documents, there is no letter or personal report from other relatives. A cousin survived a concentration camp and lived in the Netherlands in the 1970s. I remember him visiting Rio de Janeiro. A fragile figure of whom Werner did not say much but mentioned his survival from a concentration camp. Perhaps it is from his family the picture of the bar mitzva of Sam Stern (PH-888) in the collection. Also, in the collection, a postcard from Hermann to Gertrude during World War I is another clue I did not follow. Maybe there's a woman somewhere who, like Erika, told her daughters and nieces the story of this family. Who knows this book helps finding other pieces of this puzzle.

---

[46]Karl May published, in Germany, supposed reports of travel experiences. It turned out later that he had never left his country.

[47] Despite having recorded video testimony and said I could use it in the research, Heinz and his wife did not sign the authorization to use the images. So, I opted to maintain their anonimity. All other cases, people were filmed during the interviews and signed authorization for image use. Therefore, there is no point in maintaining anonymity.

2.1.2. Olga Helene Blank

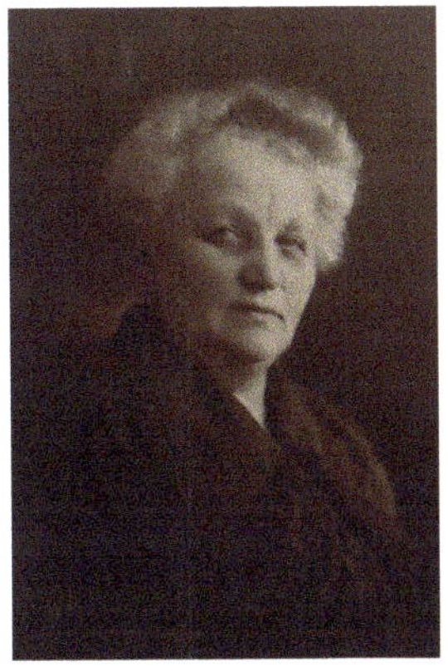

Olga was the daughter of Russian Chaja Blank and the Hungarian Ladislau Vamos. Chaja was the daughter of Michael, whose original surname was Stark. Probably because he had a non-Russian family Micael adopted the new surname so he and his family wouldn't have to deal with the inconveniences of being considered a foreigner in Russia. He became Micael Blank. The family lived in Odessa, where there was a large Jewish community since the end of the eighteenth century. However, probably due to the repeated Pogroms (1821, 1859, 1871, 1881, 1905, 1914), the statistics changed radically and in the early twentieth century the population of Odessa was about 30% Jewish.

Figure 60: Sofia Blank (PH-1130).

Between June and October 1905, hundreds of Jews were murdered in Pogroms. In August of the same year broke out the "bloody Sunday" triggering the Russian revolution of 1905, "a vigorous prologue to the revolutionary 1917 drama" (Trotsky, 1922). Micael Blank, Chaja's father and Olga's grandfather, died that year. He was then 47. It is not known whether his death was a direct consequence of any of these events.

By then the family had their homes destroyed several times. The birth certificate of Chaja Blank was translated into German in October 1905, when she adopted the translation of her name, Clara. By coincidence of dates, one can imagine that there is a connection between prejudice against Jews, political events in Odessa and the family's moving to Mittweida in Saxony.

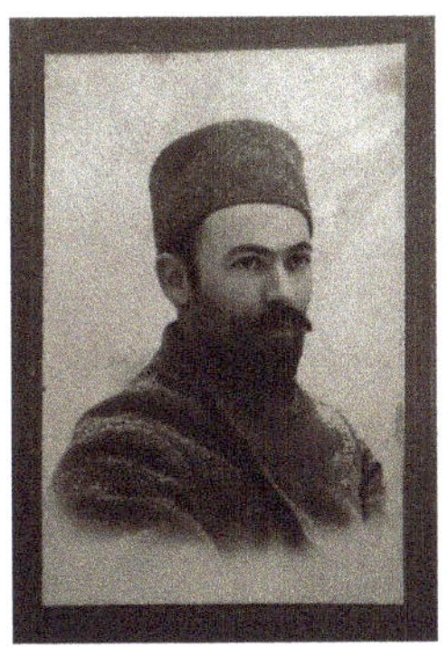

Figure 61: Photo of Miron, Chaja Blank's brother (PH-1126).

In the family genealogy [48] systematized by Erika Hasenberg, Olga's sister, the reason for the family's immigration is attributed to Michael Blank's death. A child's point of view is that of everyday events, different from those used as historical landmarks. Erika was probably unaware of the historical and social context of the period and placed the justification as a consequence of the affective loss and not of the social and political causes that led to this loss. Indeed, in

---

[48] Figure 5 shows the simplified family tree, systematized by Erika. The one I mention here is available digitally in Olly and Werner Reinheimer's Archive.

the justification for a radical change like this, both mourning and social difficulties must have contributed to the decision. This subjective dimension is also an important part of decisions such as that, but they are often left out of the analysis of historians and social scientists: varied scales (Revel, 1998) enrich history by reinforcing social milestones and showing its consequences in everyday life for ordinary people.

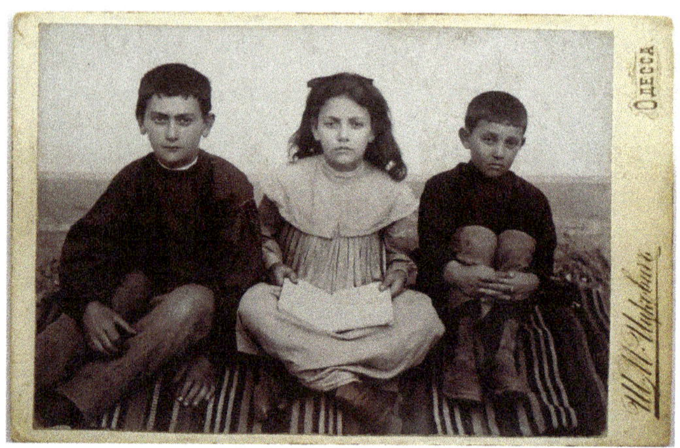

Figure 62: Clara, Mitja e Jasha, in Odessa, 1905 (PH-1127).

The family immigration to the West is not an individual case. Restrictive decrees, administrative pressure and Pogroms in Russia have led to a massive immigration of the Jewish population. Between 1881 and 1914 there were about two and a half million Jews that left Eastern Europe (Marrus, 2002). Another substantive contingent left the country in 1917. A part of the Blank family, however, remained in Odessa, another went to the capital of Azerbaijan, Baku, one of the cities that experienced a rapid industrialization process, leading to the emergence of a middle class, as indicated by post cards and data included in Erika Hasenberg's family genealogy.

Sofia Blank, born in 1857 in Odessa, was the daughter of a rabbi and had 4 sisters and a brother[49]. When Micael died, Sofia moved to Mittweida along with her mother-in-law *Babushka*[50] and her eight children. This German city was relatively important due to the presence of the Technical Institute of Engineering and its textile production with mechanical weaving looms, remarkable until the end of the 20th century. The literature speaks of urban characters who probably composed a rich cultural life due to the students and professors of several countries that attended the university. This Institute was one of the biggest institutions of technical education in Germany. The

---

[49] She had with Micael nine children, Anna (1881-1962), Rosa (1883-1940), Lisa (1885-?), Miron (1887-?), Manya (1889-1979), Jasha (1891-1930), Chaja 1893-1985), Mitja (1895-1941) and one born dead.
[50] No longer remembering her grandmother's name, Erika used the noun in Russian to refer to her

city lived off of this relationship with the school through hostels, inns and shops that served students, teachers and their visitors.

Sofia set up a boarding house, where she served meals for students, in a central street. Her home address was Tzschirnerplatz, 13 (DO-15). We can suppose that the pension was there, perhaps on the ground floor of a townhouse. Ladislau Vamos, was the son of a Hungarian banker. The lad was an engineering student. He used to go to the boarding house where he met Clara. Olga was born in 1914 as a consequence of this involvement. According to Erika, class difference was decisive for Ladislau's father to reject Clara getting married to his son. This created on Olga indelible marks. Even married women as individuals had an inferior condition to their male parents, husbands, the family and the children themselves. The condition of a single woman with a child at the turn of the twentieth century was not only inferior but morally recriminated.

One of the categories to refer to a single mother was "illegitimate-mother"; like her children, she was a moral hazard to the family and an existential threat to society. Children also considered illegitimate, or bastards, were the proof of this social crime. Erika talks about the echo that this moral recrimination had in the relationship between Olga and her mother: *"I always had the impression (after being an adult) that Clara, in her subconscious, blamed Olly for stealing part of her life by throwing her in the shade and with the aura of "seduced and abandoned, because there was never much affection among them"* (CO-104).

When I made the first effort to systematize Olly's career in 1998, I interviewed several people who had been part of the couple's relationship. Only then did I find out that Olga was the daughter of a single mother. The continuous fabric of kinship impacts in different ways groups that do or do not emphasize consanguinity. Several works in indigenous ethnology point to the presence of inner alterity to what we call consanguinity. The body of the newborn child must be worked so that it is not identified with other non-human animals. This is an example of how the identity of alliances needs to be constantly reinstalled.

Information about Olly's father, which eventually came to know her biological father, was not disclosed to subsequent generations (son and grandchildren). It was thanks to the research that the information came to light. The non-consanguinity of Hasenberg and Olga was for a long time replaced by the mistaken interpretation that Clara's husband was the German physicist Werner Heisenberg. If she was not the daughter of a "legitimate" relationship, at least the family shared the physicist's notoriety. It took some time for the misunderstanding to be dispelled by artist and intellectual Fayga Ostrower in a conversation with me. The identification of the physicist with our relative probably arose from Erika's recognition of similarities beyond their participation in the engineering field (Werner Hasenberg has some patented some of his creations) for she declared in 2015 that their signatures was also very similar. She got in touch with the physicist's signature in the Alexander Volta Museum in Como.

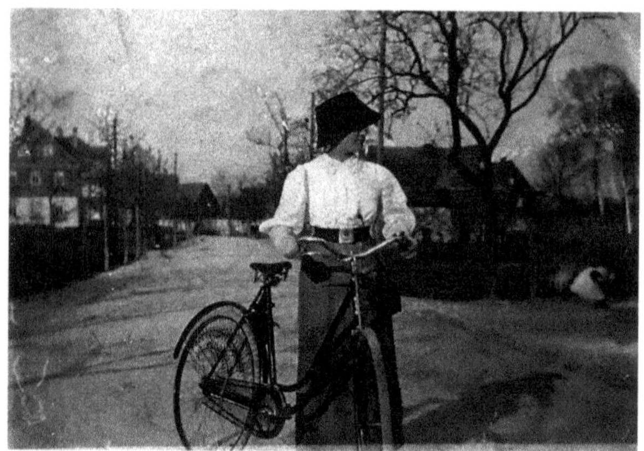

Figure 63: Clara in Mittweida, Olly's city of birth.

The Slavic origin of the Blank family should have continued on the name Ilonka[51] that Olga was supposed to receive. However, the German law of the time precluded the assignment of foreign names. Even though she was born in Germany, Olga did not have German citizenship. Although the etymology of the word nationality indicates the relation with the nation, that can be translated in the domain of the language, customs and national symbols, it is mainly a legal bond between a person and the State. Nationality can be given by origin or by request. The first one is granted by the State at birth in accordance with the laws in force in the country.

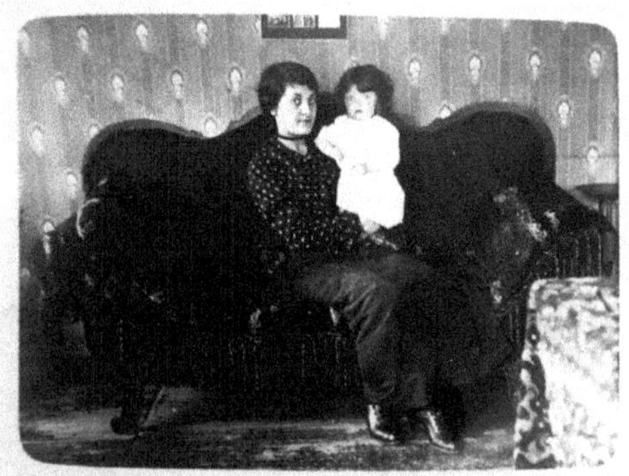

Figure 64: Clara and Olga, in Mittweida, 1914 (PH-1121).

---

[51] Which can be translated to Helena

In Germany, as in all European countries at the beginning of the twentieth century, the right to nationality followed the principle of blood – *jus sanguinis* – that is, it was directly related to ancestry. This principle was related to the great European migrations of the nineteenth century and aimed at giving legal shelter to the children of emigrants born outside a given territory. This nationality by bloodline affiliation, however, instituted second-class citizenship for people who, like Olga, were born in from foreign parents. For these "citizens" several different rules applied, instituting distinct sets of rights and duties[52].

A Russian girl, Olga had the status of a foreigner. If thanks to that it was possible for the research to find traces of her trajectory, these "traces" are the indications of the physical and financial control of the German State over foreigners. Later, these and other official records were used to persecute, arrest, and murder all those who didn't fit the standards considered Aryan by National Socialism.

This control made necessary authorization to change cities within the country. So, leaving Mittweida for Berlin required the registration of the new address. From these documents we verified arrival and departure dates and residence addresses. Compartmentalized in "moral regions" (Park, 1979), much more segregated than today's cities, these dates and addresses allow us to assume *ethos* as well as ethnic and social identities from the differential distribution and pattern of use of urban equipment.

Agier's critique on the notion of *moral region* (2011) points to the importance of observing situations rather than naturalizing space from a set of actors in relation to each other, ignoring transformations in time. The city becomes the scene of several groups and although there is a relationship between people and space, the emphasis is on the transformation of these relationships throughout the day, between the days of the week and the months of the year. Time then appears as a category as important as space.

In a historical investigation it's more difficult to recover the temporal changes in relation to the districts and their frequencies. Therefore I infer the *ethos* of this family from historical accounts of the proximity of more or less orthodox groups, of dwelling in more or less segregated regions, in the presence of more or less working classes, and of the testimonies bequeathed by Olga, Erika, Rene, and by the

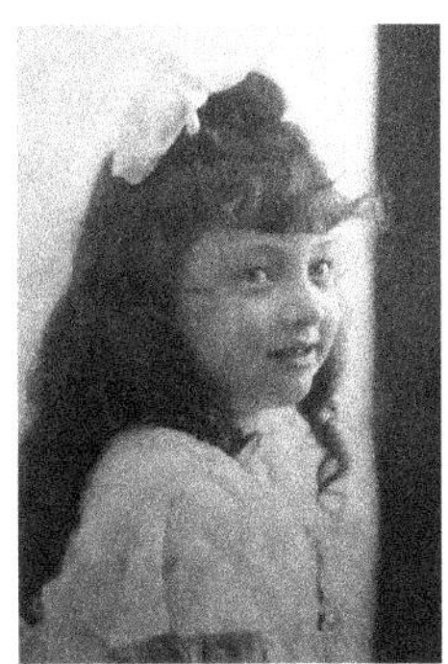

Figure 65: Olga Helene Blank, c. 1920/21 (PH-1117).

---

memory of conversations overheard in my childhood. Here, the social practices of the family are inferred from the location of the schools that the children attended, the proximity of leisure spaces and synagogues, and thus whether the practice of Judaism was orthodox, liberal or non-existent, deducing the configuration of some moral values.

Olga was born on January 28th, 1914, at 2:00 p.m. With brown hair and very vivid blue eyes, she arrived six months before Austria declared war on Serbia, kicking off the Great War. In 1918, Clara took her to Budapest to meet her biological father but he had married another woman[53].

In 1922, Clara Blank moved to Berlin, where her aunt Anna was living. She went with her mother, daughter and grandmother: Sofia, Olga and *Babushka*[54]. Olga tells (MA-33) that Sophia was very religious but did not impose the religion on her granddaughter. Olga escaped from religion classes to play in the garden of Bertolt Brecht's house. Wagner Seixas Mello, an actor and theater director who worked with the artist in the 1960s, recalls that she mentioned having met Brecht. Aware of the information that could contribute to the construction of her image, she seemed to make the most of these data, 'creating' stories of herself. From a certain biographical instrumentality she seemed to produce a past that justified her actions in an emerging cultural field in Rio.

By 1920, Berlin had integrated its suburbs, rising from 6,700 to 87,000 hectares, making it the third-largest city in the world, after New York and London. The opening of new port facilities and transport reforms[55] contributed to the growth of trading (Richard, 1993). This development attracted migrants from everywhere, but the promise of marriage to Werner Heisenberg was certainly as or more important than the opportunities the city presented for Clara and her family's decision to move there.

However, the city's economic flourishing coexisted with a heap of unhealthy housing. One of the most precarious areas of Berlin was in the 1920s the combination of East European Jewish immigration with the poorest part of the population (Geisel, 1993). The *Scheunenviertel* (literally, barn quarter), where Bertolt Brecht lived.

---

[53] Twenty years later, Clara sought Ladislau again apparently to help bringing Olga from Germany to Brazil. Ladislau Vamos moved to São Paulo on August 3rd, 1925. Son of Desidério and Thereza Vamos, he was born on September 18th, 1891. He married Valéria Kollar Come and had a daughter, Heda Vamos. In 1949, the Oficial Diary (document DO-58) registered in São Paulo the opening of an ice cream company on behalf of Ladislau and other partners, Sorvetes Cremosos Vamos Ltda, indicating that their refusal to help was not due to his economic situation. Without access to the descendants of Vamos, I do not know the reasons for his immigration to Brazil. The family probably fled the Hungarian dictatorship. Between the middle of the nineteenth century and the first decades of the twentieth century, Brazilian immigration policies encouraged immigrants of non-black European origin to "fill the void" and form a potentially eugenic population (Koifman, 2013).

[54] *Babushka* died when she was 103 years old, according to Erika's testimonies in 2014; 106, according to the family tree; 111, according to Olly's manuscripts.

[55] Tempelhof airport was built in 1924, opening the possibility of international exchange

Remembering that Sofia, *Babushka*, and Olga were Russian and Olga's mentioning about the gardens of Brecht's house, I imagine they lived in or near that block.

Clara probably lived with them until the end of 1922, when she married Werner Hasenberg. Hasenberg, as Ladislau Vamos, had studied at the technical school of Mittweida. At that time, he attended Sofia's boarding house, where he played the piano to earn some extra money. During World War I, Clara worked in a factory as a technical drawer. For Werner Hasenberg's training as an electrical and electronic engineer, technical drawing is the language through which projects are presented. Her ability to perform this task may have helped the couple's meeting, encouraged by Sophia who wished for her daughter a marriage that would lessen the familiar embarrassment represented by Olga's presence.

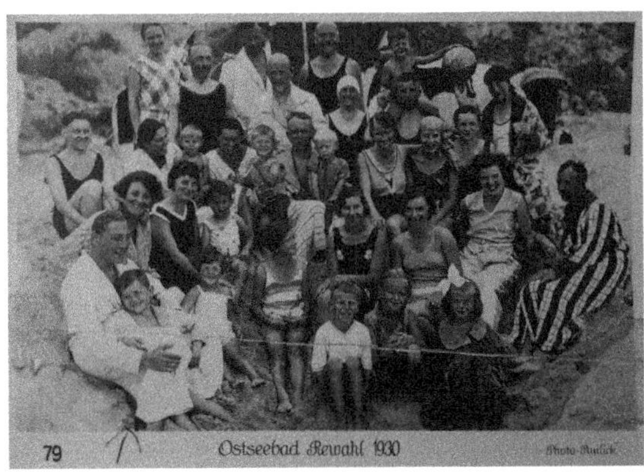

Figure 66: Werner, Clara, Egon and Erika Hasenberg on the left, front row.
Ostsee, Germany, 1930 (PH-1014).

After the marriage, Clara adopted her husband's last name. They lived in Gosslerstraße in the working-class district of Friedrichshain, not far from Scheunenviertel. Werner Hasenberg belonged to a new social category that emerged with the expansion of commerce and the tertiary sector, the employee. He worked for important lighting and communications companies such as Ozram and Telefunken.

This professional category, subjected to rationalized work, also inaugurated the frantic activity of the new metropolis, with a culture of pleasure that contributed to the emergence of the myth of the golden era of the twenties. To some extent the increasing intensity of work was compensated for, but it was also a reaction to the disappearance of the authoritarian structures of the imperial era and the attenuation of sexual taboos. Employees thus contributed to boosting the installation and diffusion of technologies of the entertainment industry: the phonograph, the radio, the cinema, and also photography, sport and weekend travel (the weekend became a commodity).

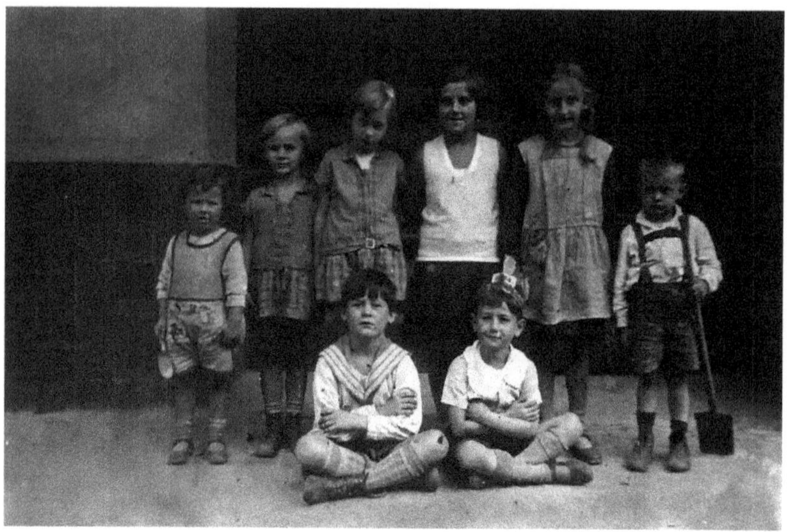

Figure 67: Children from the neighborhood, Berlin. The vulnerability of the Jews was so great that any child could go to the police and get a family arrested. In front, on the left, Egon Hasenberg. On the right-hand side, the neighbor's son who denounced the Hasenberg family for being Jewish (PH-1057).

This new social actor was deprived of the support that the union organizations gave to the working class, thus not having the protection that the worker's status granted. Fully subordinated to the positions they held in the companies where they worked, they were subject to rigorous competition (Strohmeyer, 1993). This competition probably contributed, along with the recession and persecution of Jews in the 1930s, to the family's immigration to Brazil.

The couple had two children, Egon (1924-2014) and Erika (1927-2015). Shortly after Egon's birth, they moved to Jagowstrasse in Moabit, an industrial neighborhood where there was the prison from where Olga Benario liberated Otto Braun in 1928. Levetzowstraße, the liberal bourgeoisie synagogue, was in this neighborhood, but it has no record of the family's attendance. Erika does not remember her mother being devoted to religion until Sophia's death in 1945[56], when she "rediscovered Judaism". This flexibility with religion did not stop her from expressing fury when, in 1948, Erika told her about her conversion to Catholicism.

---

[56] Sofia immigrated to France along with her daughter Manya and family. She survived the concentration camp thanks to the black-market trade that Manya performed (on some survival strategies in concentration camps see Spiegelman, 1995). Soon after the liberation of Paris and her exit from the camp, Sofia died of cancer.

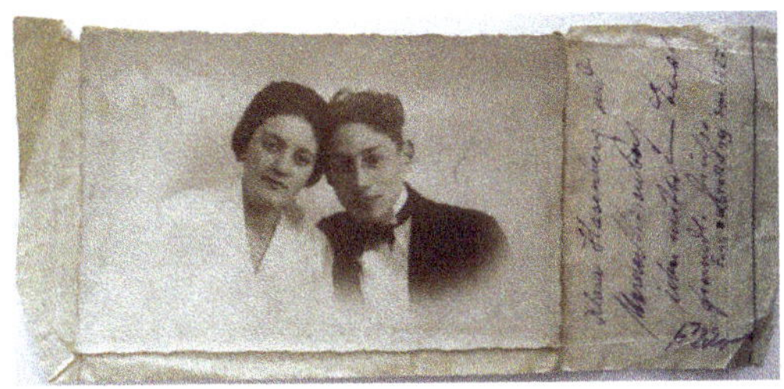

Figure 68: The description of this card reads: Clara and Werner Hasenberg, radio's exhibition, September 1927 (PH-1076).

On October 29th, 1923, at 20:00 hours, the radio entertainment service (Huynh, 1993) was inaugurated in Germany at the height of the post-World War I economic crisis. The success of the radio industry can be grasped by the number of specialized magazines discussing technical issues and broadcasts. Even the newspapers made room for commenting on radio programs. The electronics area was, therefore, a rising area in Germany during that period.

Olga reports that, with her stepfather's knowledge, the family had the first radio manufactured from a box of matches (MA-33, p.24). That was probably the reason he was offered a place at the Kaiser Wilhelm Institut some years later. However, his ethnic background prevented him from taking office.

The family's social situation can be deduced from information regarding the education given to the children. Olly, Erika and Egon attended school and had at least piano lessons as extracurricular activity – learning this instrument was part of the training of all the relatives mentioned so far, Werner Reinheimer also played guitar[57].

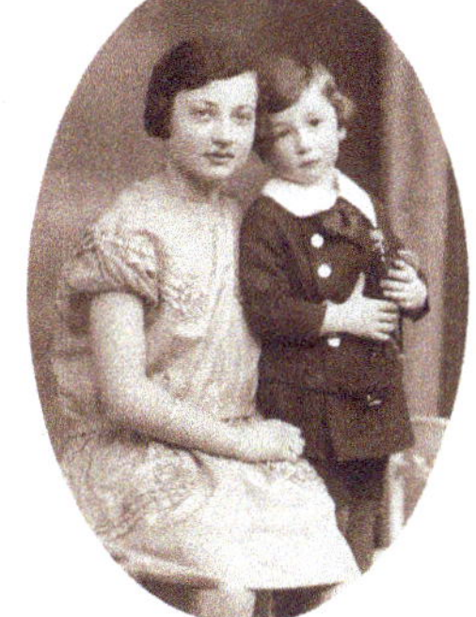

In addition, Clara's sister, Anna, who lived in Berlin when the Blank moved there, was married to Grischa, a bank clerk. Probably, they also had a reasonably comfortable financial situation. So, the Hasenberg and presumably Olga, Sophia and *Babushka* were spared of

Figure 69: Olly and Egon, Berlin, 1927 (PH-1069).

---

[57] Duarte and Gomes (2008) call attention to the relationship between study and habitus, arguing that the conditions of access to formal education are related to incorporated dispositions and associated with the idea of self-control and civilization. These abilities are culturally characteristic of the middle-classes and elites, transmitted to the younger generations from birth. This family *ethos* is inseparable from the neighborhood universes, work and extended circuits of coexistence. These circuits in which the elites move are made up of selective meshes, increasingly restricted as nearer to the top. The "distinction" logic depends precisely on the consciousness of the broader environment in which it manifests itself. That's why early on stimulation of formal education is encouraged and also other activities in which cultural and social capital is incorporated.

the intense bitterness of the economic crisis through which Germany passed from 1929 until the departure of the majority of the family from the country in 1935.

In March 1929, Heinrich Brüning rose to the post of chancellor and inaugurated the period of authoritarian measures. In October of that year, "Black Thursday", which triggered the economic crisis in the United States, hit Germany, which was trying to rebuild itself from the devastation of the World War I, mostly with US investments. The crisis deepened and unemployment became massive. Between 1929 and 1933, the politicization of streets led to increased violence through attacks and clashes between small groups of armed activists, Nazis, Communists and Social Democrats.

Probably the growth of anti-Semitic sentiment led Werner Hasenberg to seek other options. Initially, his intention was to go to Paris, as indicated by some postcards and conversations with Erika Hasenberg. However, the couple and both children ended up going to Rio de Janeiro where Philips Company offered an engineering position. That same year, in September, after the departure of the family, the racial laws of Nuremberg came into force, which defined consanguine kinship made one Jew or non-Jew.

According to Erika, Olga stayed in Berlin waiting for a groom who would be traveling but never returned. We could also imagine that she had chosen to finish the technical course she might be taking before she moved out of the country. In the meantime, she would sell what the family had left behind. At the age of 22, in April 1936, Olga left for Brazil.

2.2. A FABRIC OF FEELINGS

There are still few studies on immigration to Rio de Janeiro, especially when compared to the states of Paraná, Santa Catarina, Rio Grande do Sul, São Paulo, Minas Gerais and Espírito Santo, which received the highest percentages of immigrants of various nationalities (Gomes, 2000).

The first immigrants classified as "Germans" arrived in Brazil before independence. They were traders and craftsmen attracted by the economic possibilities that emerged with the opening of ports in 1808. The use of quotation marks marks the distinct meanings of the "German" category as an inclusion/exclusion criterion[58].

---

[58] As anthropologist Giralda Seyferth points out, "before 1871, the German language characterized German nationality but not necessarily citizenship. In practice, individuals who entered Brazil and belonged to teutonic minorities in Russia, Hungary, and Poland considered themselves "Germans" and attempted to join the immigrants of that origin. Among the German-speaking Austrians and Swiss, one finds, in the literature on colonization, Germans of the Volga, Swabians of the Danube, Germans of Lodz, Germans of Sudeto" (1988: 4). Therefore, caution is needed to not naturalize the condition of "German". Marked this care I will use the term without quotation marks. The same caution should be observed with all ethnic categories cited here, including the notion of "Brazilian".

Some attempts to fix German immigrants in southern Bahia failed in the first decades of this century. In 1819, the founding of Nova Friburgo with "Swiss" immigrants also failed. Seyferth supposes these failures may have redirected German colonization to southern Brazil (Seyferth, 2000).

Those first German residents in Rio de Janeiro had few numerical expressiveness, but a lot of visibility among the other foreigners. In 1821, they founded the Germania Society (*Gesellschaft Germania*), the first demarcating association of Germanic ethnicity in the country (Seyferth, 2000). The migratory flow to Rio de Janeiro lasted for a long period until the 1930s, but the contingent was relatively small. This set was heterogeneous being made up of rich merchants and other immigrants of varying classes at the same time[59].

German immigration to Rio de Janeiro had a distinct character from that which characterized the colonial centers in the south of the country. Rather than the result of a specific policy directed at farm families, immigration to urban centers had no stimulus or subsidy and was individualized (Michahelles, 2003). However, urban immigrants maintained links with those who concentrated in the southern region of the country through a network of institutions such as the press and the Teuto-Brazilian schools and synods of the German Evangelical Church.

This interaction leads Seyferth (2000) to speak of a shared ethnic identity, built as early as the nineteenth century and inspired by the ideals of Romanticism and German nationalism. This identity was also crossed by Brazilian social and cultural events and conflicts. It was therefore the result of the experience of immigration, of German cultural singularity, but also of the historical process and community life in Brazil (Michahelles, 2003).

Michahelles's work, while centered around World War I, analyzed some sources from the late 1920s and revealed "the establishment of social boundaries of ethnic membership and the existence of a variety of ethnicities, which brought together the German-speaking population and updated such limits". It also showed how in literature "it was possible to recognize the affirmation of an identity that could be called Teuto-Brazilian" (2003: 170) that tried to define the German-speaking population residing in urban nuclei from the term "colony" even if they were not located in areas of ancient colonization.

The "German colony" thus had ethnic visibility resulting from various commercial, cultural and sporting institutions such as the Beneficent Society, the Evangelical Church, the German School, the Gymnastics Association, the women's

---

[59] These groups instituted in the city cultural, sporting, charitable, and religious organisations that functioned as markers of ethnic membership. According to Michahelles (2003: 17), "the 1940 census indicates the presence of 9,475 German citizens and 945 Brazilian citizens living in the city who spoke German". However, several immigrants returned to their countries of origin. In 1924, 10,000 Germans residing in Brazil were repatriated. At the same time, the Teuto-Brazilians of the South came to the federal capital and São Paulo, in search for better school education and social ascension. Therefore, the density and constitution of this group varied from year to year.

clinic, the German Hospital Association, the Women's Association and the various singing associations, which formed the wider community of *Rio-Deutsche* (Germans in Rio). This group was articulated through an ethnic identity as opposed to a larger whole, corresponding to the "Brazilians" (Michahelles, 2003)[60].

The works that deal with immigration in Brazil in general are dedicated to national ethnic groups. In the case of Germans, they deal mainly with Protestants, or Jews as a whole, although recognizing their internal differences of language, religiosity and/or nationality. There is no specific work on Jewish-German immigrants to Brazil or Rio de Janeiro, much less progressive German-Jewish. However, the subject of race and ethnicity either implicit or explicit in discourse and legislation on immigration is common to all researches dealing with national minorities. This subject usually refers to the end of the nineteenth and early twentieth centuries and the discussion about nation in Brazil.

From 1880 to 1920, the intense migratory flow helped believing in the imagined white nation in the future causing all scientists to discuss the issues of colonization and immigration as a 'race issue'. Racism was incorporated into the nation's planning practice: "A modern Brazil, whitened through the broad encouragement of European immigration" (Seyferth, 1993: 179). However, this project for creating a Brazilian "race" sometimes considered the Jew as a positive contribution, others a negative one. These distinct forms of valorization of the Jews have been associated with various diacritical marks, including nationality, social and cultural status, and also to orthodox habits.

In counterpoint to the Jewish stereotype[61], there were those individuals and groups who presented themselves as a complex, multifaceted reality who applied for visas. So, many Jews were able to enter the country when anti-Semitic discourses were hegemonic in Germany and were on the way to becoming State policy. According to Lesser, 36,000 Jews of different nationalities arrived in Brazil between 1929 and 1945 (1995).

---

[60] The *Rio Deutsche Zeitung*, for example, a newspaper of great influence in the German community, was published in Rio de Janeiro between 1921 and 1941 (SEYFERTH, 2000). This, and many others, were characterized by a discourse that emphasized the economic, political or cultural contribution of the Germans in Brazil, ideally expressing their membership to the German ethnic group.

[61] As the idea of race was vague, it served to corroborate either the positive prejudices or the negative ones about different social groups. Regarding Jews, Lesser speaks of "two types" of Jews who would have had different receptions in Brazil: the "true" and the "enemy". The "enemy" would be that one of the stereotypes always reductionist since the stereotype is related to the designation of preconceived convictions and/or opinions about individuals or groups. It involves simplifying a limited choice of physical, mental, and behavioral characteristics to qualify or disqualify groups and individuals. This 'selective cognition' (Preiswerk and Perrot, 1975) serves to reinforce our perception of others, which also involves a definition of ourselves (Epstein 1978). Loaded with values, usually negative, these labels are always ways of reinforcing identities (Seyferth, 1993).

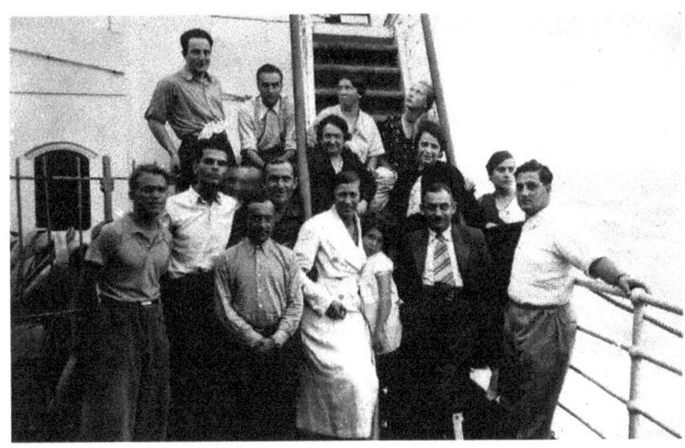

Figure 70: Werner on the ship heading for Brazil, the last one on the top left, 1935 (PH-01).

Werner described, in the same text where he narrated his departure from Germany, the arrival in this idyllic place that was Rio de Janeiro in 1935:

"After long weeks, finally, when the fog rose, there was our paradise. When the sun rose, it lit up a beach that was unbelievably beautiful. Soft waves played with the sand, and farther afield rose the white mansions with their gardens and palm trees. The ship approached, the first cars, the first men and finally we arrived. Rio de Janeiro was sun, light, laughter and music. It was the exact counterpoint of Germany, gloomy and militarized. The people were completely different, they had time for games. In front of stores that sold records, people stopped, sang and with simple boxes of matches they were able to reproduce a crazy drum. The women did not march, but they were almost dancing, in the streets and on the beaches. Everything here was different; the colors were more alive, and people were not ashamed of them and wore them. They spoke aloud, but with unbelievable tenderness. Friends and acquaintances embraced and kissed each other as they greeted each other. This all delighted me. I liked it" (Reinheimer, 1983).

Werner, Clara, Egon, and Erika Hasenberg had embarked for Brazil three months earlier. They traveled on tourist class, but had to stop at the Tenerif port, where they stayed for three or four days, due to a problem on the ship. The trip was not set as an escape, at least not for the 8-year-old girl. Erika said that crossing the Equador line justified a fancy party, for which they dressed her as "night". It was the institution of an imaginary frontier, where below the Equator the roles could be reversed and to these migrants/tourists was allowed the simulation of their colonial fantasies.

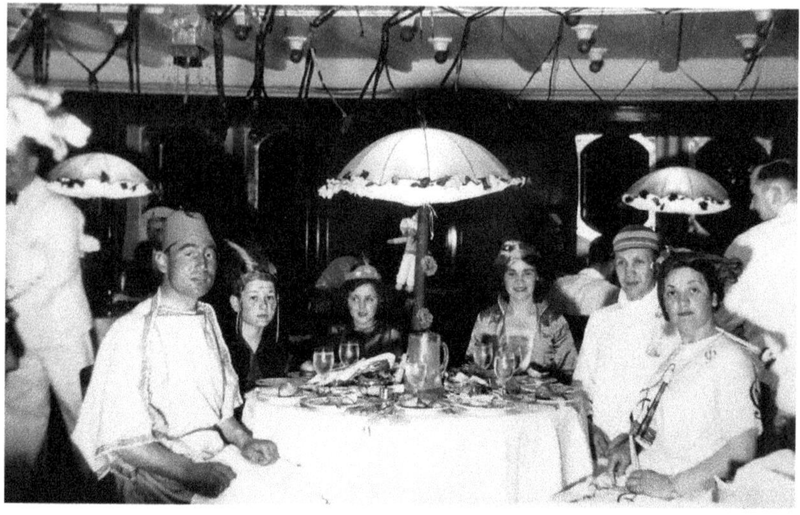

Figure 71: Werner, Egon, Erika, Clara and an unknown couple, dressed in costumes for the party on the ship bound for Brazil, 1935 (PH-1011).

By telling about the costumes, Erika laughed, remembering her mother staging the stereotype of what appeared to be a "Greek figure" with the son's violin as an accessory; of the father who wanted to imagine himself as a "Turk" in a tunic with a red hat and her indigenous brother. Sometime later, browsing Erika's old photo box, a picture of the four around a table shows these costumes, described so vividly. If the photo kept the memory alive or if she created a fantasy about the party based on that photo, we will never know.

The perception that this was a tourist trip could be contradictory to Erika's refusal to speak German and the stating of her anguish over Germany, which she only visited again in 2008. But we need to remember that memory is not only composed of one's experiences, but also of feelings and experiences of others. The story of the family and friends' family members who suffered consequences of war helped compose Erika's affective memory of Germany, which she couldn't forgive.

When they landed in Rio de Janeiro, they were received by another Hasenberg family who, knowing of their arrival, mistakenly imagined that they were relatives. From this information it's possible to have an idea of the size of the German immigrant's group in the city in that period, as well as to perceive the existence of an effective system of communication between them. Werner Hasenberg was hired to open a new film and acoustics department in Rio. The company sent someone to greet them at the port and accommodate them in their new home. This new house was on a street parallel to Rodrigo de Freitas Lagoon. They lived there for four years.

In 1935 Hasenberg had already patents registered in Germany and at the university he had contact with Albert Einstein and Werner Heisenberg Nobel Prize winners in 1922 and 1932, respectively. Olga remembers to have met them (MA-33, p. 28). He was received in Brazil as "pioneer of electroacoustics" (Correio de São Paulo, 1937). In Rio de Janeiro, he installed acoustic systems in cinemas, concert halls and in the Urca and Atlântico casinos.

Olga arrived in 1936 and went to live with Clara, Erika, Egon and Werner Hasenberg. Initially she worked as a sales clerk in a store, in General Osorio Square, where she sold the fabric flowers she made. She became involved with the Carioca community of Jewish refugees, which included going out, going to the beach, dating and getting married to each other. Werner Reinheimer and Olga Blank met through this group. Ira S. and Edith Weitzfelder, for example, who also belonged to this group met Olga and Werner in the 1930s and 1940s, respectively.

Ira, married Heinz, who arrived in Rio in 1936. Her husband and her came and "called" their parents after they had settled. Both met in Ipanema, where they still lived when interviewed, in 2014, when she was 99 and he was 100 years old. The option for Brazil, on the part of Ira was because she had relatives there. Heinz tried to go to the US but could not. As they gave him a tourist visa to Brazil, he went and stayed.

Ira got her authorization by saying she was going to work as a peasant, even if she had never worked the land. Anthropologist Jair de Souza Ramos (2004) mentions this strategy as a common one to obtain permission to stay. She was born in Moscow in 1915 and left there in 1918 because of the Russian Revolution. Ira was part of the two million people mentioned by Hobsbawm (2005) who emigrated because of the Soviet Revolution and thereby deprived the state of much of their skilled cadres. Through Poland, Ira and her family went to Germany and, in 1936, to Brazil.

Edith Weitzfelder, former Rosenfeld, was born in Karlsruhe, a neighboring town of Pforzheim, in July 1928 (and died in Rio a few months after our last meeting in 2014). From a wealthy family, her mother was taken to Auschwitz camp in 1942, where she was murdered. Her father died in December 1945, after facing the crossing of Lake Geneva to take his daughter to a shelter. Edith was then 17 years old. She went to a refugee camp in Montreux until they found an uncle in São Paulo at the end of 1946. Ernest, her uncle, agreed to take responsibility for her. After losing almost all her relatives, and finding herself almost alone in the world, Edith sought marriage as a form of compensation[62].

---

[62] Edith Weitzfelder, a tall woman with large bones, strong and affirmative voice, corroborates the stereotype about German women. Her apparent strength, however, was not maintained when after almost seventy years she mentioned the suffering during World War II. Talking was a new torture and silence a way to keep what was rebuilt.

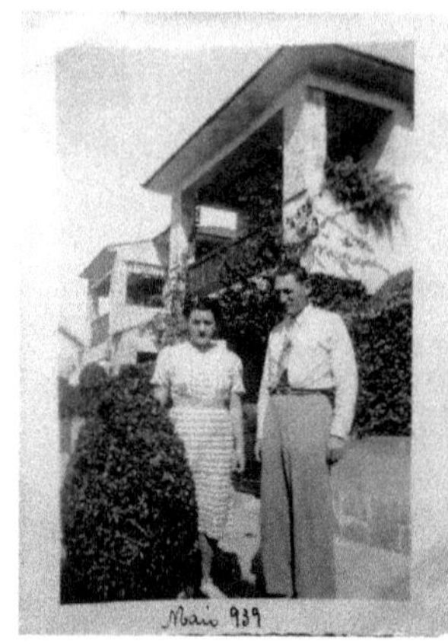

Figure 72: Clara and Werner
Hasenberg, Ipanema, 1939.

Again, it was her daughter who was interested in reconstituting the family story. Part of this story is told in the book that recounts how L'Oréal bought from the Nazi the house the family was forced to abandon. The book was incorporated into *Olly and Werner Reinheimer's Archive*, as well as a copy of the German diary that her father kept during his confinement in the concentration camps.

In the late 1940s, setting up a family seemed the best way to recreate her "roots" – a term used in her testimony – that had been torn from her. Her marriage was arranged by acquaintances who told her there was a German Jew in Rio in search of a wife. She met Joseph in 1949, they married in 1950 and had two children[63]. While the children were small, Edith kept a suitcase with passports ready for any eventuality. Remains of her past. Joseph was part of Olga and Werner Reinheimer's group. The four became friends and Edith attended the Reinheimer couple's house until their death.

Edith spoke of a certain performative disposition (Bourdieu, 1983), that is, certain propensities, tendencies, or inclinations, especially regarding the use of the aesthetically oriented body in Olga's personality, since they met in 1949: "*I met Olly when I came to Rio. I was 21. I was expecting my first child, Daniel. We lived nearby. She came often to visit me and said, "I do not like the tidiness of this house". She stirred everything. This pot has to go here; this table has to go there. Made some great changes, I really liked it. I think she was quite right. Except my husband came home and had a chill. He said, what happened here? Everything changed! The furniture, everything. I said, it was Olly who was here*".

In the 1930s, the debate about the German immigrants' descendants returned to the national scene motivated mainly by Nazi invaders in the colonization areas[64].

---

[63] Part of the family's story can be found in the project Names, in search for 6 in 6 milhion: http://projetonomes.weebly.com/uploads/1/4/7/0/14704412/6_em_6_milhoes_final_comp e http://projeto nomes.weebly.com/ano-2.html. Part of the family history can be found in the Names project, looking for 6 in 6 million: http://projetonomes.weebly.com/uploads/1/4/7/0/14704412/6_em_6_milhoes_final_comp and http: // projetonomes. weebly.com/ano-2.html

[64] At the end of the nineteenth century the German ethnic character gained national visibility with the expansionist rhetoric of the Pangermanic League. The "German danger" was debated in the Brazilian press and on the political dimension, under the influence of the Monroe doctrine, through the keyword "denationalization". The Germans were accused of wanting to form a state within the Brazilian state, to turn the three southern states into a true German colony or simply to claim the political emancipation of the south, creating an independent State. "Colonization was interpreted as "colonialism" and the colonists accused of being agents of German expansionism, when in fact what was constituted in some southern areas of the country was a Teuto-Brazilian culture and ethnic citizens certainly not assimilated and strongly

National Socialism appeared in Brazil through propaganda and the control of some institutions such as shooting societies and part of the German-language press, creating directories of the Nazi party. The intention to assimilate the descendants, by force if necessary, through a Nationalization Campaign by the Estado Novo[65] intensified the debate.

The Campaign preceded the ban on Nazi activities in Brazil. The Estado Novo produced a policy of nationalization to assimilate the immigrants' descendants from all backgrounds, between 1937 and 1945. It was put into practice mainly in the southern areas of the country. This campaign interfered with people's daily lives in order to integrate immigrants into a supposed national identity (Seyferth, 1995). The urban centers were less affected by these xenophobic manifestations of the State and the Brazilian population, but not exempt.

In the years leading up to the outbreak of World War II, the situation in Europe was unsustainable for Jews and other peripheral groups such as homosexuals, Roma and foreigners in general, as well as for people with some physical disability and people who disagreed politically with National Socialism. In November 1938, a Pogrom known as Kristallnacht, Crystal Night, destroyed synagogues, trades and private houses of Jews throughout Germany. The commercial establishment of Werner's father in Pforzheim was one of those affected by the destruction. To defend the local synagogue on November 10th, 1938, Hermann wore his First World War uniform and stood in front of the temple. Hit by a gun handle, he lost his sight.

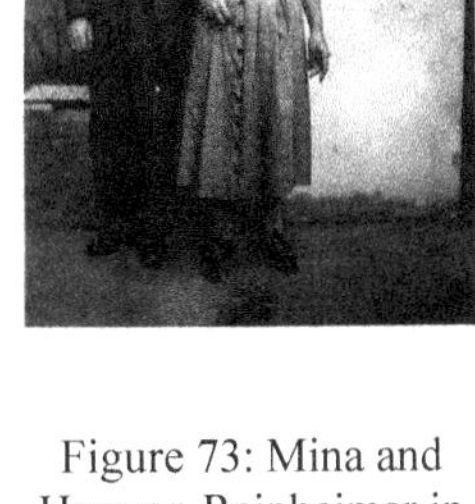

Figure 73: Mina and Herman Reinheimer in São Paulo, n/d (PH-1138).

On October of that year Werner had obtained permission to bring his parents to Brazil. Mina and Hermann arrived on February 9th, 1939, at the port of Santos. Until 1940, half the Jews of the town where Mina was born, Weingarten, either emigrated to various countries or were deported, among them, Mina's parents, to Gurs and Auschwitz. Hermann's two brothers and two sisters were killed by the Nazis. Selma, Abraham's daughter, one of these brothers, managed to flee to the United States.

---

identified with a Germanist ideology, but by no means willing to assume the role of potential citizens of the Reich" (Seyferth, 1988: 21). Perhaps for this reason, even today the term "German" is used in many Brazilian places as a category of accusation for those who do not belong to the group.

[65] Between 1937 and 1946, when Getúlio Vargas presided Brazil with a centralized power regime

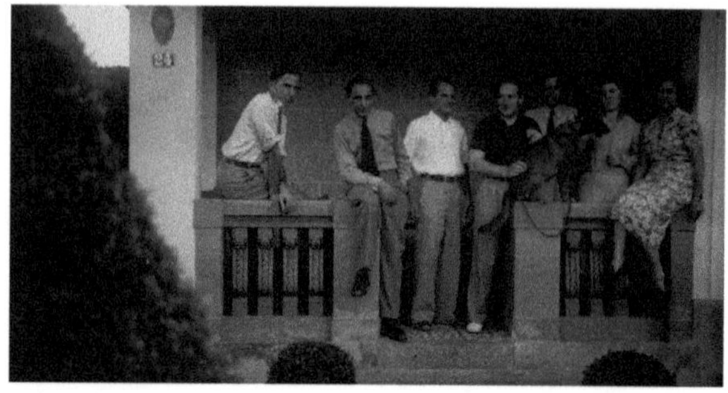

Figure 74: Olly, Werner and some unrecognized people in São Paulo, around 1938 (DIA-1186).

Olga and Werner never talked about what happened in Germany. Werner was irritated by sudden noises: a door that slammed with the wind, fireworks, the ringing of an unexpected visitor, or even the sound of the telephone. The unspoken did not hurt less by being silent. The weight of survival was as great as the pain caused by the absence of those who were gone.

Mina and Hermann disembarked in the port of Santos and went to live in Tremembé, São Paulo. Far from the city center, the district attracted European immigrants, mainly Germans, for their topography and climate, near the Cantareira Mountains. The German presence was still marked in the 1960s, when the neighborhood had the "German News" newspaper that disseminated information about the country and dedicated a page to the memory of the Germans who marked the neighborhood (Bazani, 2008). Hermann died in 1957 and Mina, who lived until 1966 (OD-35), went to live in the Israeli Religious and Charitable Society, founded in 1937, by the mother of José Mindlin. It is no coincidence that Vera Mindlin, the sister-in-law of José Mindlin, was the second person to wear an outfit made out of Olly's fabrics (MA-33).

Still in the 1930s, Werner Reinheimer worked in trading, initially as a representative of watches (produced in Pforzheim?) and in August 1937, wines. According to the Official Gazette (DOU, 1937), he was a partner of Giannini and Acherinto, Italian immigrants who became winemakers in Brazil. According to Cytrynowicz (2002), between 1937 and 1945 immigrants in urban centers such as São Paulo and Rio de Janeiro who had urban occupations such as liberal professions, specialized trades and traders found opportunities for economic rise in the face of accelerated urbanization, industrialization, import restrictions and open development possibilities in local industry and commerce. These prospects for advancement were not conditional on ethnic characteristics but rather on the urban profile, the educational and professional background of immigrants, and the objective opportunities for industrial development and forms of community organization, even if these were not geared to women.

An example offered by the author is the case of the Italian and Jewish immigrant Giorgio Mortara, who emigrated to Brazil to take over the post of president of the Brazilian Institute of Geography and Statistics (IBGE) and coordinate the 1940 census, after having been removed from office in 1938, in occupied Italy. Cytrynowicz (2002) argues that an immigrant, refugee from fascism, becoming the coordinator of the Brazilian census, when discussing the "desired" parameters of settlement in Brazil, indicates that in everyday practice anti-Semitism in Brazil can not be compared to what was seen in Europe[66]. Prejudice was present in the acting of the Brazilian Integralist Action fascist movement and party between 1933 and 1937. However, the history of Jews and anti-Semitism in Brazil do not overlap. In the 1930s, "the Jewish community maintained at least three radio programs in Rio de Janeiro and São Paulo, at a time when radio was the main means of mass communication and controlled by the Vargas government" (Cytrynowicz, 2002: 400).

Although the Vargas dictatorship as of 1937 and the Integralist movement gave visibility to the anti-Semitic discourse of the Brazilian elites, this did not prevent the formation of a German Jewish congregation. Until 1936 the German Jews in Rio frequented the religious services of the Belgian community that, later, gave origin to Copacabana's Synagogue. From that year they began organizing to bring Rabbi Heinrich Lemle and his family, with the help of Lilly Montagu, president of the World Union for Progressive Judaism in London. He was supposed to stablish a liberal congregation in Rio[67]. The first board of the congregation was formed in January 1942.

Erika remembered that her father took her and her brother to attend the services of this synagogue, while Clara took the streetcar downtown Rio: "*at Easter time, my mother would take a streetcar and go to Lapa, because some houses there sold Matze. They were round in a blue paper ... Yeah, a thick paper, right? Like this. And she did this alone. I don't know how many she bought, two or three of these things. To have Matze at home on Easter Sabbath. I remember that, too. Do you know how I used to like Matze? I used to make a cup of chocolate, yes!? With Nesquik and chocolate. She broke into small pieces and did like this (gestures). It would look like a pudding and I*

---

[66] "Anti-Semitism was present in the 1930s and 1940s in important government circles, especially Itamaraty, and its most serious consequence was the secret circulars that restricted the immigration of Jews to Brazil from 1937 onwards. This anti-Semitism produced terrible episodes, such as the story of the three thousand visas to non-Aryan Catholics that the Vatican asked the Brazilian government and which, for the most part, were eventually rejected, according to the book of historian Avraham Milgram, and hundreds of tragic stories of refugees who could not enter, as Maria Luíza Tucci Carneiro shows in her researches. In this sense, there is no doubt that the policy of the Brazilian government was conniving with anti-Semitism in Europe. Although the Estado Novo had ideological nuclei attuned to extreme right regimes, such as those of Portugal and Poland, with Italian fascism and even with German Nazism, one can not, however, define it as a fascist or Nazi regime, historiographically speaking" (Cytrynowicz, 2002: 396).

[67] http://arirj.com.br/origem/ accessed February 13th, 2015.

ate it". This was also how Olga and Werner offered Matze to their son and grandchildren.

Remembering these episodes, Erika justifies her conversion to Catholicism by the lack of relations with the Jewish community. It is important to know, however, that she married an Italian whose personal history of passing through orphanages had a strong link with the Catholic Church as a substitute for family ties.

In 1939, Olga and Werner were married, three weeks before the arrival of Mina and Hermann. With the marriage, she abandoned her family name and the middle name, becoming Olga Reinheimer. Since the end of 1938, the two were living in São Paulo, Werner in Rua Fernando de Albuquerque number 64 and Clara, Olga, Egon and Erika, at number 68. At that time, Egon studied at Mackenzie, a school with imported pedagogy from the USA. Werner and Olga's moving there was probably to prepare the reception for Mina and Hermann. The marriage, authorized in December 1938, by the State of São Paulo, was held on January 20th, 1939 and Mina and Hermann arrived on February 9th (DOU, 1938). Receiving Werner's parents with a new family was certainly a way of minimizing the distance of family and friends, the loss of the butchery, Herman's sight and the life they had known so far. However, there was no atmosphere for partying. The wedding seems to have taken place only in civil, since there is no mention or party photos.

Six months after she was married, Olga got pregnant. Erika narrates this period, between the announcement of pregnancy and birth of the baby, as a moment of peace in the family, back in Rio de Janeiro: *"I remember putting my ear in her (Olly's) belly, excited to feel her son's movement. I was 13. Olly had her feet swollen by the pregnancy and walking to search for a house was difficult for her. But we found in Ipanema at the end of the streetcar, I don't remember the name of the street, it was a cute little house. René was born in a clinic; I can not remember which one. Werner took me to see him. It was his father's face, red-headed. I was aunt at 13. This was a very good time. I remember that Olly and Werner called themselves "matzi" and maetzichen was René (it came from the word pipmatz, or bird)"* (CO-104). Hence the signature of Werner being a little bird pooping (Figure 75).

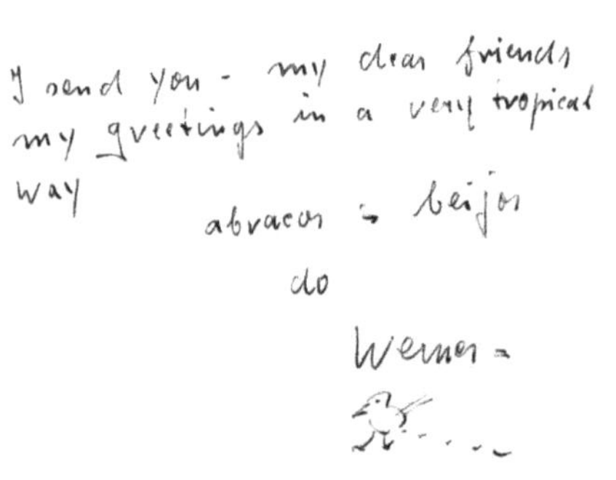

Figure 75: Werner's signature with the symbol of affection between the couple.

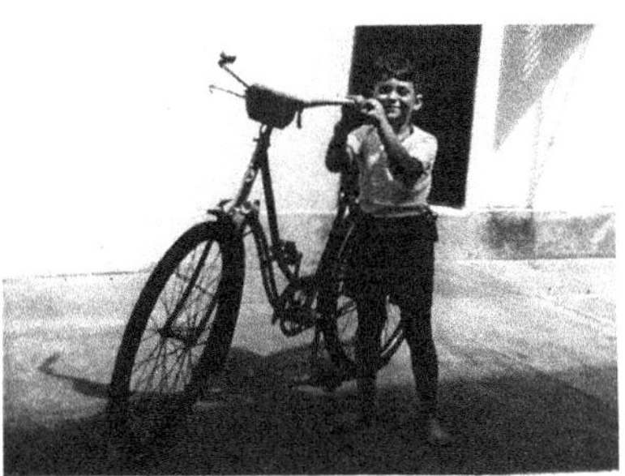

Figure 76: Rene, Bar 20, Ipanema

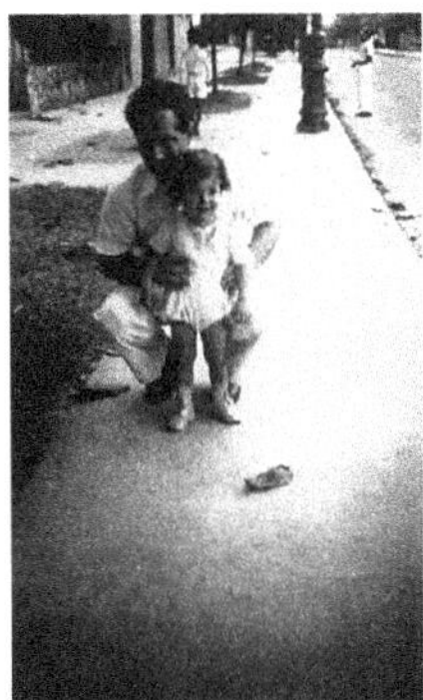

Figure 77: Werner and Rene, Ipanema.

The apartment where the couple lived as soon as they got married was in the area known as Bar 20 (there was a streetcar stop named after the Bar that originally existed there). A block in Ipanema with two-story buildings. The street presented the landscape of a small, cozy town before urbanization in the 1960s. The streetcar stop was four stations after the Hasenberg house. Erika studied at Andrews College, on Botafogo Beach. The same streetcar that took her home took all the other children from other schools who lived in Ipanema. Erika was friends with Billy Blanco, Durga (owner of the Oxford course) and other residents of Ipanema with whom she kept in touch over the years by letters, telephone and e-mail.

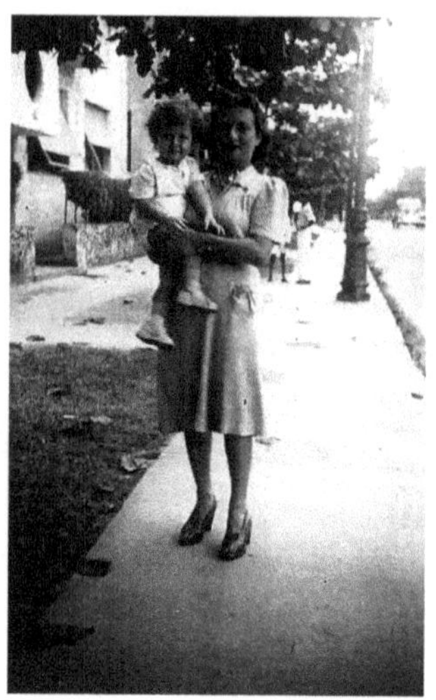

Figure 78: Olly and René, Bar 20, Ipanema, 1940 (PH-89).

On March 22nd, 1940, René Renato Reinheimer was born. For registration, the witnesses were Rudolf Rothgiesser and Josef Leipziger.

Germans, Rudolf, and his wife, Josephine, were Werner's friends until their deaths. They all shared the same political values. Rudolf was born in Berlin and arrived in Rio in 1936. When he arrived, he was a Pforzheim's jewelry seller. Josefina seems to have gone first to Argentina. Whenever they could, they went back to Germany. In 1998, when I interviewed them, Rudolf complained: *"There is nothing left from our philosophy"*.

The story of the name chosen for the child refers to Werner's past. When fleeing Germany, his position in the party was occupied by someone who was killed shortly thereafter, his name was Rene. The son's name was a tribute to this fellow. However, the notary required a "national" name and the translation then made the baby have the same name in two languages, René Renato (which means reborn, twice).

Although it was a homage to a colleague of militancy, the meaning itself does not go unnoticed. The name indicates a rebirth, or two. Whose or what? Rebirth after the dispersion of the families in the Holocaust? After anti-Semitism and war? Rebirth after the bombing that killed Werner's colleagues. After the weight of being an "illegitimate" daughter, redeemed in the constitution of her own family?

In Olly and Werner's trajectory I investigated two families[68] that have become one, but also another form of kinship, a membership that has as its common thread suffering, loss and migration. In anti-Semitism and in the migratory processes of the 1930s and 1940s, the set of common experiences defines each family in itself and the set of families that lived or fled the Holocaust and then had to overcome the difficulties of arriving in a new country and the impact of international political events in the new context. The experience of the refuge in immigration as a symbol of membership, the "Jewish diaspora", identifies all Jewish immigrants who have gone through humiliation, loss and abandonment (of themselves and others). Ernst Renan in his attempt to define what a nation was in 1882 called attention to suffering as a more potent union factor than happiness (Renan, 2008)

Refuge gains a symbolic strength to unite through the memory of the unspeakable. Several authors speak of the silence, of the difficulty of people who lived the years of 1933 to 1945 in Germany and other countries invaded by Hitler or countries that had relations with Nazism. Suffering seems to be potentialized in collective identification when what matters is not what each person lived, but the silence that materializes in each one all the experiences, including that of having survived. This is how the union of two families means the rebirth of these families and the hope of happiness in the construction of new subjectivities.

This is how the suffering experienced by the Jews since the beginning of the nineteenth century, mainly (the various Pogroms in Russia and the Holocaust in Germany), are perhaps their greatest identity strength. Contradictory, what caused so many lives to be lost is what unites around an identity people with different religious and political beliefs, nationalities and diverse generations. Suffering then begins to identify not only individual families, but also all those who identify themselves in some way with that membership, ethnic or religious, Orthodox and laity Jews[69].

In the 1940s, the experience of refuge and the beginning of World War II probably had some influence on a possible revision of the couple's anti-Zionist ideas. In his son's photo album, which accompanies the first ten years of his life, there is a pin from a fundraising association for the founding of the State of Israel. In 1944, through the documents of the collection, one learned that the couple received an invitation to the feast of Shewuot of the *Jewish youth of the whole world* who called

---

[68] I am working with Duarte and Gomes' definition of family as "a more or less broad network, from which some are distant and others approach, in a complex game in which what remains is the recognition of a common thread, linking family, locality and fishing "three dimensions of common membership" (2008: 84).

[69] These experiences are transmitted between generations through various institutions of memory that exist in the world. They may have been stronger in Germany, stage of the definition of specific norms for framing people in the category of undesirables, making persecutions a state policy. Institutions such as the Documentation Center for National Socialism in Nuremberg, Topography of Terror or the Jewish Museum in Berlin present the persecutions (in the latter case, to the Jews and, in the first case, to the various groups such as Sinti and Roma, homosexuals, foreigners, disabled people and people with mental disorders) as a way of talking about a past that should not be repeated. However, it can also be perceived by those who identify with the Nazi-fascist type of thinking as a celebration of Hitler and his proposal.

the *Israelite youth* for a *proclamation of youth to youth* on the subject *Us and the religion* that happened on May 28th at the Botafogo Football Club. Moral support was expressed when uniting around the cultural values and history of the Jews.

The Second War had just begun. President Getúlio Vargas maintained economic relations with Germany. Several immigrant associations faced restrictions imposed by the Estado Novo. However, the German Jews were the most vulnerable group. In the 1930s they had to take refuge because they were persecuted for their ethnicity; between 1939 and 1942 they had to find strategies to circumvent the official restrictions and anti-Semitic discourses and after 1942, with the declaration of war to the Axis, they were confused with their executioners, the Nazis.

Even so, there was room for complaints. Cytrynowicz quotes the editorial of Rio de Janeiro's weekly magazine, "Aonde Vamos?" (Where are we going?) of March 1945, which "showed a haughty stance of the Jewish community, claiming without any embarrassment a position from the federal government on immigration". The editorial exalted the lack of prejudice in Brazil by referring to the supposed "racial democracy" an expression invented by Artur Ramos to justify the financing by UNESCO of an important research in the 1950s in Brazil. The member of the Jewish community questioned the contradiction of this idea with the attitude of Brazilian authorities in placing German Jews "in the same position as other subjects of the Reich" (2002: 416).

There were also complications in a war between all European countries which affected mixed families. Heinz spoke of difficulties at that time by being married with a Russian immigrant, since he was German. With Russia and Germany on opposite sides and Brazil assuming distinct positions before and after 1942, the request for safe passage to travel, for example, meant that only that immigrant spouse of the country with which Brazil was allied at the time received authorization. Thus, during the war, the couple, apart from having to ask permission to travel, were unable to do so together. At least this complication, Olga and Werner did not have.

However, invisible threads formed a web of worries. The city of Pforzheim as a whole was involved in the war. In 1944, 18,622 workers, including at least 10,000 in the defense sector, came from Pforzheim. Its industry was fundamental for the development of technological innovations. In some areas, on-board radios had up to 50% of their parts produced in Pforzheim. On the outskirts of the city there was a factory for production of anti-aircraft shields. In addition, the city had a key role in the rail transport of military organizations.

Being central for the Germans, the city was almost completely destroyed during a British air strike on February 23rd, 1945. In 22 minutes, 17,600 people were killed. Bombs and the firestorm struck the old city, killing nearly a third of its population. After the bombing of Hamburg and Dresden, this was the third deadliest Allied attack during World War II. With 98% of the city center destroyed, Pforzheim was one of the most devastated cities during the war. In May 1939, the city had 78,743 inhabitants, in December 1945, 42,402. If information on concentration camps had not yet reached the general public, this bombardment was enough to know that most, if not all, of Werner's acquaintances and relatives had died in this war.

Perhaps the best description of the feelings that linked people across the Atlantic was Stephan Zweig's, writing about World War I:

> Between those who are close and the distant ones, float invisible threads of love and worry, a fabric of feeling, infinite, now covers the world, night and day. How many words are whispered, how many prayers said to impassive space, how much longing love floats through every hour of the night! The atmosphere quivers continually in mysterious waves whose names unknown to science and whose oscillations no seismograph can record: but who could say if these desires are impotent, if that immeasurable desire, which burst forth ardent from the deepest layers of the soul, also does not travel distances such as the vibration of sounds and the electric shudder? (Zweig, 2013: 199)

A tour around what was in the past the main area of the city shows the 5 buildings that still have pieces of what was their architecture before the bombing. In the middle of the Black Forest, the ruins of the Liebeneck burg resists with difficulty the green of the forest that dominates (Figure 79).

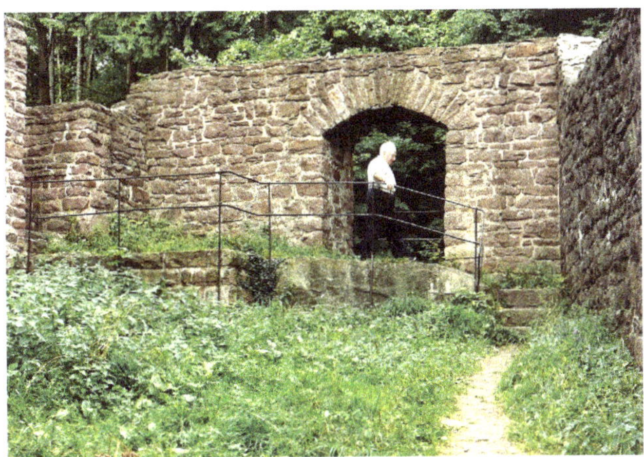

Figure 79: Werner on his last trip to Germany, 1988, in the Ruins of the Liebeneck Burg.

The Reinheimer and the Blank witnessed in the first decades of the twentieth century Germany becoming a Republic, the Western world divided between capitalism and communism – although it was later possible to perceive that it was indeed a dispute for distinct forms of liberalism; the transformation of prejudice against the Jews into a new social phenomenon that came to be identified by the term anti-Semitism; and had to leave the known world to take refuge in a new land with completely different language, customs, values and climate; and in the meantime they lost almost all their relatives and friends.

In Brazil, contact with people who had similar experiences should make the drama and the sense of identity loss less drastic. This happened through various institutions. During this time and during the 1950s, Werner, Olga and René attended twice a year a recreational association located in Nova Friburgo[70], "Recanto Saudoso" (Figure 80). The owners were Henry and Kätte Witchell and the members were immigrant or immigrant descendants: the Walter, Roost, Brock, Hanzele and Tante Magda. On walks, horseback riding, the guitar played by Werner with everybody singing and the parties these immigrants reinforced the feeling of membership to a world of their own, distinct from the universe of Carioca values. The feeling of familiarity was so great that in letters from 1950 (CO-81, CO-73, CO-75), I learned that René, then at age of 10, went by himself because his parents were going to São Paulo, probably to visit Mina and Hermann.

Nova Friburgo and Petrópolis are the main experiences of colonization with immigrants in Rio de Janeiro. According to Carneiro, the choice of this region for the establishment of a colony of immigrants from Canton of Friburg, Switzerland, was due to the climate that was "considered closer to the region of origin of these immigrants" (Carneiro 2000: 45). The contact with foreigners contributed to the creation of networks of solidarity and sociability among them.

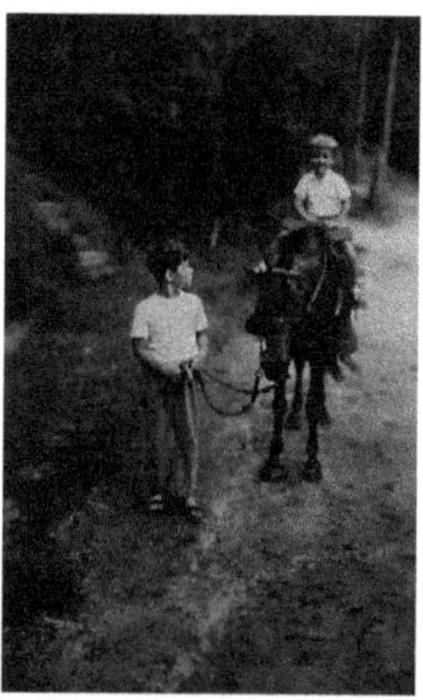

Figure 80: René (pulling the horse) in Recanto Saudoso, Friburgo (PH-500).

However, if the trip to Petrópolis or Friburgo was not a problem for the couple, another difficulty arose: the image of the Jewish-Communist, especially German. According to Lesser, this image began to be built after World War II. Another author,

---

[70] The city was cited above as the first failed attempt to install Swiss immigrants in Brazilian soil in 1819.

however, situates its emergence as a modern political myth from the Revolution of 1917 and the fascist movements (Motta, 1998). According to Motta, these were the temporal frameworks both of changing the content of prejudice against Jews from a religious dimension to a social and political one, and of the emergence of the "myth" of the Judeo-communist conspiracy by joining the conservative discourse of communism and Judaism.

The notion of myth supposes for the author a fabulous narrative usually related to an immemorial time, bearer of an explanation for the origin, with moral teachings; an illusion opposite to reality; and the idea of a dynamic construction that incites to action. The myth of the Judeo-communist conspiracy would thus be a "modern political myth" endowed with elements of all these definitions. It is less interesting to question the temporal frames of this myth, which is the subject of dispute among historians, than that the image contributes to the complexification of the issue of anti-Semitism and xenophobia.

According to Motta, this myth of the Jewish conspiracy for the establishment of a communist dictatorship was the result of an association between "revolutionary militancy and communism to the figure of the Jew presented as the ultimate artifice of the "red peril" (1998: 93). The impact of the socialist formation on the Jews was so important that some authors place the political option and not the national provenance as the main identity mark among the Jewish community formed in Brazil today (Lourenço Neto, 2008 and Bahia, 2007). This overlapping of Judaism and communism led to persecution of militant and non-militant Jews in the 1930s (Blay, 1989).

According to René, Werner Reinheimer had joined the Communist Party in Brazil as soon as he arrived. Thus, he had some involvement with the local politics, besides his activities in the commerce. According to poet and musician Geny Marcondes, he was accountant for a group of German communists in Rio de Janeiro. The people I interviewed and who met him spoke of his sympathy for communism and, by contrast, of their own political stances and the fear of being associated with his sympathies by calling him the nickname "festive Communist". Besides we know that in the 1960s, after the civil-military coup, he was arrested and questioned for his political involvement. I found no information of any reflection of it during or shortly after World War II. Certainly, being German, Jewish and Communist during the Cold War should not have been easy and one way of dealing with it must have been to engage with the Jewish Left. It probably comes from there connecting with institutions like Kinderland and the Scholem Aleichem Association.

In Rene's letters to his parents, he refers to Kinderland summer camp, the Scholem Aleichem Association ASA, and the People's House (CO-77, CO-01). Founded in 1952, Kinderland was an offshoot of the AFIB – Brazilian Jewish Women's Association – former Vita Kempner (life struggle), created by a group of immigrant women from Eastern Europe. The project aimed to continue the work with "war orphans" with commissions organized in different districts, regions and states of Brazil.

The group developed cultural activities such as the Reading and Debates Circle on current social and cultural order inspired by national and international press articles and *Yiddish* literature. There was also the "I Peretz club", where adolescents participated in cultural activities (theaters, cinemas, lectures) followed by debate. The camp was composed of colonists, coordinators and monitors. They went through a training course that sought to convey knowledge about the child, the activities that would be developed and the spirit of collective and group coexistence, as in a *shtetl* (village) (Bahia, 2010).

Both Kinderland summer camp and Scholem Aleichem Association, founded in 1964, were important for the consolidation of networks of solidarity and Jewish sociability. These institutions had a political role in national society in shaping the young children of the members' families in terms of discussion and action on social causes. According to anthropologist Joana Bahia (2010), especially in the beginning, these organizations fought for the preservation of the *Yiddish* and progressive culture, while at the same time seeking integration with the Brazilian people in the struggle for economic, political and social emancipation. The cultural activities promoted by these associations had as objective, in addition to maintaining integration with local society, the improvement of the point of view of a socialist formation.

As all the founding fathers and mothers of these institutions have died, it was not possible to discover how Werner and Olga approached them. However, it is known both by personal communication, and by Rene's letter that Rene himself was part of "I Peretz club" and ASA's choir. In this letter, he talks about the visit to the Casa do Povo (House of the People[71]), the reading club and the theater where they would watch "Of men and mice", that *had been showing for a few months at Teatro de Arena-SP.*

The text by the American John Steinbeck speaks of the impact of the Great Depression mainly on migrations workers from urban peripheries. Through a set of moral values and subjective references, Steinbeck

> "Constructed a historical reading that sought to interpret, denounce and portray the problems posed by the historical evolution of the United States, whose developments were to a large extent the gradual increase of the hegemony of monopoly capitalism and its ramifications over the most diverse corners of the social life of the country "(Kölln, 2014).

Steinbeck's text speaks of a solidarity with the dispossessed. Therefore, both the visit to the *Casa do Povo*, as well as the theater and the reading club are part of the process of formation of youth within the moral values of socialism, described by Bahia (2010) mainly in relation to Scholem Aleichem College of São Paulo. For Olga and Werner besides the socialist formation, it was about inserting their son in the progressive

---

[71] A Jewish institution in São Paulo.

Jewish community of Rio de Janeiro. In this perspective, it is necessary to agree with Bahia (2007) and historian Lourenço Neto (2008) when they argue that one of the important forms of differentiation of Jewish groups is their political and ideological position, generally more important than nationality: liberal or orthodox, progressive or Zionist, communist or capitalist are internal dividers, some being crossed by others.

2.3. THE CONSTRUCTION OF ONESELF AND NEW FIELDS OF ACTION

In 1950 the couple completed fifteen years in Brazil. A relatively stable group of friends had already been established, among Jewish and non-Jewish immigrants, descendants of immigrants and Brazilians. In 1952 they moved to the apartment in Visconde de Pirajá, between Farme de Amoedo and Montenegro streets, this last one renamed now Vinícius de Morais street. This would be their residence for the next forty years. The change from Bar 20 to the middle of Ipanema is not unimportant, since neighborhoods are not homogeneous in the distribution of moral values (Velho, 1989).

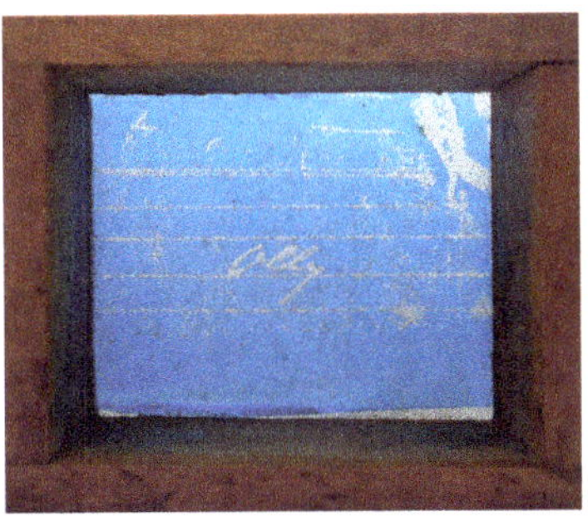

Figure 81: Silk-screen with Olly's signature (PAO-16).

An important part of the changes was the investment by Olga in a profession and, along with her, a name at the same time artistic and legal, Olly Fabrics. The pseudonym was her nickname since she was a child. In 2014, during Erika's testimony I asked about Olga, she repeated the name aloud and amended: *I always called her Olly. I find it strange to use Olga.* The transformation that a name change entails can be thought of in her case as a process that began in her change in civil status, when she married. It continued in the transformation of her childhood nickname into a legal entity when she entered the artistic field and, for the first time, worked for herself and not for her family[72].

---

[72] Several authors point out that, even today, from the time when women are born, they are subjected to a kind of work different from the paid job. This last one can be chosen today depending on the social class to

The prestige of a recognized name is the power to consecrate objects (the label effect or signature), that is, the power to value and obtain benefits from that operation (Bourdieu, 2004). Bourdieu shows that any cultural product is a product not of an individual, but of a system that includes individuals, values, and institutions. The production of belief is precisely the construction of a system that obliterates itself by making the objects appear as products of a single individual. Reputation also contributes to the work's monetary value. And this reputation is gained through a process of producing the efficacy of the objects and the *creator*'s name.

In anthropology, naming is an important part of a person's social construction. Initially, the artist was presented by her artistic pseudonym accompanied by her husband's surname. Throughout the 1960s, the family name disappeared and only the pseudonym began to be used. Although this is the conquest of a proper status, independent of the husband, Mariza Corrêa (1995) shows how the careers are configured quite differently when they are conjugated in the feminine.

Olly had already begun to work with art before moving to the new apartment. According to Geny Marcondes, herself, Olly and Maria Teresa Vieira created a Children's Arts Club, which ran on Saturdays from 1:00 p.m. to 5:00 p.m., between 1951 and 1953. In 1951, they worked in Geny's house's garage, on Nascimento e Silva Street. In 1952, it was in the Brazileiro de Almeida College. And in 1953 at a branch of the Brazilian Music Conservatory located between Copacabana and Ipanema. While Olly taught ceramics, Geny taught music and Maria Teresa Vieira painting and drawing. Moving to the new apartment brought Olly closer to the area where most of the neighborhood's intellectuals and artists lived and with whom she had established relationships even before moving.

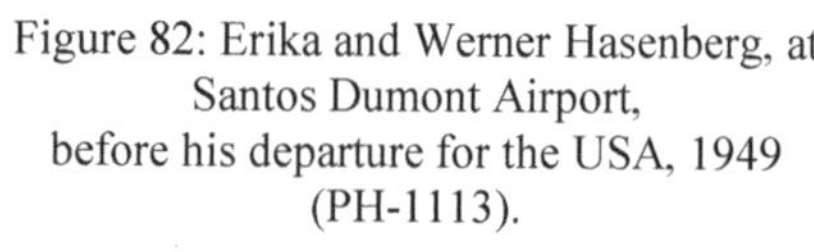

Figure 82: Erika and Werner Hasenberg, at Santos Dumont Airport, before his departure for the USA, 1949 (PH-1113).

However, a subjective dimension may also have had an impact on this change of direction: Olga's stepfather, being German, was unable to renew his contract with Philips, a Dutch company, after the war. This made him re-emigrate to the US. Werner Hasenberg went to Princeton University, where Olly's mother followed a few years later. The country's immigration laws divided the couple, for after the war

which they belong. Young and old women work at the home for their father, brother, husband and children only because they are women, in the service of others who can not or do not want to work as they do (Tiburi, 2018).

ended, the borders were open to Germans, but not to Russians. Olly's sister married an Italian and they moved to Rome in 1950. In that year, Rene was 10 years old and Olly probably found the time to invest more intensely in her professional career.

Several times she justified her entrance in the artistic world because her son did not *need as much attention anymore*. This justification can be understood in several ways. On the one hand, it was necessary to found her entry into a labor market so that she did not seem negligent with the house and the family. On the other hand, the mention of the child may have a much more extensive meaning than the phrase seems to imply. At least two of my respondents indicated that the couple's son was their liaison with Olly and Werner. Rene, in addition to effectively expanding the couple's web of relations with the parents of his peers and friends, probably also contributed in translating nuances of local meanings and values to his parents.

The couple's financial situation was not comfortable, evidenced by the constant complaint in letters about Werner's difficulty in paying the bills by himself. Thus, unlike the representations of an inner need that would lead an artist to devote herself to art, context and material needs probably led her to invest in something that already aroused her interest before, the artistic work associated with textile production.

Fayga and Heinz Ostrower were close friends of the Reinheimer couple. She was born in Poland in 1920 and immigrated to Germany in 1921. He was German and a Communist. Both Jews took refuge from Nazism in Brazil in the 1930s. The two couples met before they were married. It was a *boat brotherhood*[73], that is, a sense of kinship formed between those who came together on the same ship or had many similar experiences. The reference comes from the film by Sérgio Oksman, *Irmãos de navio* (Boat brothers) (1996). The closeness between the two couples, as well as the distinction between them, can be seen in Olly's claim for not being invited to Fayga's house other than for birthdays and year-end parties. She was bothered for not participating also in the meetings with intellectuals and artists.

Fayga had studied graphic arts at the Getúlio Vargas Foundation in the 1940s, where she took woodcutting classes with German artist Axl Leskoschek (1889-1975). In the 1950s, she engaged in the local artistic strife by adopting abstract language. In 1954 she began teaching at the Museum of Modern Art of Rio de Janeiro. Fayga, like other people living in Ipanema, including immigrants, Jews and non-Jews involved in art, probably led Olly into contact with Margaret Spencer, her first art teacher in Brazil[74].

The fact that one does not know exactly what stimuli led Olly to devote herself to art removes the individualistic character often implied in the rhetoric of entering into the artistic field. Olga lived in a neighborhood whose language was that of aesthetic and customs renewal. Her youth in Germany had been close to that same grammar.

---

[73] http://www.sergiooksman.com/irmaos_eng.htm
[74] Document M-33, probably written in 1986, tells about her having met many artists at a friend's house in the 1940's.

Physical objects are only a small part of the reciprocity ritual process which is consumption as a language. Something else as important or even more important to consider is name sharing. Who indicates whom and for what is part of an information control system that has the power to direct and define who changes status: from unknown to known, from being dispensable to being indispensable.

As Douglas and Isherwood put it:

> In fact, what is being transacted in the highest realm is actually shared knowledge about a network of mutual trust. Real goods are the visible tip of the iceberg. The rest is a classified submerged catalog of people's names, places, objects and dates. The main activity is an ongoing attempt to standardize your values as accurately as possible. What is being kept in the highest sphere, and contained therein as far as possible, is creativity. Alternative ways of doing things can be glimpsed, alternative types of knowledge suggested, but here in the privileged circle of superconsumers of the highest position decisions are taken on patronage. To sponsor is to support the channeling of resources. (2013: 205).

The coincidence between needs, desires and possibilities may be what led her to seek artistic training in other expressive techniques such as painting in fabrics. It was through artist Marília Rodrigues that I learned about Olly's participation in events at the Escolinha de Artes do Brasil: *"She was very attached to Augusto Rodrigues and Noêmia Varela. Intensive course of art in education. He did it for teachers from all over Brazil. The teachers who were already in action, professionals came to do this specialization. Focus were in all directions. Folklore, philosophy, art history. Then people were called in to give lectures. It was not just teaching, training. It was very comprehensive. Many artists were called to talk about their work. There were a variety of artists. I think that's where I met Olly"*.

Through Olly's curricula and manuscripts, she declared ceramics was the first arts training she made in Rio de Janeiro as Margaret Spencer's private student. However, notes on vegetable dyes in a São Cristóvão Athletic Club notebook indicate that her interest in fabrics could have existed long before. The club existed with this name until 1943, when it was renamed São Cristóvão Futebol e Regatas. The notes, therefore, may be from the early 1940s, indicating her interest in other creative processes and their techniques, notably concerning tissue (MA-06). The date declared by her as the beginning of her work with painting in fabrics is 1957, well after the work with ceramics. Even so, the beginning of the work is certainly after the technical apprenticeship necessary to execute it.

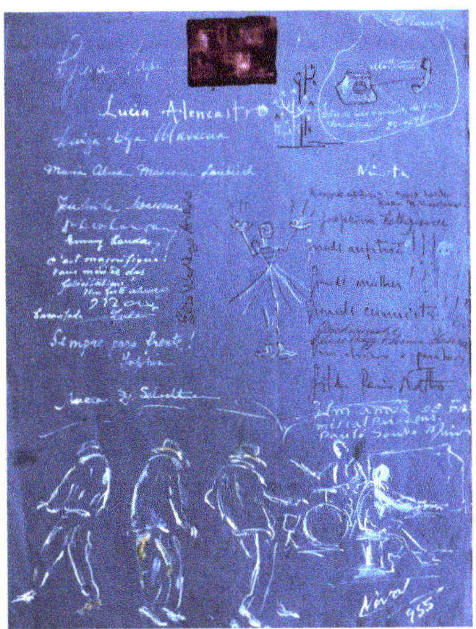

Figure 83: Records of visitors to an exhibition of ceramics produced by Olly, 1955.

American artist Margaret Spencer founded in 1948, in Rio de Janeiro, the Escolhinha de Arte do Brasil (School of Art of Brazil) along with Pernambuco born Augusto Rodrigues (1913-1993), Napoleão Potiguara Lazzaroto (Poty), Darel Valença and Lúcia Alencastro Valentim[75]. The "Escolinha" was part of a movement that had relation with the New School, of the 1930s, and through it with Fernando Azevedo and Anísio Teixeira, but also with John Dewey's philosophy, Viktor Lowenfeld and, mainly with philosopher and theorist of the arts Herbert Read (1893 - 1968). In 1941, the British Council organized in Rio de Janeiro an Exhibition of Drawings and Paintings of English Children, whose presentation was written by Read (Sardelich, 2011).

In 1943, in his book "Education through Art", Read had systematized his educational perspectives through art, starting from a non-interventionist teaching principle, based on the stimulus to *free expression* as a way of developing creativity and imagination, without establishing a priori rules (Itaú Cultural, 2015). The idea of *freedom* gained its own pedagogy. The school taught different artistic expressions (dance, painting, theater, drawing, poetry, etc.) and initially worked in the premises of the Castro Alves Library of the Institute of Social Security and Assistance of State Servants – Ipase (Bacarin and Noma, 2005). A certificate that Werner donated blood

---

[75] The first three mentioned have drawings or engravings in Olly's collection. Lucy Valentine and Margaret Spencer may have works among those whose signatures could not be recognized.

to Ipase's Hospital in 1950 leads me into believing that maybe Olly would have given clothes cutting classes there (DE-04-B, MA-33, MA-63).

In 1950, Olly attended private classes at Spencer's house in Del Castilho, on a private street in the Klabin factory (MA-37). Soon after, these classes were transferred to MAM-RJ. She complained she did not understand Spencer's noninterventionist pedagogy (MA-33). However, later, this was how she presented different techniques to her grandchildren, that is, the way she showed the use of a certain technique was always one among others that should be discovered in relation to the material and not a form that should be learned from the teacher. As poet and sociologist Ligia Dabul (2001) shows, the process of learning artistic techniques is one of the ways in which artists produce from the inculcation of dispositions, especially through exercises. Imitation, experimentation, and repetition are procedures generally used by teachers to gradually establish continuities and discontinuities with other artistic practices.

Douglas and Isherwood (2013) drew attention to the differences in consumption in more or less restricted social fields. Membership in an Orthodox Jewish community has much more restrictions on individual choices, although there is more support for members when they face some sort of problem. Conversely, transit through a wider social field leaves individual freer in terms of their choices, but also with less support.

The contemporary artistic world is marked by the values of individuality and singularity, although these values can be articulated with others in quite different ways depending on the time, place and group of which we speak. René points out that one of the changes he felt when leaving Bar 20 was the loss of community ties partly due to the architectural structure itself. In the new apartment they no longer lived in one of several two-story houses. It was now an 8-storey building with four apartments per floor, without space for common life. However, as will be seen, Olly's increasingly intense approach to the world of artistic production has made the bonds of membership to communities such as Jewish and immigrant and their descendants less prominent than the actual artistic exchanges. This new network of reciprocity, however, continued to be largely formed by immigrants and/or their descendants, Jews and non-Jews. Now the thread linking each other was not ethnicity but aesthetics.

In 1953 Olly participated in the II Salão de Arte Moderna of Rio de Janeiro (Modern Art Salon of Rio), with her production in ceramics. In the following edition of the same event, she won the acquisition award[76]. Her first studio was set up with the financial support of the classes she gave in the garage of Geny Marcondes' house. A document in her archive points to 1955 as the year of transferring the registration of her brand, Olly Fabrics, to a new address (DFC-04; DFC-11; MA-63).

According to newspaper articles (MROW-G-01), an intoxication from the ceramic's chemistry made her, as off 1957, to start dedicating herself strictly to

---

[76] This award is actually a way of becoming part of the museum collection. Having her piece acquired by the Museum of Modern Art was the prize.

painting in fabrics. In 1958, designer Norman Westwater invited her to have her first individual at the Contemporary Art Gallery (MROW-G 23). The relationship between fine arts, furniture design and interior design was intense and went through mutual complementation in terms of presenting their work. Therefore, the designer's invitation was another decisive step in legitimizing her work with the restricted circle of artists and intellectuals who reformulated the representations and values of modernity in Rio de Janeiro.

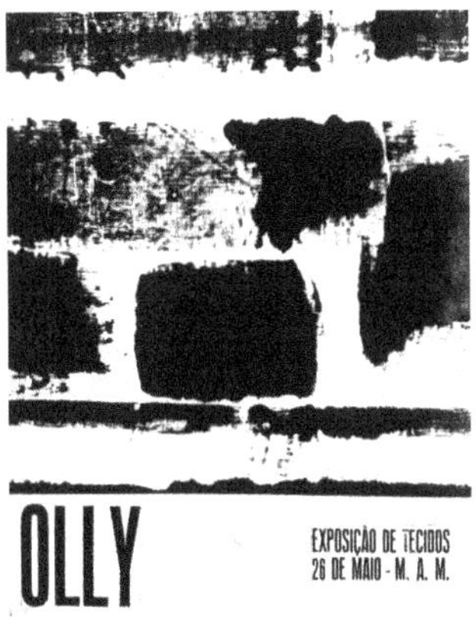

Figure 84: Poster of Olly's first individual exhibition at MAM, in 1960.

Modern, as a temporal and not "stylistic" classification, is considered here from the beginning of the twentieth century. The artistic modernity of which Olly was a part, relates to what was instituted mainly from the late 1940s with the inauguration of modern museums, biennials and art galleries aimed at modern artists. Although the galleries have instigated the appreciation of the living artists who had produced in the early twentieth century, modern art and modern artists – here, and especially in the next chapter – concern mostly those that emerged from MAM-RJ's art workshops and other museums of modern art, in other states, and which were in some way linked to abstraction and later styles until the early 1980s.

Artistic manifestations are a universe composed of several worlds in cooperation and the forms of cooperation between the different professionals involved in the production of the goods characterize these worlds. Art then appears as a phenomenon that is the result of the interdependence of various activities and therefore restricted in its freedom to the economic, political and organizational constraints of each of the processes that constitute it (Becker, 1982).

Decoration through its recognized professional activity, industrial design, interior design or furniture design follows a series of conventions partly determined by the characteristics of the material used and/or the techniques of production. Thus, cooperation has not only positive but also restrictive sense, denoting the influence that each system can have when intervening in the final form of production. Being part of this group of people, who were instituting what would become the new modern conventions, was as much presenting herself from what those social actors were producing, as producing things consistent with the discourses of self-presentation, that is, that "matched" their proposals. And, as Campbell (2010) shows, the perception that certain things match is part of social and cultural conventions, therefore they are socially invented.

Some social actors who participated in this network that instituted new values and representations produced a double gesture. Fayga Ostrower, Franco Terranova and Aloísio Magalhães may have been some of the most representative examples of this production of an artistic discourse associated with a social discourse that inserted them into different symbolic universes by constructing their own meanings and contributing to the production of interpretations about them and their context. These actors created the conditions for the definition of new artistic practices in Brazil that over time have become different fields of activity: design (in several of its specific areas such as fashion, interiors, graphics, jewelry), architecture (mainly landscaping) and art.

In the next two chapters, I enter the second half of the twentieth century, concentrating attention on the artistic dimension of Olly Reinheimer's practice. It should be noticed throughout the work the contrast between ethnic membership, in conflict with the different currents of Judaism and in relation to Werner's political positioning, in the first half of the century, and the insertion of the actors in a network of immigrants and their descendants and of an intellectual middle-class crossed by the ideology of the singular individual, freedom and choice, in the second half of the century. This difference of focus is related to the diversity of materials available in one and the other time period, as well as to social contexts, but especially to Olly's life *project* that has gained previously unknown proportions.

This later period is marked mainly by the actions and information about practices and rhetoric by and about the artist. Thinking about the impact of Werner's relationship on her production seemed as important as reflecting on any social actor from the mesh in which the individual trajectories are constructed. The horizon is McClintock's (2010) critique of a feminism that does not include either non-white women or men (white and non-white). Therefore, I have set out to investigate the trajectory of this artist, considering her husband and the peripheral themes that appeared in her trajectory as a political and aesthetic subject.

Olly and Werner's trajectories allowed me to explore gender and class, private and public spaces, marriage and the market boundaries, with a view to reorganizing values in the artistic field at the beginning of an industrialization that marked the denial of power relations, but in doing so reaffirming them. Gender, class and ethnicity were mutually constitutive of the modern identities that emerged from the cultural field formed in the 1960s and 1970s. However, in the process it was necessary to account that in any analyzed context, some people are closer and others more distant and therefore have more or less incidence on the events, discourses and meanings that are produced.

Working with the couple as a heuristic unit, or as a system of complementarity, seemed to be confirmed by some interviews I conducted with other couples. One of them in particular had some moments that made visible the division of social work and memory within the marriage. Asked about the arrival of her parents, the interviewee looked at her husband, who gave some tips for the answering of the question. Then, to remind him of the names of the cities from which his parents came and later to speak about the meaning of Jewish progressism in the past (a subject related to Kinderland and ASA, institutions to which she held a post) it was the wife's turn to give the tips for the answers.

Although each one, within a long marriage, constitutes an individuality, there are crossings that consolidate with coexistence. The political position of one contributes to the work of the other, without the other needing to verbalize what is already established as "the couple's". Another example was the testimony of an artist who was questioned about her political ideology and replied that her husband was a socialist. At the same time, her husband's profession as a geographer certainly had an influence on the artist's form of seeing the maps and using them as artistic expression.

Olly did not discuss politics. However, Werner's participation in most of her activities made him an intrinsic part of her aesthetic subjects' grammar. It is in this sense that although he hardly appears in this second half of the century, when the central theme is her work, his presence is ubiquitous.

From here the material does not follow a chronological order, although it began in the 1950s and ended with the death of both social actors, in 1986 and in 1992. Between 1950 and 1986, the emphasis was on the subjects that crossed the construction of Olly's artistic career presented from some of her major exhibitions and collections. Other productions like theater costumes, for example, would need new research.

The notion of *career* here is derived from that produced by Dabul to think of contemporary painting, that is, a "repertoire of events related to [artistic] production distributed over time in order to demonstrate ascension and constructed and acted to attest to the capacity of a social actor to create meaning through [production]. Flexible and highly linked to the circumstances of its presentation, a *career* can range from initiatives that prove that ability in a consensual way to the people with whom an [artist] relates (such as a prize in a certain Salon, an exhibition in a certain place and a valued thematic), to the presentation of her relations with a group of specialists, perceived and valued only by those who map her (such as having a work in the studio of a painter known by the teacher and by some colleagues)" (2001: 194).

The *career* then is the affirmation of paths of creation over time, affirmed by events that confirm the capacity of a social actor to create meanings with her artistic production, also indicating the network of relations that operates this confirmation. However, there are no pre-defined stages of how to build an artistic *career* in modernity, since the paths, as well as instances of consecration and areas of recognition of activities can be diverse. An artist who lives and works in an inner city has a social space and is subject to completely different aesthetic conceptions from an artist who lives in a city like Paris, for example. Between the two poles, there are a multitude of variations on what can be considered a "successful" artistic *career*, with the values, institutions and agents linked to it. However, as Goffman (1985) would put it, there is a moral dimension in the way these *careers* affect people's *ethos*.

CHAPTER 3

Stop, Look, Listen: When the Dead Die, Are They Really Dead?

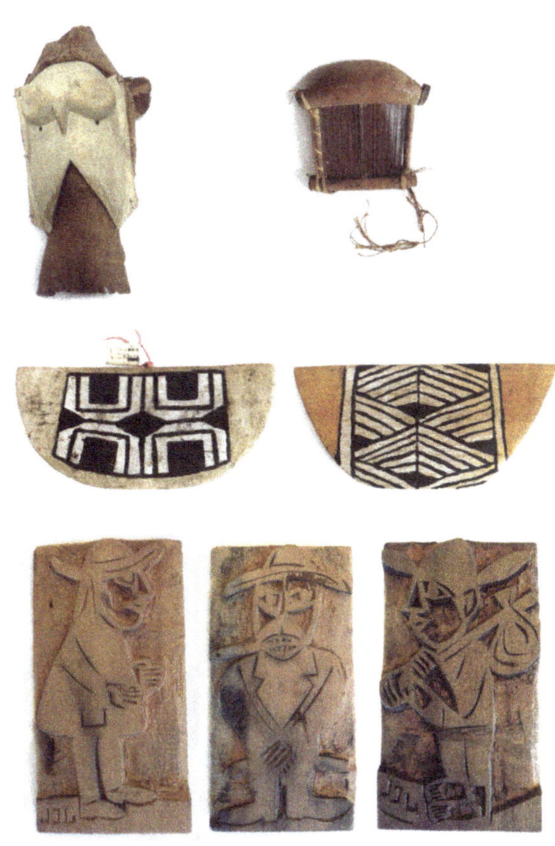

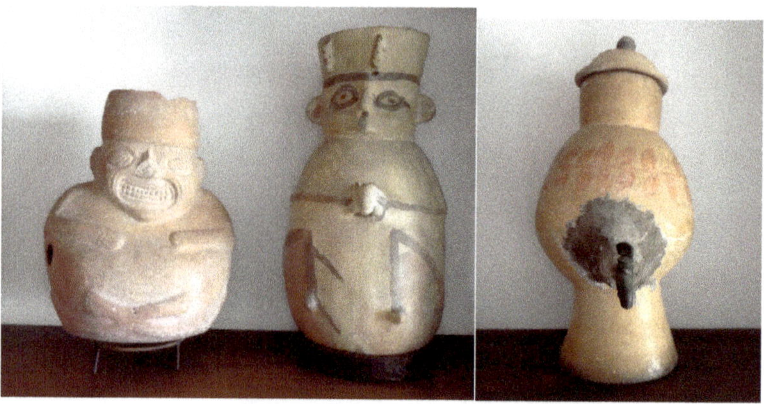

Figure 85 (1-9) : Things accumulated by Olly and displayed in her apartment.

3.1. OBJECTS AND PERSONS: THE RECIPROCITY SYSTEM IN ARTS

In this chapter, I analyze the collections as social technologies of building memberships from the distribution of objects through the domestic space. I argue that the verticalization of urban space, as well as industrialization, played a fundamental role in this process. I start from the idea of a *mercantile racism* that appropriated peripheric groups for the construction of *consumption spectacles* that forged identities for consumers, but not for the original producers. I then analyze the role of collecting as a strategy to materialize the ambiguous place that a Jewish, white, heterosexual, married, middle-class woman occupied in the process of social transformation that Brazilian industrialization entailed.

The inclusion of feminist debates, black movements, and ethnology in their aesthetic bias was a way of challenging social, sexual, and racial boundaries. To transgress these boundaries was the way in which the new middle-class, of which the couple was part, found to subjectively produce themselves. Social, sexual and racial boundaries were crossed, sometimes to be questioned others to be reinforced from new assumptions. White women were supposed to work, but they were not yet in the history of the disciplines involved. They could also have certain privileges of a freer social life, but they had to conform to heterosexual normality and the ideology of marriage.

Urbanization and industrialization were accompanied by the expansion of urban jobs in the areas of services, administration, supervision, planning, public works, civil construction, health, artistic and cultural production, among others. New cinema and bossa nova[77] were part of this context. A new middle-class consisting of engineers,

---

[77] New ways of producing and thinking about the movies and the music in Brazil.

architects, economists, doctors, administrators, lawyers, and other professions required a higher level of education in the country and the expansion of higher education. This context facilitated the acceptance of feminist demands for the entry of white middle-class women into the labor market.

It was during the 1950s and 1960s that the first generation of Carioca Jews, children of immigrants that arrived in the immediate pre-and post-war period, born between 1930 and 1940, entered the university, benefiting from these transformations. At the universities, this generation has found a new world of friendships, relationships and professions. The graduate study was an important path of social ascension and the public service an option to the instability that the parents experienced in the previous generation.

Duarte and Gomes call attention to the individualizing project implicit in the investment that the education of children requires: "Studying implies much more than the payment of tuition. There is less need of a financial investment than the presence, even if in tension, of an individualizing project" (2008: 140). It is an ascension *project* that requires a specific *ethos*. There must be an individualization project as a force of transformation, linked to the idea of freedom and equality, but also to the notion of choice, considering the limits imposed by social norms. The child's education is, then, the social action that explains this individualizing project as constituted of steps to be followed from a strategic evaluation of the socio-cultural situation in which the family was immersed.

In general, Jewish immigrants of German origin married each other. However, from the next pre-and post-war generation onward, perhaps due to the influence of the university entrance and of the transformations that modernity brought to the family institution, the mixed marriages came to predominate. The couple's son did not escape these rules. As soon as he graduated in engineering, he became an employee of Furnas, an electric State company linked then to the Ministry of Mines and Energy. At the university he met his first wife, who, like the following two, was Catholic. This indicates a relaxation of the couple's ethnic ties, as well as the relevance of the professions mentioned above in the social and economic context of the period, but mainly reinforces the idea of individualization as a process of circulation in different groups and social environments. This was necessary for the coexistence in urban space where the expansion of the webs of interaction required the coexistence of people with often antagonistic ideals. In the case here, perhaps the most paradigmatic is the professional coexistence between Jews and former participants in fascist regimes.

From the 1950s onwards, social ascension coincided with socio-spatial changes in the city of Rio de Janeiro, driven by public investments in infrastructure, mainly transportation. It can be added to the successive changes that had been redesigning the city since the 1940s and the opening of the Pasmado Tunnel linking Copacabana to Botafogo. It allowed former elite neigborhoods to expand to the shoreline of Copacabana, Ipanema and Leblon.

Copacabana was the first neighborhood to be verticalized in the 1930s. In 1946, the city government approved 12 story buildings to be built, consolidating the process of replacing houses and villas with buildings with several apartments per floor. Small-scale civil construction entrepreneurs of Jewish origin played a part in this transformation. Ira and Heinz were part of this change, having their construction company been responsible for several buildings in Copacabana, Ipanema and Leblon, during the 1960s and 1970s.

Copacabana's loss of status was associated with the compensation of the cost of land in the late 1950s and early 1960s with the construction of one-bedroom apartment buildings and a code of postures that allowed the construction of contiguous and tall buildings. It made it difficult to aerate and transformed the landscape into a forest of "armed cement". As a consequence, Ipanema and Leblon, mainly from the 1970s on, became the destinations of the Carioca middle-class (Keila and Limoncic, 2010).

It was after the Second War that the International Style of Modernist Architecture transformed the urban setting, although Walter Gropius, Le Corbusier, Mies van der Rohe and Frank Lloyd Wright, some of its main propagandists and practitioners had already been active for a long time (Hobsbawm, 1995). The historian Lilian Schwacz (2006) points out the contrast between the vertical architecture of these large buildings that invaded the metropolises in the 1950s and the vivid colors of the popular festivals, the whitewashed houses and the neighborhoods that still resembled images of the homelands of many migrants. The festivities and many other popular references were counterbalanced by the rapid tempo of the metropolis. The coexistence of opposing poles had multiplied both by the accelerated disappearance of past memories and by the valorization of this past, contributing in stimulating the search for furniture and objects of rural groups exchanged for modern ones.

Counterpoint to and in support of this modernity, folklore had been an important theme since the late nineteenth century, gaining new meanings until the 1950s. Anthropology historian George Stocking Jr. (1982) retraces the trajectory of anthropology in Europe to show how the idea of folklore is part of this story. Just as in Brazil, folklore and anthropology have emerged in some countries as two distinct areas of knowledge. The author analyzes this relationship by contrasting the forms of constitution of anthropology in the colonizing countries and their involvement in the building of Colonial Empires (*empire-building*) and in the peripheral European countries in which anthropology supported to a certain extent *nation-building*.

While the former reflected on the often dark-skinned "outer" and distant "others", the latter, devoid of colonial empires, reflected on inner alterity. These two traditions, "primitive" versus "peasantry" (or indigenous in the Brazilian case), were differentially denominated in Germany, giving rise to folkloric studies and to ethnological studies, *Völkerkunde* and *Volkskunde*. Folklore then emerged as the study of close alterity, revalued by the romantic movement. This movement's protagonists were the ascending middle-classes who despised the French-style and defended a cult of sincerity, simplicity and nature. From this came the opposition between

Civilization and *Kultur des Volkes*, a term first used by the German philosopher Herder (Vilhena, 1997: 271).

Alterity in relation to civilizational models was then the foundation of the modern nation, at once authentic and culturally "backward". Paradoxically, this same delay would be the privileged way of protecting the national particularity. These singularities, however, were always "discovered" when they were about to disappear in the process of urbanization and industrialization. The folklorists' aim, at its origin, was thus an attempt to reconstitute a lost totality.

The notion of authenticity is linked in this case to the absence of an original to counteract. The anonymity of authorship was then a condition for the constitution of this field of study. These manifestations were also linked to the idea of totality from the point of view of the production, circulation and fruition of the works, unlike the "cultural industry" in which production and circulation would be dimensions external to the "people" consuming the products imposed from outside.

In Brazil during the 1920s, the field of folklore was still a heterogeneous area of study, formed by amateur dilettantes such as Amadeu Amaral, Mário de Andrade and Sílvio Romero, considered the founding fathers of the discipline. In that decade and in the following the studies on folklore reached their peak valuing the idea that the soul of the people would be in the peasant rural life. It was considered authentically national, 'expression of the people', which was not contaminated by foreign culture. As a discipline, folklore became important during the Estado Novo when the integration of the indigenous into the national culture was discussed and folklore became part of the Ministry of Education.

Anthropologists Carla Dias and Antônio Carlos de Souza Lima showed how in the late 1930s the formation of the idea of a "people" or of the "popular" also went through the constitution of a collection of objects of the material culture from cities in the Northeast and Minas Gerais that eventually invented the associations between the nature of those geographical regions and the social realities that were found there with the idea of a nation homogeneous in diversity. According to the authors, *hick, regional, folkloric, popular*, were referred to distinct regimes of conception and enunciation that led to actions of nationalized collecting and national staging through devices such as exhibitions, catalogs and books (Dias & Lima, 2012: 203).

Dias and Lima showed how the identification of the national supposed processes of collecting objects of material culture from arbitrary systems of valuation and signification historically determined that can be seen as broader processes of nationalization of social life. Brazilian regional diversity had been perceived until the beginning of the 20th century as a sign of inferiority. In the National Museum of Rio de Janeiro, a Hicks' collection was inaugurated in 1918 and a Regional one was constituted between 1930 and 1950. In 1939, the Brazilian Historical and Geographical Institute (IHGB) inaugurated the section "Types and aspects of Brazil" (Daou, 2001), with articles illustrated by Percy Lau. But the values accorded to those collections in those different periods were not the same. For the modernists, diversity was considered part of the national wealth.

In the 1940s, folklorists and social scientists, mainly from São Paulo, had established a close relationship by sharing the value of fieldwork, largely stimulated by the courses given by anthropologist Dinah Lévi-Strauss. These courses were offered at the Society of Ethnography and Folklore, supported by the Department of Culture of the City of São Paulo, which was headed by the writer and folklorist Mário de Andrade and later by art critic Sérgio Milliet. At the end of this decade, the National Folklore Commission (CNFL) also drew attention to these manifestations and the different perspectives from which to perceive this production.

Anthropologist Luiz Rodolfo Vilhena (1997) studied the trajectory of folk studies between 1947 and 1964. During this period, a series of national congresses were held in several states of the country to discuss the subject, as well as to defend these manifestations and the establishment of a government agency to coordinate research and preservation efforts. This agency was created in 1958 under the name of Brazilian Folklore Defense Campaign (Campanha de Defesa do Folclore Brasileiro). An expressive contingent of intellectuals was engaged in the valorization of popular culture, conceived by them as an object of research and as the basis of national identity. This was also a period of transition in the development of the social sciences in Brazil, which sought to consolidate since the 1930s with the creation of the first graduate courses on the subject.

Part of the Folklore Movement attempted to consolidate folklore as an autonomous discipline through the creation of graduate courses at philosophy universities. Defining the idea of "people" linked to the peasantry and a "purist" notion in which it would be closer to "nature" and less marked by foreign customs[78] was part of the process of specifying what the folkloric phenomenon was. The 1950s was the decisive moment of the battle for the recognition of folklore as one of the social sciences, but it was not effective in Brazil. Folklore has become mainly a subject of disciplines such as anthropology, sociology and the arts.

During World War II, it was inaugurated the idea of a "national character" that singularized each nationality transforming the nations into an object of analysis of anthropology. In the same period studied by Vilhena, sociologist Gláucia Villas Bôas (1992) identified folklore as the most researched subject in the Brazilian human sciences including other disciplines besides anthropology and sociology. Ethnic groups were then divided into indigenous groups, immigrants and blacks. Part of this set is the study of the social scientist Dante Moreira Leite (1969[79]) on the "Caráter Nacional Brasileiro" (Brazilian national character) published almost twenty years later. This character was regarded as something "natural" that should be preserved

---

[78] In this process, there is a discussion on orality in which an opposition between originality and authenticity associated with illiteracy and oral culture was constructed in relation to the inauthenticity and literacy of the written culture typical of the elites and much of the internationalism of the workers' movements. However, this debate goes beyond the scope of the subject analyzed here.

[79] Due to the presence of the book in the couple's library I opted to include it in the ethnographic references instead of the bibliographic ones.

from possible deviations. Although the anthropological studies, which sought to characterize the Brazilian originality, did not mention the folklorists, both perspectives were looking for the traits of an authenticity of Brazilian culture. Effectively those studies ended up generating this supposed authenticity that was inscribed also in Olly's work.

The folklore movement included an effort to reconcile the national and the regional, guaranteeing the specificity of each region without sacrificing the unity of the nation. This relationship is not always explicit, but it is always an underlying assumption. The preservation of national unity then went through two basic dissonances that were the opposition between the regions and the opposition between "people" and "elite". It is from this period also the so-called "community studies", whose most representative author is perhaps German anthropologist Emilio Willem for whom the culture of the interior of Brazil was the background for the investigation of the processes of cultural change. These studies, which were concerned with "hick culture", were also of interest to folklorists as a way of defining the regional stereotypes that would compose national unity. In the same way, the magico-religious world studied by the ethnologist Eduardo Galvão would be part of the "folkloric characteristics" of the Amazonian indigenous groups.

The praise of mestizaje was one of the main biases through which Brazil was given originality over other nationalities, that is, its unique character would be "a historical product of the "integration" of the ethnic strata that made up Brazilian society" (Vilhena 1997: 159). Criticized as an ideology that masks social inequalities, this bias was associated by Vilhena with a "populist nationalism" that contributed to the formulation of an idea of "Brazilian culture" representing a certain decadent agrarian aristocracy and the sons of social oligarchies.

Another aspect of these studies assumed a notion of "Brazilian culture" that, even crystallized, denounced the unequal character of Brazilian society. The context of the accelerated process of capitalist modernization propitiated the emergence of new readings about this society. The choice of Brazil as the locus of implementation of the UNESCO Project on Race Relations produced a new line of interpretation of modernization through social structure. The dependency and underdevelopment theorists tried to verify the possibility of carrying out a project of modernity for the country. To the idyllic vision of a national *ethos* was added the dimension of conflict between strata and ethnic groups. Both perspectives reconcile the idea of preservation of a national basic unit and the alienation of foreign influences.

However, for those intellectuals concerned with class differences, syncretisms would mask social inequality among the different strata of Brazilian society. Although Unesco Project researches did not reach a common sense, some books by authors that reflected on the social stratification and the supposed Brazilian underdevelopment constituted Werner's readings and were subjects of his debates in his web of relations. Therefore, the appropriation of these themes and the collection of objects from these groups was not done from a simplistic perspective but was imbued with the contradictions pointed out by the various studies and debates that appear in the literature of the couple's library.

Social Sciences' institutionalization in Brazil led to the organization of institutions of self-legitimation that contributed to the production of specific intellectual identities that defined fields of study, with their scope and limits. These fields excluded a series of manifestations that were not considered as objects of these new disciplines because they did not fit the institutionalized criteria. These exclusions then found other social spaces in which to build their legitimacy.

The effectiveness of the Folklorist Movement was not merely instrumental, promoting rewards and expectations for those who engaged in it. There was an emotional awareness to the theme that made it recognized by society allowing advances in its objectives and engaging other social groups. The main coordinators of the Folkloric Movement were based in Rio de Janeiro, although they maintained their regional references. From the 1950s onward, a major market for mass symbolic goods was witnessed in the main Brazilian cities and, from the following decade, the cultural sphere became increasingly governed by a market logic.

Folklore, regional themes and miscegenation have come to be seen as increasingly conservative, obliterating the conflicts and inequalities. Manifestations that were previously related to this area of study began to be examined under the prism of "popular culture". Folklorists were the first to make a systematic discussion of this notion. It now gained reality in the practice of a set of actors that connected fashion, design and art. And even though they were linked to museum institutions; they began to form private collections with these objects.

The nation-building process also went through the structuring of a range of institutions that established common signs with which to communicate with other nations. It is in this context that we consider the modern artistic language and the particularization of pictorial subjects. It allowed the constitution of a common repertoire for classification and attribution of value to comprehensible works and themes in an international market. In this market nations built their singularities in relation to different conceptions of the "Other". Thus, as anthropologist José Reginaldo Gonçalves (2007) called attention, the constitution of the new museums in general included a tense relationship between different ethnic groups, social classes, nations, professional categories, the public, collectors, artists, cultural goods, agents of the State, etc.

In Brazil, while "modern" art was constituted by a process of individualization (Reinheimer, 2014), a cultural field based on the "popular" and other internal "primitives" was designed. In the 1950s, a search for antique furniture, baroque statuary and objects from what was beginning to be defined as "folk art" was organized in the interior of the country. "Many future contemporary art dealers such as Fernando Millan and Jean Boghici were involved in this collection, conducted both by public and private interests". According to art collector Jean Boghici, Jânio Quadros indicated Mário Pedrosa for head of culture and the poet Ferreira Gullar worked for the Cultural Foundation of Brasília. Both invited Boghici and José Carlos de Oliveira to collect "popular culture" objects in the interior of Brazil. For three months the two devoted themselves to this task (Bueno, 2005: 390).

The pre- and post-World War II immigration played a significant role in structuring the modern art market of the second half of the twentieth century in Brazil. Between 1947 and the end of the 1960s, most of the gallerists and collectors of modern art were foreigners who fled the war and/or its consequences and played a fundamental role in building the foundations of a certain modernity in the arts, theater, cinema and television (Bueno, 2005).

Part of the national bourgeoisie that was at the head of modern institutions, museums and biennials, was linked to the media. The 1950s in Brazil represented an expansion of the web of art consecration, with specialized agents and fixed exhibition venues, such as salons, museums and art galleries. Between 1947 and 1952 there were the inaugurations of the: MASP – São Paulo Art Museum (1947); MAM-SP – Museum of Modern Art of São Paulo (1948); MAM-RJ – Museum of Modern Art of Rio de Janeiro (1949); São Paulo Biennial (1951); Paulista Salon of Modern Art (1951) and National Salon of Modern Art, in Rio de Janeiro (1952).

Modern art museums became the main exhibition spaces, legitimizing and consecrating the producers and artistic products of the time, and the biennial became poles of information and formation of modern movements (Bueno, 2005). Architecture played an important role in the consolidation of the field, since a part of the modern art market arose from the initiative of some architects and designers in exhibiting artists' production in their furniture stores. Thus, in Rio de Janeiro and São Paulo, until 1959, the exhibition spaces for modern production were mainly furniture stores that served as galleries.

According to sociologist Maria Lúcia Bueno, "the core of collectors responsible for a regular trade was almost all foreigners of Jewish origin. The scenario only changed at the turn of the 1970s, with the consolidation of capitalism in Brazil, when the image of the Brazilian art buyer appeared" (Bueno, 2005: 390). The names of artists of the 1930s and 1940s gained economic value through art dealers such as Pietro Maria Bardi and Giuseppe Baccaro who sought artists who were consecrated, living but forgotten by Brazilian collectors. Ismael Nery, Tarsila do Amaral, Antônio Gomide and Anita Malfatti, were put back into circulation mainly in auctions. In this context, contemporary production found a "precarious and highly competitive commercial circuit, where supply was always higher than demand". The specialized galleries survived economically using the strategy that also existed in the 1960s: showcases and events promoted contemporary artists, but sales promoted the established names of modernism from the 1910s to the 1940s (Bueno, 2005: 398).

It was in this context that Niomar Muniz Sodré redefined MAM-RJ's performance. Sociologist Sabrina Parracho Sant'Anna (2011) divided in two this museum's constitution history. While from 1948 to 1952, when Raimundo Otoni de Castro Maya directed it, the project consisted mainly in the construction of a past as a way of aiming for the future; as off 1952, when Niomar Muniz Sodré took over the direction, to 1958, the museum gained as a project the constitution of a becoming, establishing a mediation between the desired future and the one that was to come. This desired future had great influence from the foundations of the Ulm School of Design and names such as Gropius, Mies van der Rohe, Paul Klee, Wassily Kandinsky, Malevich, El Lissitzky, Moholy-Nager and others. However, the past has never completely left the horizon of this museum. In part, modernity in Brazil was built, as in Europe, compared with the past of ancestral cultures. In this period, it was not so much a matter of guaranteeing the legitimacy of a new way of thinking and of producing art, but of producing a distinction between European and Brazilian modernity, sometimes inserting Brazil into Latin America, others constituting a Brazilian peculiarity independent of Latin-America.

Between the late 1940s and early 1950s, the emergence in Europe of a new museum concept played an important role in this process. The ideals of museums' popularization began a process of spectacularization, opening these institutions to larger audiences. Conferences, libraries, temporary exhibitions and film shows have become common techniques to these memory spaces. In Brazil, the political horizon of this period was developmentalism, with progress as a motto. Until the 1970s, museum teaching in Brazil focused on training for identification, authentication and preservation of objects. The museum was then thought of as a space in which the idea of Brazil was represented, through collections of families of the ruling and elite classes. This conception changed only when, in the 1970s, Gustavo Barroso founder of the National History Museum in 1922 and of the museology course in 1932 ceased to be responsible for the training course in museology (Gonçalves, 2007). Contrary to this view, museums of modern art stood as symbols of modernity, and modern architecture was one of the main ways of representing this planned future.

The construction of MAM-RJ was also the establishment of a system of gift and counter-gift, where collectors, patrons and businessmen converted social capital into economic one and vice versa. The purpose of the institution became not only knowledge, production and dissemination of modern art, but also the constitution of a Carioca cultural field analogous to the role of other similar institutions in other states.

Sant'Anna shows that, contrary to what would happen in the management of Niomar Muniz Sodré, the first phase of the MAM-RJ was turned to a frustrated attempt to equate the Brazilian achievements with those of Europe. The social art had been consecrated in the 1930s and 1940s, having Cândido Portinari and Emiliano Di Cavalcanti as its main representatives. The national themes and forms were in continuity with a modernity that found in Brazilian and in the exotic otherness certain relation with the primitivism of European Avant-garde, being alterity emphasized by these two artists as the poor social classes rather than ethnic groups: Portinari's main subjects were the retreatants and the life in the small rural towns, while Di Cavalcanti had as one of his main themes the poor women of the tenements.

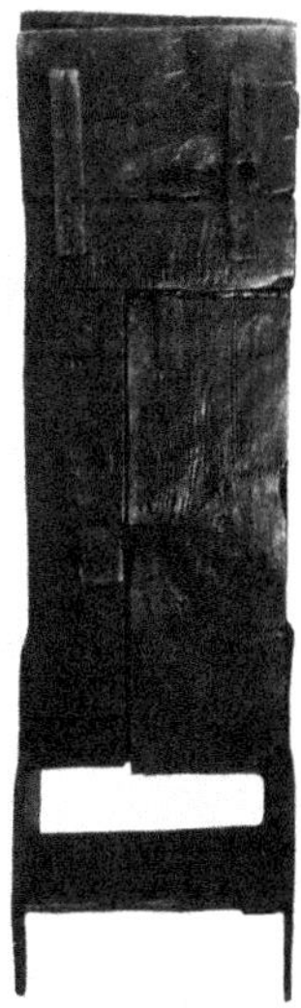

Figure 86: Cabinet designed and produced by Márcio Mattar.
Same one as in figure 30

Behind the exhibitions of museums there is a complex system of social and symbolic relations that allows their formation and guides their functioning. The Northeast ceramics exhibition, organized in 1953 at MAM-RJ, was related to modernism through a request from David Rockefeller, brother of MoMA's founder Nelson Rockefeller, to gather pieces for an exhibition of folk art of the Americas. The subject was present in MAM-RJ's statute through the encouragement of "folk surveys". Rodrigo Melo Franco de Andrade, leader of SPHAN[80], was also a founding member of MAM-RJ. The exhibition of the Northeastern pottery was thus both a form of presentation of alterity to civilization, but mainly of continued disciplinarization and internal production of that other. MAM-RJ, as well as the National Museum and other Brazilian modern art museums, actively participated in the process of legitimizing and naturalizing the production of a certain regionally identified material culture. The modernity in steel, plastic, vinyl, glass and even wood, ceramics and leather, if produced with rulers, compasses and squares, was the counterpoint of the rusticity of wood, ceramics and leather worked with the hands, without the intermediation of instruments of measurement, standardization and obliteration of manual labor.

It is indicative of the importance of these object systems (Baudrillard, 2004), of which the artists were part, the manuscripts in which Olly detailed, about some objects in her collection, to whom they belonged, in what situation they were changed

---

[80] Service of National Patrimony, History and Art.

and/or who should they be returned to. She also used the objects to tell a little about her relationship with the persons mentioned: how much she liked someone, what one day saddened her regarding someone else, what moment of the relationship made her happy. These are objects loaded with meanings that persist and retain both their memory and the subtle presence of all this web of relations that participated in her social life: *"The French critic **I have borrowed**[81] from Sergio Campos Mello. The magazines, I returned. The book I got from Carmo. He wanted to borrow but did not take it. He also never took the thick paper I gave him"* (IN-04). The book about Roberto Marinho's collection was Marc Berkowitz's gift, of which she says she has won also other books.

These manuscripts are from 1986, the year in which she passed away. The artist seemed to want to continue through her objects, and in these writings, she authorized people to borrow, take back what belonged to them or asked the returning of what was hers. The exchanges should then continue after her death, which she knew imminent. *"I gave a book to Gilberto Motta that he hasn't given me back. He says it's petty to ask for my book, after about 5 years"* (IN-04). This exchange also involved the loan of works for exhibitions, as can be seen in the correspondence with Frederico Morais about sending two paintings for a show on the "Constructive Movement in Carioca Art" that took place in 1985 at the Banerj Gallery (CO- 21). Membership in the circle of reciprocity was also confirmed by the invitation of curator Rossini Perez for her participation in an exhibition in honor of the Atelier de Gravura (engraving studio) in 1984, following its recovery after the 1978 fire (CO-111).

Unlike the research on the production of knowledge by academics or intellectuals struggling for institutionalization, the actors observed in this research were not concerned with establishing, let alone agreeing on, what would be "popular culture", "indigenous groups" and their productions. However, the fact that there is no systematicity in the explored subjects by the set of actors involved in Olly and Werner's trajectory does not mean that there were no theoretical and political foundations and, therefore, categories mediating the relations between the actors and the realities on which they acted and contributed to building. Her universe was that of art. Thus, "popular culture", "indigenous production", as well as "regional productions" and/or related to the religions of African matrices, were reclassified as "indigenous art", "pre-Columbian art", "black art", "Popular art".

A series of negotiations had to be carried out so that this production would gain this new status. The first that we can mention is that in specific cases of "black art" and "folk art", some objects were removed from anonymity and their producers were identified through their names and their life stories. Folklore or "popular culture"

---

[81] I added emphasis on the expression "I have borrowed" because in Portuguese Olly used a "poetic license" allowed to those who do not have Portuguese as their first language and that often persists in grammatical structures or accents in the new language even after decades of using it. This emphasis aims to remember both the status of immigrants of those social actors and of Jews, whose stereotype includes always being a *foreigner* (Simmel, 2005).

began to identify producers as one of the ways to recognize, not so much the quality of the producer of the object, but the "aesthetic look" of the collector, art critic and/or art dealer.

3.2. CONSUMING ART, CULTURE, AND WASHING MACHINES

The expansion of consumption, both in scale and in the diversity of forms, constituted what Baudrillard (1995) called "consumer society": a society, which is related through consumption, makes things a way to tie individuals and groups, classify and give meaning to the world. The reasons for consumption can be varied, what is common is that things are not consumed just because of their utilitarian functions.

In this society, things organize themselves as collections that allude, respond and point to one another in reciprocal movement. This process of referentiality also includes the people who produce things, in the broad sense of the term, as well as the institutions that legitimize these productions. However, in collectionism we realize that production and consumption are not watertight stages but interconnected social processes. Whoever does the object manually is not necessarily who turns it into a symbolic good to be consumed. This has been an action of people who occupy certain social positions and negotiate with the cultural field, from their consumption, to produce those objects as constituents of a narrative and/or classification.

In the third quarter of the twentieth century individualization was also related to the increasing differentiation of products and social demand for prestige. The expansion of the artistic field is due in part to this broadening of the market with new publications on great painters or musicians, consumed in the 1960s and 1970s, mainly by the middle-classes. Several collections on "great artists", for example, can be found in Olly and Werner Reinheimer's library. These groups, in general, have projects of social ascension based on individualization and the nuclear family through cultural formation as a sign of distinction (Velho, 2003). Culture becomes at the same time an exercise, a commodity for promotion, a knowledge and a statute. The consumption of these publications is then another indication of the strategies of social mobility and, at the same time, the agent of this mobility insofar as the exposure of these objects [the shelves or coffee tables in the houses as spaces of self-exhibition] is also a style of decoration of the domestic spaces and a distinctive taste (Bourdieu, 1998). Culture, like art, becomes the object of consumption, just like washing machines.

In consumer society, identifying these new classifications for things and people was tied to a new form of relationship and perception that makes any social group virtual and generic. The peasants, the indigenous groups, or the pre-Columbian peoples can all be transformed into investments for fashion, without their meaning being made explicit so as not to reduce their capacity to seduce the various potential consumers. Using the idea of peers' recognition circles (Heinich, 1991), from the more legitimate groups in the cultural field to the general public, this non exposure of the meaning of using those groups as a reference was a social technology through which new groups and new forms, and positions of statuses were created in the most legitimate circles of peers who shared some interpretations for the collected objects. In other words, while the not shared sense allowed for greater flexibility in the consumption of meanings by the wider circles, among the peers, the sharing of meanings constructed new groups, positions and statuses.

Collecting for private middle-class people, no longer for the nation-state nor for the wealthy classes, was one of the forms of production of new subjectivities, things and collectivities. In *Olly and Werner Reinheimer's Archive* and in their web of relations, collecting in its broadest sense as the habit of joining things to which its accumulator attributes common properties or characteristics and through which it produces a specific form of world knowledge, may be thought from three *ideal types*: antiquarianism, souvenirs and collections (Stewart, 1993), or from another theoretical corpus, the collection of souvenirs, fetish objects, and systematic collection (Pierce, 1994). These three forms of collecting allowed me to think about the strategies for forming these collections, how they constitute the individuals who accumulate them, and how they project these people beyond themselves through these objects and sets of things.

***

For the poet Susan Stewart (1993), antiquarian societies which first appeared in England in 1572 varied in the ways in which they formulated their values and were suppressed during the Jacobin period because of their power to revive alliances between knights. The literary critic Marjorie Swann (2001) shows how the construction of identity founded on land in the sixteenth and seventeenth centuries England was intertwined with the modes of representation through which the fields came to be portrayed as a space full of physical objects by the antiquarianists. The influence of antiquarianism caused writers to become collectors, assembling, organizing, and displaying artifacts that symbolized the identity of noble landowners.

The wars in England gave a sense of urgency to the registration of threatened objects, just as industrialization in Brazil served as justification for various projects of "salvage" and "rescue" of Brazilian popular and indigenous material culture. Swann (2001) draws attention to the genealogical construction efforts of nobility members who sought to incorporate individual and collective identities by meeting and displaying objects in curiosity cabinets. Stewart (1994) argues that antiquarian collections were politically motivated and supported, usually in order to authenticate the history of the kingdoms. Collecting, in general, is at the same time a form of individual construction, of projecting an image to its accumulator, and sometimes can also constitute a form of construction and/or authentication of collectivities.

In relation to time, the antiquarian, in turn, is a way of appropriating the past, at the same time distancing itself from it. To maintain an antiquarian *sensibility*, a rupture with historical consciousness is necessary, creating a sense that it is possible to make the appropriate culture part of another reality in time and space. This was the way of the peasantry's objectification, the aestheticization of rural life that made that style of decoration of domestic spaces the survival of a purer, although diminished past. It was also one of the forms of the construction of the "noble savage" also redeemed by the aesthetics of its productions.

The critique of collecting referred to the empiricism that decontextualized the phenomena and objects and reconstructed their histories from the perspective of antiquarianist that tried to rescue it from oblivion. In the mid-nineteenth century, the term antiquarianist was replaced by *folklore* (Stewart, 1994).

While the historian seeks causal relations, the antiquarianist seeks material evidences from a past that seem to have internal relations with the present, through a radical rupture between these times. By erasing the past, it creates an imagined past to make it available for consumption, assuming an essentially aesthetic attitude. All aspects of rural and indigenous life thus become potentially collectible to the antiquarianist. Lamenting the loss of a "pure nature", the antiquarianist turns everything into art (Stewart, 1993).

Antiquarianism may be related to the type of collection described by Susan Pierce as a collection of fetishes. The fetish for this author radicalizes the Marxist interpretation in which the producer of meaning is independent of its production. The fetish would be a way of seeing the final stage as *self* constituted by the consumption of goods. For the author, these collections are separated from their context and from the spheres of social relations in which they were produced. Once the tensions and understanding efforts that produced them have been eliminated, these collections become part of a universe deprived of their accumulator. Rarely exposed, these collections are often undone over time by a lack of wider meanings beyond that of their original owner. In this sense, the things that make up these collections deny the processes by which they were constituted, just as they freeze time in a kind of purposeless limbo (Pierce, 2003). These things would thus be a product not so much of production as of consumption.

***

These characteristics above described were arbitrarily selected among the several others presented by the authors to underline the attributes that seem to distinguish some possible meanings attributed to collecting identified in this investigation.

Among Olly's many collections, I identify a few I would like to reflect upon: string literature[82], objects made by indigenous groups, objects made by pre-Columbian groups, and various other objects that could be associated with the rural world. There are approximately 61 woodcuts for the production of String brochures,

---

[82] Literatura de Cordel, or String literature is the production of booklets out of poems. The best known cordelistas are usually from the Northeast of Brazil. Their process of composition is artisanal, using in the early twentieth century the woodcut for the composition of the images that accompany the poems. The poet creates narratives and characters about the cangaço, cowboys, the drought, the migrants, the rural life and population and, consequently, a representation of the Northeast and its people. This manifestation was exalted in the 1940s and 1950s as the authentic Brazilian popular literature by Carlos Drummond de Andrade.

around 30 booklets and 4 important books on that literature in the couple's library; the objects made by indigenous groups, in addition to being more perishable due to the materials used, are less identifiable as such, so many were lost, others were donated (a mask was donated to the National Museum and, unfortunately, lost in the fire of September 2018). The karajá dolls in wood and ceramic are the ones that are most interesting for this work, totaling 5 in wood and 3 in ceramics, among the objects made by Pre-Columbian groups there are included around 90 ceramic pieces, a few in wood, 5 fabric dolls and a collection of paraca fabrics that can not be quantified because the lot was sold to an auctioneer in New York in the 1990s, and what I am generally calling things from the "rural world" are wooden and bronze pylons, coffee grinders, furniture, bronze pots, and various ceramics that represent some variations of these things.

The accumulation of series of objects supposedly of the same kind was a characteristic of the artist. In addition to the objects that have remained in the family up to the present, even if a few only in memory, I can still remember the familiar anecdote about the day she came home with a straw mat wrapped in a wooden shaft where one could see several colored whirligigs. Asked about this eccentricity, she would have replied *"a single one is not funny"*. Olly was an accumulator, but not of just anything. Several interviewees mentioned her aesthetic *sensibility*.

How to make sense of these collections?

Between 1950s and 1970s, anti-colonial struggles raised criticism of oppressive systems by colonial countries, and internally, the subalternization of groups in the context of national states was also questioned. The impact of these contestations on the artistic field led art critic Frederico Morais to begin a text about Olly's work mentioning Franz Fanon and the role of clothes in the Algerian revolution (s.d., annex 1).

In Brazil, the claims about indigenous groups seem to have caught Olly's attention. Denunciations of "genocide" had repercussions in national and foreign press soon after the dissemination of the Figueiredo Report, a result of the Investigation Committee of the Ministry of Interior (1967). The Report lead to the extinction of the Indigenous Protection Service (SPI) and the foundation of a new organism responsible for indigenous matters, the National Indigenous Foundation (FUNAI).

In the context of the Federal Legislature, several violations of the Brazilian Indigenous Peoples led to several Parliamentary Committees of Inquiry (in the Senate, in 1955 and in the House of Representatives, in 1963, 1968 and 1977), in the Legislative Assembly of the State of Rio Grande do Sul (1967) and in the Federal Executive the Investigation Committee of the Ministry of the Interior (1967), which produced the Figueiredo Report (Zelic, 2014). According to the report of the journalist Maria Rita Kehl for the Indigenous Commission on Truth and Justice,

> *"the figures show that indigenous groups were the greatest victims of the military dictatorship of 1964-88. (...)* With the overthrow of João Goulart's

government by the military coup, the plans, projects, benefits and economic incentives for the integration and exploration of the interior intensify. The Jurunas, Araras, Paracanãs, Kararaôs, Tembés and Gaviões were reached in the route of the transamazônica. In the Araguaia River Valley, the Tapirapés, Karajás, Javáes, Avá-Canoeiros and the Xavantes. In Tocantins the Xerentes. In the route Cuiabá-Santarém the Apiacás, Suiás, Caiabis, the Krenhacarores. In Rondônia the Cintas-largas, Suruis, Araras and Pakas-nova. In the Guaporé Valley the Nhambiquaras, the Parecis and *countless peoples in the extreme north of the country* (Zelic, 2014. Emphases in the original).

Relations between indigenous peoples and the state or "settlers" have always been ambiguous, marked by a combination of respect, partial understanding and fear on the one hand, and hostility on the other. In the first Vargas (1930-1945) period, when Olly and Werner were arriving in Brazil, state officials supported the indigenous groups as an icon of Brazilian historical and cultural formation, a proto-patriot who would be redeemed by government tutelage. This feature was part of the government campaign to popularize the March to the West, launched on the eve of 1938, as a project to occupy and develop the interior of Brazil (Garfield, 2000).

"As part of his multifaceted project to build a new Brazil more economically independent, more politically integrated and socially more unified Vargas turned to the symbolic value of the natives. Unlike the "exotic plants" of economic liberalism and Marxism, which the nationalist authoritarian regime sought to extirpate Brazilian soil through political repression, censorship and federal intervention in regional affairs, the indigenous groups would be defended by Vargas for containing the true Brazilian roots" (Garfield, 2000).

In August 1940, Getúlio Vargas was the first Brazilian president to visit an indigenous area, the Karajá village, on Bananal Island in Central Brazil. Vargas also expressed the desire to recognize the territory of the "ferocious" Xavante that inhabited the surroundings. Part of the national unification project was the "pacification" of this group. However, the Xavantes assassinated part of the group sent to "pacify them". The government tried to mask the incident, presenting the indigenous group as docile and with primary intelligence, only conceiving the murder as equivocal.

The state's investment in these two indigenous groups and the production by Karajá women of pottery dolls that became items of collectionism gave visibility to these groups. It is no coincidence, then, that in addition to creating clothing based on body painting and the karajá dolls, Olly took photographs with a Xavante leader in the 1960s (see Figure 88). Werner and Olly's contact with Noel Nutels and Darcy and Berta Ribeiro probably made the indigenous subject, as well as that of the national formation, part of the interests of the German couple, and access to these two groups in particular facilitated. The participation of these intellectuals in the couple's web of relations is probably linked to the migratory process, political participation and/or their participation in the cultural field.

Noel Nutels (1913-1973) was a Ukrainian Jew. He arrived in Brazil at the age of eight and was raised in the Northeast, coming to Rio de Janeiro in search of a job as a civil servant. Without being naturalized, he founded along with Samuel Wainer, Rubem Braga and the painter Di Cavalcanti the magazine Diretrizes, in 1938. There they published themes such as Brazilian problems and the advance of fascism in Europe. The magazine was composed of members and "sympathizers" of the Communist Party (Paiva, 2011), to which Werner was affiliated.

In 1940, Nutels was involved in the fight against malaria at Km 47 of the Rio São Paulo road, a site where the future Federal Rural University of Rio de Janeiro UFRRJ would be. This experience was definitive to receive the invitation to participate in the Roncador-Xingu Expedition, organized in 1943, together with the Vilas Boas brothers. In this expedition, one of the major problems detected in Araguaia, among the Karajá, was tuberculosis. Nutels then contributed to the creation of the SUSA (Service of Air Health Units) in the 1950s, whose purpose was medical care for indigenous and rural populations. During his work at SUSA, the criticisms regarding the processes of integration of the indigenous populations into the national economy resulted in the project to create the Xingu Park.

In 1963, Nutels was appointed director of the SPI, which only lasted six months because of the 1964 coup. Before, however, he requested army troops to defend the Cinta-Larga who lived in areas rich in diamonds and cassiterite. The group had already suffered a massacre in the previous year, known as Parallel 11. The dictatorship changed perspective into viewing again the indigenous population as an obstacle to the development. the Transamazon[83] construction became then the major expression of the policy of extermination of indigenous peoples (Costa, 1987).

Darcy Ribeiro (1922-1997), in turn, married Berta Gleizer (1924-1997), a Jewess and a native of Bessarabia, Romania, who was naturalized Brazilian in 1948. The couple may have had contact with Olly and Werner, in the 1950s, when Darcy Ribeiro participated actively in the creation of the Xingu Park, acting in SPI, along with friends like the Villas Boas brothers, Eduardo Galvão and Noel Nutels. The meeting may have also taken place when the Indigenous Museum was founded in 1953, but it may also have been through Berta and the Jewish immigrant community in the late 1940s when she returned to live in Rio de Janeiro. Her father died and her sister was extradited for her membership in the Communist Party in the 1930s. At that time, the party hosted Berta in Sao Paulo before her departure for Rio. In a small community of Jewish immigrants and intellectuals that of the 1940s and 1950s, there were many opportunities for these Jewish immigrants to establish links.

---

[83] A road that would cross the Amazon from east to west. Many people were killed during the work to build the road and it was never completely finished.

Perhaps it is important to remember that the Indigenous Museum was founded, according to Darcy Ribeiro, as a museum against prejudice (Chagas, 2007), based on an aesthetic discourse that sought inspiration in the production of indigenous groups. This aesthetic bias was largely a result of UNESCO's action in art, culture and education projects from the idea of a universal language as a common denominator through which people could understand and reinforce their links.

The theoretical foundation of this idea may be related to the influence of intellectuals such as Marcel Mauss, a post-war Frenchman who formulated reflections on "the nation" as a total social fact in which aesthetic and cultural dimensions were an integral part of a social system (Mauss, 1969). Mauss struck both the foundations of this international body and the formation of the intellectuals at the Escola Livre de Sociologia e Política (Free School of Sociology and Politics) in São Paulo, where Darcy Ribeiro graduated in 1946. Although his mentor was the German Herbert Baldus, the ELSP was largely influenced by French thought through teachers such as Roger Bastide and others. The ethnic groups' production's aestheticization was then part of the postwar context of which collectivism was its substrate.

Some books that are part of what remains of the couple's library may contribute to understand their interest in indigenous groups. The book "Kadiwéu", released in 1950, for which Darcy Ribeiro won the Fábio Prado prize, is in the library with an edition of 1980. Maíra, also by Darcy Ribeiro, as well as "Yanomami" by Claudia Andujar and Darcy Ribeiro, "Poemas e canções dos índios Tupis" (Poems and songs by the Tupi) by Wilson Pinto, " Réquiem para os índios", by Felicitas Barreto Costa, "A arte e o artista na sociedade Karajá" (Art and the Artist in Karajá Society) by Maria Heloisa Fénelon (research conducted by Darcy Ribeiro) and "Litjoko: Puppen der Karaja, Brasilien" (Litjoko: Brazilian karajá dolls), by Günther Hartmann, almost all from the 1970s, are indications of the importance of the theme for the couple. Some questions can be asked: were both of them interested in the subject? In other words, was there a political and social interest in the subject that stimulated it to be transformed into aesthetic matter? Is it possible to make a strict distinction between the two forms of interest in this subject?

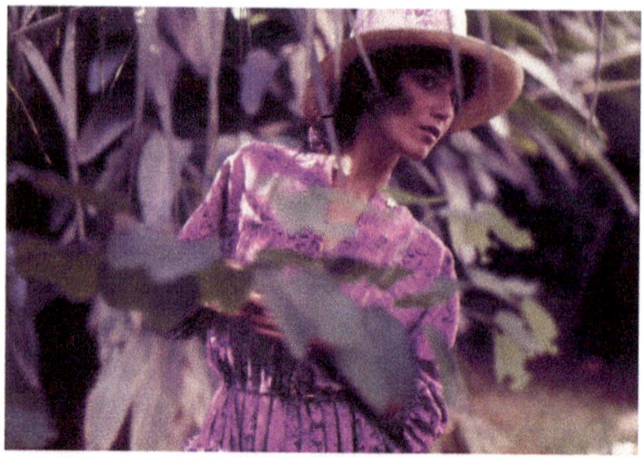

Figure 87: In 1971, a photo illustrating the column "Fotógrafos de moda" presents a model wearing Olly clothes registered by Cláudia Andujar. The photographer was born in Switzerland and contacted the Karajá with the guidance of Darcy Ribeiro, in 1958. Throughout the 1970s and 1980s, Andujar worked with the Yanomami, about whom she published a book together with Darcy Ribeiro (1978). A copy of it is in the couple's library, with dedication to Olly.

The presence of a page in the Correio da Manhã newspaper (Correio da Manhã, 1969), which contains articles on Romanian independence, English colonialism and its relation to Zionism and the relationship between Arabs and Israelis is a further indication that the discussions of international geopolitics and power relations between peripheric groups were present in the couple's house. Alaíde Pereira Nunes stated in her testimony in 1998 that *"They were very special people. She had a very sharp sensibility and he had a human content in the superlative. He lived the drama of Nazism, so more than anyone else he was aware of the pain of persecution. She was very alienated. Her sensibility was to aesthetics"*. Hence the assumption that the themes came from Werner's discussions and concerns, Olly making the visual translation of these subjects and turning the political issues into consumer goods. Marriage as a system of complementarity.

The interest of artists on indigenous groups as a subject or for their material culture, as an influence on literary and visual productions, is old and can be traced back to the 16th century with the iconography produced by artists and travelers such as Franz Post, Albert Eckout, Thomas Ender, Jean Baptiste Debret, Johan Moritz Rugendas, William Burchell and others (Belluzzo, 1999). In the nineteenth century, writers such as José de Alencar and Gonçalves Dias sought a Brazilian authenticity with romanticized narratives about the native people. The modernists of the 1920s extolled anthropophagy as the synthesis of the autochthonous with the foreigner. Regina Gomide Graz produced tapestries from the study of indigenous paintings in the 1920s, and Cássio M'Boy produced carpets in the 1930s, which he said were a blend of stylizations based on the geometry of indigenous art and Art Déco, which was in vogue (Cáurio, 1985).

The expropriation of indigenous lands imposed by colonialism followed the expropriation of cultural production removed from contexts and reinterpreted by "colonial" artists. The continuous, prolonged and direct character of the engagement between indigenous and European cultures, in several other countries, has given rise to an indigenous artistic production (Thomas, 1999, Goldstein, 2012). However, in Brazil, these contacts produced sporadic works of "colonial" artists with indigenous themes or influences. And the ambiguity of these relations has often resulted in stereotyped representations. See, for example, the work of Lúcia Kluck Stumpf (2014) on the paintings of Antônio Parreiras, a Rio de Janeiro painter who worked between 1883 and 1936. Parreiras painted idealized natives who spoke more of the elite's will to present themselves as republicans than about the natives themselves who had no idea why they were invited to be models for such a subject.

The ambivalence between natives and settlers became more accurate when, from the nineteenth century on, with the arrival of the royal family and independence, the question of national identity emerged. In considering the need to invent an identity, designers, painters and poets often turned to what seemed locally distinctive, the natural environment and indigenous cultures. But as well as emphasizing modernity, the reference to the indigenous elements came in general accompanied by connective strategies with Europe.

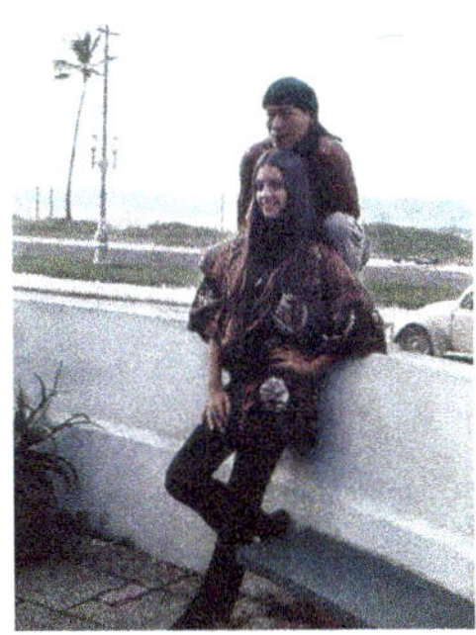

Figure 88: This photo was taken on Ipanema beach in the early 1960s. A model is seen dressed in Olly's clothes with Semuã from the Xavante group. Semuã was probably taken to Rio de Janeiro along with other Xavantes by Francisco Meireles (Chico Meireles) and stayed in Ipanema, where he lived with Meireles' family. This photo attests to Olly's contact with the indigenous groups themselves and not only with their production shown in museums and books.

However, in Brazil the recourse to the autochthonous was different from the "primitivism" used in modern European art. At the beginning of the twentieth century European 'modern' art appropriated 'primitive' motives and forms as a way of affirming new ways of producing, appreciating and valuing art. In Brazil, artists and writers sought the affirmation of a relationship that distinguished them using something valued in Europe. Unlike the way artists and designers built this distinctiveness in Australia and New Zealand, for example, using reference to specific groups Aboriginal and Maori, respectively, in Brazil the resource was for the generic native, with no emphasis on any specific ethnicity.

In the 1970s, these works criticized the condition of indigenous groups in national society. Two works are always cited by historians and art critics, directly related to the native question. In 1975, Cildo Meireles produced "Sal sem carne" (Salt without meat). His father was an SPI's director during the lawsuit against Brazilian State on the Krahô massacre in northern Goiás. The name of the work was taken from the definition given to the artist by the indigenous interviewees on what it was to be a native Brazilian. Meireles was barred from entering the park to interview one of the survivors. The interviews had to be conducted in a community near the Xingu Park.

The second work is by Anna Bella Geiger and was produced in 1977. It is a series of postcards entitled "Brazil Nativo/Brasil Alienígena" (Native Brazil/Alien Brazil), through which the artist denied a national cultural unity. Concomitant with the construction of the Transamazon Road and the tragedies of indigenous massacres, the State, from 1964 to 1988, used mestizaje as a propaganda strategy on the common root of Brazilians. A set of postcards sold in newspaper stands featured an abstract entity, the autochthonous, dancing, hunting, or playing with animals. On the back of the postcards one could read: "Native Brazil". For each of the postcards, Anna Bella Geiger recreated the poses and compositions with her daughters and friends, on the balcony of her apartment. If these Indians were Native Brazil, the photos of them were of Alien Brazil and there was, between one and the other, an abyss and not communion.

However, if these works are relevant due to the respect and recognition they grant to indigenous culture in the broad sense, what is their effective contribution to broadening interest and attracting support and understanding to indigenous political claims? In Australia and New Zealand, the production of colonial artists based on indigenous production has formed interactive relations with social contexts, with artistic production and contexts mutually defined. Those contexts could change and be disruptive to each other (Thomas, 1999).

In Brazil, however, artistic production never had an impact on the social realities experienced by indigenous groups. If Olly and Werner had any knowledge of postcolonial theories, Olly's work did not criticize colonial images and ideologies, nor did she question whether indigenous groups could represent themselves in modern art. The idea of authenticity seemed to prevail, without the awareness that this was indeed the production of herself, of a subjectivity conceived as "authentically Brazilian", and not a critique of the idea of an indigenous essence instrumented by distinct groups over Brazilian history. Perhaps for this very reason the work attracted attention, for giving continuity to the common sense of an identity that was particularized through the autochthonous.

The artist used as a base for the set of clothes inspired by the Karajá, their body painting, as well as the Ritxoco, that is, the ceramic dolls produced by the group's women. When figuration and abstraction were no longer elements whose disagreement served to define the places occupied by the social actors of the art world, the body metaphor of neoconcretism and performance came into focus. The indigenous body and the female art of the ceramists were taken to produce the fantasy of "difference" in "modernist" performances. The connoisseurs and consumers of her works wore, literally at least, the indigenous cause. According to the couple's son, "*it was a passion. Everyone wanted a costume with Karajá paintings. The house was always full after this exhibition*". It is a matter of realizing that, although the indigenous has been a constant theme in Brazilian literature and art since the arrival of the Europeans, it has not been the same over time. By the end of the 1960s, the categories of perception and evaluation of the world had changed and the appropriation of the indigenous as a subject had new implications.

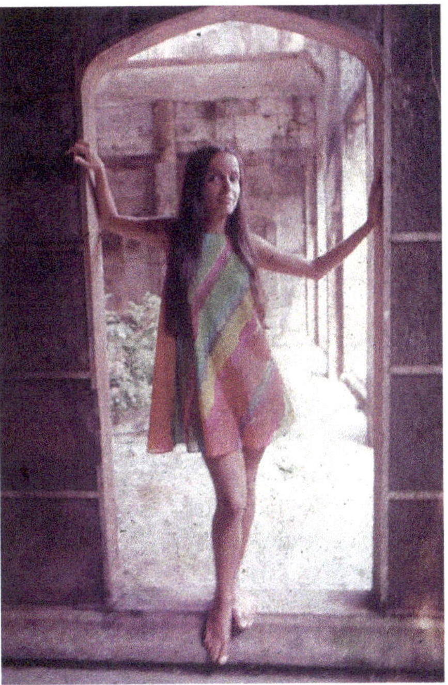

Figure 89: Photo by David Drew Zingg (DIA-824).

The karajá corporal painting is a way to mark the social hierarchies and the place of each person in that society. Ceramic dolls, in turn, initially produced as children's toys, gained recognition and began to be produced for commercial purposes, aimed at an indigenous art and crafts market. Since in this group the activity of the pottery belongs exclusively to the female domain, the dolls are ways of accessing the Karajá female worldview (Chang, 2010).

The Ritxoko have a polychromatic decorative painting with geometric motifs in jenipapo black and urucum red and share a series of common formal features with the Karajá body painting. "The Karajá use geometric patterns and associate these motifs and their combinations lines, greeks, stripes to body parts, to terrestrial and aquatic fauna" (Ferreira Filho e Silva, 2012).

For the Karajá potters,

> "Making "doll's families" with the use of traditional graphic patterns and presenting children with these "families is a way of reaffirming their role in transmitting knowledge about the Karajá family constitution, the life cycle and also the graphic elements and formal (modeling) that belong to communal knowledge "(Ferreira Filho e Silva, 2012).

According to anthropologist Manuel Ferreira Filho e Silva (2012) the ceramicists generally do not speak Portuguese and rarely circulate outside their villages without the male presence. Therefore, the circulation of artifacts depends on male mediation. Even if the evaluation of the works is dependent mainly on the artist's relation circle, these artifacts signal to traditional gender roles. However, the result of the dolls' commercialization returns to the families in the form of consumer goods such as DVD, TV, gas stove, clothes, cell phones, guaranteeing other forms of prestige for their producers.

In January 2012, the Karajá dolls were registered as Brazilian Intangible Cultural Heritage. Olly's work at MAM-RJ in 1969 had nothing to do with this patrimonialisation process. However, the role of the group of professionals linked to MAM-RJ, who was in some way connected to design in general, but mainly to architecture, furniture and interior design, made an important contribution to the appreciation of the Brazilian indigenous and popular material culture. In this process, clothing represented on of the media through which indigenous issues entered the homes of a Brazilian intellectual and economic elite.

The reference to cave paintings[84], pre-Columbian production, popular production and the Karajá are even more likely to be read from the idea of colonial domination and subalternity if we pay attention to what they obscure in Olly's work. The only reference to Judaism appears in the pictures of singer Maria Bethânia wearing clothes from the Karajá line[85]. Her work made almost no reference to Judaism and Germany.

---

[84] Olly's visit to Sete cidades, a newlly instituted National Park where cave paintings were found was also used as reference to her work.

[85] The image can be found in Olly and Werner Reinheimer's Archive. The referece to find the photo is (DIA 127). Unfortunately, I could not get the singer to agree to its publication here.

It seems interesting that the only visual reference appears exactly in the essay that had Maria Bethânia as the subject.

The singer was already recognized as representing a certain modern Brazilianness, young and tropical, largely associated with popular themes due to her relationship with MPB (Brazilian Popular Music) and tropicalism. She carried, therefore, the symbol of a group Olly sought to identify herself with. The Jew as an ethnic category was then integrated into the condition of Brazilianness and an identifiable minority to others like the natives and popular manifestations, in their dimension of subalternity and periphery. If we take the paradigm of the "artist as an ethnographer" (Foster, 2014), what stands in the shadow can then be taken as an integral part of a shift from the art theme of capitalist exploration to colonial, ethnic, racial, and gender oppression. This is the continuation of an earlier movement, but it gained momentum in the 1990s.

The materiality of Olly's work suggested a racialization of this artist. Her ambiguous position, woman, Jew and immigrant placed her in a privileged position to appropriate the cultural production of peripheric groups, being herself eventually considered part of one of these groups. In the cultural appropriation of indigenous, children, black cultural production, Olly was also to some extent subverting values, attributing value to what was considered useless. She brought into the market what was the filth of white, bourgeois, enslaved society, that is, using what McClintock (2010) calls *marketing through difference* that is the extravagant display of the right to ambiguity.

This movement becomes even more significant if we consider various other social actors who were making the same move to bring up the production of socially marginalized groups as a way of rebuilding their social position. "The staging of symbolic disorder by the privileged can merely dispel questions from those who do not have the power to display ambiguity with comparable license or authority" (McClintock, 2010: 115).

The sense of rusticity that was constituted in relation with the native and popular material culture mixed with the modern one was constructed mainly during the 1960s. Part of this process can be seen in the decorative magazines of the time. Those collections made by Boghici, Fernando Millan and José Carlos de Oliveira became common practice. The artist's daughter-in-law told about the trips to the interior of Minas Gerais and Rio de Janeiro and the purchases or exchanges of furniture and other things used in the houses where they visited. These stories are part of a certain family mythology as the two strolled through the cities in the interior entering the houses and offering new furniture and objects in exchange for those used by the locals. The stories were told as part of an aesthetic learning process that led Olly's daughter-in-law to initially produce "rustic" wooden furniture during the 1960s and 1970s, and later to develop other diverse artistic works of her own.

Indigenous objects, mainly basketry but also pottery, were thus blended with time-worn furniture and utensils, ex-votos, string literature, and "modern" furniture and pictures to create a style of decoration related to an intellectualized middle-class, largely formed by immigrants or second-generation descendants. The action of time on objects and the wear and tear were conditions for the creation of a system of values alongside new objects associated with a determined style that valued the contrast with the popular in the construction of a "modern" future.

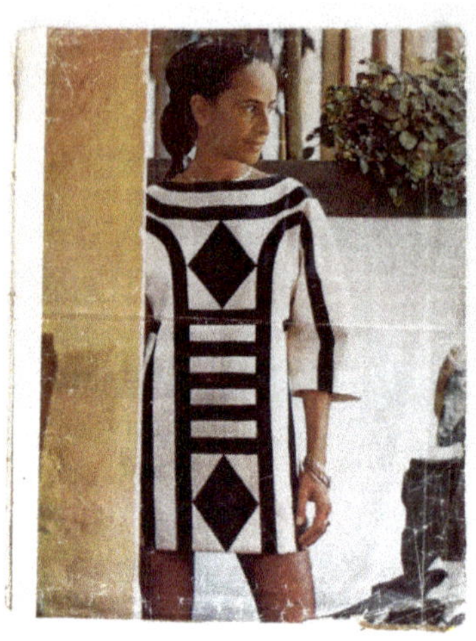

Figure 90: This photo was taken in the 1970s, by Marisa Alves de Lima, the model is the singer Maria Bethânia. She is wearing a dress like the one found in L.C. Barreto film producing company. The image is another page of the article reproduced on figure 106.

This process of forming a class taste followed the period of institutionalization of social sciences in Brazil. In the late 1930s, the arrival of several French and German professors was part of the process of structuring sociology and anthropology in the Country. Analysing the trajectory and production of Herbert Baldus (Darcy Ribeiro's German tutor), anthropologist Luiz Henrique Passador (2002) concluded that, as early as the 1940s, it was not only the boundaries between literature and anthropology that were tenuous, but between these two and visual arts as well. The trajectories of Olly and Werner point to the maintenance of these exchanges between social sciences and the arts in later years. In the 1960s, Olly stated that the subject of pre-Columbian cultures was an influence of the director of the museum of ethnology in Peru. In Brazil, Darcy Ribeiro and Noel Nutels certainly influenced not only her work but also that of other artists.

Her rhetoric was in tune with some values associated with antiquarianists and fetish collectors, on the one hand, and travelers and ethnographers, on the other. She stated several times that her paintings (Jornal Diário de São Paulo, 1966) were not things taken from books or copied, but things that marked her, from her experiences. She did not, however, think about the meaning of these things. Meaning was created by her work and these supposed experiences that she never elaborated. Being there, wherever she went, seemed to give her enough authority to appropriate the productions of these groups as the basis for hers. A supposed aesthetic sensibility, which marked her webs of relations and the values at stake in the thematic legitimacy, was capable of turning women into artists. However, it was not all women, but the white, married, heterosexual middle-class ones.

For these women, to perceive aesthetically the indigenous production was to be in tune with a political dimension, it was to challenge a certain type of colonialism that attributed formal inferiority to the production of these groups, but it was also to invest in the idea of "saving" what capitalism and industrialization were destroying by attributing to these groups a certain purity and to themselves the superiority to save them. The sense of a *sensibility* analogous to the modern Western one was reiterated in its consumption and collection. The history of these collections became the history of their accumulators.

Probably, her gender condition was fundamental to the impossibility of transforming her collection of indigenous objects from the personal dimension to a patrimonial one, from a *situational illusion* to a *collective illusion*. It is not about not having volition in the valorization of her collections. The existence of a file in which she kept the evidences of her production seems in itself a sign of a memory project. Since collecting is generally associated with the masculine dimension, with metaphors of conquest and slaughter attached to the practice (Price, 2000), probably the fact that they were composed by a woman was part of the difficulty in producing for these collections classification systems and interpretations.

Still, the karajá body painting gained meaning through Olly's textile production. This meaning linked to the indigenous group, however, did not remain with the passage of time. This became clear when, in 2014, one of her dresses was found in the collection of the film producer L.C. Barreto (Figure 90). Delighted at the outfit, the person who discovered it used it in an event for which it appeared to have been specially produced: an exhibition for director Stanley Kubrick's commemoration of the 50th anniversary of the film "*2001: A Space Odyssey*". The tradition of indigenous body painting printed on clothing disappeared and what remained was a geometric style that linked several different productions of the 1960s and 1970s.

Another form of interpreting this collectionism found in the material investigated is what Stewart called souvenirs (1993) and Pierce (1994) memories. These are sets of objects that gain unity of collection only by their association with a person, their life story, or a group of people, as a couple or a family as if it were a collective person. Stewart presents souvenirs as devices of objectification of desire which, unlike systematic collections, contract the world and expand the *self*. The author presents the souvenir as a memory outside the body, or a substitution of memory experienced by the object.

The souvenir speaks of a context of origin through a language of longing, for not being an object that arises from need or use value, but from the demands of nostalgia. It generates narratives that refer to the past, to the inside, not to the future, or to the outside.

This form of collecting can be identified in *Olly and Werner Reinheimer's Archive* in the numerous tourist catalogs, postcards and slides of mostly European places visited by the couple. Organized in city-named envelopes, the one hundred and ninety-four (194) publications, folders and books, not including slides had five Brazilian destinations and all other materials were referred to European cities, museums, events and artists. Only a set of 3 Peruvian postcards, along with an announcement by H. Stern[86] on the Gold Museum in Peru.

The five Brazilian destinations are: a folder of the Hotel Baleia Branca, owned by Norman Westwater, dating from 1960; a brochure from the Feira de Caruaru in Recife (a fair where String literature is sold), which was accompanied by a booklet of what appears to be the programming of a music event at the Feira de Caruaru, dating from 1976; a brochure of Sete Cidades (park where the cave paintings were found), in Teresina, together with the leaflets of this park; a travel guide to São Luís do Maranhão and a brochure about the city of São João Del Rei in Minas Gerais, the latter undated. It is through this "touristic" material that one perceives the collecting character and the *archival gesture* (Marques, 2015) that besides acquiring and storing the material representative of the trips' memories, they classified them according to destinations. I did not try to map the couple's trips, which could be done by comparing the photographs and other documents with this "touristic" set, but it is possible to imagine that perhaps this material was also organized by times traveled.

Thanks to this gesture of *mise en archive*, along with the collections of books and indigenous, pre-Columbian and popular objects, it was possible to follow the processes of self-construction undertaken by the couple throughout their lives. The collection then comprises a double movement of self-externalization in objects that are seen and of interiorization or expansion of themselves through allusions to the various facts for which souvenirs are the reduced model. Souvenir collections offer individuals ways to see and say something about themselves. The possession of these objects is an affirmation of membership to the prestige generated by the event, the travels. It is like a genealogy that shows the presence of certain wealth in the family for several generations. Souvenirs are the intimate dimension of a collectionism that is primarily self-collecting – while the fetish objects built the artist herself, they also contributed to the institutionalization of industrial design and what later became fashion design in Brazil.

As Werner seems to have never surpassed his departure from Germany, I am taking the touristic collections, especially those referring to European cities as his collections and those that have been reference to Olly's work as her collections. While his collections symbolically marked his biography, hers can be used for the singularization of her artistic production, although it is not possible to construct particular cultural biographies because they have not been object of patrimonial actions. These collections did not undergo any process of public visibility that would

---

[86] A jewelry design and production company owned by a German jewish who arrived in Brazil in 1939.

allow them to acquire collective approval that would confer a certain sacredness on them (Koppytoff, 2008). That is, these things were not effectively transformed into systematic collections, with the singularization of the collections themselves, making them part of *collective illusions* (Lopes, 2017).

Processes of singularization are subject to the flows established between people and things producing values of social use that define the collections as social goods or patrimony. These flows are what allows us to observe the mutual constitution of things and people sustained by regimes of value understood as degrees of value coherence interchangeable according to the situation of commodity or of singular object (Appadurai, 2008). This process of mutual constitution through the singularization of collections in this same period and web of relations can be observed through Franco Terranova's relation with some of his collections.

3.3. STORIES OF EX-VOTOS[87], CARRANCAS[88], AND CANDOMBLÉ

Anthropologist Zoy Anastassakis (2014) shows that there were two discursive strands in the process of institutionalizing the teaching of design in Brazil. One of them bet the mixture of modern industrial rationality with autochthonous and local popular cultural values and another focused only on the dimension of industrialization and rationality, closer to the guidelines of the Ulm School of Design. Some of the personalities linked to this second strand were Joaquim Tenreiro, José Zanini Caldas, Sérgio Rodrigues, Michel Arnoud and Norman Westwater. Lina Bo Bardi identified herself with the first line, having devised a school project in Salvador along with Hans Köellreuter, among others, for the articulation of the industry with local production.

Olly related, in one way or another, with all the names mentioned here, from both strands, and all of them had relations with MAM-RJ. Köellreuter was married to poet and musician Geny Marcodes Ferraz who, together with Olly and Maria Teresa Vieira, organized the Children's Arts Club (see chapter 2); Zanini Caldas was the founder of some of the houses used as stage backdrops for photographing Olly's clothes (Figures 8, 106, 119, 120), it was in Norman Westwater's store where the artist made her first solo show in 1958 (see chapter 2.3) and Lina Bo Bardi was director of MAM-BA in 1960, when she exhibited at this museum.

In order to be institutionalized as a disciplinary field, professionals from different fields tend to produce discourses of differentiation from neighboring fields aiming for autonomization (Bourdieu, 1968). Anastassakis (2014), showed how this happened in Brazil in design in relation to the fields of art and architecture. The field was initially denominated *industrial design*. These three areas of activity, industrial design, art and

---

[87] The gift given by the faithful to her/his saint of devotion in consecration, renewal or thanksgiving of a promise.
[88] A sculpture with human or animal form, produced in wood and used at first in the prow of the boats that navigated in the San Francisco river. It was believed it keept bad energy and gosts away.

architecture, had until the end of the 1960s, the decoration shops and museums of modern art as a privileged space to introduce themselves and meet their consuming public. In the dispute to be constituted and to differentiate, conflicting discourses were produced of what should or should not be conceived as design in Brazil. However, when we distance the attention from pedagogical projects, articles and curricular structures to observe interactions between people, exhibitions in modern art museums and architecture and decoration magazines, we realize that the division between art, architecture and design and the dispute over whether design should or should not have "local color" is not as clear. In the chain of social life, these *fields* (Bourdieu, 1968) were complementary, leaning on each other for the constitution of lifestyles, values and practices.

Looking at the list of exhibitions that MAM-RJ organized between 1952 and 1984, it is possible to understand the importance that this institution had in Olly's trajectory and, probably, with more or less impact, of other actors mentioned here. The 1960 exhibition at MAM-RJ was probably important for Itamaraty's decision to finance her trip to Peru to teach painting in fabrics in Lima (which had a considerable impact on her artistic production), leading her to acquire objects of pre-Columbian ceramics that constitute one of her collections. Similarly, the artist's trip to the park of Sete Cidades is probably related to the exhibition on the same subject presented by the institution in 1973. However, this museum is not the only reference in her life, nor for the analysis here undertaken. In addition to the interviews conducted to obtain reports of life in movement, I compared information from *Olly and Werner Reinheimer's Archive* documents with the documentation of several of MAM-RJ's exhibitions and also the Franco Terranova collection (this one still in the process of systematization).

In MAM-RJ's exhibitions during the 1950s and 1970s, some references to what would constitute the "local color" in that context are evident. This "coloring" was divided by me into what I called three great thematic sets: those related to textile manufacture (1), those that could be classified as internal or external "alterity", that is, primitive, autochthonous or popular (2) and those related to children's production (3). I have enumerated the ones that occurred between 1952 and 1969 so it is possible to see the frequency with which they happened in that period:

1. "Modern French tapestries" (1952), "Lurçat" (1954), "Abstract Tapestries" (1956), "Genaro's Tapestries" (1957), "Argentinian Tapestries" (1957), "Fridl Loos" (1958), Olly painted fabrics (1960), Gina tapestries (1961), "Hilda" (1961), "Hilda Campofiorito Tissues" (1962), "Tapestries of the Atelier Douchez-Nicola" (1963), "Dresses and Tapestries "(1966), "Eila's Tapestry" (1968), "Rumanian Contemporary Tapestry" (1968), "Olly Reinheimer" (1969) (15 exhibitions);
2. "Ceramics of Vitalino and the Students of the Institute of Ceramics" (1952), "Primitive and Modern Art in Brazil" (1955), "Folklore Prints and Sculptures of the Northeast" (1964), Popular Peruvian

Folk art (1965), Ex-votos from the Northeast (1965), "Hungarian Folk Arts and Crafts" (1965), "Primitives" (1965), "Folk Art" (1966), "Aspects of Ghana Culture" (1968), "Exposition of Czechoslovak Culture" (1968), "Hungarian Crafts" (1969) (11 exhibitions);

3. "Children's Painting" (1952, 1953), "3rd Children's Art Exhibition" (1954), 4th, 5th, 6th, 7th, 8th, 9th, 10th, 11th, 12th and 14th "Children Painting Exhibition" (1955, 1956, 1957, 1958, 1959, 1960, 1961, 1962, 1963, 1965), "Japanese Children's Painting" (1958), "International Children's Art Exhibition" (1961) "Children of MAM-RJ" (1964) (14 exhibitions). From 1952 to 1965, every year they had at least one children's painting exhibition. This kind of exhibition disappeared in the following years.

In the 1970s, references to *black art* appeared with "Africa, black art", for example, and the art from the insane with the exhibition "4 Artists from Engenho de Dentro". The shows related to fabrics, tapestries and clothes disappeared in the 1970s, being the last one "Contemporary French Rugs X Biennial of São Paulo", in 1970.

Afro-descendant, Afro-Brazilian, naïve, popular, diasporic, Afro-oriented, with African matrix are classification categories that aim to totalize a heterogeneous set of artists and works. This classification is sometimes based on the origin of producers, others on the subject treated, or on the bias of a supposed African canon for artistic production. All these terms carry an adjectivation that is not present in productions and artists considered universal, western, generally white men of economically privileged groups (Menezes, 2018).

In the nineteenth century, art critics such as Luiz Gonzaga Duque Estrada when talking about "still life" produced by Estevão Silva (1844-1981) revealed a racializing tendency of the production of art criticism in Brazil that lasted long after that period. Characteristics considered racial were taken as determinants of the work's final result, as if there were a particular instinct that determined aesthetic choices and inventiveness. Authors like Nina Rodriques (1862-1906), Mario de Andrade (1893-1945), Luíz Saia (1911-1975), Arthur Ramos (1903-1949), Mario Barata (1921-2007) and Clarival do Prado Valadares (1918- 1983) related behavioral and cognitive characteristics to the color of the skin, essentializing with greater or less intensity the production of Afro-descendant artists throughout the 20th century.

Until the 1980s, the subject of African or Afro-Brazilian art was mostly of interest among social scientists, Africanists and ethnologists, and it was only afterwards that it came to the attention of historians and art critics. However, through Olly and Werner Reinheimer's collections, it was possible to witness the interest of collectors in the construction of value and meaning for the production then classified as black or popular. Far from being a scholar, Franco Terranova could be considered a curator, collector and gallerist. His interest was not in the research on Afro-Brazilian or popular religious production, but in the aesthetic quality and in the production of an exchange market for these goods.

It was mainly non-black artists who were recognized as representatives of this strand – Djanira da Mota e Silva, Carybé, Mario Cravo Jr., Pierre Verger, among others – for approaching their production of cultural, stylistic and thematic traits of what Afro-Brazilian expression could entice. Before the end of the twentieth century, however, adjectives that referred artistic production to descent or African subjects were not used, requisitioned, or contested with the frequency with which they came to be later. Often the term was rejected for an art without adjectives, identified with universal canons, or accepted without question. This was the case of the collections of Franco Terranova's ex-votes and carrancas and the objects of rural groups that became pieces of decoration on Olly's home.

Agnaldo Manuel dos Santos was one of the few exceptions that escaped the invisibility/anonymity rule of black artists, one of the axes around which the central demands in the field of arts are organized today. The recognition of the subject generally designated as black or Afrodescendant, but not that of black artists has been a way of allowing themes to be represented by others, but to prevent self-representation by those who experience the racialization of their bodies.

Abdias do Nascimento was the first intellectual to articulate the theme of Afro-Brazilian art as a political-artistic tool of anti-racist militancy. In 1950 the Museum of Black Art (MAN) was created, from the discussion of blackness' Aesthetics, in the 1st Congress of the Brazilian Negro, realized by the Black Experimental Theater in 1950. The accumulated collection was exposed only once, in 1968, in the Museum of Image and Sound, in Rio de Janeiro, and the collection did not get its own headquarters.

Several exhibitions of Afro-Brazilian art were organized in the 1950s/60s by Lina Bo Bardi, such as the *Bahia Exhibition* at Ibirapuera, in parallel with the 5th São Paulo Biennial in 1959, the *Afro-Brazilian Sculpture Exhibition* and individual exhibitions of Emanuel Araújo, João Alves, Agostinho Batista Freitas, Agnaldo Manuel dos Santos and Carrancas from the São Francisco River, with works by Mestre Francisco Biquiba, all of them in 1961, in MAM-BA, *Civilization of the Northeast*, at Solar do Unhão, in Salvador (1963) and *The hand of the Brazilian people*, at the Art Museum of São Paulo, in 1968. Ex-votes, carrancas and objects of candomblé and costumes of orishas gained relevance for the first time with these exhibitions.

Following this aspect of valorization of popular production, Franco Terranova, owner of the first gallery of modern art in Rio de Janeiro, the Petite Galerie, and important figure in the panorama of modern art in Brazil, constituted over the decades three important collections for the analysis here undertaken: the São Francisco River's carrancas, ex-votes and modern and contemporary Brazilian art. Upon entering the apartment that was Franco Terranova's (today it belongs to his widow) I came across a carranca and a sculpture by Agnaldo Manoel dos Santos (among other things that have no relevance for this analysis). In the adjacent room to the entrance hall, two metal and black leather chairs with Bauhaus like lines and a wooden shelf, with a few sets of objects forming small collections, as well as books contrast with a rustic wooden table in the center and a wooden ex-vote, both worn out by time. It is this contrast between two conceptions of design that prevailed in the 1950s and 1970s, in Brazil, creating new aesthetic and life styles and political activity for this intellectualized middle-class in the main Brazilian capitals of the period.

Foreigners who came to Brazil in the inter-war or post-Second World War and were involved in some way in the process of constitution of a relatively autonomous artistic field were fundamental in this process. They were collectors, art marketers, art critics and artists such as Franco Terranova, Pietro Maria Bardi, Terzo Lombardi, Marc Berkowitz, Jean Boghici, among others.

The construction of these new aesthetic dimensions was corollary of a process that had in the abstraction its greater support and in this sense the relation with psychological knowledge can not be minimized (psychiatry, psychology, psychoanalysis – the *psy knowledge*). I have been affirming a reciprocal cooperation between art and *psy knowledge* to constitute themselves as autonomous fields: while art relied on the idea of the unconscious to abandon the technical domain in the representation of reality as a criterion of evaluation of artistic quality, the *psy knowledge* supposed the idea of abstraction and expression as the empirical basis of the unconscious. Jung's theories are perhaps the most well-finished form of psychoanalysis's use of art, and the collections of artistic productions of psychiatric patients the form participants in the art world found to appropriate the knowledge and practices of *psy knowledge* in the reformulation of this universe's values.

However, in Brazil, the role of anthropologists in the constitution of a modern artistic field has been little investigated. Anthropology was fundamental for subjects such as *black art, indigenous art* and *folk art* to gain socially recognized senses. These categories, although metonymically associated with Brazil, were geographically located. The Northeast, and especially Bahia, for example, became the cradle of *Brazilian black art.* Largely this was a consequence of anthropological works, such as that of Melville Herskovits. In the 1950s, Herskovits stated that Bahia would be the place where contact with Africa would have lasted longer. However, he was not the only one to contribute to this ethnic regionalism. Gilberto Freire had launched in 1926, in the First Regionalist Congress, a Manifesto (Freire, 1996) that defended the national union around Brazilian regions and not around Brazilian states. The Manifesto was reprinted in 1952.

If regionalism intended to outdo the states, this did not happen. In the Manifesto, Freire briefly presented the elements used by the various intellectuals who participated in the Regionalist Movement to form what we now recognize as artisanal production of the various states of the Northeast. Several authors have already analyzed Freyre's regionalism, considering Bourdieu's (1982) critique of the participation of geographers in the reification and naturalization of cultural divisions from the "natural" landscape. Freire was, in Brazil, one of the main responsible for the national and international dissemination of the miscegenation ideology. However, the author's interest in this research lies in the fact that if, for him, Recife was the ideal model of miscegenation for having a homogeneous amount of mixture, the contribution of the African part on that mixture came from Bahia. Its regionalist defense reified the nature of the different Brazilian states in local popular production.

Agnaldo Manoel dos Santos (1926, Itaparica-1962, Salvador), author of the sculpture that stands in the entrance hall of Franco Terranova's apartment (as well as the sculpture in figure 18), is part of a group of people and categories which were classified as artists and artistic from the 1950s onwards. Intense industrialization and economic growth transformed the social landscape by stimulating Salvationist discourses that converted everyday practices and values into regional, ethnic, and/or national "traditions". The artistic recognition of Agnaldo counted on the participation of sculptor Mário Cravo Neto, with whom Agnaldo learned both the craft of woodworking and the "African" theme. At the time of their acquaintance, in 1952, Mario Cravo worked with wooden sculptures of candomblé orishas and also regional themes such as cangaceiro[89], capoeira[90] and berimbau[91].

Agnaldo himself had contact with Pierre Verger who presented him to the African sculptural work in wood and Terzo Lombardi, an art dealer in São Paulo, who suggested that he make sculptures based on the ex-votos. His participation in the Luso-Brazilian Colloquium, in 1959, put him in contact with the pieces of the Dundo Museum in Angola. This foreign perspective, distinct from what would be valued by the community from which Agnaldo himself came, is confirmed in the "quasi-ethnographic" text of Clarival do Prado Valadares, who argues that the artist's neighbors did not appreciate much of what he produced, "but the whites did".

Between 1952, when he met Mario Cravo, and 1962, when he died, he participated in the 6th Baiano Art Exhibition, in 1956, in the IV São Paulo Biennial, in 1957, the National Salon of Modern Art, in 1959, and in several individual exhibitions in Rio, São Paulo and Bahia. In 1966, Agnaldo was awarded posthumously at the 1st Black Art Festival in Dakar.

In terms of *indigenous art*, Darcy Ribeiro was instrumental in reformulating the ethnographic values of indigenous objects, projecting this perspective primarily from the Indigenous Museum in 1953. The exhibits of the museum's collections were not the only form of disclosure. The consumption of the production of indigenous groups was stimulated by the institution that served as a kind of commercial mediator.

According to museologist Mario Chagas, in the initial moments of the Indigenous Museum, the activities divided "into "thematic and rotating exhibitions", technical assistance with the collections (Conservation, disinfection, protection, restoration and classification), production of audio-visual documentation, ethnological research, loan

---

[89] Cangaço was the banditism phenomenon of Northeast Brazil in the late 19th and early 20th centuries. This region of Brazil is known for its aridness and hard way of life, and in a form of "social banditry" against the government, many men and women decided to become nomadic bandits, or cangaceiros.

[90] Capoeira is an Afro-Brazilian martial art that combines elements of dance, acrobatics, and music

[91] The berimbau is a single-string percussion instrument, from Brazil. Originally from Africa, the berimbau was incorporated into the practice of the Afro-Brazilian martial art capoeira.

of collections to colleges and television programs, national and international museological exchanges, the realization of combined sessions of music concerts, film and guided tours, which were the "great success of the Museum". However precarious and inaccurate the data on the activities and visitors of the Museum, it is known that in 1954 there were 66 film sessions, 25 indigenous music auditions, 12 special receptions and conferences, as well as countless guided tours. The visitors, although in an insignificant number 6,716 people during the year 1954 received a differentiated service with "information about the SPI, its organization and work", on the "operation and purpose of the Museum", "on uses and customs of our (sic) Indians, in general, of objects and tribes focused on exhibitions, in particular" (Chagas, 2007: 182).

According to the author, "it seems that visiting the Indigenous Museum in its earliest days was a kind of entrance into another territory, whose rules of reading and behavior needed to be learned. By placing himself as a liberal defender of the "indigenous cause", the Museum was also a voice authorized to speak for the "other" and to say that the "other" and "we" are not only different but also similar. Even though the generic use of the indigenous category was relativized, the Museum did not stop using it and did not fail to rehearse a discourse that, in practice, generically absorbed this indigenous within the scope of the national. Assuming a role of information and formation house for new mentalities, the Museum wrote and presented its narrative and also said what kind of reading should be done" (Chagas, 2007: 186).

Some objects similar to those exhibited and/or marketed by the museum can be found today at handcraft fairs such as basketwork, rattles, zoomorphic benches, masks, rain sticks, combs, utensils made from gourds and ceramics. Among these, some are recognized by the name of the group that produces them. But their practices, beliefs, histories, struggles and social organizations have not been popularized. Their names are known only as the manufacturers of those objects and they function as a label that supposedly guarantees ethnic authenticity for the products. If karajá dolls, for example, are recognized as Brazilian cultural patrimony, the claims of the Iny people, as the karajá demand to be known, do not have ample visibility.

The same happens with several other indigenous productions. Many pieces can be found among Olly's things, as well as in the homes of the well-known persons I interviewed and/or her partners[92]. Thus, Rio de Janeiro seems to have been a pole that disseminated both indigenous artisanal production and an imaginary about these groups and the Amazon[93].

---

[92] I tried to access to the Indigenous Museum visitors' books from the time it was founded until the 1970s to see Olly's presence at exhibitions and events, but the museum had been closed for some time.

[93] It seems important to add that the northern indigenous groups, especially the ones from the Amazon, were for a long time considered the only real Brazilian Indians for being considered "pure". Anthropologist João Pacheco de Oliveira (1998) criticizes the essentialization undertaken by North American cultural evolutionism, French structuralism and Brazilian indigenism (mainly Darcy Ribeiro) who described indigenous groups from the idea of tradition. If the indigenous objects considered "art" were those related

Even though Olly used a specific group to be represented in her work, the Karajá, the collection of indigenous pieces she accumulated seems to have artifacts produced by distinct groups, which gives this collection the appearance of a collection of "art" or "artifacts" as a specific social type whose aggregation can be thought of in terms of the colonization's violence. According to historian Jens Andermann (2004), it was in the turn of the colonial order towards the capitalist means of production that there was in Brazil a proliferation of visual representations of objects and indigenous men and women through paintings, sculptures, photographs and caricatures. However, by the middle of the 20th century, indigenous peoples continued to be treated as historical objects, valued for their supposed contribution to national history, but without due discussion about their rights and citizenship.

If geographically "black Brazilian art" was localized in Bahia and "indigenous art" in Amazonia, "popular art" was linked to the interior of Minas Gerais, the Northeast in general, and specially the São Francisco River. The reclassification of objects found in the interior of Minas Gerais was probably a continuation with the modernism of the 1920s and its search for Brazilianness. The Northeast and the São Francisco River were related to the entry of new technologies and the role of two collectors, Italian Franco Terranova and French Jacques Van de Beuque[94]. The fact that the carrancas were being abandoned both by motor boats, and by medicine that explained diseases from categories for which the carrancas could not contribute, made these pieces part of a changing imagination. Many carrancas' sculptors also produced ex-votos and both sculptural forms became an adventure for Franco Terranova.

The gallerist's collection had a principle of aesthetic organization and a selection of examples in order to represent a relationship to a world in extinction. His emphasis was on a classification of carrancas drawn from their context and placed in a relationship created by seriality. These would be the significant elements for Pierce (1994) in the conformation of a systematic collection. For Stewart (1994), this would be the form of collection itself, as opposed to souvenirs. For this author, while souvenirs invent a subject, subjects invent objects with their collections that are metaphors of the past in the present. The collection replaces history by classification, creating an order beyond temporality, completely aestheticizing the things' use value.

Unlike Olly, Terranova also invested in designing his collections and projecting his reputation on collected objects. Through the visibility his collections gained in books, newspaper articles, and exhibitions, we learned about his efforts to get the objects, the motivations that led him to collect them, and the meanings these collections acquired in the places where they were exhibited.

---

to these northern groups, several other indigenous groups were left out of this process of valuing of their material culture.

[94] About this second collector and the museum he founded, the Casa do Pontal Museum, see the works of Ângela Mascelani, 2006.

In addition to the museums and art galleries where they have won exhibitions, several critics and art historians (Clarival do Prado Valadares and José Roberto Teixeira Leite), museologists (Silvya Menezes de Athayde), intellectuals (Jorge Amado), politicians (ambassador Haroldo Costa) and others that crossed several of these categories (Quirino da Silva and Wilson Rocha) produced texts for the catalogs, contributing to the construction of these collections' values.

As Lopes (2017) argued, there are as many motivations for collecting, as types of collections. However, the legitimacy strategies of collections are important clues about the purposes that characterize collectors. The gallery owner Franco Terranova was, in fact, an art dealer. When questioned about the sale of part of his collection of ex-votos, he justified he was mainly a dealer[95]. *Marchand* is a classification that is at the same time honorific because it is related to a consecrated dimension of western society, but inferior in the hierarchy of the artistic world for it maculates the aura of purity and sacredness that supposes that this social sphere is devoid of economic interest. Collecting, as well as owning a gallery that "discovered" new names, purified the mercantile character of his performance. Unlike collectors themselves, who construct their narratives abstracted from all sorts of consumption, making collectible objects a form of self-referentiality and seriality independent of the economic universe, Terranova did not make these things strictly *objects of luxury*.

The reclassification of carrancas and ex-votos brought new social actors into reciprocal relationships. The pieces became part of an exchange circuit in which artisans and mediators participated in the transformation of values. Agnaldo Manoel dos Santos, for example, participated with Franco Terranova in the search for carrancas in the São Francisco river. According to the catalogs, he was the one who presented the gallery owner to Francisco Biquiba Guarany. Agnaldo and Francisco thus became part of this web in which, along with carrancas, ex-votos and other social mediators constructed the values of this new "artistic expression". These are, however, two names and not the categories to which they belonged. Northeastern and northerners, blacks, indigenous and the poor from urban centers did not gain more attention from the public authorities themselves. Nevertheless, aesthetics was in this period a struggling tool for many of these intellectuals and one of the possible ways to understand it is perhaps thinking about the relationship between folklore and anthropology in Brazil.

The dimension of an individual particularity was one of the ways out of a generalizing discourse that located this production as part of an anonymous collectivity. Although this period was indelibly linked to evolutionism, naming the producers of these things was a way of building an alternative to folkloric anonymity. Vitor Galdino (2018) shows the social trajectory of the idea of anonymity in relation to that of authorship. The notion of the author appears in the seventeenth century as a form of social control: to attribute a name was to blame someone for the speech, that

---

[95] This was his widow's report in a personal communication with the author, 2017.

is, in this period anonymity was an opposition to the *status quo* represented by the British crown, that is, a form of freedom of speech. This anonymity condemned in the seventeenth century as a transgressor was redeemed in the eighteenth and nineteenth centuries as representative of a popular authenticity, the origin of diverse cultural identities, including national ones. From the second half of the twentieth century onward, anonymity was criticized as a double strategy, on the one hand, for not recognizing the creative capacity of individuals from peripheric groups and, on the other hand, as a way to allow the misappropriation of this production.

In ethnology, aesthetics was also an attempt to produce a new reading that would transform the inferiority attributed by evolutionism into a form of equality, even though this equality was not yet being discussed in terms of citizenship. However, the aesthetic bias did not acquire universal value, but served to reinforce the national dimension of things and people. Agnaldo, for example, in 1963, was presented to the international public by historian and art critic Clarival do Prado Valadares in a book, in English, recounting the artist's biography, his poor origin and his manual work until his death by schistosomiasis and Chagas, diseases typical of places without basic sanitation. Poverty guaranteed the dimension of authenticity by its removal from a civilizational bias located in the erudition, almost a justification for the lack of action of the State before these groups. The national dimension was due to their ethnic membership since Agnaldo was black, and the theme linked to the religions of African matrices.

In 1966 the first Black Art Festival was organized in Dakar, Senegal, with the support of UNESCO. The event was supported by the poet Léopold Sédar Senghor, who later became president of the Republic of Senegal, which had become independent in 1960. Thirty-seven (37) countries were represented in the show. Art critic Clarival do Prado Valadares was part of the Brazilian delegation. He was also a member of the jury, along with Professor Estácio de Lima of the University of Bahia, the former Brazilian ambassador to Ghana, Raimundo de Souza Dantas, the anthropologist/folklorist Edison Carneiro, the representative of the Center for Afro-Oriental Studies Waldir Freitas Oliveira, the director of the Institute of Afro-Asian Studies, Candido Mendes de Almeida and the painters Rubem Valentim and Heitor dos Prazeres. The festival was partly the result of a movement initiated by a small black bourgeoisie that was formed during the period of colonization of the African countries composed essentially by colonies employees, specialized workers, merchants and liberal professionals who had access to French universities in the first decades of the century. Among them was Léopold Sédar Senghor (Oliveira, 2018).

Thus, to name these artists and to value a production classified as black was also to insert Brazil into a trading market headed by a white bourgeoisie and its collections of popular objects, ex-votos, etc., with only a few black artists nominated. Nowadays, the expression "Afro-Brazilian art", even if it has had a variable meaning according to the context, interests of the moment and the actors in question, echoes the racial connotations of its origins and the erasing of the subalternization of bodies in the subsumption of that production to the notion of Brazilianness and its corollary, miscegenation. In this sense, the body has now been one of the main supports for contemporary artists' work for rejecting race as a colonial construction but emphasizing the impact of their creation on the body and experience of racialized subjects.

Agnaldo's sculpture that appears in figure 18 was a character of one of Olly's idiosyncrasies. Hilda de Azevedo Soares, founder of Cineduc, an NGO that worked with education through movies, was neighbor and friends with Olly. When I interviewed her, she said the artist had a relation of respect and fear for this sculpture. At certain times she would send the sculpture to her friend's house, for she thought the sculpture brought bad luck. Then she would make peace with the piece and bring it back to her house. This anecdote gains social proportions if we account that the artistic production classified as Afro-Brazilian was until recently linked to the religions of African matrices and was first in evidence in the researches on this social dimension, before gaining the attention of art critics and historians. However, it also explains the ambiguity of the relationship of this white elite with the production (and its producers) classified as popular, *naïf, black, indigenous*, etc. which is always marked by a distrust typical of liminality.

The ideology of miscegenation through which Brazil became known, thanks mainly to Gilberto Freire's publications, was thus an important dimension from which to build these new artistic categories, incorporating the dangers represented by the margins as part of the national construction. Depending on the author of the text and the producer or artistic product analyzed, the emphasis could be on African, indigenous or popular culture. Clarival do Prado Valadares, for example, emphasized Agnaldo's relationship with Africa, while Darcy Ribeiro emphasized the importance of the indigenous in the conformation of a Brazilianess.

It is important to note that, in Brazil, modernism of the early twentieth century repositioned the arts in terms of social prestige. Thus, if by the end of the nineteenth century, names such as Horacio Hora, Arthur and João Timótheo da Costa, Crispim Amaral and Estevão Silva represented by their social origin the hierarchical inferior place that the arts occupied in Brazil, from the beginning of the 20th century, medium and upper classes, generally white, were represented (Chiarelli, 2015). In the 1950s, black artists began to emerge again, not so much from the more legitimate classification of their production as art, but with an adjectival art, "black art" or "popular art", offering their share of authenticity in the conformation of Brazilianness.

This adjective was a skewed attempt to overcome a hegemonic evolutionist bias. It transformed the linear representation of art history that automatically attributed inferiority to all "others" in a particular artistic *sensibility*, thought from a primitivist fantasy of origin and childhood (Price, 2000). The "primitive", represented here by the native, the Negro, the producer of string literature or the pre-Columbian producer, an image of a radical otherness, offered a possibility to denature ways of seeing the world and with this, a possibility of producing culture criticism. However, its plastic expression was categorized from descriptive terms – "black art", "primitive art", "folk art" – which recognized the universality of *aesthetic sensibility*, even though they remained conceived as hierarchically different. Always identified by a white middle-class elite from the ideas of tradition and authenticity, these groups were denied the possibility of self-representation and of producing outside the parameters assigned to them.

It is necessary to draw attention to the difference between the material analyzed by Sally Price (2000) and the one presented here. While the author speaks of generic categories that do not name their individual producers, what I observed in the material investigated was the construction of some names to associate the ideas of "popular art" (Geraldo Teles de Oliveira – GTO, Mestre Vitalino, Antonio Poteiro, Cariri, Ciça, among others) and "black art" (Agnaldo Manoel dos Santos). There seems to have been in Brazil both an investment in the construction of a generic category "primitive art" and in the recognition of some of its individual producers. A visit to the Edison Carneiro Folklore Museum in Rio de Janeiro shows a room dedicated to "folk art" where almost all the exhibits have their authorship identified. Indigenous production, however, was not associated with private producers in this period and its recognition as an artistic expression is still disputed today.

In some books on art history it is possible to find references to *indigenous art, feather art, textile art* as representing the beginnings of art made in Brazil by indigenous groups. However, among anthropologists and even among some members of indigenous groups recognized as artists there is no consensus on the value of being treated as an artist. Anthropologist Ilana Goldstein has drawn attention to this dimension, showing how the Brazilian example is very different from that found in her doctoral research among the Australian aborigines, where the idea of an "autochthonous art" has represented the construction of new senses for the art making and the ways this can be directed to the community as a whole (Goldstein, 2018, personal statement). The disputes between recognizing or not indigenous production as artistic are only partly related to the fact that indigenous production is not a separate dimension from other spheres of social life, for if there is a relatively autonomous artistic field in the "West", this production also does not happen independently of other social spheres.

Trying to escape presentism without falling into historicism (Stocking Jr, 1999), it is important to ask questions to the past that are based on the knowledge accumulated in the present but accounting for the problems of the time. At the same time one needs to mobilize synchronic and diachronic perspectives to account for the moments in which the city, intellectual life and art conform in a convergent sense (Pontes, 2008). What temporal relations are present in the forms of private collections found in this research? Collectionism can be understood here as the search for a sense of permanence as exteriority in relation to its accumulator, as a social action that reproduces and surpasses the duplicity of permanence and absence manifest in the collected things (Lopes, 2017).

This sense of exteriority has distinct temporalities depending on the type of collection to which it refers. Hierarchizing the temporal extension of the three ideal types proposed here as reference, we can think of the collection of souvenirs as a collection that only acts in the present. If they are nourished by an idealized past, just as the other two models, souvenirs only produce the subject in the present. Rarely does a collection of souvenirs remain beyond the physical death of its accumulator, and even if it does, objects are usually dispersed within the family and do not remain linked to the building of the prestige of its original owner. Therefore, they are not objects with a temporal extension.

What I called the Antiquarianist collection, that is, the collections accumulated by Olly – indigenous, pre-Columbian and popular – projected status in the artist's textile production, but this status was not maintained by the lack of a narrative construction of meanings and a visibilization project for the collection. If the hierarchy of goods is part of the values hierarchy of social groups, shaping the status of individuals and groups according to models and types of reciprocity and redistribution of individual and collective surpluses (savings and accumulations), collections that achieve social visibility contribute immensely for the projection of the collector status. However, the possibility of recovering part of the history of these sets of things puts the past in focus, opening spaces for investigations of their meanings.

Based on an investigation of non-institutionalized collectors, that is, of non-patrimonialized collections whose accumulators use technological mediations to disseminate their collections, anthropologist José Rogério Lopes (2017) suggests that the incorporation of a manifested *ethos* as an observable attitude is necessary so that the act of collecting is renewed as a practice in subsequent generations, updating the grounds and criteria for discrimination. Perhaps it is no coincidence that Olly's sister introduced the collection of her mother's buttons to which Erika had given continuity (and is kept by her daughter).

Three metal boxes contained a world of senses. Separated by colors – black, white and colored buttons – the boxes denounced a classificatory principle. The delicacy of that collection of mother-of-pearls, wood, and leathers lined four generations of women. These buttons represented not only the connection between the past and the present, but also a gender alliance that linked experiences and reflections to the stories heard and the possibility of telling them to others. And this bond was made through seams that aligned affections, women and generations. Constituents of a determined *ethos* in this family they probably helped Olly to perceive the accumulation of things as the subjects' extensions. It is no coincidence that the Reinheimer's son has collected coins and stamps and that I am collecting knowledge about the family.

The motivations, the criteria of discrimination and the way of projecting oneself into things were transformed between the generations represented by the social actors investigated here. From Clara's buttons to Olly's indigenous, pre-Columbian and string literature sets there were very distinct self-production practices that need to be related to the social and historical context to which each of these women belonged.

The collection for Olly marked the beginning of her *career* recognition, being thus conditioned by the perceptions of the various actors involved in the typical interactions in the environments in which she was. Art museums, ethnological museums, archaeological sites and professionals linked to these *traditions of knowledge* (Barth, 1993) constituted perceptions characteristics of the identity bonds established throughout her collecting. The clothes drawn from these interactions incorporated these bonds and transmitted them to whoever consumed them.

However, these values established throughout the time of collecting and producing her fabrics and clothing did not extend beyond her life span. This is partly due to the fact that she has not invested in building a public sense for her collections since the public sense also depends on the social context.

The meanings of things are debtors of the movement of things, or things-in-motion (Appadurai, 1990), as well as of the values and social relations around this movement. The process of recovering the importance of things in the social world can not minimize the fact that this world is also constituted of values and social relations. Thus, the recognition and legitimacy of objects as collections was conquered by the discourses and actions undertaken by the accumulators, but also by the actions and discourses of other social actors in other webs of relation and the conditions of possibility of the contexts in which they developed. The construction of a collection's meaning then is not perennial, as the example used by Susan Pierce (1994) shows, and its changes point to the power struggles involved in the attribution of meanings and value systems tied to those meanings.

If the work of constructing the value of "black art" collections, carrancas and ex-votes of Terranova gained social recognition between the 1950s and 1980s, in the long run, social changes and dynamics produced a reflux in the meaning of those collections and in the very idea and social interest for this type of production. With the death of Franco Terranova, the family sought a well-known auctioneer to sell the collections of ex-votos and carrancas and he informed them that there was no market for those pieces in the artistic world. Their aesthetic and consequently economic value had declined vertiginously, they were left to represent the biographical trajectory of their collector and the historical period of the Brazilian art to which it was linked.

Nowadays, the search for works with African ancestry content that have been in vogue since the 19th century has been replaced by the focus on the artists' African ancestry, which poses new questions to the debate and the universe of contemporary art (Menezes, 2018). Some exhibitions and events gained prominence in the second decade of the 21st century. Particularly in 2018, a year that "celebrates" 100 years of slavery abolition in Brazil[96], the exhibition Afro-Atlantic Histories (MASP and Tomie Ohtake Institute) was part of a series of other events that proposed the construction of counter-narratives on self-representation and representation of others in various cultural fields (Reinheimer, Araújo and Santos, 2019).

The meanings constituted throughout the 1950s to 1970s was not based on the political struggle for the equality of right between different peripheric groups and a

---

[96] Slavery abolition in Brazil is an event that more than celebrated is used as a moto for black movements to denounce racism in contemporary Brazilian society.

national elite, but on the construction of the subjectivity and the prestige of members of a white middle-class. From the 1970s on, the national totality gave way to a fragmented vision that emphasized the identity of particular groups and social categories. The claim of groups for representation and formulations of cultural diversity, multiculturalism and multiculturality led to the proliferation of museums and heritage (Gonçalves, 2015), as well as reviewing classifications that stereotyped groups from an external perspective. Increasingly, the representations of peripheric groups have been considered legitimate only if it comes from an internal membership and not from an external mediator, as was the case of the collectors mentioned here.

It is to this participation of new groups and new discursivities in the artistic field that authors like Hal Foster (2014), Terry Smith (2012) and Hans Belting (2006) have called attention, referring sometimes to an "ethnographic turn" that has readmitted that aesthetics are neither neutral nor disinterested and that the social reading of the artistic manifestations can result in interesting and valuable productions for the artistic world.

Therefore, to some extent, the loss of value of these collections is related to the question of representativeness that has come to play in contemporary art as well. Peripheric groups have gained in the artistic field the right to tell themselves the meaning of their things. The case of Terranova's collections helps to realize how recognition of the value and meaning of collections can shift from a dimension of aesthetic legitimation to the hierarchically subordinate dimension of history.

However, the fact that values established throughout the artifying period for those collected objects or things produced from them have not been maintained after the death of their collectors does not mean that these objects have not connected generations. The objects accumulated by Olly and Werner and the fabrics produced by Olly based on them are the axis around which this investigation has developed. The same goes for the Terranova family that organizes and systematizes the collection left by Franco. Unlike the economic elites who often donate their collections to museums or make up their own private foundations, the collections described here did not gain patrimony status, nor did they retain the social visibility they had during the life of their accumulators. Yet the "power of objects" (Weiner, 1987) continues to serve for subsequent generations to make statements about their identities, goals and fantasies.

I was interested here to understand how, from the 1950s to the 1980s, in Brazil this phenomenon was incorporated in the practice of a set of social agents that contributed to transform aesthetic values and to constitute an artistic field based on nationally and internationally coherent practices and discourses. The collection observed from the materials of the Reinheimer couple and Franco Terranova was a technology among others that contributed to forge new values from the classificatory rearrangement of the material production of some groups until then perceived as peripheric and considered from disciplines such as history, anthropology and archeology. But this collection served also for my repositioning within the Brazilian anthropological field, just as it has functioned as a form of repositioning of those who are involved with the collections of Terranova, each in its professional sphere.

The collections, as a result of *situational illusions* (Lopes, 2017), are projections of individual attributes or projects of constitution of status and, in this sense, of legitimation of attributes not yet necessarily recognized individually and socially. When they gain their own biographies and become singular, they come to represent *collective illusions* gaining diverse meanings related to the memory of groups, states, historical periods, events, etc. Thus, collections are always constituted in the interaction between the subject and the collected things, or between the social actors who identify collective meanings in the logics of organization that generalize the collections and the institutions that exhibit them. A chain of authenticity is formed in this process, that is, the memory and recognition, over time, of what the person built. This did not happen for Olly's collections, nor was it maintained for Franco Terranova's collections of ex-votes and carrancas.

Modern art museums actively participated in this process (Shapiro, 2007) of *artification* of private collections, taking these popular, black and indigenous productions as a way to attribute Brazilianness to the modernity of the design produced on national soil. In 1960, a photograph of the architecture and decoration exhibition at MAM-RJ shows the architect Sérgio Rodrigues in a living room simulation. There, the furniture in modern lines, Bauhaus style, are mixed with the only book which cover is visible, *Les arts sauvages Océanie*, in front of which you see a wooden object representing an orisha. This mixture of the modern straight lines (parallel and perpendicular), the industrial materials (metal and polyurethane) and the sinuous curves with the "natural" materials (wood, leather, cotton, plants, among others) are the elements that conformed the new style of this middle-class that was constituted in Brazil from an alliance between the collection of these new artistic categories and the design of furniture, interiors and fabrics/clothes. These individual producers, Agnaldo, Mestre Vitalino, and others, were the national exemplars illustrating the broad categories generally forged in Europe and the United States: *primitive art, black art, folk art*.

Over time and criticism on the construction of these generic categories, the collections lost exchange value. However, the names of some producers classified as artists have maintained recognition, even if often with a more historical and anthropological than properly aesthetic value.

CHAPTER 4

Textile and Feminine Production in the Middle of the 20th Century

This piece, for example, she says, showing a cloth whose important details are leaves and dry branches, had the participation of Patricia. At the age of 7, she already shows a tendency for art, says Olly forgetting her work and thinking about the little granddaughter, like every doting grandmother"
(Folha de São Paulo, 1975).

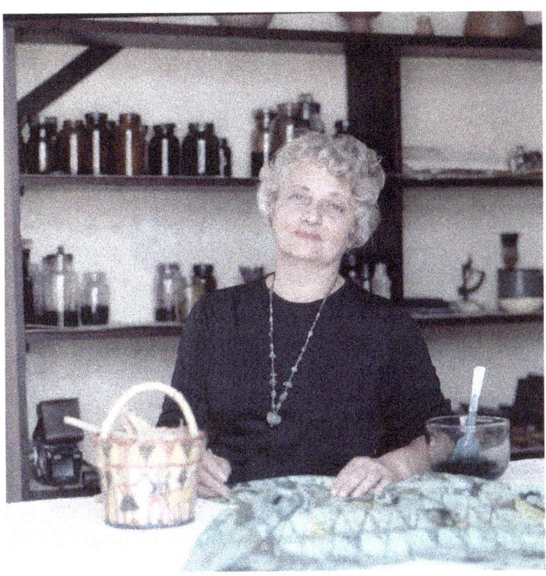

Figure 91: Olly in her studio. Behind her, there is the chemistry she used to produce her own ink. However, she also experimented with producing paints from various natural materials such as earth, seeds and flowers.

4.1. FROM STUDENT TO ARTIST: EXCHANGES THAT OPERATE A CONVERSION

The entrance of Niomar Muniz Sodré, in 1952, as executive director of MAM-RJ, inaugurated a new project for that institution. The new statute, established in 1951, withdrew the mention to "folk surveys" and replaced it with "studies and achievements in plastic arts, including popular arts" (Sant'Anna, 2011). Instead of the search for an abstract folklore as a way of producing a national symbology, consistent with the debates of the 1940s, the museum sought to identify itself with a changing society in which the groups, although stratified, shared time and space. The country, which was sometimes treated as part of Latin America, sought to see itself no longer as an environment of backwardness, but with the optimism of a modernity for which it assumed an active role. It was imagined that modernity would redeem the ills of Brazilian society. This "popular" also presented itself from a new "style of decoration of the domestic spaces" specific of a middle-class, formed to some extent by the immigrants of the immediate pre or post-Second War.

In Sodré's administration, MAM-RJ begun having its own artistic training courses and publicizing the exhibitions in the city's periodicals. It is worth remembering that at that time, printed material was the most important source of information. People often read more than one newspaper and some periodicals had morning and evening versions. The institution also began to organize conferences, publish a newsletter, and search for a headquarters of its own. Both the museum and the artists related to this institution begun to occupy the pages of Correio da Manhã (Morning Post) a newspaper owned by the museum director's husband, Paulo Bittencourt and other periodicals, entering into the daily life of their readers. Yvonne Jean, an art reporter at this newspaper, along with Mário Pedrosa, Jayme Mauricio and Flexa Ribeiro, produced numerous positive reviews about the museum, its activities and the artists who had a direct relationship with it.

The perception that Brazil needed a place to exhibit modern art was replaced by the idea that it was necessary to create a demand for it. As part of this project, a new headquarter was idealized and designed by a renowned modernist architect, Affonso Eduardo Reidy. The building was erected in the newest sign of Brazilian modernity, Parque do Flamengo[97], where "nature", through the landscaping of Roberto Burle Mar

x, was accommodated to the needs of technology, through an urbanism that privileged with the main symbol of that moment through the expressways, the speed.

Sant'Anna (2011) draws attention to the fact that the definitive headquarters' work began by the school block, which denoted the museum's "didactic vocation" and its project of building a modern Brazilian art. The training courses began in 1952,

---

[97] Idealized to be the Tropical Central Park, it was the first active leisure park in Brazil. The first equipment installed in the park was inaugurated in 1965 and its architectural and urban design was conceived by the same architect who designed MAM-RJ. http://www.parquedoflamengo.com.br/sobre-o-parque/

with a free studio by Ivan Serpa, painting classes by Milton Goldring and modeling by Margaret Spencer. In courses, students and teachers built new meanings for artistic practice. A rigorous teacher, Ivan Serpa's didacticism combined freedom of creation, which excluded other technical and expressive possibilities such as teaching perspective, for example, and severe criticism as a way of constructing meanings for the modernity. MAM-RJ's art courses sought to form artists that could later be exhibited there, but were also frequented by an audience with varied goals that would later constitute the consumers of that modernity they were producing.

The category *freedom* appears as significant in several social dimensions in this period: from gender to art teaching, passing through the political system. But the notion is permeated by contradictions. In art, the representations about the artist's freedom do not consider the objective conditions of the work's production and the artist's renown, which in practice means the work's recognition. However, freedom is a value used in differentiating periods of pre-modern artistic production.

In a person-to-person communication, art critic Frederico Morais (2014) mentioned the presence of *"bored housewives"* in MAM's training courses in the 1960s. It is very likely that in the 1950s, women of white middle-class have also attended the courses probably in search of a hobby to overcome the boredom of class-imposed idleness (McClintock, 2010), but probably also in search for training that could be turned into a professional activity. The investment of the museum in industrial design led to courses in graphic design, engraving and work on fabrics, techniques that can be applied in a variety of ways in the labor market.

In modernity, on the one hand, the advent of abstraction and new forms of expression has brought greater openness to the participation of women in the hierarchically more legitimate expressions of art. On the other hand, the emergence of industrial and graphic design opened new fields of professional investment linked to art from a subordinate dimension. Perhaps that is why the writer and feminist Betty Friedan (1971) in 1963, suggested that, at first glance, the arts appeared to be the "ideal solution" for women. In the making of art, work and pleasure are not opposing dimensions, and remuneration does not appear as the ultimate goal and therefore does not place the white middle-class woman in a radical opposition to the values of class, gender and race coined for her throughout the 19th century: professionalizing, but not working – after all one of the main representations of the artistic world is that its doing is mistaken for pleasure – and having an occupation that does not focus on making money – role reserved for men.

Hierarchies of artistic objects were still gender influenced. Some types of objects and practices were considered masculine and others feminine. Applied arts, often referred to as handcrafting, were situated at the base of a hierarchy since Renaissance. In this hierarchy, pure arts – resulting from a process of reflection rather than manual labor – would be at the top.

If craft was one of the ways of thinking the association between industry and art, this was in itself a gendered relationship. Industry-related professions were largely male-oriented, just as the materials used were hierarchical in terms of gender value.

Leather, wood, and metal were regarded as more noble materials and related to masculine making, while fabric and ceramics were feminine dimensions of the industry. This relationship between materials and gender was homologous to the relationship between nature and culture, with the craftsmanship and the feminine being associated with nature and industry and the masculine, with culture.

Industrialization, which came with this new conception of modernity, ensured women greater access to the labor market in general, including in the art world. However, even with the increased possibility of women joining consecrated artistic production, they were still less likely to achieve recognition than men. This recognition, when won in life, was often not perpetuated to the point of inserting them into the history of Brazilian art, even if Brazil is an exception in the gender curve of the art world by the number of women who participated in the constitution of a relative autonomy for the field or that contributed to this by their performance in other areas. Curators Ana Paula Simioni, Elaine Dias and Maria de Lourdes Eleutério (2015) argue that in Brazil, the greater presence of women in artistic field is probably related to the devaluation that culture in general has in the country. Although active in the present, very few are remembered beyond their lives. Olly was one of those progressively forgotten.

Feminist writings on creative women tend to consider that partnerships with male artists create invisibilization of female work. Described and understood by critics and historiographers as "wives", "companions", "sisters", "lovers", or "daughters" of artists, they were frequently and subtly denied the right to authorship, "the most valuable statement in the field of arts and culture" (Simioni, 2007,90). This analysis, however, makes room for imagining that women who entered the artistic field unmarried or with affective and family ties with men whose professional activities were not related to this field have achieved visibility and recognition more easily. This was not the case for several artists. Celeida Tostes, for example, performed at about the same time as Olly and in the same circle (see Figure 14, various pieces of Celeida decorating Olly's apartment). Both had their importance recognized when mentioned to people who knew them. However, no book, study or exhibition about them was realized after their deaths. Simioni (2007) shows through the case of Regina Gomide Graz how the absence of women from the artistic field was not so much due to the lack of intellectual or artistic qualities, but to successive and more or less institutionalized practices of exclusion.

Through a study of female researchers in Brazilian anthropology, Mariza Corrêa (1995) shows that there was in this field a lesser recognition for researchers married to male anthropologists than those who tried to make a career on their own. Corrêa speaks of a continuum that goes from female wives to single women to argue that the attributes of the female condition cover the social characters of married women who lose their professional identity to gain an identity as wives. These anthropologists' partners, in the cases studied by Corrêa, or artists, studied by Simioni, describe social expectations about women in general, which are broken by the action of "single" women in the sense of women who are not linked to a partner in the same professional activity, are not married to a colleague by profession.

Olly was able to sustain her own name and reknown while she was producing, but the gender social and political battle is not fought only in the present tense of action. It is also about remaining as a symbol, an example for new generations, women who helped in the past to build the present. Therefore, the gender issue itself must be thought of in time and space in relation to invisibility and recognition, important dimensions of this struggle.

Nathalie Heinich speaks of recognition circles ranging from peers, more legitimate groups in the field of art, to the general public. She makes this reflection from the Van Gogh case, thinking how he was recognized by his peers before his death, but only a century later achieved international recognition. Reputation is about how the hierarchies of objects and people change over time and space: in posterity, artists can both gain recognition and oblivion.

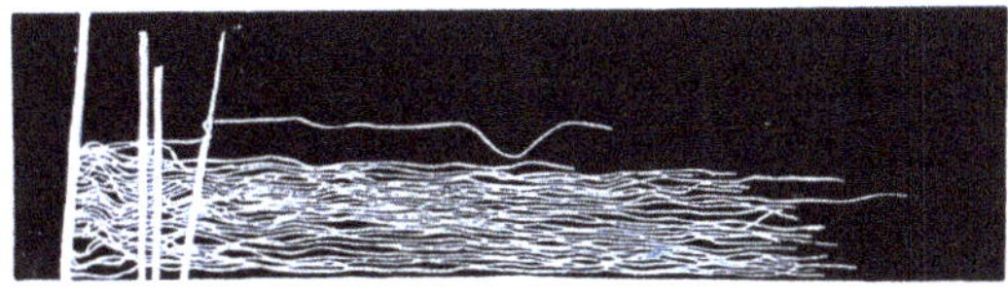

Figure 92: Printmaking by Olly. s.d.

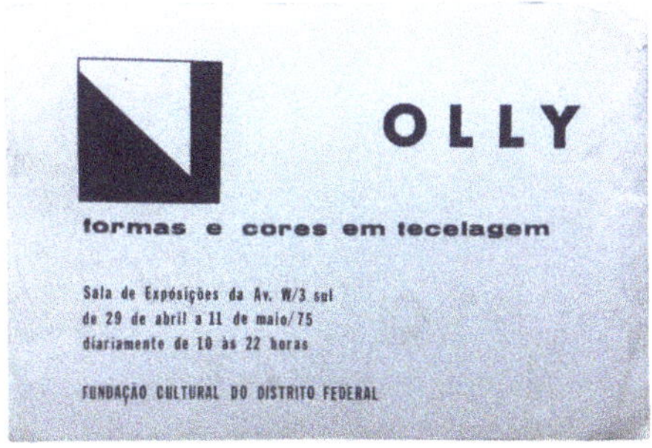

Figure 93: Poster from an exhibition that does not feature in any of the artist's curricula.

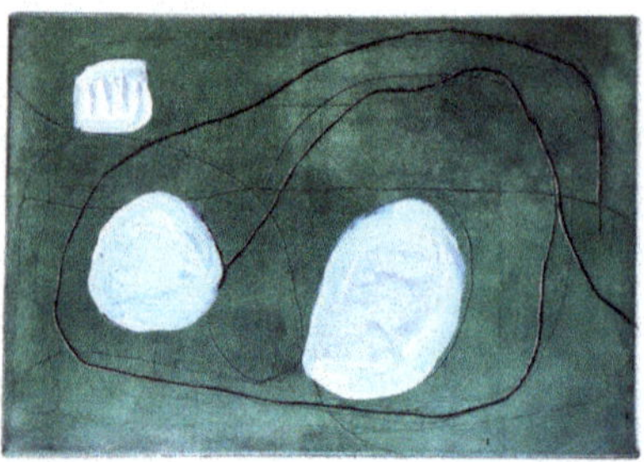

Figure 94: Printmaking produced by Olly. s.d.

These hierarchies pass through value categories that constitute objects and people as more or less artistic. These values are constituted in relation to several factors such as the materials and techniques used and the mesh of institutions and social actors in which the candidate or the artist circulates. Thus, the obliteration of courses, teachers, experienced techniques and institutions explicitly explains the hierarchy of the system, making important dimensions for the understanding of social processes "disappear" from the history of the constitution of the fields. James Clifford (1994) provided a framework where some of these dimensions are considered to show how art and culture are part of a complex hierarchical system. Therefore, thinking about a textile production, which resulted in clothes, made by a middle-aged European woman – Olly was 44 when she had her first exhibition in 1958 – in a context when youth was becoming very important, helps to understand various class, ethnic, generation and gender conversions and reconversions that had to be made in the process of building her *career*.

Bourdieu (1996) calls attention to the primacy of youth that the intellectual field values which is more related to the negation of the economy and the representations of domination and power that money and the bourgeoisie imply, than chronological age. Still, Olly's chronological age probably would not have helped her enter the artistic field if her proposal were to produce contemporary art rather than textiles.

The constitution of MAM's Art School in the early 1950s, as well as the transfer to this institution of the ceramic classes that Olly attended with Margareth Spencer, probably put her in contact with other possibilities. She also became a pupil of Renina Katz (part of the contents of the course "Color and Form" are in *Olly and Werner Reinheimer's Archive*), Fayga Ostrower (Composition), Milton Ribeiro (Graphic Arts History and Theory), Kazuko Abe (painting), René Leblanc (Drawing), Ivan Serpa (Painting), Milton Golbring (Painting), Zélia Salgado (Painting), Santa Rosa (Painting), Frank Schaefer (Painting), Hilda Schulenberg, Robert Delamonica (Engraving), Johnny Friedlander (Engraving).

According to the testimony of her friend Edith Weitzfelder, Olly taught ceramics since the 1940s. At this time, when exhibiting her work in Galeria Exclusividade, she met Russian art critic Mark Berkowitz. However, in her Curriculum Vitae and in the newspaper columns about her work it seems that her entrance into the artistic universe began with MAM's classes. References to previous artistic practices were found in other documents and through interviews. Photography is another dimension of her experiences which is not mentioned: she took photography classes at ArtCenter in 1974. In a letter (CO-97), she talks about Photosessions, which could mean photograph sessions of her work, although it seems less likely for there are annotations on photography as if they were course notes.

Ceramics, a minor art, gained prominence when given as part of MAM's educational project. In the same way, photography was associated with propaganda and journalism, not yet constituting a technique compatible with others in artistic production, such as drawing and painting. Her participation in MAM-RJ's workshops was then decisive for the construction of an artist's career and to produce a work in the sense of the reiterated confirmations a *career* suggests. Participation in these workshops constituted much more than technical learning, it created a sense of group membership, even if it was open and implied the constant inclusion and exclusion of members and that within this large group, MAM-RJ's students and teachers, there were subgroups, more or less recognized, such as Grupo Frente, for example, made up of students from Ivan Serpa's course and the professor himself. This membership was also due to participation in exchange circuits, directly or indirectly related to the institution.

To the system of reciprocity that was formed among the founding members of the institution (Sant'Anna, 2011), the art courses included the artists and their productions. Olly, for example, constituted a collection of art with various works that were the result of exchanges commented on throughout her life, or enumerated in the manuscripts she left. In a manuscript she comments on how Serpa was a strict teacher, until he saw her painted handkerchiefs and suggested an exchange (IN-04).

The fabric painted by Olly and exchanged with Serpa, represented her incorporation into the modern artists' mesh of relations, that is, a web of mutual obligations. Participation in this system from fabrics and clothes had a double aspect of being permeated and transformed by both the maker and the wearer.

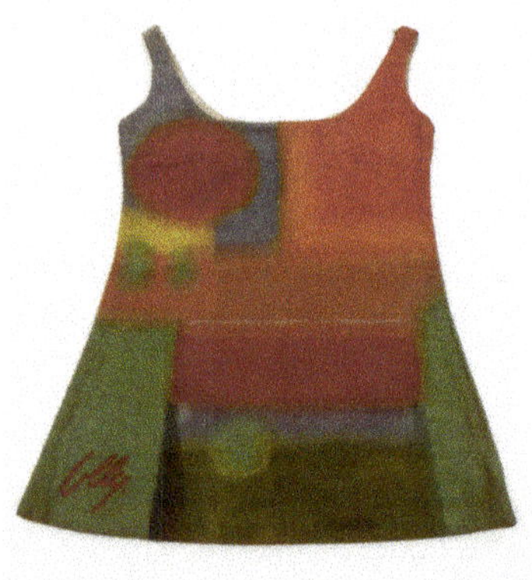

Figure 95: After Olly's death, Werner offered her entire collection to MAM-RJ. The donation process took 15 years to be analyzed and, at the end of this period, only two pieces of clothing were accepted and are now part of the museum's collection. This is one of them. MAM-RJ Collection. Photograph: Patricia Reinheimer, 2018.

From this system of generalized exchanges, in which all are mutually involved, the consumer society (Baudrillard, 1995) produces its values, while the products exchanged constitute the subjectivities of its consumers (Miller, 2009). The modern identity of these social actors and institutions was constructed through the circulation of objects and values and information they symbolized. The donation of works to the museum and the exchange of works between artists stimulated the entrance of other institutions and social actors in this system, expanding it and opening space for other participations in the process of construction of this modernity.

Maybe that's why the artist Marília Rodrigues (1937-2009) remembers Olly from the perspective of trading: "*What I think is Olly's very important trace is her generosity as an artist and as a person – to exchange information, to open up, to encourage. Our age difference was enormous. Of course, I started working and getting help very fast, but of course at the stage I was in and at the stage she was I was getting a lot more than I could give. So, this generosity is a very important trait. And it was not only me who received. She was generous, open. When she organized those nuit de parfum, with those fantastic outfits, even in Franco Terranova's Petite Galerie, it was dazzling, those models all wearing Olly's clothes. Beautiful clothes*" (testimonial, 1998). Several respondents stressed what they called "generosity". Although this may be an individual assignment, its consequences are social.

Hetty Goldberg, was manager of Forma furniture store at the time when Olly was exhibiting her work there. She described a situation in which she listed both Olly's creativity and *generosity*: in the early 1980s, Forma decided to launch a line of decorative fabrics. Hetty, who until then had made all the store windows, decided to invite a professional to do this one. She went to Casa Alberto, a clothing store for formal occasions, which indicated their window-designer. The professional spent all day making a showcase that was quite traditional, from the manager's perspective. Since the collection's inauguration would be the following night, she called Olly who lived a block from the store. The artist arrived, took off her shoes, went into the shop window, and undid the work the designer had been working on. She picked up all the fabrics' samples and started tying them. Gradually they formed a five-foot-wide colored ball that occupied almost the whole window. Mixed fabrics of all colors and, next to them, a single lounger. *"It was one of the most beautiful shop windows Forma has ever had"* (Hetty, 2015).

Generosity is the most complete form of the total prestations referred to by Marcel Mauss (2003). Its voluntary character conceals the economic and obligatory dimension of retribution. The benefits are imposed and interested, and it is in this process of receiving and reciprocating that social structures and hierarchies are built and destroyed. An example of an interrupted or destabilized relationship due to a misunderstanding as to who owed what is in a drafted letter that Olly left in her archives (MA-10). Marina, the recipient of the letter, had at some point obtained work for the artist's husband. It also seems that Marina was ill, or so she was trying to convey in order to justify the cancellation of two jobs commissioned from Olly after the services were already under way. The letter is an outburst that lists the various exchanges developed between the two parties over time, accusing Marina of lack of respect for the orders cancellation. Olly recognized the various things that the recipient would have done for her and her husband. But the variety of forms of offering, receiving and retributing in the reciprocity system, as well as the disinterested character that is used as a formal model of behavior in the artistic field, opens space for misunderstandings regarding the evaluation criteria of the various currencies used in the exchanges.

Participating in collective or individual exhibitions was also part of this system. As already mentioned, Olly's first solo exhibition was held in 1958 at Galeria Contemporânea, at the invitation of Norman Westwater, designer and owner of the furniture store, Mobília Contemporânea, where the gallery was located. Norman came to Brazil in the early 1950s, fleeing a war-torn Europe. In the mid-1950s, MAM-RJ began announcing the construction of the Escola Técnica de Criação (Technical School of Creation). Based on the principles of the Ulm School, the aim was to train technical professionals to intervene in the world from the industrial design perspective. However, the School gained independence and became an autonomous institution, the Escola Superior de Desenho Industrial ESDI (Higher School of Industrial Design) (Sant'Anna, 2011). Westwater taught at ESDI in the early 1960s. He was also one of the first members of the newly instituted ABDI (Brazilian Industrial Design Association)[98].

---

[98] Westwater's personal archive is in England, with his widow, Nedra Westwater. This is a very rich collection from the 1950s to the early 1960s, when Norman participated in the Brazilian design training

According to Olly (MA-33 s.d.[99]), about the event in the Galeria Contemporânea, art critic Mario Pedrosa spent hours watching the exhibition and described her work as musical. It was then that Niomar Muniz Sodré invited her to exhibit it at MAM-RJ. In addition to large exhibitions, the museum organized exhibitions of its students, "despite having constantly requested exhibitions and refused them as often and quickly as they were suggested" (Sant'Anna, 2011: 117). In the internal bulletins, Ivan Serpa's children's classes gained prominence, and every year during the 1950s the children's work were exhibited. In 1953, the works of ceramic students were presented alongside the masterpieces of Mestre Vitalino, popular and erudite constituting this planned modernity, but also the popular as a phylogenetic origin of humanity, homologous to childhood for ontogenesis.

Mário Pedrosa played a key role in the presentation of the Grupo Frente, as well as other exhibitions of the museum's students, as he assumed the role of associate of the museum and member of the institution's board of directors, art critic and museum official. This was the case for Olly's first exhibition at this institution in 1960. In 1949 Mário Pedrosa had defended his thesis, "From the affective nature of form in the work of art", to the chair of art and aesthetics history of the Faculty of Architecture in Rio de Janeiro. Geometric abstraction was a way of seeing in practice some of the central concepts he defended there.

Pedrosa was interested in the mechanisms of human perception. He believed that art had a fundamental role in transforming *sensibility* in order to develop an awareness of its historicity and the possibilities of a libertarian and democratic context. Abstraction was the way to achieve this new *sensibility* in a global way, not in the sense of following international trends, but rather of a communicative possibility. His posture also had a political component related to the Brazilian and international contexts concerning both the Communist Party and the Cold War. At the same time, it produced a tension with industrial design, since defending abstraction was to defend art as an expression and not as a technique.

In the 1950s there was still a predominance of an aesthetic paradigm linked to the 1940s' modernism. In Brazil, the legalization of the Communist Party in 1945 led to the affiliation of artists of diverse aesthetic conceptions, who supported in various ways the party's organization. These artists offered works whose sales value was reverted to the party; recognized personalities were nominated for various posts. It multiplied the lectures focused on agrarian reform, the misery of the people and

---

through the design of decorative and bathroom furniture and stage design for theater and Carnival parades. In 1968, he was responsible, together with Karl Heinz Bergmiller, for the English representation of the first Design Biennial of Rio de Janeiro, Industrial Design 68, held at MAM.

[99] I suppose many of the manuscripts in Olly and Werner Reinheimer's Archive are from 1985 and 1986, that is, the interval between Olly's second and last and fatal stroke. After the second one, Olly was left without mobility on the right side of her body and began to write with her left hand. Her handwriting on some manuscripts indicates the approximate date. The dating is also deduced from the content of the writings.

suffering. Often, "indignation toward social conditions was shifted to the materiality of the picture by dignifying suffering, poverty and misery in the aesthetic record" (Reinheimer, 2014). Thus, when the 1950s began, Figurative art was still tied to specific subjects and work was evaluated ethically and morally rather than aesthetically.

Pedrosa's struggle against the instrumentalisation of artists in favor of political interests and to the detriment of aesthetic issues was also a consequence of participating in various debates at the congresses of the International Association of Art Critics – AICA[100], in which he was present. In these congresses the nationalisms that resulted in two wars and the role of art in the maintenance of peace were debated between the lines. In these debates, the individual and subjectivity appeared as resources to which artists should turn to find issues that specifically concerned the interiority in which to found an autonomous art. The main argument was the artist's notion of *freedom*, which matched the Cold War mood.

"Abstract representation posed the challenge of assessing intrinsic issues to the practice of painting, such as the use of textures, the balance of shapes and colors, and the distribution of these in the space of the canvas, paying attention to the composition as a whole, without reference to heteronomous dimensions to the artistic phenomenon" (Reinheimer, 2014: 20). Hegemony of abstract painting over figurative one as an important part of the transition to this new way of doing and speaking about art has been, in Brazil, largely an achievement of Mário Pedrosa. However, it was not only due to the critic. The exchange of information and the sociability among artists, teachers and students in MAM-RJ's workshops contributed to the fact that they were all gradually adhering to abstraction as a path to new forms of artistic expression that emerged in the second half of the 20th century. Sociologist Lígia Dabul (2001) shows in her ethnography of the Parque Lage School of Visual Arts, in the late 1990s, how to construct the identities of artists through didactic devices that consolidate ways of dealing with space, time, the body and artistic materials that are considered significant, legitimate by certain webs of reciprocity.

If art critics' texts are important tools for legitimizing new artistic proposals, other devices should also be considered when thinking about the emergence of any artistic strand. Olly left notes (MA-41, MA-10) that are clues to some of the didactic strategies for assigning meaning to abstraction. It is a summary of how one thinks the question of movement and balance in modern art, from the use of the line. Line can use various lengths, thicknesses and shapes to give the picture *movement*. These forms of graphic representation and the spaces they create are associated with speech and music, creating meanings that did not necessarily exist in earlier times.

Lines that can be thin or thick; interrupted, such as the spoken phrase; with the voice rising or falling, as one sings; can be waved, as in the baroque. They are possible conventions for the interpretation of a visual representation that is abstract,

---

[100] French acronym for Association Internationale des Critiques d'Art.

that is, that does not have an explicit subject. This canon is used today in the reading of any representation, even figurative ones. A nude pencil drawing, for example, is considered more or less *static* according to the stability of the lines' thicknessess constituting it. MAM-RJ's courses were thus so important for the construction of abstraction hegemony and the beginning of a new conception of art as Pedrosa's public defenses of this form of representation. The conventions created and learned in class built a language of their own about art and artistic creation whose meanings were shared among students, artists and intellectuals and disseminated among a wider audience in the columns of the periodicals. In Olly's formative years, these were some conceptions of what was considered legitimate in artistic production.

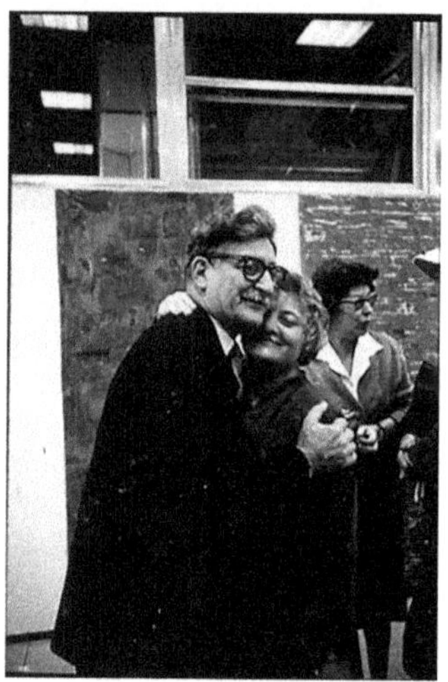

Figure 96: Roberto Burle Marx hugs Olly in her exhibition,
MAM-RJ, 1960.

The artist exhibited her fabric production in MAM-RJ in 1960. The exhibition was titled Olly Tecidos (Olly Fabrics) and consisted of fabrics paintings that were not figurative. They were combinations of colors, lines, and abstract shapes. The fabrics looked like canvases, without chassis. Unfortunately, I did not find any color photos of this first exhibition, but comments from art critics and other social actors attest to the reception that caused the color combinations she used. Poet João Cabral de Melo Neto (1960) wrote in a book dedication that she did *"poetry with colors"* and art critic Frederico Morais (1975) called attention to *"her chromatic wisdom"* as one of her *"greatest qualities"*. Decades later, almost all respondents to the survey still commented on the color of her work.

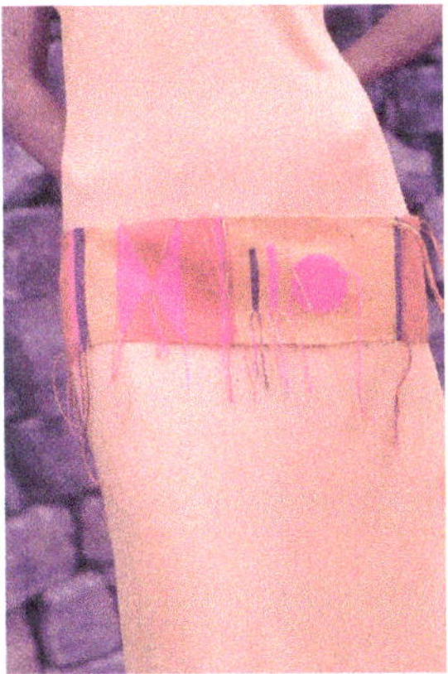

Figure 97: November 1974 (DIA-405).

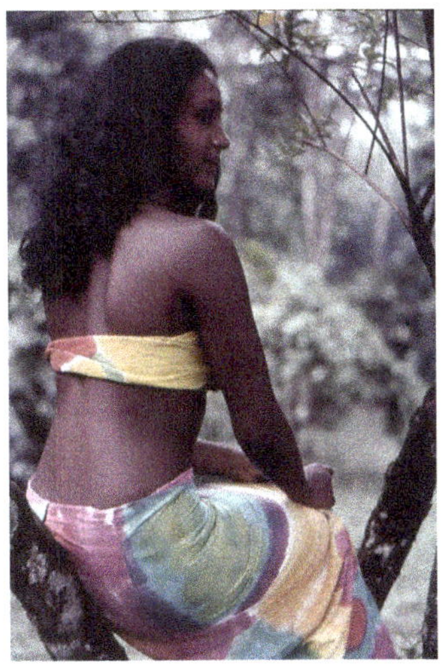

Figure 98: Vera Manhães, 1969 (DIA 553).

After Rio de Janeiro, the show went to the Salvador Museum of Modern Art in Bahia. There, Olly reunited with Norman Westwater and met his future wife, Nedra, who narrated one of these encounters (Interview, 2016)[101]:

---

[101] Nedra and Norman spent their honeymoon in Olly and Werner's apartment in Ipanema when the tenants were traveling.

"Olly Reinheimer was in town to prepare for the opening of her exhibition, Olly Fabrics. As Norman had business to do, I agreed to see her and invite her to spend the weekend at the Baleia Branca (White Whale), which was how we named our house on the island (in Itaparica). She was not in her room at the Hotel da Bahia, so I crossed Campo Grande street to the Castro Alves Theater. I found her preparing her display, in the hall, a vast softened space with curtains from ceiling to floor. Though I did not know her well, the small, sturdy figure pacing from side to side, adjusting the screens while giving orders to a group of assistants, was unmistakable. She looked intimidating.

— "Mrs. Norman", she said, smiling like a child.

— I laughed. "Not yet!" I said.

— "See, I want you to choose a wedding present. Any length of fabric you like. But you can not have it now. Only when the exhibition is over".

— I stuttered thanks and tried to focus on the fabrics, a mixture of bold, hand-painted figurative and plant designs, subtle patterns and batiks, printed in blocks. The color orchestrations were extraordinary, ranging from furious to the most sublime adages.

— Each one is a work of art! I said, confused "I'll need Norman to help me decide".

— "You are perfectly capable of making your own choice", replied Olly[102].

(From this trip we find in the archive the pamphlet of the White Whale mentioned in the previous chapter.) In item 4.3 the cloth that was offered to Nedra was witness to Nedra's testimony, in 2015).

The exhibition was the result of Lina Bo Bardi and Odorico Tavares' invitation. From the Salvador museum it went to the II Annual Salon of Curitiba, at the Museum of Modern Art of Curitiba. In 1951, the architect Lina Bo Bardi, Pietro Maria Bardi's second wife, contributed to the establishment of the Institute of Contemporary Art (IAC), the creation of a collection of costumes (or Costume Section, as Bardi preferred) and two fashion shows at Museum of Art of São Paulo – MASP.

---

[102] Excerpt from her unpublished memoir, "An Island in Brazil".

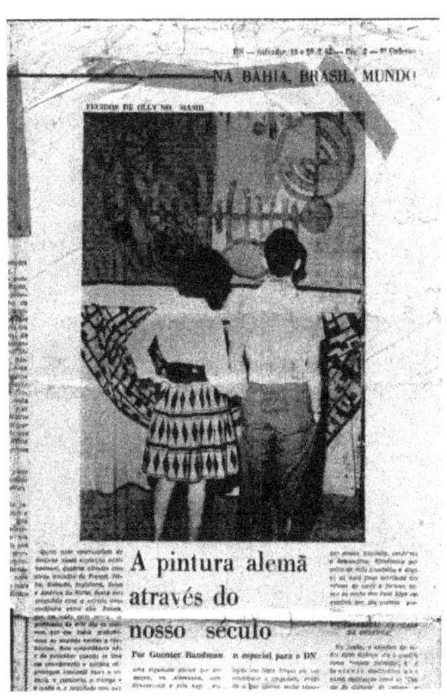

Figure 99: Detail of DN Magazine page, 1961.

Journalist Odorico Tavares (1912-1980) supported the creation of the Museum of Modern Art in Salvador, designed and directed by Lina Bo Bardi, Pietro Maria Bardi and Assis Chateaubriand. Tavares directed in Bahia the newspapers Diário de Notícias, Estado da Bahia and Radio Sociedade da Bahia and, later, TV Itapoan. They were all companies of the Chateaubriand Associates. Therefore, as in Rio de Janeiro, the participation of the media in Bahia was fundamental for the publicity of MAM-RJ and its proposal. In one of the disclosures of Olly's exhibition in Salvador, in DN magazine, we see the photo of her work next to a column on "German painting through the century" (Bandman, 1961). The article speaks of the similarity between German painters dispersed by other countries and their relation to expressionism (Der Blaue Reiter, Die Brücke etc.) and names like Kokoschka, Emil Nolde, Pechstein, among others.

The article is illustrated with two of Olly's fabrics, hung on a wall at the top of the photograph. At the front of the tissues a couple watches with their backs to the reader. The artist is not mentioned in the text, nor does she need to be. A week before, an article in the same magazine talked about her immigration trajectory, her work, and its accumulation with domestic occupations (Guerra, 1961). Throughout the 1960s, several newspaper columns talking about her work make references to the fact that she did not abandon her domestic "obligations" with her son and her husband.

1960s and 1970s in Brazil marked the reverse of English industrialization. In the nineteenth century England it was necessary to negotiate the limits of the family by withdrawing women from the paid labor market and building a theater in which the family and home were reserved for the feminine dimension and paid work and political power to the male one. In the second half of the twentieth century, Brazil had to renegotiate this theater since there was a demand from both industry and the feminist movement for women to enter the paid labor market. If the removal of women from the market was the basis for the obliteration of domestic labor and its consequent devaluation as a way of defining femininity, it was necessary in the second half of the twentieth century to find ways of negotiating with this ideology.

The arts were most consistent with the entry of these white middle-class women into the world of paid work, since the ideology that supported the creative spheres was that of the gift, rather than that of financial gain[103]. In the nineteenth century, an isolation cord of racial degeneration was created around those women who worked publicly and visibly for money. White gloves were one of the ways to socially separate work from idleness (McClintock, 2010: 320). In the twentieth century, women occupying a social position analogous to the use of white gloves entered the labor market, affirming it as an important step for feminism, once again making invisible women who never stopped working.

Anne McClintock discusses the relationship between industrial capitalism and patriarchy and finds in domesticity a space of confluence. The very formulation of a border between public and private, between work space and domestic space was a way of keeping the contradictions of liberalism hidden behind cleavages of gender, class and race. When Olly calls attention to her not abandoning the domestic work, it is at the same time a way of staying within the acceptable limits of patriarchy and bringing out the contradictions it engenders. While confirming her value as a woman within heterosexual and bourgeois norms, she presented a revolutionary structural condition of economic and professional freedom. Working was a transgression asserted by reinforcing her role as a "family woman", wife and mother. What she exposed was not so much her professional work, as this was to some extent expected from middle-class women during Brazilian industrialization. She exposed the domestic work, the place mothers and wives assumed, converting the subordination into affirmation.

---

[103] Currently, this discourse of financial disinterest and the lack of commitment that founded artistic modernity is no longer accepted without restrictions.

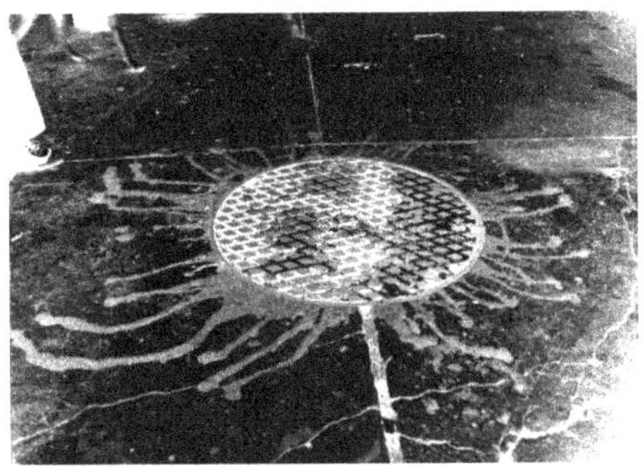

Figure 100: City sewer photography: The subject appeared in the interview with Fayga Ostrower in 1998, when she mentioned Olly's creativity. According to Ostrower, Olly would be walking and suddenly would say regarding a culvert, "that's beautiful", and the culvert would be used in her work. This manhole appears on her collection in a diapositive and enlarged in paper, in a negative version reproduced here.

To some extent, emphasizing domestic work, she put it in evidence and included it in the calculation of the commercial value of her professional work. The contradictions of the industrial world appear then in gender, ethnic and class dimensions. Aesthetically they can be summarized in the event of the manhole photographed to be transformed into a sun (Figure 100). At the same time, it was the exposure of the "abnormal" dimension – the culvert, the indigenous body, popular production, domestic work, the primitive and the irrational – transformed into art that endowed normality to a white, heterosexual, middle-class woman, whose professional condition made her "modern".

The convergence between wife, servant and slave was part of the reinvention of the domestic space by keeping the family in the "natural" sphere and reserving the political dimension of civil society to men to whom the liberal notion of sovereign and rational individuality was restricted. The idea of natural submission – women, slaves, servants, and colonized – was thus the other *par excellence* of the notion of a rational liberal individual. The domestic sphere, as the realm of natural submission, as well as the primitive, scope of racial subjugation – domesticity and empire – are essential elements for the formation of the liberal imagination (McClintock, 2010). However, in the nineteenth century, the rational accounting of the market necessitated the domestic space as an arena of incorporation of the quantification, measurement and surveying systems. Exposing domestic work in the context of Brazilian industrialization was thus a way of making explicit the imbrication of the public sphere and the domestic space by exposing the social and economic value of women's domestic and manual labor. But to do so, the artist relied on her privileges of class, gender and ethnicity over other oppressions.

During the exhibition in Salvador, art critics Jayme Maurício (1961) and Clarival do Prado Valadares (1961) wrote about her in Correio da Manhã, praising her clothes and her success in Salvador. It is not a coincidence that a photo of Olly's work illustrates the article on the German Expressionists. Nathalie Heinich (1991) called attention to the forms of insertion of modern artists in the context of art history. It is necessary to create a "hermeneutical space" within a system of interpretations in which the name of an artist is relevant to several different areas. Identified in this space, the artist is distinguished from her peers and then specialized critics establish her greatness.

The authoritative speeches of professors, art critics and galleries with their public evaluations, whether in workshops or in texts for exhibitions or newspaper columns, establish relations between her work and art history, creating spaces where the artist may or may not come to be inserted either by art historians, historians, psychologists, sociologists or anthropologists. Having an authoritative speech in the period in which one is producing is one way an artist can confirm her ability to produce meaning for a set of actors. Exposing one's work in shows, receiving prizes and being acquired by a clientele are other ways of affirming this capacity, leading to what could be called an artistic *career*.

Expressionism was the space in art history, the differentiation was in charge of Jayme Mauricio himself specialized critic contributing, along with Pedrosa, Berkowitz and others for the establishment of her greatness. The difference between Olly and other artists would be the fact of making a "Brazilian fashion" that, Mauricio associates with interior design, industrial design and typography. The artist was at the same time inserted into the art history and industry through design.

In the 1950s, Gilda Melo e Souza defended her thesis on fashion in São Paulo. The book was published only in 1987, that is, the beginning of the institutionalization of fashion as a higher education in Brazil. It was only in 1978 that the intersection between the clothing industry or the textile industry and fashion began to appear in several of Brazilian Institutes of Higher Education. However, only in 1986, the term fashion was again used in the title of a post-graduation work. Only in 2004 did the Ministry of Education approve the National Curriculum Guidelines for undergraduate courses designating that curricula in fashion education should follow the same educational guidelines as design courses. Currently, courses in fashion have changed their nomenclature to "fashion design", including several disciplines of design theoretical repertoire (Bonadio, 2010).

The association of the artist's work with typography, which gained modernity with Jan Tischichold (1902-1974), was one of the ways used by actors of the time to treat garment design as part of a broader field of design in process of institutionalization in Brazil. Mauricio defended the phenomenon as typically psychological, as well as economic, and still described her creations as posing artistic questions: *"Olly will perhaps be the most qualified contribution to what can be called "Brazilian fashion", solving with her fine creations in cotton and silk, the problem of color and form"* (Maurício, 1961). The following day, Clarival do Prado Valadares (1961) added: *"If, Olly uses the sewing cloth for her painting, she does it with the same dignity as the poet who writes his poems on any paper"*. Psychology, literature, history and industry were being used to interpret her work and constitute a positive value for the textile industry at a time when it became part of mass consumption in Brazil, but lost ground with the introduction of synthetic yarns.

In the nineteenth century, industrialized goods were associated in advertising to the moral values of the British empire. Textile productions manufactured with semi-industrial techniques by middle-class white women in the mid-twentieth century were featured in newspaper columns and illustrated magazines as the way to a creative Brazilian industry. To some extent, it was intended to compensate for the loss of market due to the maintenance of pre-industrial forms, together with the lack of renovation in the machinery system and the entry of the synthetic fabrics with the creativity of a feminine production that attributed to the Brazilian fabric characteristics both tropical and familial.

Olly's work fits in the same context as Rhodia's campaigns with women photographed with clothing that refers to collections with names like coffee and sun, among others (Bonadio, 2014a). The merchandise had played a role of justification and propulsion of the conquest of Africa. In Brazil, the merchandise justified and impelled the conquest of an internal market in part with the use of national icons. The sun, the coffee, the sea was what was being sold on the clothes and fabrics, but also the modernity of the mini-skirt, the sexual "liberation" of women, the entry of women into the labor market. In nineteenth-century British imperial propaganda women disappeared. In the 1960s and 1970s women were both the commodity and the consumer. They are the ones that appear in the photographs dressed in sun, sea, with maps on their skin and with karajá body paintings[104]. This is about the fetish of the commodity, that is, its exchange value and its potency as a sign (McClintock, 2010).

In the exhibitions we can perceive some social relations mobilized by the artist. It shows how *careers* are related to social memberships. As much as the affiliation to abstractionism, it was important that her artistic productions were related to the world of design, which was compatible with MAM-RJ's political project to stimulate the association between art and industry as a way to enhance a singular, national modernity. In this case, it is not an ethnic but institutional affiliation, in the sense of a group of social actors consecrated in the artistic field as critics, producers or consumers/collectors that corroborated specific producers and their productions as being in harmony with the values the institution sought. MAM-RJ gained recognition as an institution for the training of modern artists between the 1950s and the end of 1970. Regardless of the evaluation of time, there was a predisposition to positively qualify the work of those who had been trained in this institution and preferably exposed there. This probably explains in part why the courses mentioned by Olly in her curriculum are exclusively those held at that museum.

Once identified as a student/artist formed in MAM-RJ's courses, her *sensibility* was attested by the authority of critics and gallery owners. Therefore, other possibilities would open up. She had been knitting since at least 1953, when Edith

---

[104] See Figures 30, 87, 88, 89, 90, 97, 98, 104, 106, 108, 109, 110, 114, 119, 120, 121 and 122.

Weitzfelder said she learned some knitting and crochet stitches from her. But it is possible that her craft training is related to the technical schools of Berlin. The approach of her work with art was also made by the erasure of her craft training, which included fashion and design. The reference to modeling classes taught by her was made in the oldest curriculum of the collection (DE-04-B). In all of the following, modeling courses are no longer mentioned.

In the search for school records in Germany, Olga Helene Blank does not appear in the Berlin Research Institute of Education. Therefore, one is not sure of the school she attended, neither in the elementary and middle school nor possible technical schools. However, the quality of the clothes' modeling she created in the 1960s and 1970s and the fact that she taught modeling in the Escolinha de Arte of Brazil (Little Art School of Brazil), the Pestalozzi Institute and in the School for Children with Hearing Impairments and the fact she was working with ceramics long before she started taking courses in Brazil suggests that she did some kind of training, which probably includes courses in cutting and sewing.

Edith Weitzfelder (1998), friends with the Reinheimer couple since the 1940s, said she lived in the same village in Bar 20, in Ipanema, where they had a pottery group. Ceramics, as well as weaving, were the disciplines directed at women by the Bauhaus (Simioni, 2010). Probably, the other Berlin schools of Arts and techniques, in that period, shared the same pedagogical structure.

Cut-and-sew learning may also have been done through specialized German and Brazilian magazines. As in Mittweida she was very young, it is possible to suppose that it happened in Berlin. Two schools in the area of design and fashion were famous at the time: Lette-Verein and Reihmannschule. Between 1932 and 1933, there was also Bauhaus which was not as important at the time as the other two.

Lette-Verein and the Reihmannschule were in the Bayrische Viertel (Bavarian district), an elegant neighborhood in which many intellectuals such as Albert Einstein, Erich Fromm, Gisèle Freund and Erwin Piscator lived. There were also many Jews who attended a local Orthodox synagogue. The Reihmannschule, founded by Albert Reihmann in 1902, had textile workshops and training in fashion and design.

The Lette-Verein School was founded in Berlin in 1866 by Wilhelm Adolf Lette as an association to promote the "acquisition of skills by the female sex". They had technical courses such as Commerce, Domestic Sciences, Photographic Education, Telegraph, Typographers School, Book Binding and Metallography (Cytrynowicz and Cytrynowicz, 2015). This school has a file with drawings and modeling of several of its students that deserves to be investigated in the possibility of finding something with Olga's name on it.

It should be remembered that much of Berlin city was destroyed during World War II. The collections were partially reconstituted by the donation of some documents that survived in the hands of their private owners. However, many of these same owners either had to flee the country during the war and even those who remained had part or all of their belongings destroyed. Therefore, although no records have been found, it is possible that Olga was a student of one of these courses. These are just assumptions, but even if she did not attend any of those schools, it is likely that the encouragement of the participation of women in the industrial sphere linked to industry has been the subject of magazines, radio and perhaps other media in Berlin when she resided there.

In an exhibition catalog (MROW-G 61, 1961), Pedrosa and Jayme Mauricio comment on her work, exposed along with tapestries by Fayga Ostrower, Nicola, Ismael Nery, Lisete Meimberg, Douchez, Consolar and Brennand. In many newspaper columns she had already been introduced as a weaver. Like pottery, tapestry had been one of the privileged courses for women at Bauhaus. Paul Klee, along with first student at that school and later teacher Gunta Stadler Stölzl, studied the relation between color and form and the use of natural pigments to dye the threads for weaving. Olly, in addition to producing her paints with industrialized chemicals, also did research on paints with earth, plants and flowers (Figures 27, 91). This was a constant investment in her *career*.

While sewing was a way of gaining some financial autonomy for the poorest women, clothing was, throughout the nineteenth century, the place of class and gender contradictions. As McClintock (2010) argues, the idleness of upper-class women was exhibited in dresses produced by working women under very harsh conditions. In the 1960s, Olly became economically independent in her marriage based on manual labor that had in the past meant subordination of class, race, and gender. The implied exchange in her work, the fabrics transformed or not into clothing and decorative objects, was a direct exchange between a white middle-class woman and others of higher classes – rarely men.

The presence of peripheric groups in these exchanges was not so much in the exploitation of their work by the artist, but in the representation of those groups as a discourse of membership in which the artist was herself holding an ambiguous position before the national Brazilian elites. The possibility of contamination of these elites in relation to the *foreigner*, that is, the danger of ambiguity was contained by the exchange of money (McClintock, 2010). To a certain extent, this ritual exchange of money for artistic production was a form of confirmation of the elites' fantasy of control over this intellectual middle-class. This constituted an important part of the cultural field of the period and, above all, a control over this and other women who were entering the labor market. Industrialization in England, Brazil and a number of other countries was based on the textile industry, as well as slavery, sugar and spices. That is why Hobsbawm (1977) says that when one speaks of industrialization, one necessarily speaks of cotton and slavery.

Olly was designing, painting and sewing her own fabrics and clothing in the 1960s, just as she did the housework. In so doing, she challenged the ideology of female idleness. This emphasis on domestic work was both a way of asserting herself as an intermediate class between the elite and the working classes and a way of reinforcing her German ethnic background. Her "cleansing craze" (testimonial, 1998) can be interpreted as part of a poetics of social discipline and racial purification (McClintock, 2010), serving as part of purification rituals that seek to legitimize the imposition of cultural values on the part of someone who occupied the place of ambiguity: woman, Jew, German, artist, white, heterosexual, middle-class. Some of these attributes serve to neutralize or contradict others.

Regina Gomide Graz, one of the first Brazilian artists to make tapestry had introduced Art Deco in the country through her cushions, rugs and curtains. There was, therefore, some recognition for this practice. Although hierarchically occupying a place of lesser visibility vis-a-vis other artistic materials and techniques, the identification of MAM-RJ's teachers with the Bauhaus's orientation placed tapestry, together with decoration and clothing in privileged places in relation to other historical periods of artistic production in Brazil.

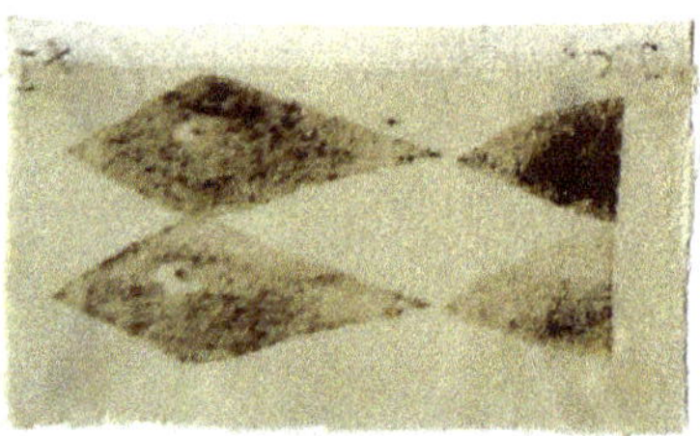

Figure 101: Example of Olly's wood stamping, with stereotyped fish that resembles pre-Columbian motifs (PACA-30).

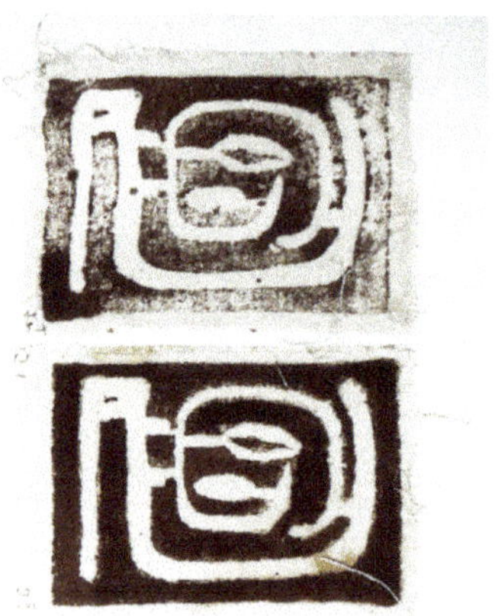

Figure 102: Example of Olly's wood stamping, with stereotyped bird that resembles pre-Columbian motifs (PACA-26a).

There was a proximity of MAM-RJ with the political field in the initial two decades of the institution. This is evidenced both by the presence of important politicians in the exhibition photographs of this period, as well as the sponsorship of exhibitions at the institution and students abroad.

Brazilian industrialization made human contribution in the new world of machines seem seductive. Works such as Olly's seemed a possible solution to legitimize women's entry into the labor market without challenging the female role. This woman was helping build a place of Brazilianness for a national industry that was stagnated against the international market. A newspaper clip, whose origin has not been identified, exalts this: *"Achieving originality among the innumerable masters that heavy industry has developed is a very difficult task. She achieves it with one of Bauhaus' ideals: to embellish the utensils or products of daily use"* (MROW-G 58, 1962).

In 1966, she returned to Lima to exhibit once more at The Art Center. On both trips to this country, she visited archaeological sites and acquired ceramics and Paraca fabrics. Lourdes Mello (Interview, 1998) told me she returned from Peru *"in love. She said she's never seen such a colorful place"*. According to her, the artist changed her chromatic range and incorporated figures in her work after these trips. Abstractionism had already done its job. In assuming MASP's leadership, Mário Pedrosa declared that he was dismissing "militant criticism" and assuming a less aggressive and more neutral position (Pedrosa, 1960, emphases in the original). His entrance at MASP represented then not the institutionalization of abstraction as a style, but of a certain *freedom* or the obligation of innovation through experimentation with supports, techniques and materials that would mark contemporary art for the next decades.

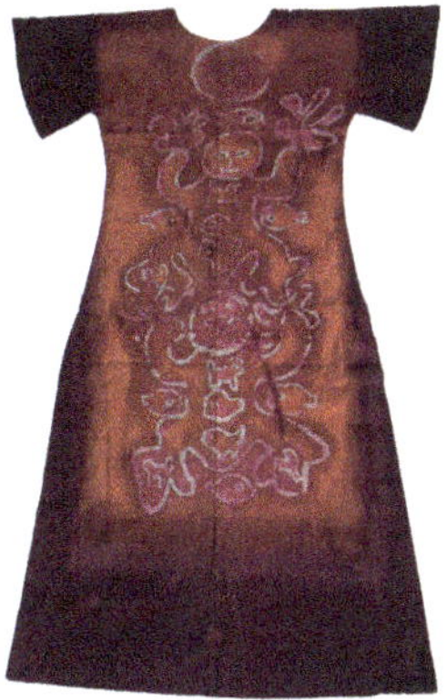

Figure 103: Dress of pre-Columbian inspiration, donated by Maria Luíza Leão to the author, in 1998 (PACT-24).

MASP had a collection of pre-Columbian objects. Probably, as a way of valuing this collection, in 1966, Olly was invited to make a show in that museum Pinacoteca. The event consisted on showing 40 pieces of pre-Columbian inspiration. However, it was not only the thematic coincidence that inspired the invitation, but also the interest of

Pietro Maria Bardi for the clothing as part of an industrial system in interface with artistic production.

Founded in 1951 at MASP, the Institute of Contemporary Art (IAC) offered courses in fashion, design and advertising. Pietro Maria and Lina Bo Bardi promoted in 1951 and 1952, two fashion shows that initiated the formation of a collection of clothing. According to Bonadio (2014), Bardi questioned the separation of "pure" and "applied" art that underpinned European museums.

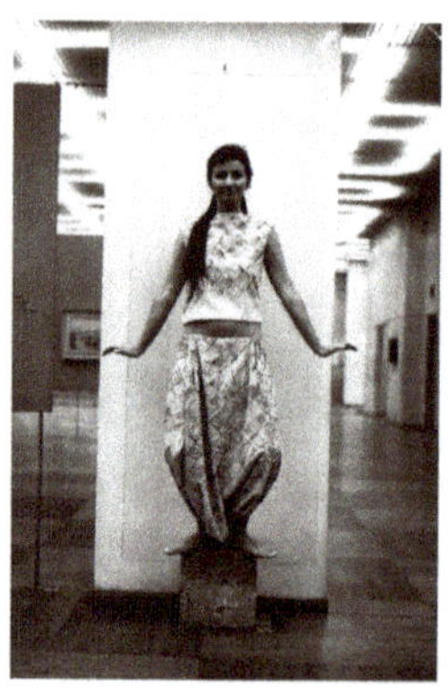

Figure 104: Photo taken at MASP, 1967 (PH-637).

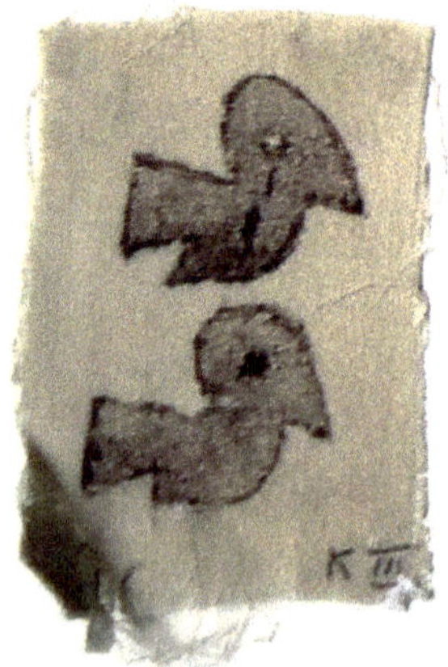

Figure 105: Example of wood stamping in cotton fabric (PACA-32).

Affiliated to the National Fascist Party, since 1926, Pietro Maria Bardi arrived in Brazil in 1946. Part of Mussolini's nationalist project was founded on the valorization of industry, architecture and fashion as much as Italian art. Bardi, who directed MASP from its foundation in 1947, until 1988, brought some of those ideas to the institution. Habitat – Arts in Brazil Magazine conveyed his projects and the ideas of his collaborators. It published some texts defending the development of a Brazilian identity for fashion design made in the country, path followed by his wife, Lina Bo Bardi.

What Olly presented in 1966 had no direct relation to a Brazilian identity, but with a Latinity of which Brazil was a part. The pre-Columbian cultures inserted the country in this Latin continent, at the same time presenting Latin America from a particular modernity by the approximation and valorization of its "primitives". It was, therefore, at the same time to distinguish itself from European art, maintaining with it a strategic identity, a modernity that was constructed in opposition to the antiquity of its internal alterity. The abstraction that had been the focus of Olly's exhibition in the MAMs of Rio, Salvador, and Curitiba had been replaced by a form of figuration that referred to a different idea of origin.

Three years earlier, in 1963, the São Paulo Biennial presented the exhibition "Pre-Hispanic Peru: 3000 years of art". The pre-Columbian exhibition was divided into three geographical areas: Peru (Pre-Hispanic Peru 3000 years of art), Argentina (Argentina Art before history) and Colombia (Colombia Museo Del Oro/30 pieces of Prehispanic goldsmithery) and for each one was produced a specific catalog. But this show was the result of previous efforts. In 1956, the Ambassador in Mexico, Carlos Martins Thompson Flores and Francisco Matarazzo Sobrinho began to negotiate an exhibition on pre-Hispanic architecture. In August of the following year, the newspaper O Tempo reported that there would be a Special Room in the IV Biennial, in the sector dedicated to Architecture. Entitled "4000 Years of Mexican Architecture" the exhibition would have examples of the pre-Columbian architecture until the Mexican Modern period, with emphasis on Olmeca, Teothihuacana, Totonaca, Toltec, Zapoteca and Maya cultures. The exhibition was promoted by the Sociedad de Arquitectos Mexicanos and held in MAM-RJ, MAM-SP and MAM-BA, and ended not participating in the São Paulo Biennial (MAZIERO, 2015).

As a result of the exhibition, in 1963, it was founded the Museum of Art and Archeology of the University of São Paulo, later renamed the Museum of Archeology and Ethnology (MAE). With the exhibition's success, the Bienal tried unsuccessfully to organize a show in 1965. In 1967, the Bienal presented an exhibition of pre-Columbian Peruvian architecture. In 1974 Regina Célia Colônia, who had written an article about Olly for the Ipanema newspaper (Colônia, 1972), released her first book. A collection of poems that had the title Sumaimana, a Quechua word that indicated the author's fascination for the culture of pre-Columbian peoples. In 1978, the Ema Gordon Klabin's Cultural Foundation inaugurated with a collection of these peoples. That same year, the First Biennial of Latin American Art was founded, and "in Caracas, at the First Ibero-American Meeting of Art Critics and Plastic Artists, Carlos Rodriguez Saavedra spoke of an original pre-Columbian coherence" (Sant'Anna, 2014). In 1981, pre-Columbian songs and dances finally gained space at the São Paulo Bienal.

Through Jayme Maurício's article (1966) we learn that Olly's hand-painted fabrics used techniques ranging from drawing, batik, metal, wood and stone engraving, and that since her trip to Peru the artist had been enchanted by the pre-Colombian cultures. Just like shared values took her to collect objects from indigenous material culture, her trips to Lima put her in contact with Peruvian excavations, archaeologists, anthropologists, museologists and interpretations of the production of pre-Colombian peoples. If the aestheticization of indigenous production was being elaborated as a way to re-signify the role of these groups in the scope of the Brazilian national State, in Latin America this movement must have also existed. Some articles and interviewees mentioned a change in the color of the artist's work. The pre-Columbian influence now had the role of justifying a new chromatic range, and also the presence of figuration, redeemed after the 1950s (Reinheimer, 2014).

The associations between clothing, pre-Columbian material culture and colors – as before had been clothing and abstraction – attributed legitimacy to one another contributing to the construction of her *career* and her role in legitimizing an association between certain female work, art and the textile industry in Brazil. But in addition, they were also associations that built a specific modernity for Brazil through subjects, objects and people as a counterpoint to a system of modern art that had been constituted from abstraction, experimentation and abandonment of national themes. I argued somewhere else (Reinheimer, 2014) that modern art from the 1950s onwards was based on a departure from the subject, relying on technical experimentation and a new way of speaking about art. However, this departure from subjects in the visual arts was concomitant with the constitution of a field of action of design professionals and of a certain textile production that was anchored in part on national subjects (cf. Anastassakis, 2014). Both the link between national themes and the internalization of the artistic expression, as well as the institutionalization of design teaching and production in Brazil, were important allies in the museums of modern art and the Bienal de São Paulo.

In Mirante das Artes, a magazine also edited by Pietro Maria Bardi, on the same year Olly produced her show at MASP, Mona Gorovitz (1967) illustrated an article with pictures of Olly's clothes. The article in the Column Fashion & Problems was titled Fashion and Mass Consumption. The text does not speak of the artist or her show, but of the economic-social aspect of fashion, of how it became radically transformed after World War II and about the research of synthetic fibers. This is further evidence that the artist's work was not being integrated into the art system "only" for its aesthetic quality, but for the possibility that it opened to interpretations of broader social phenomena such as the textile industry and gender, class and race relations.

Textile production in Brazil was one of the main drivers for industrialization in the late nineteenth and early twentieth centuries. In the 1880s and the beginning of the next decade, Brazil had its first great industrial outbreak with the implementation of large manufacturing enterprises (Oliveira, 2006). São Paulo and Rio de Janeiro concentrated the largest companies and textile workers. Factories had a presence in people's daily lives, often including housing, leisure and cultivating land for the subsistence of their employees. The Northeast, especially Pernambuco, was the second state in the production of textiles. One of the main investor families in this industry was the owner of Casas Pernambucanas (Leite Lopes, Alvim and Brandão, 2010).

In the early twentieth century, influenced by the anarchist movements and the Russian Revolution, textile workers began to structure themselves into unions and demand better working conditions. In November 1918 the Greve do Pano (Fabric Strike) was organized in Santo Aleixo, Rio de Janeiro (Ribeiro, 2015). During the second World War, with the Brazilian textile industry being the most developed in the country, part of the economic cooperation negotiations was the "Textile Agreement" with UNRRA and CFA (respectively, United Nations Relief and Rehabilitation Administrations and the Conseil François d'Approvisionnement), an agreement that expanded national textile production (Clementino, 2012).

With the end of the war and the expansion of foreign production, the obsolescence of Brazilian equipment was made explicit. In the late 1950s, cotton yarn, a national product, was challenged with the introduction of synthetic fibers and the possibility that it opened to increase productivity due to the speed machines could achieve. In addition, from 1962 onward, the crisis that this industry faced accompanied the slowdown of the world economy. The beginning of the crisis coincided with the beginning of the tax incentive system for development of the Northeast, which led to the bankruptcy of several companies in the Southeast and brought new industries to the region where investments were concentrated.

If, on the one hand, Brazil in the 1950s and 1960s can not be considered a *clothing society* (Stallybrass, 2008), in which fabric was a currency, on the other, the fabric had a symbolic value highlighted in the idea of a national industrial modernity. This industry also represented, both the inequality of class and race that industrialization was supposed to eliminate, and the annoyance of the labor organization and the challenge to hierarchy. Olly's work was in vogue in the 1960s and 1970s also because of its flexibility/malleability/as a reference from which to interpret a diversity of social phenomena, as well as its consonance with the aesthetic values recognized in the period.

4.2. The Contradictory Meaning Of Gender: The Woman As Subject

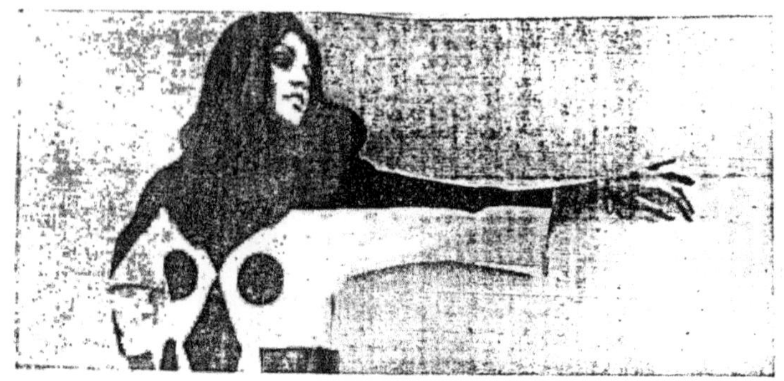

Figure 106a: photo from a two-page article in Jornal do Brasil, September 8th, 1969
(Olly-MROW-G-38).

Almost ten years after her fist exhibition at Museum of Modern Art of Rio de Janeiro Olly was invited to organize a new one in the same institution. The event took place in 1969. She allied with experienced professionals to produce the event. In that space, the garments should not be mistaken for fashion. Clothing in Brazil became, in the 1960s, an expression of revolutionary affirmation, marking mainly the issues of gender and age (Rainho, 2014) and its presentation in museums became possible thanks to various mediations and conceptual exercises that were set in motion.

In the 1969 exhibition, some of the main mediators were the photographer and the event coordinator. Photographs by David Drew Zingg (1923-2000) combined the aesthetic quality with the photographer's political aura. Zingg had arrived in Brazil ten years earlier and had already built a significant reputation by registering intellectuals and actively participating in the bossa nova circuit of Rio.

The event coordinator, director of the MAM-RJ's Institute of Industrial Design (IDI-MAM) Karl Heinz Bergmiller, guaranteed the conditions accomplishment and confirmed the design dimension represented by Olly's work. Born in the city of Bad Tolz, Germany, in 1928, he studied in Ulm between 1951 and 1953. From 1956 to 1958 he had Max Bill as an instructor, coming to São Paulo the following year with a scholarship from the Brazilian government. In 1963, he participated in the institution of the Superior School of Industrial Design (ESDI where he taught until 1998). He moved to Rio de Janeiro in 1967 to work at MAM-RJ and the following year, he structured there IDI-MAM. That same year, he organized the first design biennial of Rio de Janeiro, Industrial Design 68, with Norman Westwater's participation.

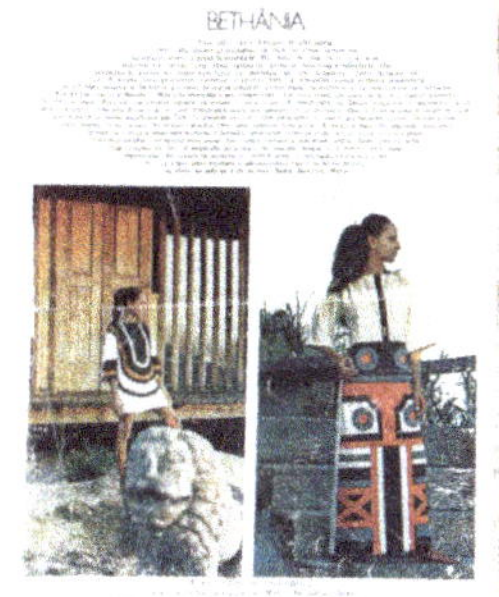 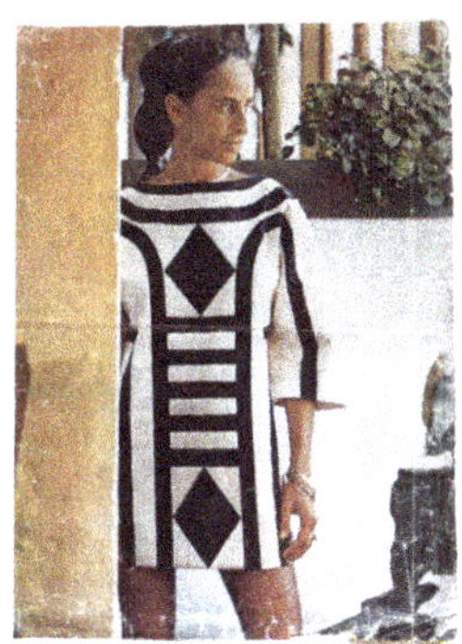

Figure 106b: Article in O Cruzeiro. "Bethânia: the Carajá fashion line". Photos and text: Marisa Alves de Lima. In the opening of the article, she appears with a skirt, short blouse and a Star of David on top of it. The necklace is passed through the blouse in a way that it seems almost to be part of the model body. Turning the page, the necklace appears again composing with a dress that could have been inspired by the graphic patterns of the Oceanic groups. It is not by chance that there is a book on oceanic art in the artist's library. The presence of books on "primitive art", "black art", and on the manifestations of various non-Western groups indicates Olly's interest in researching references outside of realism, naturalism, and classicism. Although books on Greek and Roman art are present in her library, the modern Western artists and less classical cultures like the Etruscans, Chinese, Indians, and so on prevail (MROW-G 66).

Olly's exhibition opened with what the newspaper columns called a *happening*: the models paraded some colorful dresses and others with geometric patterns, in black accompanied by ocher or orange on a beige or white background. The slender bodies of the women hinted beneath the fine colored fabrics and the stylized movements, bare legs and arms, accompanied the rhythm of music. These images were combined with the pictures of clothes and models that were projected in the screens hanging on the museum walls. The sensuality, which enchanted some, disturbed art critic Quirino Campofiorito (1969) who complained about the "*attractive*" and "*noisy*" spectacle that overshadowed the vision "*not letting the dresses created by Olly*" and the jewels by Pedro Correia de Araújo stand out.

For this exhibition, the artist cut and trimmed the clothes, delineated the patterns in pencil and some friends helped paint the models with a paint not suitable for fabric. These prototypes served for those interested in acquiring the models to make their orders. Composing today part of *Olly and Werner Reinheimer's Archive*, what was exposed was not, in the strict sense of the term, clothing. Marc Berkowitz called the set "*objects-dresses*". In testimony to Jornal do Brasil (1969), the artist justified: "*The dress is just the frame for my painting. So, I do not mind exposing some unfinished, tacked, or just cut*".

The design reminded "less is more", one of the references to the Ulm School of Design, founded by Max Bill. Since Bill's arrival in Brazil in 1951 and 1953, important Brazilian intellectuals have established a fruitful dialogue with this School. However, there were different conceptions of what design should be in the Country.

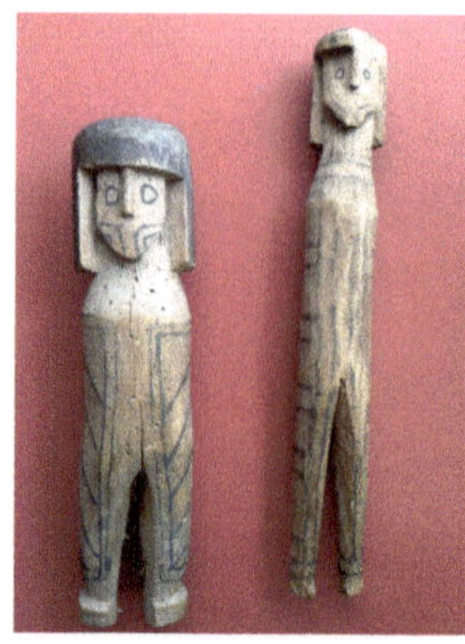

Figure 107: Wooden karajá dolls, Olly and Werner Reinheimer's collection. Photo: Patricia Reinheimer

Although in 1959, Neoconcretism[105] broke with the rationalism of the German design, the vestiges of Ulm School of Design were made noticeable in the several exhibitions that happened in MAM-RJ. Artists and designers originated or acting in Germanic countries throughout the 1950s and 1960s, as well as the direction of IDI by a former student of the School are some of these clues. Even if the numbers can not be taken as "proof" of this influence, we can see in the percentage of shows the relation of respect this institution had with the proposals of the German school. Between 1952 and 1969, 25 exhibitions organized by MAM-RJ (out of a total of 478) were from artists or demonstrations from Germanic countries, that is 20% of the total. If we count from 1959, year of the first exhibition of the group Neoconcreto, the numbers become 18 of 373 expositions, the same 20% of the total of expositions realized.

Of these, Ulm School of Design exhibited in 1956, Frank Lloyd Wright, Knoll Form and concrete artists in 1960, "The good industrial German form" in 1962 and Bauhaus in 1963, same year in which it was exhibited "Engravings and folk sculptures of the Northeast". Olly's work was the conjunction between the German proposal and the industrial project based on handcrafts.

Her works presented clothes with geometric lines and economy of colors taking as reference the body paintings and the dolls in ceramics and wood of the karajá natives. At the same time, she presented other multicolored whose reference, according to the artist, was the tropical fauna and flora. The exhibition was commented by the main critics of the period: Antônio Bento, Quirino Campofiorito, Frederico Morais, Jayme Mauricio, among others. It was sponsored by Itamaraty and, after Rio de Janeiro, according to a newspaper (Jornal do Brasil, 1969), it would follow to Copenhagen,

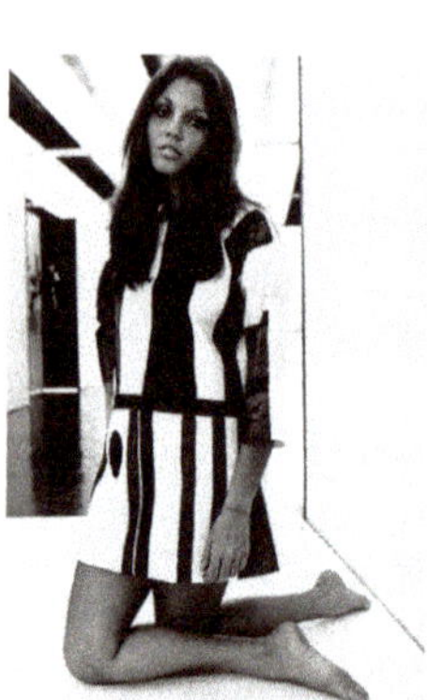

Figure 108: Model in MAM-RJ's gallery with Olly's dress. 1969 (PH-132).

---

[105] Neoconcretism was an artistic movement that emerged in Rio de Janeiro, Brazil, in the late 1950s. The artists who belonged to this movement sought new paths by saying that art was about sensibility, expressiveness, subjectivity, going far beyond geometrism defended by another movement that happened in São Paulo a few years before.

Sweden, Finland, and Germany and then return to Brazil. However, among the documents, there is no confirmation that it has been shown outside the country.

Like works of art, the clothes were signed. The exhibition poster was the photo of a woman wearing a short dress with a painting in large letters forming the museum's acronym, MAM, probably in dark orange and black. The model pointed to the interior of the museum.

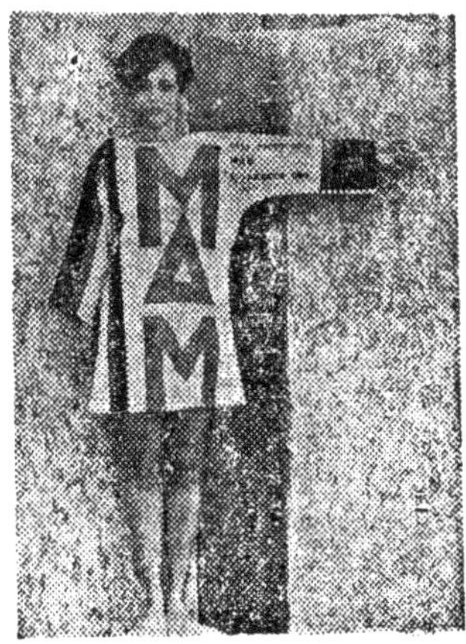

Figure 109: Poster of the 1969 MAM-RJ exhibition.

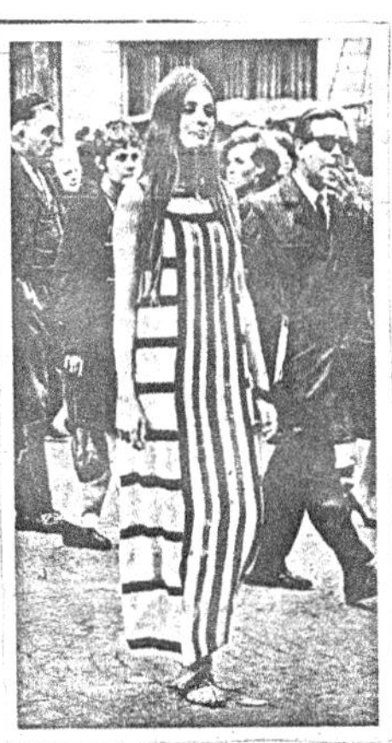

Figure 110: In a statement to the author, the model in this photo said she used Olly's clothes at the Cannes film festival (MROW-G-33).

This exhibition gained the cover of a Sunday's Newspaper special insert (Jornal do Brasil, 1969a). Antonio Bento (1969) spoke in limited editions and *"numbered dresses, like the serigraphy process"*. In that year, the first edition of the "Dicionário das artes plásticas no Brasil" (Dictionary of Plastic Arts in Brazil) was published by art critic Roberto Pontual (1969). This was a reference book for the incipient national artistic field. *Olly and Werner Reinheimer's Archive* have a copy of the book, with dedication to the couple, dated 1972.

Pontual included an entry for Olly Reinheimer, where art critic Mark Berkowitz resumed the neologism objects-dresses to refer to her work. The definition was related to the argument that clothes should not be stored when not in use, but exposed in the house, *"free, with a life of its own"* (MA-78). In explaining the object condition of clothing, Berkowitz seemed to reveal the opacity of things produced by Olly. Not only meanings to be interpreted, but a change in the relationship between subjects, through objects. The fabric regained its materiality, in addition to volume and form, gained movement and political space in the cultural field.

Sculpture was included to the emphasis in painting on fabrics given by critics in her first two exhibitions. Materiality, movement and tactibility were added to color and abstract expressionism. All this put together drew attention to the "stuffness" of fabrics precisely in a show where objects lost their function as clothing (tacked, cut, painted with improper inks, i.e. useless to wear).

The construction of the statute of art for Olly's production and of artist for the producer had the contribution of several social actors and institutions. This transition from the condition of dress to that of object can also be interpreted from what Shapiro (2007) called "artification". To this end, various explicit and implicit artifices were used. In the exhibition presentations a lexicon was used that included the way objects were presented: they were not clothes properly, since many were only tacked or cut. They could not even be acquired, so they were not meant for the market, but for aesthetic appreciation. Attention was drawn to technique and results. In addition to serigraphy, an art technique recognized mainly in the area of design, the objects presented in the exhibition were produced by multiple hands, with the participation of others in the implementation of Olly's guidelines. It is interesting that this detail has been omitted – this information was found among the artist's manuscripts.

As of the eighteenth century, the idea of art emphasized individual authorship as a determining factor of distinction. This was a way of distinguishing art from other types of artistic manifestations, such as handicrafts or folk art. It disregarded completely the fact that even "art" needed the cooperation of other actors for the production to happen. Works such as that of anthropologists Ilana Goldstein (2012) and Sally Price (2000) show how there are distinct notions of authorship between different ethnic groups and how this idea can be manipulated to fit the hierarchy of objects that the Western art system supposes.

In the West, participation of other social actors in the *authorship* of a work is what Howard Becker (1982) discusses when he uses the notion of cooperation to speak about art worlds. By mentioning collective participation in the objects' production for the exhibition, more than exposing the process of production of a particular set of objects, it is possible to take this statement as the visibilization of the *artification* process in which distinct social actors take part to effectively produce this magical transformation[106].

The reference to hierarchically legitimate techniques in graphic design, mentioning artistic styles and influences, alluding to the limitation and numbering of production which refers to the idea of rarity and authenticity, are a considerable part of this construction of an art status for the object. But more than this, to textiles and clothing it was restored the political role obliterated with industrial and capitalist society. To textiles, and by extension to clothing, it was assigned a place in the valorization and institutionalization process of industrial design, in Brazil. As objects, these dresses MAM exhibited became distinguished from the world in which they would normally exist. Neither clothes nor art works in the strict sense of the term, they were transitional things between one and another social category. Its "stuffness" made visible both its loss and its overflow of meaning. The struggles within the national State appear as central as the struggles between peripheric groups, one producing the textile, the other the pattern, one the physical matter, the other the symbolic shield. Gender, race and class in conflict relations and contradictions in the arena of consumption.

It is important to take into account the social context and the value attached to design as one of the dimensions of modernity. Clothing was part of this field of action for "modern artists", the designers, who should ensure that in industrial production *sensibility* and *aesthetic quality* were not lost. This practical interest in social life does not diminish the quality of Olly's creative work. Her ability to improvise in producing her textiles and clothes made possible their conversion into objects. She was not the only one. Fayga Ostrower, Hilda Campofiorito were some of the other women who produced textiles and from them clothes, furniture coverings, curtains and other utilitarian objects.

---

[106] See Bourdieu (2004) for an analysis of the artistic field as a belief system.

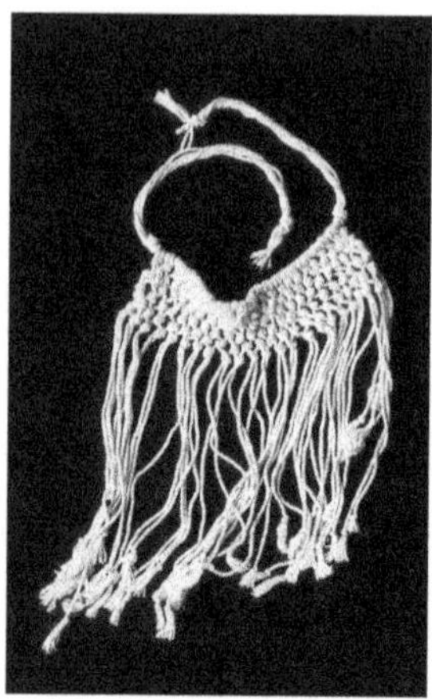

Figure 111: Accessory made of natural cotton by Olly (DIA-823).

The examples of clothing Olly showed at MAM-RJ, instead of being presented as a fashion collection, were treated as art objects. In addition to being hung on the walls as pictures, visitors were provided with space to write the impressions the show had caused them. Consistent with the objects presented, a raw cotton fabric was used for signatures and comments. A group of admirers appears as part of a web of relations, complemented by experts who write columns in the various newspapers in Rio de Janeiro – Jornal do Brasil, O Globo, Última Hora, Correio da Manhã, O Jornal, O Dia – and a book about artists (Roberto Pontual's dictionary), where her production, among that of several other artists, was presented by a recognized art critic making several references to people, countries, institutions and styles.

In this comments/signatures' fabric one can read, in red, *"Brèsil, je t'aime"*. France also appears in two articles on the exhibition. One mentions a supposed statement by model Duda Cavalcanti about having taken 15 dresses designed by Olly to Paris as *"the weapon to stand out among the French"* (Jornal do Brasil, 1969). According to the newspapers, Duda participated in the film *Un choix d'assassins* (1967), in which she used some of the artist's dresses. In another (O Globo, 1969a), the artist Sonia Delaunay is cited as a precursor of the decorative painting on fabrics, creating, between both artists, a line of continuity. Olly's production is at the same time inserted in the French cinematographic context and associated with a well-known Ukrainian artist living in France who produced textiles. The effectiveness of this resource can be measured in the testimony of jewelry designer Clementina Duarte who, when speaking on Olly almost thirty years later, linked her again to Delaunay's pioneerism (Interview, 2015).

The reference to France, and not to Germany, is understandable if we take into account the argument of the inexistence of a "Brazilian fashion", which, in the opinion of the art critic Antônio Bento (1969), made Olly's experience still more "*fruitful*". Again, the term used to speak of the works she created to accompany the clothes is part of the grammar of art and the language was French. Bento (1969) commented that it was inspired by "*pre-Columbian forms and ideograms and the painting of the Carajás, [making] true **assemblages**, using fibers, shells, snails, rolled pebbles and other cool stuff*" (emphasis added).

In Roberto Pontual's art dictionary, Mark Berkowitz divided the exhibition into four sets: 1) clothes inspired by Peruvian subjects; 2) dresses inspired by tropical birds, flowers and light; 3) ordinary dresses, not painted, but taking advantage of native Brazilian material, such as snails, banana trees bark, etc.; 4) Karajá motifs, in rustic fabric and earthy colors.

So, it seems understandable why Germany was not the reference country. It was no longer a matter of constructing the artist's legitimacy through her ethnic origin, or in reference to German expressionism, but a Brazilian fashion, in opposition and also in continuity with a French fashion made by a modern Brazilian artist. It is in this context that her statement should be understood: "*I am Brazilian, and what matters most to me advertising abroad is the colors, shapes and the eminently Brazilian spirit. At this point, my dresses inspired by the karajá dolls are the most important. Those who resemble flowers and birds are representative of the tropical thing. They always please. But there are other tropical countries. The Karajá, on the contraty, are pure Brazil*" (Jornal do Brasil, 1969a).

Therefore, Sonia Delaunay is another hermeneutic space, this time eminently feminine and related to textile production. This was intended to insert Olly in the history of a certain artistic production through the artifice of the so-called *decorative art*. MAM-RJ and institutionalization of design as a project to build modernity is the guiding thread of this exhibition. The idea of *decorative art* was a way that Brazilian modernity could be presented as "*the perfect plastic unit*", "*support for decorative art of the best category*", in clothing that achieved "*the very difficult synthesis of the regional with the universal, with an elegance and apparent ease*" (O Globo, 1969). While furniture, magazines and buildings were considered design objects, fashion was a *decorative art*, made mostly by women. Therefore, it was not without ambiguity that fashion was elevated to the category of design. It was the feminine dimension of this modernity.

Sociologist Ana Paula Simioni (2010) speaks on the hierarchy of artistic genres constituted since the sixteenth century in the artists' process of formation and consecration. In such a system, the classification established painting as "loftier", while "applied arts" would be "lower", seen as domestic dimensions and, by extension, feminine. The type of interpretation that separates intellectual work from manual labor, ascribing to the latter the feminine dimension, is what underlies Ingold's (2002) criticism of an epistemology that separates nature and culture by an internal and external logic, imposed by human reason. In nature, the transformation would come from a pre-established rather than a rational design, while in culture it would be human intelligence to shape things.

In the nineteenth century, women were conceived as inferior and only capable of performing "smaller arts". Tapestries, considered important artistic genre in the Middle Ages, were devalued by its relation to feminine dimension. In the late nineteenth century, *art nouveau* produced a revaluation of the textile supports with the resumption of artisanal methods as a way of overcoming the alienation of the industry. Still, the most valued jobs were made by men. Simioni (2010) presents some cases of men and women working together in which only the male work was recognized: Sonia Delaunay and Robert Delaunay, Camille Claudel and Auguste Rodin, Franz Arp and Sophia Tauber-Arp, Diego Rivera and Frida Kahlo, Hannah Höch and Raoul Hausmann, Vanessa Bell and Duncan Grant, Lee Krasner and Jackson Pollock, and in Brazil, Tarsila do Amaral and Oswald de Andrade and Regina Graz and John Graz are some of them.

Bauhaus and the Ulm School maintained this separation, encouraging women to attend the artistic modalities considered craftwork: ceramics and weaving. Historian Vânia Carneiro de Carvalho showed how objects can be associated with specific genders in long term processes that involve many dimensions of social life. Olly did not question the gender division in the art system. Her insertion in the artistic world was in part an attempt to recover a certain value for textile and garments, seeking professional recognition with a work whose aesthetic qualities can be considered as potentiating the strong social meanings of the raw material. Through these senses we see how gender was nourished by power relations structured also in terms of class and ethnicity.

Feminism has at times assumed the normative stance that women should equate with men by abandoning domestic work. These works eventually built new norms without recognizing women who did not give up their role as mothers and wives as also contributing in the fight against hierarchies related to gender. In the same way, women who sought recognition in the artistic field without necessarily challenging the established parameters had, in their time, impact on the reconfiguration of gender relations. But they also partially contributed to the continuity of class stereotypes and subalternization processes of various groups when they assumed the right to represent them.

Hilda Campofiorito, Fridl Loos, Fayga Ostrower as well as Madeleine Colaço, Marlene Trindade, Arlinda Volpato, Salomé, Vivian Silva, Cândida and Minnie Sardinha, Maria Thereza Camargo, Joana de Azevedo Moura, Sonia Moeller, Heloisa Crocco, Ivandira Dotto, Vera Stedile, Maria Angela Almeida Magalhães, Gilda Azevedo, Maria Kikoler, Bia Vasconcelos, Erika Turk, Ana Goldberger, Concessa Colaço, are some names that together with Olly Reinheimer contributed to modify the Brazilian artistic world in the middle of the 20th century. All of them worked the textile production, some also transforming this production into clothes.

Throughout the 1960s, *happening* had established itself as one of the ways to elevate Brazilian fashion to the category of art, bringing it closer to the status of French production. In São Paulo, Pietro Maria Bardi organized shows at MASP's Pinacoteca. In Rio de Janeiro, the Museum of Modern Art did the same, and Ipanema boutiques, which began to emerge in this decade, used the street for their events (Veste Sagrada, Gipsy, Aniki Bobó, Fragile, Bibba, etc.). According to historian Maria do Carmo Rainho (2014), the collapse of *haute couture* as a privileged system of garment production also led to a change in the spatial distribution of values and commerce in the city. Downtown Rio fell into decay and commercial stores began opening in Copacabana in the 1940s and in Ipanema two decades later. The streets also began to appear as revolutionary, especially after the beginning of the civil-military dictatorship, when fashion photos began to take place on the streets, often simulating the participation of young people in political demonstrations. David Drew Zingg, along with Evandro Teixeira, became famous for producing fashion photography, at a time when there was still no such specialization (Chataignier, 2010). Both registered Olly's work.

The production of this artist was affirmed using the legitimate devices of construction of a Brazilian fashion established in the period, besides allying to recognized or rising people in their areas of professional performance. *Happenings* with photographs by David Drew Zingg, as well as *ambiance* by Bergmiller were complemented with information on the exhibitions in Europe and the consumers of this production: Duda Cavalcanti who took the artist production to Cannes, engraver Tuni Murtinho, ambassador Wladimir Murtinho's wife, who took her garments to India, as well as *"artists and artists' wives, people from TV, film and radio"* who took their outfits to *"Europe, South Africa and the USA"* (Berkowitz, 1969).

Two years later, Betty Friedan bought the poster from that exhibition, along with four dresses created by Olly (s.d. MA-33). In the same manuscript where Friedan was mentioned, the artist cited other consumers of her production: Elisabeth Bishop, Clarice Lispector and Irene Kassorla. Friedan was in Brazil, invited by Rose Marie Muraro, publisher of Vozes, for the launch of her book, "The Feminine Mystique" (1971), at the Museum of Modern Art of Rio de Janeiro and at the Mário de Andrade Municipal Library in São Paulo. The book "became one of the main triggers of the so-called second feminist wave that swept the West" (Duarte, 2006), beginning in the 1970s. Irene Kassorla, American psychologist, published the book "Nice Girls Do" in 1981, where she debated female pleasure and women's frustration over orgasm and desire.

Poet Elizabeth Bishop lived in Brazil between 1951 and early 1970s. She did not hide in her poems the difficulties as a lesbian woman, an orphan and a traveler without roots. Clarice Lispector, Ukranian born, arrived in Brazil in 1922, fleeing from Eastern Europe's pogroms. In her first job, she was the only woman in *A Noite* newsroom, the most important print media organization in Rio de Janeiro at that time (Franklin, 2010). In 1974, she published "Onde Estivestes de Noite" (Where have you been this evening), a collection containing short story "O morto no mar da Urca" (A dead person in Urca's sea) (Lispector, 1974). A chronicle, fiction and first-person commentary, the tale contrasts the death of a stranger to the joy of trying a dress made with a textile painted by Olly.

It is not coincidence that those four women are cited in the same manuscript. Olly grew up in Germany between 1914 and 1936. It was an intellectual and political atmosphere in which the feminist movements, since the nineteenth century, have passed through powerful protest moments. However, the participation of women in the Great War was followed by a setback in the achievements of autonomy, although during the struggle it constituted an experience of freedom and responsibility for the valorization of women's work (Thébaut, 1991). The artist's mother, Clara Hasenberg, for example, worked on the development of technical drawings during that War.

In Germany, political rights were granted to women in 1918. The idea of female professions also had its emergence at that time, albeit at the cost of an overload of domestic labor. Historian Michelle Perrot (Thébaut, 1991) suggests that women's experiences during the war were a strong contribution to the emergence of the modern couple, based on individual achievement rather than family. In the 1920s, in Europe, female emancipation could be seen in short hair and clothing, but the change in women's daily lives was almost inexistent.

The free choice of spouse began to be applied to young men and women, bringing the issue of new spaces and approaches. The period between wars was marked by contradictory movements and signs of liberation from the burden of a female "nature" (Sohn, 1991). In the 1920s, emerged in Berlin, new representations for reform in the legal system for women. For those whose parents could not afford to study, the dream was to be a typist and join a white-collar staff. Material independence and sexual freedom were some of the characteristics of this Berliner woman.

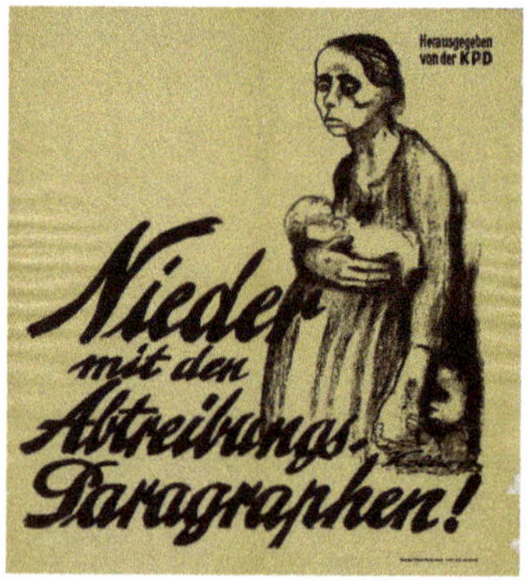

Figure 112: Käthe Kollwitz's Litography (52.5 x 48.4 cm) "End paragraph 218", 1926. German Historic Museum, Berlim. https://www.bild.bundesarchiv.de/

Sexual revolution claimed the creation of sexual education courses in schools and the deletion of paragraph 218 of the German penal code. This paragraph dealt with the penalty applicable to women who practiced abortion. Several family planning offices opened throughout Germany, especially in the working-class neighborhoods. Kätte Kollwitz's[107] prints of female suffering, poverty, and insurrection shocked Germany in the 1920s. Kollwitz's husband was one of the doctors responsible for family planning in Berlin. She created for the communist party a poster that became famous, calling for an end to Article 218 (Walle, 1993).

In this period, one way for women to gain some financial independence without challenging the values of bourgeois morality, especially because it was done at home, was through sewing. According to Perrot (2011), the diffusion of the sewing machine in the second half of the nineteenth century contributed to the rationalization and division of labor in the garment industry. Singer was a well-known German brand that disputed the market with several others. Having one of those was an ambition many times obtained on credit. Another less profitable feminine profession, also linked to clothing, was the production of fabric flowers for hats and embellishments. But in Germany, after 1933, women's emancipation was denounced by National Socialism as a result solely of Jewish influence (Bock, 1991).

Olly's arrival in Brazil coincided with the 1937 Coup in that Country. One of its consequences was the reflux of the feminist movement in Brazil. Her first job there was as cashier in a shop, where she also sold fabric flowers she produced. Again, the civil-military coup in 1964 silenced the feminist movements, as well as other social movements in the country. However, Olly's encounter with Nedra Westwater, narrated above, reveals the artist's defense of Nedra's autonomy in making her own choices (see dialogue between them in item 4.1).

The advances of previous movements were not completely lost. Observing the organization of the couple's apartment, one notices that the artist gained physical and symbolic space along the three decades after joining the artistic field, also because of the dictatorship relaxation in Brazil and the resurgence of feminist movements. However, the idea that women should speak for themselves was already present in her behavior in 1960. Advocacy for the right to opinion was an important part of early feminist struggles. Rainho (2014) describes, in the same decade, the response of the Pontifical Catholic University of Rio de Janeiro to the demand that girls be banned from attending classes wearing miniskirts. According to the University, it was not up to the institution to control what women should wear, but the women's fathers.

It was throughout the 1960s, influenced by the black movement, the hippie movement, and other movements of social contestation that culminated in the events of 1968 around the world, that a new feminism also emerged in Brazil. "For women,

---

[107] Kölwitz played an important role in the Brazilian art world. In the 1930s she became director of the Berlin Art Academy. The fact that she supported other intellectuals and artists in an appeal against National Socialism in 1932 caused her expulsion from the school. The Communist Party organized an exhibition of her works presented in several countries. In Brazil, this exhibition marked Mário Pedrosa's entry into the artistic panorama. He was central for the axiomatic transformations in the Brazilian artistic universe after World War II, Olly's active period. On the transformations in the 1950s see Reinheimer (2014) where it is possible to read Pedrosa's article on Kölwitz in the annexes.

this feminism meant a process of re-education, discovery of one's own potentialities, and review of submission processes". (Costa and Sardenberg, 2008) The motto of this new feminism, "private is political", denied the radical separation between the private sphere (family and personal life) and the public sphere. In Brazil, 1975 marked the final entry of women and related issues into the public sphere and the achievement of a political and symbolic autonomy. This year, Folha de São Paulo Newspaper published an insert in commemoration of the International Women's Year which included an article on Olly: *"Clothes to Wear and Hang on the Wall"* (Folha de São Paulo, 1975).

In the artistic field, Ana Maria Maiolino, Iole de Freitas, Maria do Carmo Secco and Ligia Pape[108], among other artists, produced works that dealt with stereotypes in relation to women, influenced by the writings of Heloneida Studart, Rose Marie Muraro and Carmem da Silva. "From the engravings of Anna Maria Maiolino of the 60s, with self-reference to her domestic life and memories of childhood in Italy, to the concretism of Maria do Carmo Secco, who investigates domestic spaces and the use of the women's image in advertising, it is possible to find the presence of gender issues allied to a feminist concern about the role of women in Brazilian society and in the artistic universe "(Trizoli, 2012: 413).

Olly did not produce speeches about her work. I suppose she had a feminist posture due to some ethnographic data. She was not part of any feminist movement, but she did not resign herself to the "feminine mystique" (Friedan, 1971) of thinking that building a family should be the ultimate goal for women. However, keeping a clean and organized home, fulfilling the expected role of mother and wife, was not questioned but was also not an impediment to her professional life. She thought it was important to say that working did not make her neglect the domestic space and the family. This claim was less due to the work ethic, since housework was not considered as such, rather than a rejoicing in the care of the home, and its broader meaning, family and friends. By this she reinforced the worship of domesticity by presenting this work as an option that was not given to non-white women and economically underprivileged classes. Her race privileges were naturalized by a commercial racism that converted the narrative of industrial progress into a spectacle of consumption in which the various peripheric groups represented in her collections of objects and clothing were the commodities.

The cleaning of the house had at the same time the sense of a racialization of the domestic space and maintenance of the *status quo*, although it appeared as the expression of a feminism that demanded for women the right to professional and financial autonomy. Olly wanted to be identified as a good housewife, as well as an artist. Feminist criticism and empirical work on the status of housewife as

---

[108] About Lígia Pape, see Fernanda Pequeno's doctoral thesis (2013). Pequeno describes Pape's works with ants, cockroaches and video art and develops the idea that eschatology, abjection, and eroticism were strategies to escape political-partisan reality, turning to gender policy.

undervalued labor and also researches on how to maintain the household have informed about normative standards that indicate that women tend to be responsible for the basic supply and men for the extra items. While one's work is widely recognized, that of the other is treated with disdain (Miller, 2002). I can not know how was the process of winning value recognition to her work from her husband and her son, but interviews in the late 1990s and the set of donated letters from the 1970s and 1980s point to a respectful relationship both on the part of the husband and the son.

Two examples of this are: first, the statement of Alaíde Nunes Pereira: "*Olly within marriage had more weight. They were very close companions, but they did not have a marriage within the norms. I always thought they respected each other. But the world was different for both. I always admired it. He felt immensely her death. He felt alone. She filled the house. They were a very special couple*" (testimonial, 1998). The second example is the letters Werner sent to Betty White and Stephen Strauss after his wife's death. In those he declared his solitude and missing his wife. In 1988, he commented: "*Olly continues to receive more letters than I do*" (Reinheimer, 1988). In the context of the letter and the statements of other interviewees there was no grudge as to his wife's success and his relative anonymity, but rather pride.

Previous experience in Germany, as well as Werner's socialist ideals, may have contributed to facilitating her dedication to art as a profession. For socialist feminism, the incorporation of women into production is what would create the basis for the liberation of male domination and family, offering economic independence and removing them from the isolation of the home even if it has not materialized in most cases nor in the experiences of the socialist countries. If Werner effectively took his wife's professional practice as a way of thinking the participation of this family in a more egalitarian economic system can not be affirmed. However, Olly's independence within her marriage and Werner's support were highlighted by several interviewees as perceived dimensions to those who spent time with the couple.

The book that Betty Friedan launched in Brazil discussed the crisis of feminine identity. It analyzed the construction of the women's image as a perfect housewife, mother and wife. The author spoke of the importance for women to seek a social place through a profession. However, women's work does not necessarily represent the achievement of autonomy. It is possible to work and still be marked by a system of dependency, even if the female remuneration represents a large part or all the family income.

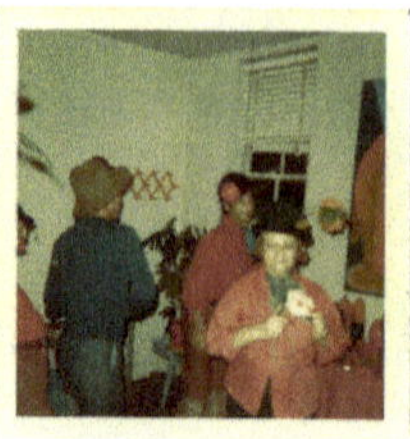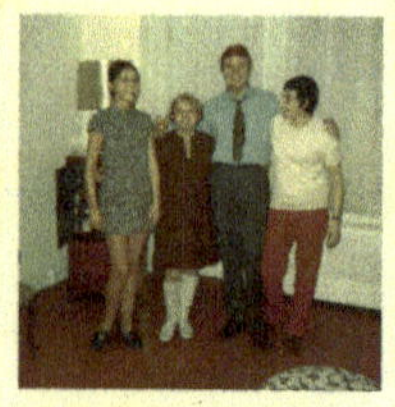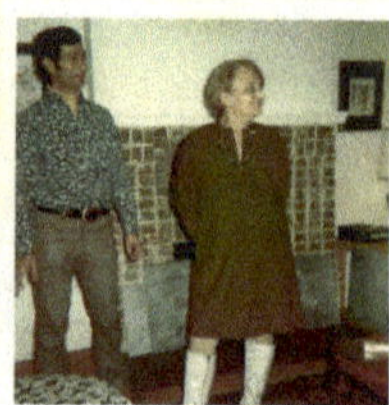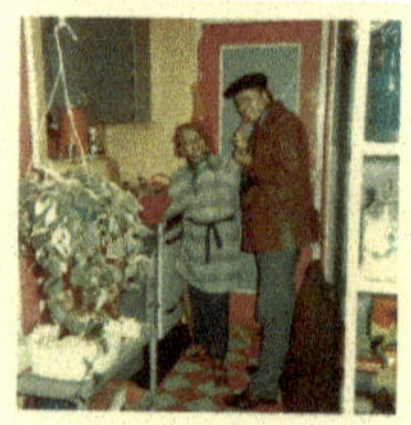

Figure 113: Sequence of the travel album to New York, July 1977. Olly traveled by herself.

However, in the couple's house there was a discourse and a practice of economic co-responsibility for the sustenance and moral autonomy of both. Olly and Werner had effectively built a relationship of mutual respect whose foundations underpinned the artist's professional development. The artistic *career* itself demanded autonomy and social visibility. She had an intense social life independent of her husband. The grandchildren, who spent many weekends with their grandparents, experienced many nights with Werner while Olly attended various events. The construction of a completely independent *career* did not match the socially acceptable and desirable expectations for the social role represented by a white middle-class woman. The fact that she was a foreigner certainly granted her a wider range of social options. However, this positioning that could be classified as feminist can not be understood only by the nationality of the couple. The various dimensions of gender, class, ethnicity, nationality, and sexuality were at stake at all times.

The absence of a discourse on women's autonomy did not invalidate the practice of this relative autonomy. However, it did not prevent also that the maintenance of the role of mother and wife, denounced by Friedan, was at times defended: in testimony, an interviewee commented on some suggestions Olly offered for the construction and maintenance of the middle-class white femininity ideal criticized by Friedan.

Artistic clothing production provided a relatively protected place from socio-symbolic violence and access to public space. In this place, Olly was part of a social web in which several women produced, received and transmitted the new values affirming the feminine accomplishment capacity of the white middle-class woman. She participated in a web of relations that linked academic, artistic and militant circuits in which these women had a privileged space, although the names of the great couturiers, in general, were masculine.

Her production was embedded in a wide spectrum of transformations. Maria do Carmo Rainho (2014) showed how the 1960s witnessed the change in the fashion system. From a class fashion to a consumer fashion (the *prêt-à-porter*). Consumption itself became multifaceted, from various social origins, and youth became a driving force. Age came to replace status as defining what was fashionable. The young body appeared as the great seduction. Fashion models ceased to be the professional models of the catwalk, and young students, artists, girlfriends and friends of photographers, artists and well-known personalities started to model. The "ordinary woman" began to appear also in magazines and clothes began to be like an affirmation of the new values.

Clothing and body became both an exception to the military regime and the affirmation of a young middle-class, sexually free, politically engaged woman with projects for professional training. Therefore, Quirino Campofiorito (1969a) praised Olly's work, but complained about the *"example of feminine modernity"*, *"all that sex-apeal"*. By the end of that decade, this new place for these women, awareness of their values and rights, and especially for Olly, the fact that she had succeeded in her work no longer prevented her from taking up work ethics as a way of affirming she was devoted entirely to her artistic production. Mentioning dedication to her *"domestic obligations"* disappeared entirely (O Dia, 1969).

The artist constructed for herself a trajectory that agreed with the feminist discourses of the period. But she did not challenge the place for white middle-class women in Brazilian society and kept in the shade the double journey of the non-white women from economically underprivileged classes. Publicity presented women using sexuality to forge a place in the consumption society as object of the masculine desire. The feminine figure that emerged in this decade was at the same time a potential subject and an object and was constructed both from liberating, political and social stimuli, and from the tradition and permanence of old stereotypes (Passerini, 1991).

Thus, if women who wore clothes produced by the artist were modern, flexible and mobile, they were still commodities. Olly eventually contributed to the normalization of white, heterosexual, middle-class women beyond stereotypes and domestic cults. She reinforced the body as a boundary for social differences. In opposition to the corpulent black women's bodies, her clothes were generally presented by very thin and tall white women (Jornal do Brasil, 1968). If in her speech she said that she first got to know the women who would wear her clothes to suit the wearer, she herself contributed to the building of a new body model for these white, modern, young, hard-working women. This body did not admit flesh. The sexualization of these "modern" women was disguised by the slavery of thinness as the object of desire.

Philosopher and sociologist Jean Baudrillard (1995) speaks of a "rediscovery" of the body under the sign of physical and sexual liberation in this period. The omnipresence of the subject in advertising, fashion and culture appears through the hygienic, dietetic and therapeutic cult obsessed with youth, elegance, virility/femininity, care, diets and sacrificial practices. The soul is replaced in its moral and ideological function. This relationship with the body reflects and also establishes the forms of relationships between people and things.

Sexuality guides the "rediscovery" of the body. The warmth of the woman is associated with the furniture, the "ambience". This heat/sexuality is the result of a game between hot and cold that is also presented through colors. The body thus becomes object of desire, but also a functional object instrumented in fragmented parts by the publicity that acts by creating a homology between the body and the objects that appear in it. The body becomes a strategy of social control mediated by a discourse of sexual freedom (Baudrillard, 1995).

According to Baudrillard, the ideological confusion that portrays the woman as sexually enslaved and proposes to "release" sexually through the "seemingly free" body, offers an ideal of woman to be consumed. The women who consume this Woman are, in fact, consumed by it. Thus, in the "confusion between women and sexual liberation, the two are neutralized" (Baudrillard, 1995: 146). If there are more rights and freedoms gained, there is what the author calls "objectification as myth" for which Betty Friedan offers in part the content, the "feminine mystique".

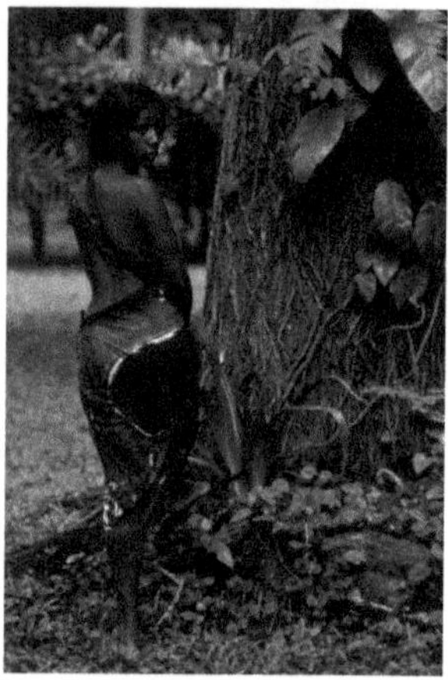

Figure 114: Vera Manhães wearing Olly's fabric.

Friedan's book denounced the manipulation of women by consumer society. Olly's work was fuel for this manipulation by using a woman's ideal to sell her products: this woman was eroticized and appeared as another commodity (Baudrillard, 1995). In many pictures to publicize Olly's work, women are closely associated with nature. The publicity that, in most cases, presented the woman as an object, made her dependent on the products she bought for the execution of her tasks, for the male conquest, or for the education of her children. Inanimate in their ability to perform actions by themselves, they became more of an object, along with those offered in advertising. In her statements, the artist affirmed the initiative, the strength and the autonomy of the women who wore her clothes. There was thus a psychological appeal as a strategy for the docilization of these bodies, whose sensuality did not depend on clothing, but presented itself through it. Her textiles then contributed to the production of a modern-looking consumption, which in the not so long-term would be the focus of criticism of the coming feminist movements. In the arts, feminism gained momentum mainly in the 1970s. In the USA, artists such as Miriam Schapiro questioned both the artistic hierarchies and the representations of this woman objectified by the propaganda. She did so by subverting the canons and modalities of the artistic field until then despised by its "feminine" content. Miriam Schapiro's work "Anonymous Was a Woman", for example, used supposedly "feminine" and "domestic" things like tablecloths, napkins and small embroidered textiles taken from their context and displayed as artistic objects (Simioni, 2010).

4.3. WEAVING SYMBOLOGIES: THE ENCHANTMENT OF CLOTHES

According to museologist Teresa Cristina Toledo de Paula (2006), in Europe, the study of textiles and clothing gained visibility after the 1845 launch of the classic anthropological guide *Notes and Queries* by the Royal Anthropological Institute. The booklet was an attempt to offer colonial administrators, soldiers and missionaries' guidance on how to objectively observe and report colonized peoples. Descriptions of forms of fiber production, weaving, textiles, ornaments and their instruments of production, as well as the questions that should be asked to guide the observation led to the collection of specimens that constituted collections of various types.

For example, collections were made in museums in Lyon, Riggisberg, London, Paris and Quebec based on specific criteria such as technology registration, aesthetics, representativeness in the cultural context and conservation status. At the end of the First World War these museum's textile collections numbered tens of thousands of units named as decorative and/or applied art, organized chronologically, by country or region, with catalogs of the most important producers. The ethnological and ethnographic museums, in turn, formed collections seeking to bring together textiles that were representative of cultures, presenting the life cycles and the different customs of evolutionarily organized peoples.

According to Paula, until the twentieth century, weaving and textile activity were generally male in most of colonizing Europe. Weaving and tissue processing techniques were brought to the colonies by skilled men from Scotland, England and Germany. Only women spun, that is, they prepared the yarn for weaving, still mostly for domestic use. In general, fabrics collected in museums were signs of practices considered masculine: flags, uniforms, and other objects related to battles, wars, and revolutions. While women's textile production was classified as *decorative art, minor art, crafts*, the fabrics of the male universe were about "travelers", "scientists", "men of God", "museum men" and "historians" (Paula, 2006).

In Brazil, presenting indigenous weaving, with all its tools (spindles, looms, bags, baskets, fibers, fabrics and threads) was considered until the beginning of the twentieth century as a proof of the civilizing process. In common sense, the activity of weaving was considered indicative of the removal of the natives from the condition of nature and entry into the sphere of culture. The first indigenous textile objects documented in Brazil appear in a photo of the Museu Paulista. These are two bags attributed to the Botocudos[109] in 1911. Consistent with this evolutionist perspective, in Brazil, weaving was historically a slave activity, afterwards an activity for freed men and poor women.

The first text about textiles in a Brazilian institutional publication was in the Museu Paulista magazine, in 1951: a summary of the thesis of Gilda Mello e Souza, followed by articles by Brazilians and foreigners about sambaquis[110], Tupi tribes and Amazonian caboclos. Textile production in Brazilian museums have always been part of other collections. However, the museum practices in relation to this production were not defined. Exaggeration for the absence of accumulation criteria, concomitant with expressive gaps in groups, periods and regions, indifference to expository forms, instability with the constant transposition of collections from one museum to another, without the necessary documentation informing the origin of things and superficiality in the registration of forms and collection criteria were the focus of these collections until the middle of the twentieth century.

One of the first ways to singularize a textile set in Brazil was through the production of pre-Columbian Andean groups (Peru). Thus, in 1964, a donation by Oscar P. Landmann created perhaps the first collection of textiles and fragments in Brazil, in the Museum of Art and Archeology, later renamed Museum of Archeology and Ethnology. Throughout the 1960s and 1970s, what seems to have been a dispute between the Paulista, Nacional and Goeldi museums (Paula, 2006) in the formation of pre-Columbian Andean tissue collections was also one of the ways to insert the country into a South American antiquity, attributing to Brazil a temporal depth that contradicted the idea of a "young nation".

Among Brazilian indigenous groups, western vestments were an introduction of the settlers initially adopted mainly for ritual occasions. Without the moral connotation that the clothes had for Europeans, the corporal painting among those groups would be the closest social phenomenon to clothing as a way of marking social status, age group and gender. As a visual language, those paintings mark individualities characterized by cultural symbols that distinguish the members of one group from others (Ribeiro, 1978). There is a symbolism of form and color described by anthropologist Berta Ribeiro to which Olly had access in the several books on the subject present in her library. The terms "art and life" were used by Berta to speak of the indistinction of an artistic sphere separated from religion, economy and family, a characteristic opposed to industrialized societies.

The indissociability verbalized in this way, "art and life," was how Olly spoke of her work in several columns, when she gave interviews about her exhibitions. The same kind of social magic that is able to turn different body paintings into forms of status, gender, and age identification can turn clothing into art. As anthropologist Alfred Gell pointed out, "aesthetics is a type of *moral* discourse that depends on the

---

[109] Botocudos is a generic denomination for a set of Brazilian indigenous groups.
[110] Archaeological remains in the coastal regions

acceptance of initial articles of *faith*" (2005, emphasis in the original). Turning things into works of art is then the product of a technology of enchantment, a certain magic embodied in the material worked by the artist. The same kind of magic that makes a body painting turn a teenager into an adult can also turn a dress into art, painting, or sculpture.

This transubstantiation is always the product of various mediations. The magical qualities of the fabrics produced by Olly were also constructed by her critics, through some repeated artifices throughout her trajectory. Since her first exhibition, she was presented as one of the most restless students and a source of pride for MAM-RJ (Mauricio, 1960). Painting, engraving, drawing, and ceramics techniques appeared in almost every report about her work as a way of denying (often explicitly) that her work was fashion, or that her clothing was fashion. Mario Pedrosa and Jayme Mauricio, for example, presented it at the first exhibition at MAM as the *"owner of an absolute technique"* and the clothing was transformed into *"framework [for her] drawings"* (Jornal do Brasil, 1969).

The work presentation invented it as an art form through a proper grammar: Chromatic ranges, formal values, *"plastic ordering with decorative purpose"* (Valadares, 1961), painting done directly on fabric, creativity, inventiveness, research and technique were some of these terms. Olly also used a particular artifice of the creative world; she titled her works. Since her first exhibition at MAM-RJ, critics have already drawn attention to this detail, which did not belong to the world of "applied arts". In 1961, Valadares compared it with the poet who also names the poems. Adding legitimacy to this discourse the consumers were important figures of the art world, politics and the economic elite.

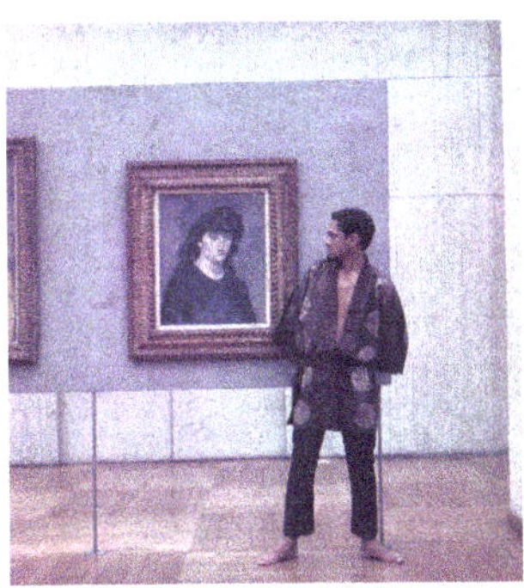

Figure 116: Wagner Seixas Melo
at MASP, 1966 (DIA 873).

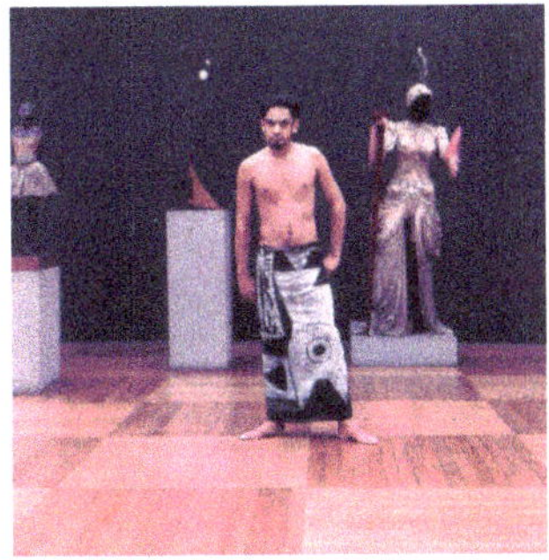

Figure 115: Wagner Seixas
Melo at MASP, 1966
(DIA 926).

Exhibiting in museums and art galleries and having the work presented from artistic techniques was part of the strategies employed. There was talk of a weaver, a painter and a draftswoman who exhibited fabrics that could be attached to the body, like clothing. Only in a second moment the information was complemented by saying she also displayed dresses, kimonos and other costumes. The clothes seemed to be an unfolding of her first performance: weaving, painting, drawing and ceramics.

In 1966, attention was paid to the show at MASP's Pinacoteca, between Cézanne, Renoir, Van Gogh and others, and then at the Petite Galerie in Rio de Janeiro. These were two consecrated art centers in their States. Pietro Maria and Lina Bo Bardi had an investment in clothing as well as an interest in design. Petite Galerie represented an aesthetic and administrative modernity, since it proposed art as a possible investment for the new middle-classes, in installments (Maurício, 1966).

The following year, the association of her work with cinema and Paris was reported in several newspapers (Correio da Manhã, 1967). Theater work also accumulated adjectives. Her clothes were given a *"dramatic quality"* (Jornal do Brasil, 1968), one of the elements of the scenic language in the play *"Stanislaw and the Angry Sex"* by Max Frisch, directed by Wagner Seixas Melo (Figure 115, 116, 117, 118).

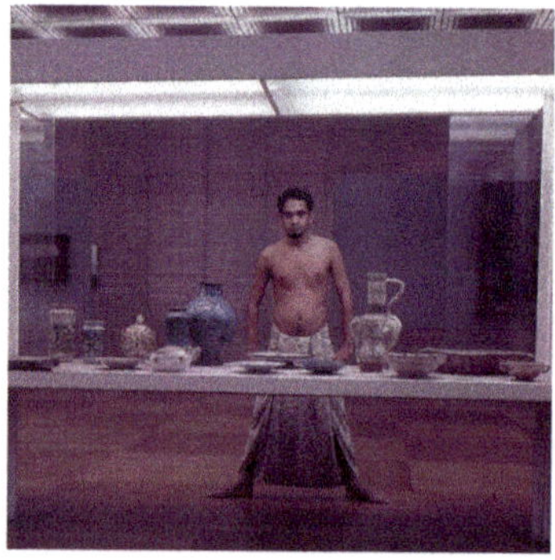

Figure 117: Wagner Seixas Melo, MASP, 1966.

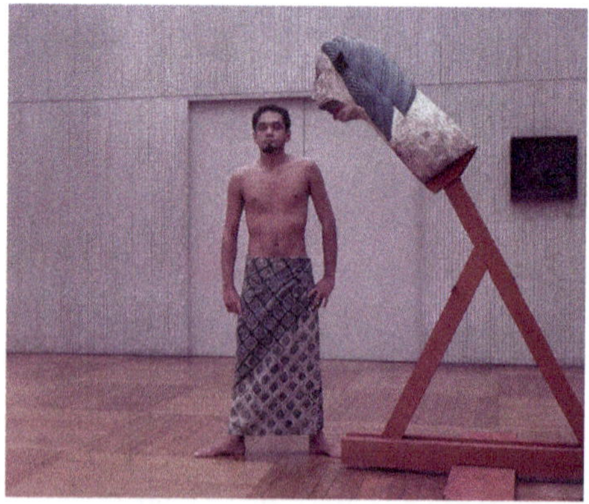

Figure 118: Unknown model, MASP, 1967.

However, this artistic dimension was accompanied by the devaluation associated with "decorative" and "feminine" work. To compliment Olly's standards, Pedrosa used adjectives such as "delicate" and "sweet". Depending on the periodical or the column where it was commented, the titles and subjects tended to be either the fashion or the art dimension of it. However, especially in the 1960s, they mentioned her German origin, her marriage, and domestic work: *"she knows how to divide the hours of the day, to devote herself to her art and to her home"* (Guerra, 1961).

Maurício argued that she was perhaps the most qualified contribution of what could be called *"Brazilian fashion"*, to make up the *"elegance of women"* (MROW-G-61, 1962). The columns in the 1960s were more explicit about decorative, fragile and dreamlike qualities: *"Hands that create dreams for women's vanity"* (MROW-G-58, 1962). It was necessary to assert her courage, mentioning humility.

In addition to a gendered adjective, the idea of "decorative" was an intermediate valuation between technology and art. The craftsmanship of Olly's work was extolled by the manufacture of her paints, with her own secretive recipe. Cotton was her favorite material, several times mentioned in the columns. This created a contrast between the "natural" craftsmanship of her work, and the industrial dimension of clothing, represented by the synthetic fibers that invaded the market.

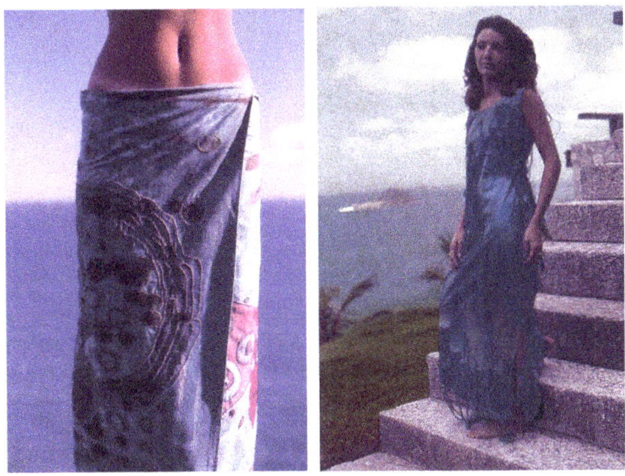

Figure 119: November 1974.

With difficulty in reconciling the art terms in a "decorative" work, Valadares used Herbert Read to speak of the opposition between the value of manual labor in relation to industry and drew attention to the impossibility of taking advantage of it in industrial design, since it would be lost the *natural quality of manual making*. While we perceive the notion of a nature associated with the feminine (as opposed to technology as culture), we also see how this was a way of proposing a less mechanical world. The feminine was presented as an ally of the industry, as the same industry demanded more labor, also offered by women.

Bauhaus was mentioned several times (MROW-G-58, 1962), always affirming the value of *sensibility* applied to objects of daily use. Human and machine coming together to produce the acceptability of an industrialization that was advancing at large paces. The feminine dimension seemed to be what would redeem this industry, sometimes associated with the poorer groups, in the clear link between the two groups and nature as opposed to masculine, culture and technology. Women and peripheric groups would then be the redeemers of a process of dehumanization denounced at that time.

After 1969, the artist began to paint and then embroider on top of the paintings. Some designs were produced based on aerial photos, with the painting and the embroidery made on the cartographic spots. The representation of nature was not new to her work, but had never appeared in the form of maps, geographic and subjective. Technology of knowledge professing to capture the truth about a place, the map anticipates the spatial reality. Instrument of power, it is the representation of colonial territorial control. Without reference to what territories she used, we can only imagine that perhaps the representation of peripheric groups was complemented with the aerial reproduction of their territories.

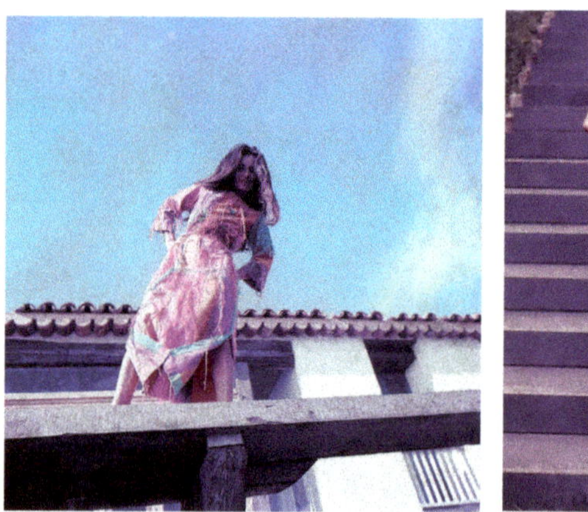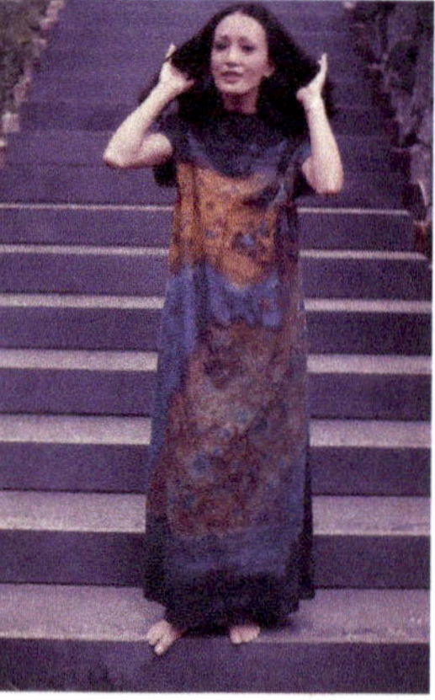

Figure 120: Models photographed at achitect Zanini Calda's house.

In 1972, Olly presented herself in the Jornal de Ipanema (Ipanema's Newspaper) as someone who allowed to rediscover herself: *"you can only find yourself if you allow yourself to be lost. Those who never get lost can not see themselves from another angle. And, therefore, one does not even know if one wants to be what one thinks one is*" (quote by the artist in Cologne, 1972). At MAM-RJ's 1969 exhibit, she had already presented experiences of embroidery on fabric in a work she called Bumba-meu-boi[111]. In these models, loose threads were purposely left to represent horsehair, oxens' tails, and birds' feathers. But the importance of displacements in her creative process, as well as her anguish, became a subject later on, after the impact of the Karajá theme had been surpassed.

As much as "*her source of inspiration*", as she declared in 1975 (Giobbi, 1975), in the elaboration of new subjects, colors and forms, her travels abroad Italy, Greece, Germany, Switzerland, Spain, USA, Mexico, Peru, Turkey and to the interior of Brazil, Sete Cidades[112] and the Northeast, for example also constituted a device to legitimize her work. From these trips, her production became a translation of direct contact with these worlds. The authority of this translation was guaranteed by the direct experience of having been there. The maps then appear as the transcription of this process of subjective reorganization. The impact of travel on her inner universe, constructed her distance from Europe, and also her identity in relation to Brazil. But perhaps, mainly, it was the external projection of an autonomy conquered for herself and other women in the metaphor of territorial control. She claimed for herself the adjective of traveler, just like the fabrics that appeared in European museum collections.

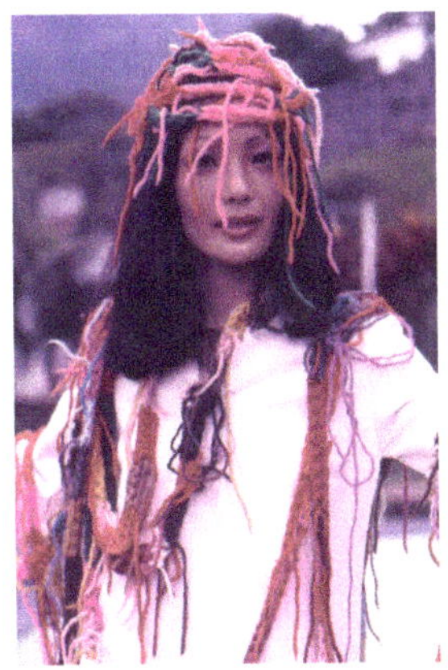

Figure 121: Satio, November 1974.

---

[111] Bumba Meu Boi is one of the folk festivals in Brazil. It happens in several places with different characteristics. It is a prank that has an ox as one of the main characters. The dances happen around the ox made with a wooden frame and covered with embroidered fabric, inside which a person makes evolutions, giving life to the caracter.

[112] A National Park in the North of Piauí, created in 1961, and known for its rupestrian paintings.

Clothing represented the inner and outer world of the artist. Thus, the transition from artistic object to clothing, that is, the transformation of the artistic object into exchange value, was compensated by the incorporated symbolism. The people who bought her work were transformed into pioneered "territories" that had the modern woman exposed: mother, wife, professional artist, traveler.

Olly's speech, however, was that the personality of the wearer should be understood so that the right costume was produced. This independent and professional woman, on the one hand, mother and wife, on the other, was identified inside the buyer and exposed by the clothing. Interior and exterior were thought of as a whole, of which the details and the materials used were part: *"in all her works the fundamental is the value of the material. So, everything matters, existing in every detail a work as a whole"* (Moura, 1975). Every detail was part of a whole, the consumer was not so much transformed as unveiled by Olly's clothing. The trips were then to the outside, to different worlds, but also to the interior, of herself and of the consumers. It involved the transformation of self and others through the process of production and consumption of clothing. An important part of this construction was the inalienable objects (Weiner, 1992) her several collections that materialized those experiences exhibited in her apartment, where her buyers went to choose their textiles.

Once the legitimacy of her creative process had been established and the meanings for her work had been produced, chance and improvisation obliterated the hard work. Thus, in an article titled *"Forms and Colors an Encounter Embroidered in Fantasy"*, Elisabete de Moura (1975) quoted the artist as describing the discovery of a new artistic expression: *"It was by chance. One day my dress (it was very pretty) was ruined. I tried to dye it again, but the colors were already saturated. I tried to embroider the damaged part and found it to be beautiful"*. Technical knowledge was transformed almost into a gift, a "perception" of the aesthetic potential of that double procedure: *"With time, the initial enthusiasm grew and with it the research, study, work and desire for renewal"* (Moura, 1975). Work was thus transformed into study, desire, research, a liminal enterprise that further erased the frontier of art as a professional occupation that requires exercise, labor and by which payment is demanded.

This transformation of the work of art into gift, *sensibility*, is part of the process of building *careers* in the artistic field. This *sensibility* is in fact a set of conventions shared in a web of reciprocity, where everyone "recognizes" in each other this distinctive skill for the attribution of meanings to objects, subjects and techniques that will themselves constitute this sensibility that confirms the elected ones. People, objects and values participate in this web of recognition where everyone is built in the very process of selecting and being selected, recognizing and being recognized, building and legitimating the values constructed through what is exchanged, but also what is held as inalienable.

Thus, as important as the knowledge of new places, peoples and cultural expressions in the geographic and symbolic displacements realized by the artist was the incorporation of new actors to her web of reciprocity. The director of the Museum of Ethnology of Lima (CO-117), for example, whom she met in her trips in 1961 and/or 1962 was mentioned at the time of the show at the MASP Pinacoteca, in 1966. It would be interesting to know with which archaeologists and collectors she had been in contact on those trips. The established web of relations was important enough that in 1970 the Peruvian Embassy entrusted her with collecting donations for the earthquake victims that struck Yungay city that year. In *Olly and Werner Reinheimer's Archive* a document (DEV-18) lists 125 people and institutions and cash values, perhaps, relating to those endowments.

Some of the Brazilian names on the list are Augusto Rodrigues, Vera Mindlin, Jayme Maurício, Margaret Spencer, Beryl and Emiliano Di Cavalcanti, Tuni Murtinho, Sérgio Campos Mello, Maria Leontina, Mário Pedrosa, Enrico Bianco, Candido Portinari, Jorge Amado, Carlos Flexa Ribeiro, Lígia Clark, Ivan Serpa, Antônio Bento, Carlos Scliar, Roberto Burle Marx. Some of the institutions were Escolinha de Arte do Brasil, Museum of Modern Art of São Paulo. The names listed composed the cultural field that projected the values that constituted a *sensibility* that founded a new *style of decoration of the domestic spaces*, from 1950s to 1980s, extolling several peripheric groups hitherto considered alienated as producers of mass consumer goods. There, the web of Brazilian social actors expanded to incorporate actors from other Latin American countries.

Some letters of presentation in the collection show her trips also as devices to expand this mesh. In 1977, Maria Frias, from the Brazilian embassy in Rome, indicated Olly to Ives Saint-Laurent (CO-03); In that same year, João Paulo de Pimentel Brandão presented her to a decorator in London and to Orlando Galveas, of the Brazilian Embassy in Athens (CO-190); in Paris, she met Clementina Duarte (Interview, 2015), through Violeta Arraes, Miguel Arraes' sister. Maps, as well as embroidery and weaving, were then ways of creating the bonds between people and fabricating the social through representation of the territory. Analogous to what the settlers did in the nineteenth century, the cartographic representation appeared again as a power device.

Ritually weaving can mean a unification, intertwining, bonding gesture. Annette Weiner and Jane Schneider (1989) talk about textile and human experience from ethnographic work in small and large, pre-capitalist and capitalist societies, dealing with the symbolic potentialities of the material properties of fabrics. The textile has propelled social organization and political life through history. "As an ornament, wrapped or stacked for exchange or preservation of heritage, the fabric helped social groups to reproduce and gain autonomy or advantages in interacting with others" (Weiner and Schneider, 1989: 1).

It is these social and political contributions they underline, showing in what domains and rituals people recognize these properties in fabric, or transform them through time. Painted, embroidered, stained or dyed, textiles can be transformed into distinct colors, shapes and patterns by gaining through these multiple possibilities an unlimited potential for communication. "Dressed or symbolically displayed, the fabric may denote variations of age, gender, status, rank and group affiliation" (Weiner and Schneider, 1989: 1) and may also convey values and ideological claims.

Fabric can be made of valuable fibers and paints, with dedicated work and artisan virtuosity attracting attention from power holders, including those who build chiefdoms and states. The export of fabric produced by royalty and peasantry through history has been one of the privileged ways to earn foreign currency. Along with gold, jewelry, exotic shells, fabric was a way to lend credibility to political elites.

The textile fibers can evoke ideas of alliance and the envelopment of people in fabric the sense of protection against malevolent forces of the natural or social environment. In the burial ritual, in Judaism, after washing, the body should be wrapped in a white cotton or linen sheet in order to preserve the image of the person in life, while broadening the vision to encompass a spiritual dimension. The white fabric also has the sense of equality among all and neutrality of the dead in the encounter with the creator.

In industrial societies, however, textiles have undergone a process of subalternization by their association with feminine and manual labor. These associations are the result of long-lasting social processes that involve various dimensions and disputes also in artistic world. This process of feminization of the textile media and its association with less intellectualized activities finds its genesis in the way capitalist society of the nineteenth century deprived textile work of its condition of creation, reducing it to a mechanical task.

The hierarchy of artistic work can be traced back to Renaissance and the construction of the founding categories of modern art history. To institute artistic activity as an individual product, Vasari conferred superiority to the *creator* as opposed to the *executor*. This separation was based on a hierarchy that placed the arts that required projects – painting, drawing and architecture – a s "great arts" or "pure arts", while others were reduced to "applied arts" or "handicrafts" (Simioni, 2007).

These so-called "minor arts" were latter associated with the stigma of female labor. In the nineteenth century, there was a naturalization of women as inferior and of these jobs as feminine. Genres such as tapestry and embroidery, central in the Middle Ages, came to bear a double negative symbolic charge of female and manual labor (Simioni, 2010). Ana Paula Simioni draws attention to how Max Weber constructed his *General History of Economics*, published in 1919, Bauhaus inaugural period. For the German sociologist, the difference between *male* professions, like medicine was in the spiritual or magical component, while the textile production would be a form of *labor*. Textile factories employing mostly female labor were the first historical example of alienated labor. The workers, alienated from the final product of their work, were in charge of the manual execution of the repetitive tasks of this industry. The other side of this coin was the masculine and powerful image of the artist, "subject of all stages of his own work, from the idea conception to the final object of his creation, through ownership and free use of the means of production" (Simioni, 2007: 96).

At the end of the nineteenth century the relationship between industry and artisanal work was revised, although it did not disappear. Textile bases have found a new environment in the *Art Nouveaux* movements (French, Austrian, German and Italian) and especially in the English movement Arts & Crafts. The English textile designer and novelist William Morris proposed a resumption of the traditional and artisanal means to overcome the alienation that capitalist society imposed to the workers. Textile production, especially carpets, gained new impetus as a revolutionary artistic proposal (Simioni, 2010). His ideas circulated in several European countries arriving in Germany through the Belgian Henry Van de Velde (1863-1957).

Van de Velde organized in Berlin a group of artists, architects and industrialists who discussed the relations between art and industry. In this context was created the Weimar School of Decorative Arts, base for the Bauhaus (Cáurio, 1985). Bauhaus maintained polarizations that counter-valued such dimensions as glass and metal studios considered *noble* and *industrial* and frequented by male students who would become designers and marginalized techniques such as ceramics and weaving considered *manual* and *traditional* work appropriate for female students who would become artisans. "Thus, the school reiterated the historical tradition of the association between textile means, female labor, and work that was more alienated than properly inventive" (Simioni, 2007).

This division of labor remained within the modernist circles as can be seen by some artists' pairs where women ended up in history as "collaborators", that is, they were relegated to the margins of history, while men gained visibility: Morris's wife and sister made the carpets he drew, but their names are almost unknown; Charlotte Perriand was Le Corbusier's partner in the decorations of his buildings, but her figure was overshadowed by his fame, even though many of his creations are attributed to her; Elise Djo-Bourgeois, was the architect Djo-Bourgeois' wife. She collaborated in his decoration and textiles, but is rarely named. In Brazil, Regina Graz, John Graz's wife, was a companion in the decorating projects of her husband, responsible for the textile part. She was classified, generally, as "executor", while he appears as "designer" (Simioni, 2010).

There was no consensus, however, on the legitimacy of the designer's classification. For some, it was a profession allied with massification that meant only the loss of an "aura" of singularity of the object and therefore of the creator. A devaluing process of both object and artist. In Brazil, as well as probably in other developing countries, industrialization was for many the arrival of a development designed to compensate for cultural backwardness, and it was through the alliance with art that this idea could be conveyed to a public accustomed to the manual production, in direct contact with whoever made their clothes, furniture and other household products.

Thus, although it is important to understand the international context of definitions of artistic and sexual genres, we should not automatically transpose this context into Brazil. When ideas circulate, they are reinterpreted in the light of local situations. On the contrary, for example, the works of Regina Gomide Graz, between the 1920s and 1940s, "described as art without great aesthetic value because they were not able to transcend their condition of applicability" (Simioni, 2007), the works of Olly were valued precisely for being textiles with aesthetic quality. But that does not mean that Olly's work was better than Gomide's. It means Brazilian institutions were ready and needed for women to be taken as capable of aesthetic production with textiles.

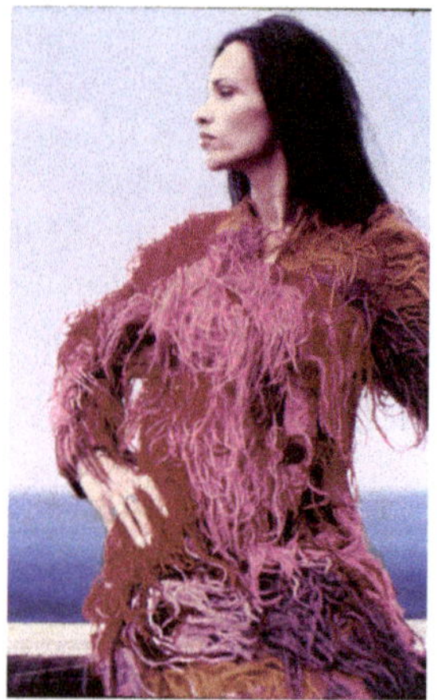

Figure 122: Model Liane Monteiro, 1974.

This difference in the evaluation of textile production of these two periods needs to consider as one of its foundations the symbology that surrounded this media. Among the Navajo, weaving is mentioned by drawing attention to care with moderation and the recommendation not to completely finish the work, leaving an opening somewhere (Scheid and Jesper, 2010). It is this "unfinished" that allows social webs to always renew themselves, including and excluding people, values and things. It was to this "unfinished" that Olly attributed the sense of horsehair, tails and feathers on the *bumba-meu-boi* collection. But this was exploited to its fullest in the 1970s.

The show at the Centro Cultural Lume, at Delfim Moreira Avenue[113], next to Jardim de Alah, was also exhibited in Brasília and São Paulo. It was elected by Mark Berkowitz, Frederico Morais and Flávio de Aquino one of the ten best ones of that year (Aquino 1974; Berkowitz, 1974 and 1974a). Embroidery and weaving became prominent, and Berkowitz, who had already created the neologism objects-dresses for the artist's work made clear the difficulty in defining something that did not fit into

---

[113] This is the avenue on the shore of Leblon, a neiboughring borough from Ipanema. See map for location on item 1.3.

current classifications: neither clothes, nor art work. Berkowitz used a typical device of the German language to create this new word, proposing a compound term from the junction of several nouns, with no space or hyphen between them: roupastapeçariasquadrosfantasias (clothes-tapestries-pictures-fantasies).

In her statement about the new pieces, the tone of fantasy and movement was present: *"The elements I have used in these pieces have an air of celebration, of theater, of joy, it is the colors of the "Bumba-meu-Boi" the Northeastern folkloric dance".* Olly explained that everything had meaning: *"Here, exposed and hung on the wall, they also have life: the wind makes them take the form of mobiles. Those are clothes one wants to touch, to feel the texture"* (Olly with Giobbi, 1975).

Among the Greeks and Romans weaving was a figure of speech that goes back to the organization of the Olympic Games. When the sixteen cities of Élida were in strife it was suggested that they send women to weave the cloak for the statue of Hera. Eight "tribes" sent two women each to perform the task that resulted in the peace achieved through the collective work of weaving.

Before weaving it was necessary to wash the raw wool, to eliminate the dirt and to remove the hard hairs. Like wool, the city was cleaned so that the fabric was well made. The preparatory operations for the weaving business thus unraveled the imbroglios of business from that small federation of women. After the fabrication was finished, the cloth was taken to the temple of Hera and the old mantle was replaced. Weaving then made peace, ordering the contradictions of cities in a unity. In order to maintain this unity, whether of the collective weaving or of the city, the ties of the federation began to be woven every four years. Peace was woven and rewoven. The wool clutter was replaced by a new, orderly cloth, where each fiber was in its place. The weaving is itself the union of opposing movements, while the carding separates, the spinning brings together, resulting in the final fabric (Scheid and Jesper, 2010).

In Brazil, mini-textiles were highlighted after the London Biennial emphasized small formats, drawing attention to the Coptic origin of textiles (Cáurio, 1985). Olly created what she initially called "witches" in reference to pre-Columbian fabric dolls. If in painting the artist had explored animal forms, in weaving predominated the geometric forms, with emphasis in the circle, although birds and fish have not been completely abandoned. Canadian artist Betty White, who lived in Brazil in the 1960s and was Olly's apprentice and helper, showed several annotations from the artist's teaching during her apprenticeship. In many of them the circle is mentioned. Olly argued that it was necessary to learn to make an almost perfect circle for then to be able to make it imperfect: *"it becomes more sensitive"* (MA 37, 26). It is this desired imperfection the axis around which the manual work, the handcraft founded the *rustic style*. The circle was perhaps the most representative figure of her work, symbolizing this calculated *rustic*, but also life, the sun, pregnancy, birth.

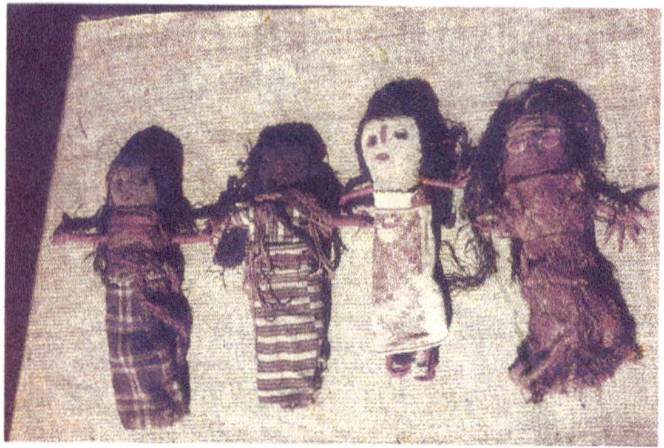

Figure 123: pre-Columbian fabric dolls, origin of Olly's mini-textiles.

Figure 124: Olly's witches

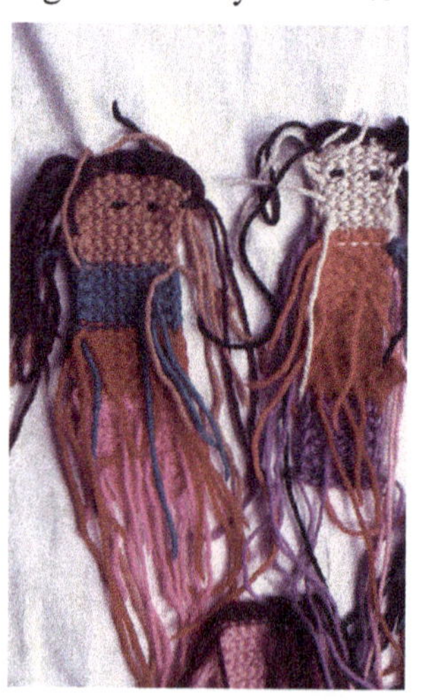

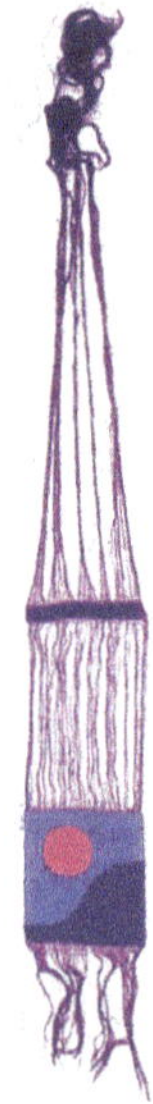

Figure 125: Mini-textile

Aline Campos Melo, wife of the painter Sérgio Campos Melo, said that when she was pregnant, she won a dress with a circle in her belly. According to her, Olly studied where she was going to put the colored shapes to enhance each other's body and work. The artist would explain this production process a few years later: "*The forms appear in certain places of the body. The embroideries are superimposed and accumulated according to a project and although retaining a casual appearance, also occupy precise places. The body would then be a frame, where the forms and colors are distributed and acquire life with the person's movement".*

Almost everybody I interviewed mentioned having or having had textiles and/or clothes produced by Olly used in ritual circumstances that marked life cycles: marriage, honeymoon, pregnancy, head of state reception. Her fabrics were not for everyday use, but for ritual moments. The circle in the pregnant women's belly was mentioned by several women. Her work exalted the creation of life, while playing hide and seek with what was about to happen. Similarly, children were a reference to her work. These references are scattered throughout the artist's house in the collection of Polish magazines on children's art, as well as in the keeping and/or exhibition of several works from her son while he was a child, grandchildren and friends' children and grandchildren. Some of them were photographed and transformed into posters, others framed and hung on the walls.

In an interview filmed from a distance, Betty White shows off her wedding dress which was sent to me latter on with the promise of returning it once the research was finished. Nedra Westwater, for her part, organized for the interview a space that looked like a small shrine. Her texts, photos, glasses were arranged in front of her like offerings to the past, this God that recreates and rejuvenates. As a writer, she maintained throughout her life journals that fed her memories' book about Brazil. She began by answering my questions, but soon she got into the subjects she selected for the testimony. She chose from the book excerpts where Olly and Werner were mentioned, and she began to read them with theatrical intonation.

Their first meeting was on a beach in Itaparica, Bahia. She remembers that Werner wore white shorts and shirt. The meeting had been preceded by a visit to a terreiro de candomblé[114]. Nedra described clothes, lines, gestures, spaces. It was almost possible to hear Werner's laughter and strong accent as he greeted the Scotsman who was to be Nedra's husband, Norman Westwater. While she read the passages, a hanging garment stood witnessing everything: the set of skirt and blouse made with the fabric Olly offered as Nedra's wedding gift revived the past in a ritual testimony (the context in which the fabric was offered to Nedra is described in topic 4.1).

Some interviewees gave me things Olly produced, others said they had passed on to their children (a towel, a weaving), others still felt obliged to justify why they would not "give them back" to me, one person has shown a sheet of paper handmade by Olly that was incorporated into a collage made by another artist whose mother was Werner's suitor after his wife's death. In all these actions, each in its own way, it was made explicit the character of building and maintaining lasting social bonds in which her textile production was part of a mesh that involved people, surpassing death and uniting different generations. This production communicated memberships, to

---

[114] An afro-Brazilian religion temple.

Brazilianness, to a creative profession, to a feminine located in the ambiguous and controversial thresholds of the standards of race and class in which the artist could be classified, to the group of actors of the cultural field of that period.

For Olly, doing the work in the domestic space did not mean her professional practice was restricted to the house. Like any artist, her activity included being present in her peers' exhibitions, participating in the events of the artistic worlds in general and maintaining contact with the possible administrators of the exhibition spaces, consumers and sponsors. What had been considered a domestic art until the 1940s, textile production and sewing, in the particular trajectory of this artist, became a profession that demanded circulation through the city and sociability with the agents of the cultural field. This refers both to a difference between earlier contexts in which sewing was accepted as a home-based profession, and to the fact that her work was valued as art, but it is also referred to the changes in white women, middle-class Brazilian society representations, the role of clothing, including the construction of a certain whiteness, and the way to consume this production.

The use of his production in rituals such as those described in the testimonies only amplified or made explicit what was already common at that moment in terms of the constitution of a Brazilianness that was based on romantic notions of origin and authenticity and incorporated *popular*, *black* and *indigenous* representations in her textile production, an industrial product in vogue in that context. This process was possible from what Anne McClintock called the *racialization of the domestic space* and *fetishization of the "primitive"*. If Olly and Werner argued for colonial struggles and against inequalities in general, they did not question the representation of the other for the reconstruction of patriarchal ideologies that played with women's work, interethnic relations between blacks, whites, Jews, foreigners, among others, and the privileges of class that allowed negotiating these dimensions.

The feminist demands and the demands of industrialization for the entry of white-collar women into the labor market contributed to the constitution of a grammar of opposition to masculine rationality and coldness. This was another way of maintaining women's double journey: a modern professional woman who takes care of the house, but in which this house is no longer only representative of a private, familiar, domestic space. It is also a place of work, of intellectual and creative exchanges. These values were not part of academic or militant discourses but were present as performative dimensions of social life. The woman's entry into the labor market thus contributed to the blurring of boundaries between public and private and to bring home the political, as well as the domestic into the work arena.

Olly's textile production could also be read as a form of domestication of textile workers' claims. Those workers were demanding better wages and working conditions. Fabrics generally appeared as a battlefield, but the textiles produced by the artist calls attention to the role of intellectual work in the qualification of the material, to some extent delegitimizing the demands of the workers by reinforcing the division between intellectual work and technical skills. If, on the one hand, this interpretation may seem arbitrary, on the other hand, it shows the unintended dimensions of social practices.

Fabrics, transformed into clothes, could also be interpreted as playing a role of docilization in the process of industrialization and class struggle. Olly's textile production, as presented by her buyers, had the ability to physically and morally transform the wearer. It was not just the communication of information expressed in painting, colors and patterns.

Sophisticated fabrics could mark prominent positions in different arenas. The manual labor and the subjects used were the great singularizing forces of her textiles, mainly because historically Brazil did not have a tradition as fabric producer, as for example India or England. The elite was one of the mediators of the processes of singularization and commodification. The State appears as another mediator at the same time promoting industrialization and commercialization of the fabrics and sponsoring exhibitions and presenting particular textile productions in special events, singularizing the product.

In the capitalist system, commodification of goods and labor tends to obliterate the value of things that once embodied the social environment from which they came. Things become impersonal and value is allocated by the market. But even if we actually believed that the market was a neutral medium, the actions of weaving, giving, and exchanging modify the quality of the fabrics and consequently the moral quality of those who come into contact with it later.

While the life of the commodity is ephemeral, the unique artifact can cross generations. But as historian Christopher Alan Bayly (2008) has noted, issues of value and community are never totally banished from the market, even in industrialized societies. However, singularity is never conquered definitively, and the life of an artifact can be as short as any other commodity if the memory of its uniqueness is not materialized and patrimonialized.

Textile production in Brazil in the mid-twentieth century was hierarchical. Producing textiles mechanically, as a factory worker, did not have the same status as painting, embroidering, and weaving manually. The social position of industrial weavers was then quite different from those that, like Olly, were associated with commodities considered free from dependence on a boss and which had a more secure market among the economic elite.

Although commodification has changed fabrics' symbolic value, this material has never been merely a commodity. There have always been, over time, "appropriate" textiles for different situations, even if these notions change over time. Thus, its production and distribution has never been determined exclusively by market forces. Looking at Olly's particular trajectory helps to realize that, while losing generic value as a symbolic product, textile production continues to have subtle meanings that need to be investigated both from the point of view of production and consumption.

It is possible to perceive the importance that was attributed to that production, feminine, based on subjects considered national: the slogan of the authoritarian governments was "Brazil, love it or leave it". As a project of modernity, MAM-RJ's emphasis on textile production in the 1950s and 1960s was also a way to attest to a certain civilizing maturity in Brazil, encouraging a perception of the social, cultural and historical density interwoven in textile materials, but it was also a way to call attention to a more palatable industrialization, its feminine side, its association between machine and handcraft, its reconstruction of a gender ideology that reserved for the white, heterosexual, married, middle-class woman not only the invisible domestic labor, but the labor market. Double journey was instituted as a modern ideology in Brazil.

In order to understand the political and public importance of Olly's production, it is necessary to remember the heterogeneity of the spaces in which her textiles could be found, although its class character needs also recognition. In her compositions there was no simple mixture between European modern art and details of a non-specific "primitive art". Her work combined modern elements with selected elements from a particular indigenous culture, a specific northeastern expression, a pre-Columbian group in particular. However, without a discursive elaboration on the meaning of these groups' choice, her clothing collection exhibited in 1969, for example, entitled Karajá, can be read simply as a result of a suitable graphic for transposing of her ideas to textiles. Therefore, even if it was to some extent a tribute to the aesthetic quality of this group and an indication that the symbolism of the indigenous graphics could be present also in the "western" clothes, this interplay was hidden.

The same can be seen in pre-Columbian production. Pre-Columbian is an identity given merely by its temporal character prior to the arrival of the Spaniards, without any mention to the distinct groups that lived in Peru before and after colonial violence. The Paraca textiles that form one of her main reference are not mentioned. If it was not for this research, this reference would have disappeared from her production.

Her work did not confer visibility to the groups. Even if her work was widely publicized, nowhere the groups and their social issues were mentioned. The name karajá, as well as paraca or popular northeastern culture, appeared as labels that always refer to the artist, the models or the museums and galleries where they were exhibited. Therefore, although design in general, and fashion design in particular, have greater visibility than "high art," recourse to the graphic design of peripheric groups did not necessarily confer these groups' prestige. Nevertheless, the social and political context and the mention to the success of the exhibitions indicate that the use of indigenous, black and popular motives were taken as an affirmation of value that had not previously occurred in Brazil.

The textile industry in Brazil was itself a symbol of colonial power, both in the most explicit dimension of the class struggle and in the role of clothing as a synonym of cultural domination among indigenous and African peoples. Unlike India, for example, where clothing symbolized political and social status, in addition to conveying notions of sacredness, purity, and pollution, indigenous groups living in Brazilian territory prior to colonial domination did not use Western textiles for such purposes. Native weavings were generally used for making baskets and nets, and body adornments that served as markers of gender, social status, and generation were generally feathers, paintings, and beads.

The indigenous body was built, in general, in direct relation with nature. Clothing was perhaps one of the earliest ways to make explicit colonial domination. Through tissue wrapping, the body was physically and morally constrained. The overlapping of body paintings in fabric is then an ambiguous way of evoking symbols, at the same time, of domination and resistance. However, if the use of indigenous and popular artistic motifs in design and in art can be criticized in retrospect as misappropriation, it has also given central place to such production in the imagination of the nation. Hence, we find today in many urban street fairs popular and indigenous handcrafts as part of a broad market for ethnic, local and regional symbols.

The use of popular and indigenous references in Olly's textiles, as well as in the collections of Franco Terranova, provided some insight into the idea of interethnic relations for wider arenas than academia and more restricted groups. Decoration and fashion magazines circulated widely and reached various social strata. However, the subject was treated superficially and in generic terms and the concrete indigenous and popular problems were not mentioned. Still, these references would not leave these values unchanged if the work of artists like Olly and others had not been systematically erased. Since the 1960s, visibility of these references does not reflect a considerable change in public opinion with respect to these and other peripheric groups in Brazil. The association between artisanal work, female producers, and autochthonous and popular material culture is a conspiracy that has not yet shown its full power.

4.3.1. Blindex Mandala

In 1978, a fire destroyed the Museum of Modern Art of Rio de Janeiro and its collections. It caused several actors connected to the institution to discuss the directions of contemporary art in the city. Several possible projects have appeared. The period of succession of vanguards and modernisms ended abruptly. "Fire had erased the past. The twisted structure at Parque do Flamengo was now tabula rasa, and the power of something new was once more felt for the Museum of Modern Art" (Sant'Anna, 2014: 7).

In the 1960s it was common for the middle classes to have a seamstress at home once a week, fashioning the models in vogue. In the following decade, the death of young political activist Stuart Angel took his mother, designer Zuzu Angel, to launch a collection that gave visibility to ready-to-wear clothing as a form of social expression. Cotton knit t-shirts have become privileged locus of manifestations: "make love, not war", "the dream is over". In Paris, a group of young artists, architects and dressmakers, who called themselves "The stylists", linked fashion to design, thinking of clothing as a three-dimensional object. In Rio, this fashion school gained followers through the Grupo Moda Rio (Rio Fashion Group), founded in 1978, which influenced the formation of other groups in several Brazilian cities (Chataignier, 2010). In 1983, it appeared in Paris a Museum of Fashion Arts. In the 1980s, it also began to emerge academic production interested in clothing, with research areas such as communication, arts, design, psychology, history and social sciences (Bonadio, 2010).

The social context in which Olly developed her work offered the conditions of possibility for relativizing the inferiority attributed to textile production due to the interest of several social actors in product design as a way to manifest modernity. Clothing appeared as one of the dimensions of this social sphere. This made the artist's work, on the frontier between art and fashion, lean initially to the first. In the final period of her activities, when MAM-RJ's proposal had dispersed and the idea of a quality fashion produced in Brazil was already a reality, she started to identify with the second classification, closer to the commercial dimension of her craft. By the 1970s, she had admitted to calling fashion what she produced, saying she would like to industrialize her creations, even if she admitted she wouldn't know how to manage it as a commercial business.

Her last exhibition was entitled *"Origins: shapes, colors, textures"* and it was first showed in 1981 at the Candido Mendes Gallery, in Ipanema. Several canvases in different sizes and colors presented compositions made of stones, shells, glass, bark, small sculptures, among other objects that seemed to compose small classification systems. The influences that geographic and subjective trips had on her production were represented there. An artist's statement about the exhibition presented her own life as a weaving fabric: *"Life is a textile made of warp and weft. The umbilical cord connects two lives, the threads intertwine, meet and disintegrate"* (Juliano, 1981). For Berkowitz, this exhibition was an introspect moment, a recapitulation of a full and rich life with many memories. They were objects, fragments, relics, moments of silence. The installation at Candido Mendes was a trip through her life. *"It was also the story of an artist for whom art and life merged and completed themselves"* (Berkowitz, 1986).

From this exhibition, the most striking picture is the one made with remnants of MAM-RJ's fire. Its title is simple and straightforward: *"Blindex Mandala (MAM-RJ after the fire)"*. This mandala was the translation of the impact that the destruction of the museum had on Olly, far beyond the ashes, twisted irons, shards of glass and unrecognizable remains. Her mandala was at the same time a magic circle representing perhaps the desire to concentrate energy to reconstruct what was the temple of modernity in Rio, but also a statement about the end of that period (Figure 7).

Simioni (2007) draws attention to the fact that art history is a discursive practice permeated by gender dynamics that crystallize into evaluative categories and hierarchies that define the objects and the people it talks about. The tensions between artistic practices and gender social expectations pose concrete obstacles for women to assert themselves as artists without, however, hindering negotiations to modify and recreate conditions in specific contexts. Textile work was an important dimension in the process of building Olly's trajectory. The magical character of the ancient tradition of weaving reappeared on the cloth painted, embroidered and woven by her during the period of industrial production (Rodrigues, 1962), and it established a particular context of construction of symbologies that guided practices.

It required several class, ethnic, and gender conversions to produce her renown. These conversions involved practices that were often ambiguous in their intentions and contradictory in their consequences. Her trajectory is important both because of the rich material that it bequeathed to us and the analyzes that it can provoke, and for the silence that was established after her death. But it is also due to the indisputable quality of her textile production that it deserves to gain visibility in the current context of institutionalization of a field of fashion studies. At a time when the subject of clothing returns to the proscenium in the Brazilian cultural and academic field, it may be time to include Olly among the recurring but often contradictory names, practices, and forms of dealing with some subjects that have contributed to conform to what has been called a Brazilian fashion world.

CHAPTER 5

And in the End, the Beginning

5.1. FROM TALENTED CREATOR TO INDISTINCT MASS

In 1984, during a trip to Europe, Olly had her first stroke, without serious consequences. The second, in 1985, left the right side of her body paralyzed. It was from this point on that she produced several manuscripts included in *Olly and Werner Reinheimer's Archive*. There she tells part of her trajectory, leaves testimonials and makes inventories. During her convalescence, she asked her visitors to sign a blank canvas and she then painted it, transforming it into her last work. It was also necessary to make sense of this experience, transforming it into art. At the end of that year, she sent a weaved piece to participate in the IV International Miniature Textile Salon, held in Mexico City in May 1986. The work was returned to Werner when the artist had already passed away.

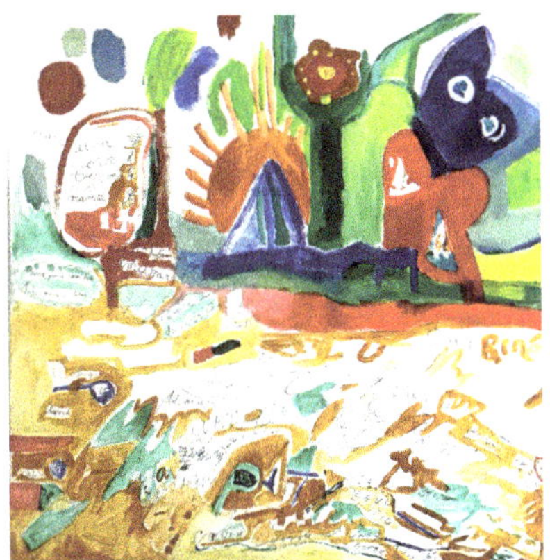

Figure 126: Signed by everyone who visited the artist in the last phase of her illness, this is Olly's farewell work.

From March to April 1986, art critic Frederico Morais organized the exhibition *"Tempos de guerra: Hotel Internacional: Pensão Mauá"* (Times of War: Internacional Hotel: Mauá Pension). According to the critic, he thought of inviting Olly, but she was already very sick. She was therefore only mentioned in the catalog (Morais, 1986). In August, Mark Berkowitz wrote her obituary: *"Olly is gone and left a void. Everyone who passes away saddens us, at least some. Only a few leave a void, they are those who occupy and mark a space with their personality strength, the importance of their being and their doing. This is Olly's case. Olly was an artist in everything she did; painted textiles, made clothes, weaved, made pottery, drew, made paper. She was a full-time artist. Olly lavished creativity. Also, in the conviviality with others: encouraged, criticized, analyzed. Olly was an artist not only in the sense of producing works, but especially in her way of seeing and living"* (Berkowitz, 1986).

To speak is to make. Language and acts of speech make things real. Heinich (2005) has already drawn attention to the fact that in art, worse than speaking ill of an artist or a work is not speaking of him/her at all. After 1986, Olly disappeared, from newspapers, art institutions, books.

Gender considerations are one of the possible justifications. French writer Macelle Marini argues that for male writers, there are three levels of recognition: geniuses, talented writers, and the unsuccessful. Among women writers there are usually only two: the genius exceptions or "the zero of indistinct mass" (1991: 367). When she typifies the categories, the author does not account the possible transformation exemplified by Olly's trajectory, from talented creator, until 1986, to indistinct mass after her death. To think that there is no intermediate possibility for women does not help understanding the practices that lead to the shadowing of women or the erasure of their names after their death.

In addition to the gender dimension, there was the fragility of the material used by the artist. Everybody I interviewed mentioned having had things produced by her. It is worth mentioning also the ambiguity of classifying these things. While some said they had, in the past, works by the artist, others said they had clothing, or fabrics. Almost all lamented the weariness of time and, with it, the absence of vestiges of these works. Perhaps the most interesting exception is Aline Campos Melo. She reacted to the requested interview in 2015, just as she had reacted in 1998: *"I still have a towel painted by her"* and added on the second opportunity: *"it is already very faded, but I like it a lot"*. When we met in 2015, I learned that the towel was passed on to the son and the daughter-in-law.

In 1984, Olly participated in an exhibition of handmade paper produced in Brazil, curated by Otávio Roth, with whom she took a craft paper course at MAM-RJ in 1982. The art critic and curator Paulo Herkenhoff directed the Instituto Nacional de Artes Plásticas (National Institute of Plastic Arts), where the exhibition was held (Funarte, 1984). After her death, Herkenhoff (in a telephone conversation with me in 1998) said he called Werner to talk about Olly and maybe do some research on her. Unfortunately, he did not take the project forward.

The multiplicity of her investments went through ceramics, fabric in multiple forms and subjects and paper making was Frederico Morais' assumption for the disappearance of an artist who, according to him, deserved to be reviewed. In a letter requesting sponsorship to exhibit her craft papers in Mexico, Olly mentioned a subject that had recently emerged as politically relevant, the environment. Perhaps more than the multitude of investments that made it difficult for art critics to locate her work, she lacked the ability to produce discourses about her choices by generalizing the particularity of her subjects. Mentioning the environment, a subject that would become a few decades later central for a middle class invested in a political project that did not challenge class division, seems to legitimize the symbolism of her production.

5.1.1. Writing a Letter is an Act of Love[115].

Olly and Werner Reinheimer's collection of objects and documents had a cardboard box with some of Werner's things. A photograph album represented different moments of his life, with emphasis on more recent trips, without Olly's presence, although she appeared in some older photos. On these trips, Werner appeared with German friends, visiting cities on the outskirts of Pforzheim.

Among the photos is his son's apartment. There, one can see the TV image presenting news about the Constituent Assembly that was established in Brazil in 1986. This was the year of his wife's death. Would democracy's return be a way to make up for the sadness of his 47-year partnership's loss? Two years later, in 1988, Werner wrote to Canadian artist Betty White about a letter he received from Virginia, USA. It was addressed to his wife. The sender, Nichole Kerchman, mailed several skeins of raw wool and asked the artist to make her "a cloud". Olly filled their lives and the apartment with colors and fantasies. The multiple objects she left insisted on remembering her absence. When I started organizing the Archive, I had been living in the apartment for over twenty years. I finished this book six years after the systematization and organization process had started. But I keep still finding things to organize and digitalize in old drawers and cabinets.

In Werner's box, letters exchanged with friends between 1989 and 1991 spoke of the pains of old age and the disappointment caused by the fall of the Berlin Wall and the dissolution of the USSR. Unlike the playful man who had always a joke ready, this box showed a man with a certain bitterness in his last years of life, his poor health, the longing for his friends, but also the joy of sharing the proximity to nature with his son. If it was not possible to return to "his" Black Forest, Teresópolis and Serra dos Órgãos[116] played an important role at the end of his life. Several pictures of flowers and their walks in the garden attest to their appreciation for plants.

In the late 1970s, Pforzheim's German historian contacted him and others of his former resistance group to write their story. The first book, published in 1980, spoke of anti-Semitism in the city, between 1920 and 1980 (Brändle, 1980). The second, published in 1985, spoke of the Pforzheim's Jews (Brändle, 1985) and the third on the main synagogue of the city, destroyed on the Night of Crystal (Brändle, 1990). Probably through Gerhard Brändle's research, Werner received the copy of the Leo

---

[115] Werner Reinheimer in a letter to me in May 1991.
[116] A mountain area in Rio de Janeiro.

Baeck Institute's Book of the Year published in 1981, where one can read an excerpt from his text *"Die Roten Trommler"* (The Red Drummer) (Eckstein, 1918).

Historical remembrance is a way of reconnecting an individual's consciousness of himself as unique and incomparable to the chain of generations and to the social groups to which one belongs. Perhaps because of this, Werner began archiving his correspondence with his colleagues of political militance. As the German sociologist Norbert Elias states, "time plays some very precise functions" (Elias, 1998: 14). Time is also an institution whose signs are interpreted in order to guide the conduct of social members. The process of writing or receiving a letter becomes an instrument of time determination when inserted into a communication system in the form of information or regulation.

The letters that speak of the dissolution of the USSR and the reunification of Germany gain historical dimension by being related to the movement of resistance to Nazism through socialist/communist groups existing in the country before the Second War. An individual experience such as writing and receiving letters becomes an event insofar as it is associated with collective political action. The experience of individuality exacerbated by immigration and the contact with groups so far removed from their origin finds a new place in that collectivity from where he had been arbitrarily removed.

Werner kept in touch with some members of the resistance group. Karl and Klara Schroth, for example, continued to live in Pforzheim, Edmund Zachar and Bob and Betty Zentall lived in New York until the end of their lives. However, the letters stored are all dated from the end of the 1980s, probably stimulated by the manifest interest of the German historian. Coincidentally, this was the period of reunification of Germany and the fall of the Berlin Wall, and therefore letters are often crossed by these subjects, giving temporal depth to their conviction of socialism and its critique of capitalism. According to a friend, *"Werner thought that Gorbachev had betrayed the Communist proposal. He neither accepted nor wanted to understand. That left to which he belonged to did not want to see that Stalinism was not the socialism they wanted"* (testimonial, 2014). However, reading the 1991 letter on the impacts of capitalism in former East Germany showed that it was not the defense of the USSR, but the defeat of socialism and the destructive force of capitalism that bothered Werner and his friends (Ostrower, s.d.).

The end of the dictatorship in Brazil, together with the renewed interest in his political participation, led him to produce some writings. Some of them have been published in Pforzheim's newspapers, others have no reference to where they may have circulated. In these texts, Werner criticized Soviet imperialism and the socialist republics under its rule, but also questioned who was interested in the dissolution of the USSR (Reinheimer, 1990). In 1991, he wrote a text about the 147% adjustment that marked the participation of retirees and seniors at the head of the Movement under that name. His texts are succinct, always have a personal tone and a certain irony. A literary style closer to a charismatic leader than to politicians or academicians.

In 1992, I was living out of Brazil. I had a return trip planed when I received a letter from Werner: *"Thank you very much for your February 19th letter. It smelled a lot of yearning for your relatives and probably also for the beach. We, the old guard, understand the intense pains of youth. When you come to Rio we will deal together with all the stuff we are going to do"* (Reinheimer, 1992). We never met again[117].

5.2. THE IMPROVISATION OF A SYMBOLIC CARTOGRAPHY

In 1952, the São Paulo Museum of Art (MASP) organized a fashion show with pieces created in its workshops and *"inspired by the fauna and flora, indigenous and Afro-Brazilian cultures and popular customs"*. Pietro Maria Bardi, then director of the museum, intended to implement a Center for Fashion Studies. The Habitat Magazine, created and directed by Bardi, summarized the actions of the museum *"in the field of design"* explaining that the *"museum intended to enter the sphere of fashion by creating a school for dressmakers and artisans who would devote themselves to the problems of fashion"* (Habitat, 1952).

The newspaper Folha da Manhã published a note about the Center and the professionals involved in the project: **German** Klara Hartoch, responsible for the museum's weaving studio, *"created weaved textiles inspired by Marajoara[118] pottery and woven straw basketwork inspired by indigenous groups"*; **Argentinian** Carybé (1911-97), *"created prints inspired by candomblé"*[119]; **Italian** Roberto Sambonet (1924-1995), *"designed most of the collection, also creating prints out of Marajoara and anthuriums[120] inspiration, and was responsible for the visual design of the event's graphic pieces, Brazilian landscape artist Roberto Burle Marx (1909-1994), who also designed prints for the collection"*. (Folha da Manhã, 1952). A few years later, Olly's exhibition at MASP was a corollary of this project.

In 1957, MAM-RJ held a poster exhibition which featured a piece from a show presented at the Neuchatel Museum of Ethnology at the end of 1955. At that exhibition, the museum showed *"modern Brazilian art"* alongside what it was called *"Primitive Brazilian art"*. It was divided into five sessions; folk art (with masterpieces by Mestre Vitalino[121]), colonial, indigenous (with the participation of some karajá

---

[117] A few days after finishing this book I received an email from German historian Gerhard Brändle: the names of Werner and his parents, Mina and Hermann Reinheimer, were included in the Stolpersteine repair project. The project aims to recall victims and resistance to Nazism by placing cubic concrete stones with 4 inches of edges with a brass plate cover that contains an individual inscription indicating where the person honored lived. In part thanks to this project of research and organization of the Archive Werner returned to his Schwarzwald (Black Forest).

[118] An extinct indigenous people that produced sophisticated ceramic works.

[119] An afro-Brazilian religion.

[120] A typical flower of tropical environments.

[121] His ceramics portrayed agrarian life in the interior of Northeast Brazil. He was brought to the urban rich areas by Augusto Rodrigues (mentioned in chapters 2 and 4). Some of Vitalino's ceramics are in Louvre.

dolls), black and contemporary art. The founder of the exhibition was the then secretary of the embassy in Bern, Wladimir do Amaral Murtinho, husband of the printmaker and Olly's client, Toni Murtinho. We can see then that the web of reciprocity included, besides social actors of the cultural field, the museums of anthropology, as well as representatives of the Brazilian State, all imbued with the formulations of a national homogeneity constituted by a *"miscigenated modernity"* from the mixing of several internal "others".

It was in this environment where Olly and Werner moved about. This investigation led once again to the relationship between 'primitivism' and 'modernism', a manifestation of the tension between German Romantic particularism and French Enlightenment universalism as one of the bases for the modern national states, and the controversies involving appropriations of so-called 'primitive' art, be it 'indigenous', 'black', 'infantile' or 'pre-Columbian'. The spectacularization of domestic consumption with the emergence of illustrated magazines on decoration and design stimulated a fetishism for alterity that was produced by a group of foreigners in order to build for themselves a membership to modern Brazilianness.

Historically the emergence of a national iconography in Brazil has been associated with the arrival of the Portuguese Court and the French artistic mission. As the literary critic Roberto Scharwtz (1987) has shown, since then we can find symbols of a particular identity that distinguished Brazil from Portugal and other European countries using indigenous groups, fauna, flora and some references to farmers, as opposed to the local elite and 'foreign influences'. Those symbols were variable depending on the situational contexts. Throughout the nineteenth century, however, the presence of these elements meant an interest in the symbolization of a national particularity. In the first half of the twentieth century those symbols where produced mainly by the Brazilian State.

Between 1950s and 1970s, the interest in "popular culture" was a reflection of a group of intellectuals and artists, many of them of foreign origin influenced by national constructions in their own countries, not the Brazilian State or the Brazilian population as a whole. From the investigation of this web of relations one glimpses at the role of immigrants in the continuities and discontinuities of the appropriation of the "other" for the construction of representations about an intellectual white middle-class in Brazil. To talk about the construction of whiteness in the country it is important to consider the unintended consequences of social actions. It was about building a dimension of membership that did not exclude others, such as religion, family, political ties, etc.

The family dimension was a presupposition for this membership that was projected from the domestic space. Contrary to a relationship between genders founded on sexual freedom, where the private was publicly produced (an example of this is Paul Beatriz Preciado's work on Playboy magazine), this web of relations produced a domesticity that built a modern woman (white, heterosexual, married) who did not question gender roles, but worked with conventions and gained new social roles with them. This "new" way of organizing space included specific forms of treating materials and an idealized temporality, not necessarily with historical depth. It was a distinctive way of using decorative objects in opposition to the standards of an elite who produced its homes with time-honored artifacts. It meant, therefore, a double distinction, both in relation to the representations of a young modernity that the media presented as sexually liberated from the family, as well as from an economic elite that was based also on the historicity of its names and historical consumption. A clear example of the latter is represented by the Eva Klabin Foundation headquartered in the former residence of the collector. Her collections include ancient Egyptian, Greco-Roman and Italian objects, among others.

I sought to emphasize the collaborative and political dimensions of the creative activities of a marginal artist, showing how modernity can also be perceived as the reproduction of previously existing forms, with variations in their situational ratifications (Ingold and Hallan, 2007). The stimulus for the use of indigenous, popular, children and black references was both an artistic renewal in the search for simple forms, influenced by European modernism, and a localist spirit that sought to express in art and architecture the vigor of life and national character. This was not simply a matter of constructing a succession narrative in which the natives would represent the past, in direct opposition to immigrants who represented the future. At that point, one imagined that peripheric groups would be integrated into this modernizing society. But in this process, one did not question the legitimacy of the appropriation of their productions in constructing the white middle-class intellectuals' subjectivities as *racialized consumption* and *commodification of "primitiveness"*.

The "collectors" and "disseminators" sought in some measure to promote the representativeness of these groups and the valorization of their production in the artistic world from a narrative that placed them in a process of disappearance in view of industrialization. This sense of disappearance was reinforced by ethnological works that emphasized the complexity of art, ancient customs and legends, and ignored indigenous life and contemporary popular groups or disqualified them as a product of acculturation. Imagining a nationality based on emblems that blended the production of pre-industrialized groups with Western artistic traditions did not mean that production based on these "other" cultures was for consumption by "nonwhites". It helped emerge a production forged by and for a white middle-class elite, immigrants or first or second-generation descendants, reinforcing a whiteness that rested on miscegenation ideology, without effectively transforming power relations.

In a version of the origins of European modernism, artists elevated to artistic classification ritual objects such as masks, carvings, and paintings that made these things valued by curators, collectors, and art dealers. This was the interpretation that prevailed in the period treated here. Later, this relationship was criticized as undue appropriation, a way of freezing cultures in time by overvaluing the notion of authenticity and obliteration of power relations produced by colonialism. These issues are still central today for understanding debates such as appropriation, restitution, multiculturalism and multiculturality.

In the social context treated here, the aestheticization of indigenous and popular production and other groups previously considered inferior is the exception that confirms the rule of an idea of linearity of human evolution and its presupposition of a universal mind. The inclusion of the production of peripheric groups in the local artistic world did not dissolve the inequalities nor the asymmetric relations. The strong presence of immigrants in this context also leads us into assuming that the construction of that imagined Brazilianness was a way for these foreigners to present themselves as "natives".

These practices had an impact on the formation of a cultural field that included, besides the so-called plastic arts, mainly furniture design and architecture, but also landscaping. Thus, the reconfiguration of Brazilian artistic world during this period happened without abandoning popular, indigenous and other peripheric groups' productions. Modern art museums were perhaps the main institutional mediators of this process.

This proposed interpretation was developed from the description of the individual and collective uses of the things that were collected, taken as reference in the textile production used in clothing design, transformed into decoration objects for domestic spaces and *artified* through various mediations. But after the mid-1970s, those same things were devoid of an artistic classification and relegated to a historical dimension.

The importance of material culture in the construction of this analysis appears in the recurrence that objects had in the research process itself. A manhole was mentioned in an interview in 1998 and reappeared among the collection's photographs and again in a testimony of a different person in 2016. A cloth was given in 1960 as a wedding gift and transformed into a dress. It was latter included in the memoires of the receiver. Latter, in 2016, it served as testimony to the reading of the 1960 dialogue that led to its exchange. A towel was repeatedly mentioned every time a couple was invited to give testimonies about Olly. The banana tree and the apartment plants were regularly mentioned by interviewees. The objects distributed among the relatives were presented to me to show admiration for the work and/or to participate in the organization of family memories. A paper made by the artist appeared on the art piece of another artist. And so on.

The way these things have entered collections helps us realize the values and ideas different groups linked to them have assumed in that period. These objects were ways of declaring identities, achieving goals, and even fantasizing (Weiner, 1987). They marked relationships between people and groups, fabricated self-images, cultivated the past, and projected a future. They had, and still do, the ability to invent the people who possessed and used them, as well as those who still possess them. This inventiveness depended not only on the objects' circulation and exchange but could also be identified in the inalienability of those things that were kept under the control of specific individuals and groups, marking the continuity of collectivities and institutions.

The path taken by Olly is portrayed here, from her birth in a city that was known for its textile production in industrial looms, through the constitution of the first collection of textile pieces in a Brazilian museum to a context of tension in Brazilian industrial textile production, the meaning of her choices (textile supports, cultural references and political orientations) were connected to important points of contact with people and things that weaved with her their recognition. Her production gains three-dimensionality, without losing creative power, as we know the different paths followed in the conformation of her threads, warps and fabrics.

The period focused here was important for the institutionalization of a regionalized artisanal production. It is possible to find "luxury" handicraft shops whose specialties are largely within the definitions described here, that is, hierarchical in regional terms, as well as materials and techniques. This is not to say that local handicrafts do not exist, stimulated everywhere as a local market of more or less legitimate producers. This local handicraft, however, is rarely found in stores that specialize in "authentically Brazilian" production, or "Brazilian handicraft".

The meanings of these things were practical, as well as symbolic. The boundaries these things demarcate are fluid and in constant motion. Its influence on people's lives, as well as being unavoidable is also varied and variable. Locals, institutions or domestic spaces where they are "showed" or "guarded" greatly influence as social, symbolic and political mediators in the process of constructing classifications and representations about the objects and social categories linked to them. Some boundaries produced, reproduced, and challenged in these processes are those that ground modern Western thinking in terms of gender, race, and class: civilized/ primitive; nature/culture; past/present; tradition/modernity; scholar/popular; national/ foreign; authentic/inauthentic.

The social actors investigated here were not bound by a single goal. If in some moments the experience of the archaeological sites was activated to confer legitimacy to her production with emphasis on the pre-Columbian influence, in another one she could use a supposed national authenticity. More than a thematic unit and a nationalistic or political discourse, Olly's work encouraged a sense of strengthening a singular subjectivity suited to the expression of modern art in Brazil and its association with design. Her creativity was not in the novelty and rupturing with conventions, but in the continuity and connection with forms and motifs interwoven in various ways by the people who were part of her mesh of social relations. This continuity, however, largely reaffirmed the structural position of the white middle class and, in order to construct a new position for this group's women, sanctioned the female double journey by explicating, rather than questioning, the work done in the domestic space, now added to the entry of these women into the labor market.

The use of indigenous motives and other peripheric groups in her work did not necessarily mean an engagement of the artist with the culture or groups criticism. Interest in these groups seemed to be only her husband's. Fauna, flora, indigenous body paintings, and pre-Columbian peoples' material culture ended up being a way of producing unconventional clothing for those who did not wear *haute couture* but who prized clothing as a way of building distinction in ritual occasions. To consume and, mainly, to wear her clothes was to incorporate, literally, a little of the exoticism of her subjects, her personality and her trajectory.

Olly and Werner were part of a social web involving immigrants, artists and intellectuals who were less occupied in reconstructing the traditions left behind, than in participating in a certain modernity *project* (Velho, 2013), partially elaborated in the frameworks of MAM-RJ, and developed between the 1950s and 1970s. Thus, although the so-called "primitive" material culture continued to be used as a reference in those decades, this was not the State use, strictly speaking. On the one hand, these artifacts of material culture were linked to an ideology of national formation and therefore were a way for these immigrants to build a national membership for themselves, that is, they were part of individual projects of insertion into Brazilian society. On the other hand, what they did was to produce a specific way for those people to present themselves through their clothes, jewelry and objects of decoration and collecting.

The *Casa do Pontal* museum is a good example of the aestheticization of objects that until then were considered ethnographic examples. Very similar to what is found in the collection of this institution are the things one can see in the Edison Carneiro Museum of Folklore, with quite different presentations. José Reginaldo Gonçalves (2007) talks about the presentation form and the visual processes that frame a certain way of looking at things as one of the devices for transforming their classification. (Reinheimer, 2007).

Two or three decades after World War II were thus the gestation years of a new way of life on the part of this new individualized middle-class that instituted for itself new subjectivities from the valuation of these objects and from the idea of creativity as *freedom* from social conventions. However, in modernity heterodoxy was a convention. The notion of creativity (Ingold and Hallam, 2007) that emerged from the second half of the twentieth century in Brazil was not only a radical form of convention, it was also about the institution of a disjunction between artist and society. This separation was instituted, on the one hand, emphasizing the rupture as a norm in contemporary art (Heinich, 1993), but, on the other hand, in the establishment of a cultural field in which the tension between the universal and the local was the constant source of production of new identities.

The construction of new lifestyles is also related to the process of individualization and large cities. Urban reality is the perfect *locus* for this process (Simmel, 2005). It is in the large cities where there is the possibility of moving about different groups, negotiating identities contextually, instead of being bound in only or mainly one web of personal relations. Olly and Werner, since arriving in Brazil, have interacted with more or less orthodox Jews, progressive Jews, Catholic and Protestant immigrants, adherents of African religious-matrices, native Brazilians and even immigrants with previous ties to fascism and Nazism. A friend of the artist said she once took to the artist's home a German journalist who mentioned an alleged IV Reich. After the end of World War II, few were likely to admit having supported

Nazism. Pietro Maria Bardi, for example, was a member of Mussolini's fascist government, although little is said about this involvement today.

This diversified sociability after World War II required the formulation of new forms of self-construction from which to build groups without referring to the values that had led to the various conflicts since the Great War. These new forms of interaction have resulted, as well as they were a stimulus, to the expansion of individualistic values, reinforcing the perception of *independence* and *freedom* that Simmel explores in several of his texts, but which finds its most finished expression in the idea of the foreigner, the stranger.

The interaction of *freedoms* in large contemporary cities is part of the process of more or less stable exchanges, alliances and conflicts that form interests, divergences, tendencies, and lifestyles. This differentiation predisposed by freedom produces new forms of individual insertion as well as disputes and conflicts that further stimulate differentiation and new ways of self-construction. *Freedom* was one of the main educational devices of the pedagogical project of the teachers of MAM-RJ, between 1950s and 1970s. This *freedom*, however, was privilege of a few.

If native art as an artifact authentically national or celebrated as an archaeological origin, seemed to have left the horizon of MAM-RJ's direction in the 1950s (Sant'Anna, 2011), re-elaborated as difference, these peripheric groups returned side by side to teachers and other actors who participated in this web of reciprocity that formed the cultural field of the period. This is how the ceramic students' works were presented alongside pieces by Mestre Vitalino in 1953. But the freedom to use these objects and/or influences for the creation of a modern art and design was the white middle-classes'. To the "others" tradition was all that was left.

MAM-RJ's modernity project never involved a complete break with the idea of origin. On the contrary, it is this origin, these works legitimized by time or by the idea of popular that, when being incorporated in the repertoire from new configurations, conferred value to the works of this new modernity that was instituted in the 1950s. A more radical rupture in this process was the way of conceiving the artist. Not someone with a special gift for academic learning, but someone who was formed from a process of *liberation* of conventions in relation to taste, creativity and a *sensibility* presented as given. This new role for the artist in Brazil was being built while it was being identified as a tool for the production of subjectivities.

It is in aesthetic education, also present in the ideals of the Escolinhas de Arte do Brasil, that it was constituted a new way of perceiving artistic producers and their role in the social world. *Freedom* appeared as a guiding thread, a category of action in the constitution of this new group of social actors, the artists of this new modernity. It was also the experience of this *freedom* that created the conditions of possibility for the invention of new lifestyles for the middle-class.

The decoration magazines in Olly and Werner's collection give an idea of the transformations these designers have aroused through an emphasis on tropical and/or Brazilian fauna and flora, as well as the revision of Romanticism to include in it not the idea of a Brazilian national identity, but the idea of a modernity from popular production. The term *rustic* appeared in this period as an allusion to this contradictory mixture.

In the 1950s, some social scientists were still opposing the "man of the city" to the "rustic man" of the countryside. Sociologist Florestan Fernandes, for example, used this term in opposition to "intelectual" in the preface of the book "Cor e mobilidade social em Florianópolis" (Color and Social Mobility in Florianópolis), by Fernando Henrique Cardoso and Octavio Ianni: "Conventionalized tolerance in race relations and the minimum of which characterizes the expression assumed by individualism and the autonomy of the person both in our *cultured man* and in our *rustic man*" (Fernandes, 1972: 168; emphasis added). Thus, if *mercantile racism* reified the subordinate place of the represented groups, without giving space for them to represent themselves, it constituted in that period a positive value for the rusticity that did not exist before.

The new style of domestic spaces decoration this set of institutional and individual actions provoked is related mainly to the manual forms of using materials such as leather, wood and ceramics. This way of using them evidences rusticity as a way to symbolize some respect for the materials and to reject industrialization as the supreme value expressed in the finishings that obliterates manual labor. But it did not consider the incorporation of the production of the groups that were being collected and strategies of artification of this production. This style can be identified in the domestic spaces and today also in the professional spaces of several people in that web, including the subsequent generations that had contact with those intellectuals, even if tangentially. The new style, rather than drawing attention to specific groups, drew attention to the value of this type of work, opening space for folk and indigenous handicrafts as objects that could be used in decoration, avoiding the norms that had hitherto been in force. In this sense, the materials, motives and forms were affirmed while the people remained marginalized. Material culture was coveted, but the indigenous and the other peripheric groups remained stigmatized. Valuation did not exclude rejection and stigmatization, which constituted a continuity between forms of celebration and maculation in the process of construction of new subjectivities.

In the nineteenth century, the meaning of leather had been reframed in order to participate in bourgeois life in Brazil. Until the second half of that century, this material was associated with harness, saddles, jackets, purses and travel accessories of the rural man and the inheritance and coexistence with indigenous groups. The refined leather of English furniture recoded the "native" repertoire and transformed the meaning of the male colonial tradition into referents of an English plutocracy that had surpassed rural habits in favor of displays of power and wealth (Carvalho, 2008).

Between 1950s and 1970s, leather came to be considered *rustic* by this group represented in Olly's *career*. That notion included the values of nature, creativity and native industry. The reconfiguration of this material was another way of putting the representation of perpheric groups in question, associating them with the notion of *aesthetic sensibility* instead of national authenticity. In other words, it was a way of speaking about the collective from the individual practices of some of its representatives. A certain notion of whiteness constituted from the idea of a universal *sensibility* capable of seeing in the "other" aesthetic qualities. However, the structural inequality that underpinned relations between the elites and these peripheric groups was not questioned.

The influence of Bauhaus and Ulm School of Design at that time was a continuation of the nationalism expressed by the Estado Novo, as well as an "idyllic reaction" in defense of traditions in view of industrialization. But it was also conservative emphasizing the idea of authenticity and purity of certain groups considered closer to nature. This *authenticity* was represented by the way the materials were handled. Modernity was maintained as an attribute of the white middle class, while to other groups remained the idea of tradition and authenticity, references to the participation in historical time and not in the present time or in the project of a future.

The engagement of white artists with cultures of peripheric groups was one way of giving visibility to issues and making their presence more and more conspicuous in all social, rural and urban, spaces. These groups' material culture was transformed sometimes into private collections, some others into inalienable objects contributing to the creation of value for fabrics and clothing. Social categories made visible in one or another context are not stable and fixed and thus served to construct varied forms of individual subjectivity and collective identities, to organize and constitute distinct ways of experiencing subjectivities and social status.

To consider the indigenous production as art in the context of contempt for these cultures can be considered a form of recognition and alliance in their struggles. However, as Ilana Goldstein points out (personal communication, 2018), there is no consensus among indigenous groups about the validity of having their production recognized as art. Meanwhile, Brazilian historians and art critics seem to have made a commitment to anthropologists not to reify this classification, which is not necessarily positive either, since the recognition of aesthetic classification means possible visibility, investment and sponsorships. Hence the debate around the expression "Afro-Brazilian art", either to request it, to challenge it and/or use it for the art world and for the black militancy is one of the ways of making visible an artistic production produced by Afro-descendants and/or on interethnic subjects.

The absence of a rhetoric engaged in social struggles should not disguise the fact that Olly's work was a response to important problems of her time. This interpretation is based on the intellectual and political interests of her husband and her social mesh, as well as the presence of these subjects in several books in the couple's library, which brought these debates into their home. Her reference was not nationalism, but a certain notion of nationality through the recognition of the influence of a particular background on creative expression.

The use of these groups – string literature, pre-Columbian, karajá and others – was a way of showing that these cultures had contemporaneity and that their meaning was a source of expressiveness also in the present and probably in the future. But the idea of authenticity ultimately essentialised them, reserving innovation to the white middle-class. Even so, these references eventually entered the domestic spaces through the media, reproductions and objects. This did not guarantee the prestige and legitimacy that the exhibitions in the galleries and the museums offered, but it conferred visibility. But the prestige was of the artist and her work, not modifying the status of the populations referenced.

Following Nicholas Thomas's (1999) analysis of the Aborigines, the question of cultural lending in general terms, such as exchange, mutual recognition or theft of colonized peoples by European exploiters, is given here considering both Olly's use of graphics and Franco Terranova's collecting of ex-votos, carrancas and the production of Agnaldo Manuel dos Santos. Appropriations have a character of unstable duality in which "to some extent there is always a combination of lending and recognition, appropriation and homage, criticism of colonial exclusions, and collusion in unequal exchanges" (Thomas 1999: 141). Therefore, the issue is not the endorsement or rejection of primitivism in principle. It is important to perceive the motivation for the production of particular works, as well as to take into account how in the long run all uses can be revised in the light of a critical perspective that leads to the role of these productions not in the construction of particular subjectivities, national symbols or indigenous traditions, but as pretexts for the groups themselves to tell their own stories and sing their own songs (Clifford, 2016). Let the focus go out of the individual and the social strata and pass to the groups from which the objects or cultural production was borrowed, in order to be in the friendliest terms of this unequal sharing.

I have tried to show that individual experiences can be varied and can lead to ambiguous conclusions about world conceptions and the art produced. I found an aesthetic production in mid-twentieth-century Brazil based on the tensions of inter-ethnic relations that underlay the period. Immersed in their social relations individuals respond differently to their desires and needs, but exposed to stimuli, moral norms and hegemonic lines of thought, it is possible to perceive certain patterns of behavior, morals and customs that configure explanatory axes that can be triggered for understanding the aesthetic choices that shape the artistic trajectories of the countries in which these artists, collectors and critics act. The construction of an imaginary nationalist lexicon is the result of the configuration and institutionalization of several professional areas, such as design and architecture in addition to literature, music, etc. The material investigated from Olly's trajectory showed the construction of a "lifestyle" expressed generally through the artifacts of daily use and/or applied in the ambiance of the domestic space.

Through fabric as a marginal material in the studies on art and culture, it was possible to perceive the role women had in some transformations and constructions of values in the period. In addition to showing how everyday things, such as furniture, paintings and decorative objects, are, in general, an implicit form of affirmation and constitution of identities, I have tried to show how reinterpretations about ethnic groups and their productions point to possible contributions that the alliance between anthropology and history can offer.

MAM's project of producing a modernity from art and industrial design has made textile production part of an incipient artistic field that relied on industrialization. Besides artists in training, several women attended the museum courses. They sought both a hobby and a vocational training. If handcrafting was in this period a way of associating industry and art, it was also a way of making industrialization a seemingly liberating phenomenon for middle-class white women by encouraging their participation as a way of introducing a certain kind of *sensibility* (feminine, primitive, naive) in the rationality of the industrial world. Textile handcraft production was also the way to make professionalization of these women more acceptable.

Women, represented by the textile handcraft, were at the same time driven to produce their own insertion in the labor market, but kept in a subordinate position in relation to the most legitimate artistic expressions. The number of women present in Rita Cáurio's (1985) survey on textile production attests to both the gender dimension attributed to this technique/material and its importance in the period. However, Olly's mentions of non-abandonment of domestic work show how it was necessary to maintain women's representations of family and domestic space while building a new image: modern, professional, and autonomous.

The affirmation of the maintenance of their "domestic obligations" was a way for these women to earn the right to this professionalization, but also to reify the double journey that only years later would be questioned by the feminist movements. If the ideal of middle-class female idleness was put in check, the double journey of non-white women, besides not being questioned, was transformed into a new ideal of behavior for all women.

In the 1970s, a renewed context would require new analytical investments to account for a female professionalization that dispensed references to "domestic obligations", even though it did not waive the practice of such activities. Further studies would be demanded also to understand the process of separation between the artistic world and fashion, which has become an eminently industrial arena. It was only in the beginning of the twenty first century that the debate about the artistic dimension of this social sphere has resumed, to a large extent, thanks to the deepening of *creativity* as a value in contemporary societies. Fashion as an artistic manifestation resurfaced in the context of elaborations about a "creative economy" (Santos, 2014).

Olly's *career* development shows the strategies of insertion of textile production within the framework of a legitimate artistic production. Other women who invested in this production were also recognized. Most of them, however, had in the textile material an ephemeral support, being identified by their works with other supports and expressive forms. Olly, on the contrary, maintained the textile production as support even when, at the end of her trajectory, she started researching the production of artisanal paper with natural fibers.

This fabric production was then a constituent part of the reciprocity system in arts between 1950s and 1970s. "Generosity" attributed to the artist was probably the measure of retribution for the recognition of her production materialized in acquisitions, invitations to exhibitions, letters of introduction to important personalities. Roughly, it is as if her "generosity" were the counter-gift from participating with her cloths in events such as the reception to the prince of Japan.

MAM's art courses forged an important instrument for production of meaning during this period, the idea of *freedom* in art. This *freedom* was linked to the notion that in art there is no right or wrong and therefore what is important is the experience. This didactic strategy put an end to the idea that to make art it would be necessary to learn techniques, replacing it with the notion that the artist is a researcher of shapes, colors, textures, materials (pay attention to the title of Olly's last exhibition).

The notion of *freedom* also gave art critics a fundamental role in the process of "discovery" and "projection" of new artists and through newspaper articles I showed some devices used in the projection of the one analyzed here and her fabrics in the Brazilian artistic universe of that period. While critics and periodicals forged speeches to invent a "great artist", Olly mobilized the webs of relations through which her work was woven between art, fashion, and design.

Latin America was called to legitimize the Brazilian textile production through the consecrated Paraca fabrics. The tissues produced by Andean groups inserted Brazil in the traditional antiquity of weaving. The appearance of collections of this material in several institutions is a sign of the symbolic value that fabrics and particularly the Paraca fabrics had in the process of building an industrial modernity with a "feminine touch" and a historical depth.

This symbolic dimension invested in textile production fed largely from its importance in the history of industrialization in Europe, especially in Great Britain (Hobsbawm, 1977). The "feminine touch" on the other hand, was a way to construct new representations on the role of women in the labor market. Transposing Karajá's body designs to her clothing was to recognize at the same time the importance of Western clothing as a social marker and indigenous paintings as a form of symbolic weaving. In addition, the mention of Karajá ceramic dolls that also featured body paintings would place women and children in this symbolic universe in which weaving, clothing and ceramics linked nature and culture, as well as the feminine dimension to industry.

There were contradictions in maintaining a "feminist" behavior and entering a professional market through clothing. But those contradictions were either unnoticed or were strategically used. One of those contractions was the sexualization of women and their presentation as objects of masculine desire. Another was the need to maintain the image of wife and mother, fulfilling the "obligations" regarding domestic work as a strategy to conquer the professional space. If the maintenance of the role of mother and wife may today be a choice for some middle-class women, in the 1950s and 1960s it was an obligation that she could not give up on the risk of conquering the antipathy of the group that was intended to become her privileged clientele. Entry into the clothing trade then assumed to be in line with traditional representations of gender roles, even if intending to transform it someday.

The traveling scientist thus resurfaced in the production of a woman who used, among other things, cartography to construct a symbology from improvisation. The white middle-class *sensibility* that was instituted by these actors was also linked to the idea of *freedom* to improvise, to unite the *rustic* to the industrial, to work with the materials and not against them, maintaining their "natural" characteristics allied to a rational design. All this should be combined in the clothing, jewelry and objects for decoration of domestic spaces forming a universe of meanings that was a declaration of membership to a particular cultural field constituted by the museums of modern art and a set of social actors linked to them and mainly participants of the Brazilian artistic worlds and of a field of design in process of institutionalization.

The symbolism of Olly's textile production appears in the speeches of those interviewed who said to have worn her clothes on ritual occasions, but also in the symbolic reorientation of the artist's house from this production and the recognition she achieved with it. On the one hand, the fabric rescued the value of the feminine, although giving it a docile appearance in the incipient industrial capitalism in the country. On the other hand, it obliterated the demands of the working class on the mundane dimensions of their production wage and working conditions inserting that production in a reverse economy where disinterest is the grammar of all interests.

Olly's erasure is related in part to the fact that she kept producing fabrics and clothing, even when fashion and art divorced from the 1970s onward. She died shortly after her attempts at something that could be interpreted as the exploration of other forms of weaving, such as the production of handmade paper and the interweaving of "colors, shapes and textures", title of her last exhibition, in 1981. At that time, fashion was already being treated as an industry. From the 1970s on, MAM did not have any other clothes or fabrics exhibitions. It is no coincidence that the project that led to this book has materialized: recently the relationship of fashion with creation has been resumed in Brazil. In this new context, Olly can be presented as another case in the process of building a "history of fashion in Brazil".

Olly's works were not only a reflection of the projects of a modern market represented by the Brazilian Modern Art Museums or the State, but they were neither merely expressions of a creative individual. The difficulty for the social sciences in dealing with artistic manifestations is to find a way to show how the production of artists is at the same time the result of improvisations and individual choices, without falling into a methodological individualism, and at the same time showing the influences from collectivities and the social context in which they participate, without diminishing the value and quality of individual work that results from them.

Olly's trajectory makes it possible to perceive the insertion of women into a generalized labor market, where the place reserved for them was at the same time a symbol of maintaining the "traditional" female role, but also disrupting that role by giving them a place in the economic and political system for building a modernity that challenged those roles. To occupy the spaces in the house, to redefine them from her professional performance, to live an autonomous social life, independent of her husband and to enjoy financial independence, were themselves forms of questioning this supposed feminine traditional role. The emphasis on Werner's involvement in her life suggests that his investment in politics has had a major influence on her creative dimension, both in the sense of the chosen subjects and in the construction of the value of her production (without detracting from the aesthetic qualities of her creations). The materials used by the artist were qualified from their gender dimension (weaving and sewing as part of the representations of a traditional feminine sphere), but the political dimension of nationality symbolization and a white middle-class that tried to separate itself from the elites' oppression over peripheric groups overlapped the dimensions of class and race to that of gender.

The motto of one of the groups that supported the civil-military coup in Brazil, in 1964, "Family, Tradition and Property", presupposed the "traditional" heterosexual marriage, that is, the function of women was reproduction and care for the home and the husband as the provider indicating a relationship between the hierarchy and the naturalization of the domestic space as a feminine place[122]. However, the expansion of capitalism pushed white middle-class women into the labor market, laying the groundwork for a reformulation of gender relations in this group. Capitalism thus appears as the positivation of the female force, reproductive, expansive and capable of encompassing all, without, however, giving women a new place in the power structure. The maintenance of subalternity is undertaken in part in preserving the hierarchically inferior position of textile production, but also in the accumulation of "domestic obligations" with women's professionalization and entry into the labor market.

There were distinct actors producing varied meanings that allowed the reinterpretation of some cultural symbols. Male and female opposition is challenged and reinforced in this game, which included art, industrial production, manufacturing, the labor market, and symbols of class, nationality, and ethnicity.

Urbanization also had an important contribution. The process of individualization that the urban environment stimulates allows people to give up their preexisting status and occupy positions in an impersonal market. The modern artistic field is one of the arenas where this market is regulated by a convention that establishes singularity as a value. Ruled by opposing forces, part of this impersonal universe of the urban environment, has innovation as its main value and reciprocity as part of its mode of operation.

Perhaps even more difficult for the relationship between art history and anthropology is the critical adjustment to histories of reception of cultural influences. Pointing to the silencing of cultural expressions in colonial relationships of control and power has been one of the ways contemporary art has forced art history to reconsider the possibilities of interdisciplinarity. There is perhaps the need for some anthropologists to abandon their prejudice against the idea that representations about individual singularity have an impact on social relations and phenomena.

Anthropology works with collective categories, even when it uses individual biographies and makes located interpretations to show how certain values or

---

[122] Very similar to the slogans we saw in the election of the next Brazilian president in 2018.

situations are constituted. The artistic field works with the idea of individual productions that mark singularities that make up the art history itself. This makes these fields, at the same time, complementary and opposites. Complementary if we take individual trajectories to think collective processes but oppose if one field denies the existence of singularity as a representation capable of constituting realities and the other refuses to see that every individual is socially and culturally constituted and, in this sense, the idea of singularity itself is a collective construct. In the social world, however, in the event of life, both perspectives build society with its complementary values and the two fields are the result of the same key ideas that shaped the modern world.

5.3. An Auto-Fiction On Reality

The Jewish burial is done with a closed coffin, and the person is naked inside it. They are buried as they came into the world so that the end be equal to the beginning. So says Tatiana Levy (2007). Until this research, I had not returned to the graveyard to visit my grandparents' graves. After all, they accompanied me in the objects inside the house and in the house itself.

One summer afternoon, surrounded by the Atlantic Forest, once again I met them and their stories in a book. Tatiana Levy narrates, in what she calls an "autofiction", the migratory process to Brazil of her Turkish grandfather. From a key that should open the door of the house from which he left in Izmir, the author retraced the path from Turkey to Brazil and from Brazil to Portugal, situating the social and political context of this history and the three generations from the grandfather to her. Her book deals with the search for an identity, the burden of carrying this story and the difficult choice of what to do with this inheritance. Making that decision involved taking a trip down unknown paths, following the curiosity to know what remained and what was left behind. This story meant opening the door to a house she did not know. To listen to silences, to say goodbye to truths and to embrace unknowns.

One of the discoveries of these journeys, hers and mine, was that exile is not necessarily only suffering. This subject is of no less importance in the case of Jewish families. For these, exile is generally related to the suffering of persecution and violence. While these are an IMPORTANT part of the story, the results of these events as complex as the reason for leaving and what has been left behind. However, those who have re-established their lives and succeeded in being happy do not seem to have the right to express it in the face of the horror of the Pogroms and the Holocaust. The farewell suffering and the uncertainty of the future often continue as success stories and happiness. But these stories defile the sacredness of the suffering of those who have not survived. It is as if surviving, and above all being happy, was unworthy.

Children tell their stories from the ship's pool and their travel experiences across unknown worlds. That was how, at 87, Erika Hasenberg remembered the costume party and the wave that broke her tooth when she was going to Brazil. The laws of

Nuremberg were far less important in her account than the captain who let her eat sweets. Memories almost sinful in the face of murder, persecution and loss.

Levy tells one of these stories of happiness in exile, at the same time showing how her imagination had been restricted to the moment of farewell and the pain of separation. It was on the reverse path to that of her ancestors that she found meaning for this migratory project that surpassed pain. As for Tatiana Levy's grandfather, for Olly and Werner the history of immigration was not made only by losses. Werner narrated the arrival in a welcoming land (Reinheimer, 1983). Although the account, fifty years later, is a reinterpretation of the past. In the present time of telling that past had the value of sounds, colors and forms of a new, joyous, funny, relaxed, happy horizon. Werner's joy of living owed, to a large extent, to Olly's gaze to the world. We can only understand one if we look at the other, as well as at the way the two universes interacted. Militancy and art constituted one another, one nourishing the other, molded by critical interaction.

Happiness does not erase suffering, but there is a choice between living with the emphasis on one or the other. Like many immigrants, to recommence implied forging a new name and a new origin for themselves. Olly used the childhood nickname to reinvent herself, to become another. Werner stood by, supported and recognized her value.

During this work of recognizing my family history, walking in the Black Forest, made me reinterpret the walks in the Botanical Garden and the garden inside the apartment of the couple. It was both Germany that was sought in this relationship with plants, as a style of decorating domestic spaces related to childhood, the rural past, before real estate speculation, demographic explosion and industrialization after the 1950s. An idyllic time. But being in the Black Forest, or in the small towns and reconstructed castles that called into question the idea of heritage, reality and historicity, also awoke in me ancient roots.

Tatiana Levy speaks of the past as being her own and realizes this while eating: "the past was not only my grandfather's past, it did not belong just to those who had emigrated. The cucumber proved" (Levy, 2007: 87). *Matzah*, a symbol of the past suffered by the Jews, dry bread that speaks of pain and misery was present in Olly and Werner's daily life, especially during *Pesach* times. But as well as the Jewish past was present, so it was the German one. Green apple, potato salad, *Meerrettich* (horseradish) brought back a past that spoke of German customs, a nationality whose strength was literally and figuratively nourished by both Jewish cooking and German recipes and ingredients. Fear stopped the words and obliterated the roots of these meals with my grandparents, but the tables of the houses I visited in the interior of Germany recounted this story and made me aware of previously unknown senses. And this story was also told by the palate.

According to Levy, "to definitively break with the past is harder than we imagine, it generates guilt, a guilt that can become mortal" (Levy, 2007: 131). The author thinks that this is why we are Jews even when we are not. I think that this is why we are still Germans, Turks, Italians many years after our ancestors have already left these lands, in every way. The past is also mine when I am reproached for not speaking German. If this "lack" was a matter of survival for Olly and Werner, today, historical atrocities are replaced by a new sense of national pride that opposes the Brazilian "Other" for the work ethic: "*You do not speak German? Lazy!*" [123]

Tatiana Levy's "autofiction" made me face some of my feelings. One was the constant oscillation between the certainty of producing something relevant and the doubt of being driven only by selfish desires to seek my story. Each difficulty lifted a wall of uncertainty and each new document with expressive information a whirlwind of emotions. Between the two extremes, the systematic work of historical survey, theoretical readings, and ethnographic research gave density to the subject and showed that Olly and Werner's trajectories represented meeting with a social mesh whose political and cultural dimensions justified my "adventure". More than a trip back to the origins, this was a work of reinvention of these origins in the light of contemporary questions. The gaps for which I had no information were filled with feelings, desires, current values, and hopes for tomorrow.

If there is a certain cruelty in the fact that life continues after the death of the ones we love, there is also poetry. If love is not enough to guarantee the memory of the departed ones – in time we forget the smell, the color of the eyes, the shape of the face – the objects are there to help us remember and recreate our dead. Olly and Werner have endeavored, each in their own way, in their collected objects and it is through these objects that I can speak about them today, tell their story, forge their past, and relive some of their sorrows and joys. In this quest for old ties, I also made new ones. This is how the future is contained in the past, having the present as a gift.

---

[123] I heard that during field work.

REFERENCES

1. Bibliography

Agier, Michel. Antropologia da cidade. Lugares, situações, movimentos. Editora Terceiro Nome, São Paulo, 2011.

Aguiar, Patricia. *Celeida Tostes: Inventando Passagens*. Dissertação de mestrado no Programa de pós-graduação em Ciência da Arte, Universidade Federal Fluminense, 2017.

Almeida, Maria Hermíria Tavares de. e Weis, Luiz. Carro-zero e pau-de-arara: o cotidiano da oposição de classe média ao regime militar. In Novaes, F. e Schwarcz, L.M. História da Vida Privada no Brasil. Companhia das Letras, São Paulo, 2006.

Anastassakis, Zoy. Triunfos e impasses. Lina Bo Bardi, Aloisio Magalhães e o design no Brasil. Lamparina, Rio de Janeiro, 2014.

Andermann, Jens. Espetáculos da diferença: a Exposição Antropológica Brasileira de 1882 In Topoi Revista de História, Rio de Janeiro, v. 5, p. 128-170. 2004

Appadurai, Arjun (ed). *The social life of things: Commodities in cultural perspective*. New York, Cambridge University Press, 1990.

Bacarin, Lígia Maria Bueno Pereira e Noma, Amélia Kimiko. HISTÓRIA DO MOVIMENTO DE ARTE-EDUCAÇÃO NO BRASIL. ANPUH XXIII SIMPÓSIO NACIONAL DE HISTÓRIA Londrina, 2005.

Bahia, Joana. De como os Ethnic Brokers fabricam seus demarcadores históricos e identitários In Associação Nacional de História ANPUH XXIV SIMPÓSIO NACIONAL DE HISTÓRIA 2007.

————. MEMÓRIAS DE GÊNERO. A CONSTRUÇÃO DE UMA ÍDISCHKEIT IMAGINÁRIA NO BRASIL. Fazendo Gênero 9, Diásporas, Diversidades, Deslocamentos, Florianópolis, 23 a 26 de agosto de 2010.

Barthes, Roland. A CÂMARA CLARA. Nota sobre a fotografia. Rio de Janeiro: Nova Fronteira, 1984.

Barth, Fredrik. Balinese Worlds. The University of Chicago Press, Chicago, 1993

Baudrillar, Jean. O sistema dos objetos. Tradução Zulmira Ribeiro Tavares. São Paulo, editora Perspectiva, 2004.

Baudrillard, Jean. A sociedade de consumo. Rio de Janeiro, Edição Elfos, Lisboa, Edições 70, 1995

Bazani, Adamo. Tremembé, pioneiro no transporte de São Paulo. 18 de maio de 2010. http://miltonjung.com.br/tag/tremembe/ acessado em 10 de janeiro de 2015.

Becker, H.S. Art Worlds. Los Angeles, University of California Press, 1982.

Belluzzo, Ana Maria de Moraes. *O Brasil dos viajantes*. Rio de Janeiro, Editora Objetiva, 1999.

Belting, Hans. Arte universal e minorias. Uma nova geografia da história da arte. In O fim da história da arte: uma revisão dez anos depois. São Paulo, Cosac Naify, 2006.

Birdwell-Pheasant, Donnae Lawrence-Zúñiga, Denise. House Life: Space, Place, and Family in Europe. Berg, New York, 1999.

Blay, Eva. Inquisição, inquisições: aspectos da participação dos judeus na vida sócio-política brasileira nos anos 30 In Tempo Social. Revista de Sociologia. São Paulo, USP, 1(1):105-130,1989.

Bock, Gisela. A política sexual nacional-socialista e a história das mulheres In Duby, George e Perrot, Michelle (org). História das mulheres. O século XX. Ebradil, São Paulo, 1991.

Bonadio, Maria Claudia. A moda no MASP de Pietro Maria Bardi (1947-1987). Anais do Museu Paulista. São Paulo. N. Sér. v.22. n.2. p. 35-70. jul.dez. 2014.

————. "A produção acadêmica sobre moda na pós-graduação stricto sensu no Brasil". In: *Iara* Revista de moda, cultura e arte. São Paulo, 2010, vol. 3, n. 3, p. 50-146.

Bourdieu, Pierre e Delsaut, Yvette. O costureiro e sua grife. Contribuição para uma teoria da magia. In *A produção da crença. Contribuição para uma economia dos bens simbólicos*. Editora Zouk, São Paulo, 2004 [1975].

————. *Les conditions sociales de la circulation internationale des idées'*. In: *Actes de la recherche en sciences sociales*. 2002/5 n.145, p. 3-8.

————. *A casa* kabyle *ou o mundo* às *avessas*. Cadernos de Campo, v.8, n.8, USP, 1999 [1970].

————. *Distinction. A social critique of the judgment of taste*. Harvard University Press, Cambridge, 1998 [1979].

————. *Regras da arte*. Cia das Letras, São Paulo, 1996.

————. Esboço de uma teoria da prática. In Ortiz, Renato (org.) Pierre Bourdieu: sociologia. São Paulo, Ática, 1983.

————. « Les rites comme actes d'institution », pp. 58-63, dans "Actes de la recherche en sciences sociales", no 43 de juin 1982 sur les "Rites et fétiches", Éditions de minuit, Paris 1982.

————. O mercado dos bens simbólicos. In A economia das trocas simbólicas. São Paulo, Perspectiva, 1977.

————. Campo intelectual e projeto criador In *Problemas do estruturalismo*. Zahar Editores, Rio de Janeiro, 1968 [1966].

————. "Celibat e condition paysane" In Études Rurales, 1962.

Brown, Bill. Thing theory. *Critical Inquiry*, Vol. 28, No. 1, Things. (Autumn, 2001), pp. 1-22.

Bueno, Maria Lúcia. O mercado de galerias e o comércio de arte moderna. Sociedade e Estado, Brasília, v. 20, n. 2, p. 377-402, maio/ago. 2005.

Campbell, Shirley. A estética dos outros In Revista Proa, n 02, vol.01, 2010.

Cardoso, Fernando Henrique e Ianni, Octavio. Cor e mobilidade social em Florianópolis. São Paulo, Companhia Editora Nacional, 1960.

Carneiro, Maria José. Descendentes de suíços e alemães de Nova Friburgo: de "colonos" a "jardineiros da natureza" In Gomes, Angela de Castro (org.): Histórias de Imigrantes e de Imigração no Rio de Janeiro. 7Letras, 2000, pp. 11-43.

Carsten, Janet. Perspectiva antropológica do lar. Palestra pronunciada na TU Delft, Holanda, 17 de maio de 2017. https://www.youtube.com/watch?v=YnvHo7zgZ3Y

Carsten, Janet (ed.). At home: an anthropology of domestic space. Syracuse University Press, New York, 1999.

Carvalho, Vânia Carneiro de. Gênero e Artefato. O sistema doméstico na perspectiva da Cultura material-São Paulo, 1870-1920. Editora Edusp, São Paulo, 2008. 368 p.

Castro, Ruy. Ela é carioca. Uma enciclopédia de Ipanema. Companhia das Letras, São Paulo, 1999

Cáurio, Rita. Artêxtil no Brasil. Viagem pelo mundo da tapeçaria. Gráfica Editora Primor, Rio de Janeiro, 1985.

Chang, Whan Ritxoko: A voz visual das ceramistas Karajá/Chang Whan. Rio de Janeiro: UFRJ/EBA/PPGAV, 2010. x, 205 f.: il.; 31 cm. UFRJ/EBA/Programa de Pós- Graduação em Artes Visuais, 2010.

Chataignier, Gilda. História da moda no Brasil. Estação das letras e cores, São Paulo, 2010.

Chiarelli, Tadeu. Apresentação In Simioni, Ana Paula. Dias, Elaine e Eleutério, Maria de Lourdes. Mulheres artistas: as pioneiras (1880 a 1930). Catálogo de exposição, 13 de junho a 25 de outubro de 2015. Pinacoteca do Estado de São Paulo, São Paulo, 2015. ISBN 978-85-8256-057-0.

Clarke, Alison J. The aesthetics of social aspiration In Home Possessions. Material culture behind closed doors. Miller, Daniel (ed). Oxford, Nova York, 2001.

Clementino, Maria do Livramento Miranda. A evolução da indústria têxtil no contexto da afirmação do imperialismo americano. XII Congresso de Geocrítica, Bogotá, 7 a 11 de maio de 2012.

Clifford, James. The Predicament of Culture: Twentieth-Century Ethnography, Literature, and *Art. James Clzfford.* Cambridge, MA: Harvard University Press, 1988. 392 pp.

————. "Colecionando arte e cultura". Revista do Patrimônio Histórico e Artístico Nacional, n. 23, 1994, Pp:69-79.

————. On The Edges of Anthropology (Interviews). Prickly Paradigm Press, Chicago, 2003.

————. Museus como zonas de contato. Periódico permanente. N.6, fev. 2006.

Collier, Jane, Rosaldo, Michelle Z., Yanagisako, Sylvia. Is there a family? New anthropological views In Lancaster, Roger & Di Leonardo, Micaela. The Gender/sexuality Reader: Culture, History, Political Economy. Routledge, New York, London, 1997.

Corbain, Alain. *O Território do vazio. A praia e o imaginário ocidental.* Companhia das Letras, São Paulo, 1989 [1988].

Corrêa, Mariza. A Natureza Imaginária Do Gênero Na História Da Antropologia. cadernos pagu (5) 1995: pp. 109-130.

Costa, Ana Alice A. e Sardenberg, Cecília Maria B.. O feminismo no Brasil: uma (breve) retrospectiva. In. COSTA, Ana Alice; SARDENBERG, Cecília (org). O feminismo no Brasil: reflexões teóricas e perspectivas. Salvador: NEIM/UFBA. 2008.

Costa, Dina Czeresnia. Política Indigenista e assistência à saúde Noel Nutels e o Serviço de Unidades Sanitárias Aéreas. Cadernos de Saúde Pública, Rio de Janeiro, 4(3): 388-401, out/dez, 1987.

Cytrynowicz, Monica Musatti e Cytrynowicz, Roney. Lilly Ebstein: uma vida entre a arte e a ciência. In http://www.lillyebstein.com.br/v1/. Acessado em 06/02/2015.

Dabul, Lígia. Um percurso da pintura. A produção de identidades de artista. Editora EdUFF, Niterói, 2001.

DaMatta, Roberto. Relativizando uma Introdução à Antropologia Social. Editora Vozes, Rio de Janeiro, 1983.

Daou, Ana Maria. Tipos e aspectos do Brasil: imagens e imagem do Brasil por meio da iconografia de Percy Lau In Rosendahl, Zeny e Correa, Roberto L. (orgs). *Paisagem, imaginário e espaço.* EdUERJ, Rio de Janeiro, 2001

Despret, Vinciane. A cabando com o luto, pensando com os mortos. Fractal: Revista de Psicologia, v. 23 – n. 1, p. 73-82, Jan./Abr. 2011Lima, Diana Nogueira de Oliveira. Consumo. Uma perspectiva antropológica. Editora Vozes, Rio de Janeiro, 2010.

Dias, Carla & Lima, Antônio Carlos de Souza. O Museu Nacional e a construção do Patrimônio In Revista do Patrimônio Histórico e Artístico Nacional. História e Patrimônio, n. 34, 2012.

Dias, José António B. Fernandes. ARTE E ANTROPOLOGIA NO SÉCULO XX: MODOS DE RELAÇÃO. Etnográfica, Vol. V (1), 2001, pp. 103-129

Dias, Nélia. "Looking at objects: memory, knowledge in nineteenth-century ethnographic displays" in *Travellers' Tales. Narratives of Home and Displacement.* Jon Bird, Barry Curtis, Melinda Mash, Tim Putnam, Lisa Tickner, George Robertson (eds). Routledge, London, 1994.

Douglas, Mary e Isherwood, Baron. O mundo dos bens. Editora UFRJ, Rio de Janeiro, 2013.

Douglas, Mary. Purity and Danger. An analysis of the concept of pollution and taboo. Routlegde, London and New York, 2002 [1966].

Duarte, Ana Rita Fonteles. Betty Friedan: morre a feminista que estremeceu a América. Estudos Feministas, Florianópolis, 14(1): 287-293, janeiro-abril/2006

Duarte, Luiz Fernando Dias e Gomes, Edlaine de Campos. Três Famílias. Identidades e trajetórias transgeracionais nas classes populares. Editora FGV, Rio de Janeiro, 2008.

Dumont, Louis *O Individualismo. Uma perspectiva antropológica da ideologia moderna.* Rocco, Rio de Janeiro, 1985.

Eckstein, George Günther. The Freie Deutsch-Jüdische Jungend (FDJJ) 1932-1933. In Leo Baeck Institute Yearbook (1981) 26 (1): 231-39.

Elias, Norbert. Sobre o tempo. Jorge Zahar Ed. Rio de janeiro, 1998.

Fabian, Johannes. 2010. "Colecionando pensamentos: sobre os atos de colecionar". *Mana*, 16(1):59-73.

Fabian, Johannes. *Time and the Other. How anthropology makes its object.* Columbia University Press, New York, 1983.

Farge, Arlete. O sabor do arquivo. Tradução Fátima Murad. EdUSP, São Paulo, 2009.

Fernandes, Florestan. O negro no mundo dos brancos. São Paulo, Difusão Europeia do Livro, 1972.

Ferreira Filho, Manoel e Silva, Telma Camargo. A ARTE DE SABER FAZER GRAFISMO NAS BONECAS KARAJÁ. Horizontes Antropológicos, Porto Alegre, ano 18, n. 38, p. 45-74, jul./dez. 2012

Foster, Hal. O retonro do real. A vanguarda no final do século XX. São Paulo, Cosac Naify, 2014.

Foucault, Michel. *História da sexualidade vol. 1: A vontade de saber.* Graal, São Paulo, 2003[1978].

Foucault, Michel. Eu, Pierre Rivière, Que Degolei Minha Mãe, Minha Irmã e Meu Irmão. Editora Graal, Rio de Janeiro, 1982.

Franklin, Margareth Cordeiro. Clarice Lispector e os Intelectuais no Estado Novo. RevLet Revista Virtual de Letras Volume 2, Número 1/2010. ISSN: 2176-9125

Freund, Gisèle. Fotografia e sociedade. Editora Vega, Belo Horizonte, 1995.

Friedan, Betty. A mística feminina. Editora Vozes Limitada, Rio de Janeiro, 1971.

Garfield, Seth. As raízes de uma planta que hoje é o Brasil: os índios e o Estado-Nação na era Vargas. *Revista Brasileira de História.* São Paulo, v. 20, nº 39, p. 15-42. 2000

Gell, Alfred. A tecnologia do encanto e o encanto da tecnologia In Concinnitas. ano 6, volume 1, número 8, julho 2005.

Geisel, Eike. Excluídos e delinquentes. In Richard, Lionel. Berlim, 1919-1933. A encarnação extrema da modernidade. Jorge Zahar Editor, Rio de Janeiro, 1993.

Giudice, Vitor. O museu Darbot e Outros mistérios do catálogo de flores. José Olumpio, Rio de Janeiro, 1999.

Goffman, Erving. Representação do eu na vida cotidiana. Petrópolis, Vozes, 1985.

Goldstein, Ilana Setzer. AUTORIA, AUTENTICIDADE E APROPRIAÇÃO. Reflexões a partir da pintura aborígine austraLiane. RBCS Vol. 27 n 79, junho/2012.

Gomes, Angela de Castro (org.): Histórias de Imigrantes e de Imigração no Rio de Janeiro. 7Letras, 2000, pp. 11-43.

Gonçalves, José Reginaldo. O mal-estar no patrimônio: identidade, tempo e destruição In Estudos Históricos Rio de Janeiro, vol. 28, no 55, p. 211-228, janeiro-junho 2015.

———. Antropologia dos objetos: coleções, museus e patrimônio. Coleção Museu, memória e cidadania. Rio de Janeiro, 2007

Grinberg, Keila e Limoncic, Flávio. Judeus cariocas. Editora Cidade Viva, Rio de Janeiro, 2010.

Heinich, Nathalie. Os objetos-pessoas: fetiches, relíquias e obras de arte. In Ciências Humanas e Sociedade em Revista. Seropédica, Rio de Janeiro, v.31, n.1, 2009.

———. *L'élite artiste. Excellence et singularité em regime démocratique.* Éditions Gallimard, Paris, 2005.

———. *La sociologie de l'art,* Édition la Découverte, Paris, [2001] 2004.

———. Le triple jeu de l'art contemporain, Les Éditions de Minuit, 1993.

References

————. *La gloire de Van Gogh. Essai d'Anthropologie de l'Admiration*. Les Éditions de Minuit, Paris, 1991.

Heredia, Beatriz M. A. de e Palmeira, Moacir. O VOTO COMO ADESÃO. Teoria e cultura. v. 1, n. 1, 2006.

Heredia, Beatriz Maria Alásia de. A Morada da Vida: trabalho familiar de pequenos produtores do Nordeste do Brasil. Rio de Janeiro: Paz e Terra, 1979.

Heye, Ana M. Repensando o artesanato: algumas considerações In O artesão tradicional e seu papel na sociedade contemporânea. Textos de Berta Ribeiro e outros. Rio de Janeiro, FUNARTE/Instituto Nacional do Folclore. 1983. 253p.

Hobsbawm, Eric. *Era dos Extremos. O breve século XX. 1914 - 1991.* 2005 [1994].

————. Industria E Imperio Una Historia Económica De Gran Bretaña Desde 1750. Editorial Ariel, S. A., Barcelona, 1977.

Hyunh, Pascal. Cidade-rádio, cidade-jornal. In Richard, Lionel. Berlim, 1919-1933. A encarnação extrema da modernidade. Jorge Zahar Editor, Rio de Janeiro, 1993.

Ingold, Tim. Estar vivo. Ensaios sobre movimento, conhecimento e descrição. Editora Vozes, Rio de Janeiro, 2011.

————. Bringing Things to Life: Creative Entanglements in a World of Materials, Working Paper #15. ESRC National Centre for Research Methods NCRM Working Paper Series, University of Aberdeen, July 2010.

————. The perception of the environment. Essays on livelihood, dwelling and skill. First published by Routledge, 2000. This edition published in the Taylor & Francis e-Library, 2002.

Ingold, Tim; Hallam, Elisabeth (org.). Creativity and Cultural Improvisation. Oxford, New York: Berg, 2007.

Koifman, Fábio e Santos, Ricardo Augusto dos. A política imigratória brasileira do primeiro governo Vargas O projeto nacionalista imposto pelo Estado Novo passava por uma política imigratória claramente seletiva e restricionista. Pré-Univesp. Revista digital de apoio ao estudante pré-universitário. Número 27 Movimentos migratórios Dezembro de 2012 e Janeiro de 2013.

Koifmann, Fábio. Ipanema de rua em rua. Do Arpoador ao Jardim de Alah. Rio de Janeiro, Editora Rio, 2005.

Kölln, Lucas André Berno. As vinhas da ira: a leitura histórica de Steinbeck acerca da Grande Depressão. Revista Trama Volume 10 Número 19 - 1 Semestre de 2014. p. 135-154

Kopytoff, Igor. A biografia cultural das coisas: a mercantilização como processo In Appadurai, Arjun (org) A vida social das coisas. Eduff, Niterói, 2008 [1986].

Latour, Bruno. 2000. The Berlin key or how to do words with things. In *Matter, Materiality and Modern Culture*, edited by Paul Graves-Brown, pp. 10-21. Routledge, New York.

Latour, Bruno; WOOLGAR, Steve. 1997. *A vida de laboratório: a produção dos fatos científicos.* (Trad. Ângela R. Vianna) Rio de Janeiro: Relume Dumará. [1988]

Leite Lopes, José Sergio, Alvin, R. e Brandão, C. *Tecido Memória.* Museu Nacional/UFRJ, 2010.

Lesser, Jeffrey. O Brasil e a Questão Judaica. R.J., Imago, 1995.

Levy, Tatiana Salem. A chave de casa. Editora Record, São Paulo, 2007.

Lopes, José Rogério. Colecionismo, arquivos pessoais e memórias patrimoniais. Editora CirKula Ltda, Porto Alegre, 2017.

Lourenço Neto, Sydenham. Imigrantes Judeus no Brasil, marcos políticos de identidade. Locus: revista de história, Juiz de Fora, v. 14, n. 2. p. 223-237, 2008.

Marini, Marcelle. O lugar das mulheres na produção cultural. O exemplo da França. In Duby, George e Perrot, Michelle (org). História das mulheres. O século XX. Ebradil, São Paulo, 1991.

Marques, Reinaldo. Arquivos, coleções, ficções. Revista Z Cultural, UFRJ, agosto de 2015.

Marrus, Michael R. The unwanted. European refugees from the First World War through the Cold War. Temple University Press, Philadelphia, 2002.

Martins, Luciano, (1987). A gênese de uma intelligentsia; os intelectuais e a política no Brasil, 1920-1940. *Revista Brasileira de Ciências Sociais*, v. 2, n 4, p. 65-87.

Mascelani, Angela. O Mundo da Arte Popular Brasileira. Editora Museu Casa do Pontal, Rio de Janeiro, 2006.

Mauss, Marcel. Ensaio sobre a dádiva In Sociologia e Antropologia. Cosac y Naify, São Paulo. 2003.

Maziero, Dalton Delfini. A arte pré-colombiana nas bienais de São Paulo: um referencial para nossa identidade cultural (1951-2003). Disponível em: http://www.arqueologiamericana.com.br/artigos/artigo_07.htm. Acesso em: 27 fev. 2015.

Michahelles, Marina. A "colônia" alemã do Rio de Janeiro: a Sociedade Germania e a construção de uma identidade teuto-brasileira. Niterói: UFF/ICHF/ PPGH, 2003.

Miller, Daniel. Consumo como cultura material. In Horizontes Antropológicos, Porto Alegre, ano 13, n. 28, p. 33-63, jul./dez. 2007

————. Home Possessions. Material culture behind closed doors. Oxford, Nova York, 2001.

————. Consumption: critical concepts in social sciences. Routlegde, London, 2001.

————. Sobre pessoas e coisas: Entrevista com Daniel Miller. Entrevista cedida por Daniel Miller em 21 de setembro de 2009 no departamento de Antropologia da University College London. In REVISTA DE ANTROPOLOGIA, SÃO PAULO, USP, 2009, V.52N 1.

————. Trecos, troços e coisas. Estudos antropológicos sobre a cultura material. Zahar, Rio de Janeiro, 2013

Motta, Rodrigo Patto Sá. O mito da conspiração judaico-comunista. Revista de história. FFLCH-USP, 138 (1998), 93-105.

Nicoulin, Martin. La genèse de Nova Friburgo. Editions Universitaires, Paris, 1981.

Nora, Pierre. Entre memória e história: a problemática dos lugares. Projeto História, São Paulo, n.10, dez. 1993, p.7-28.

Oliveira F, João Pacheco de. Prefácio. In: *Andrea Roca*. Os sertões e o deserto. Imagens da nacionalização dos índios no Brasil e na Argentina, na obra de J. M. Rugendas (1802-1858). 1ed. Rio de Janeiro: Garamond, 2015, v. 1, p. 10.

Oliveira F, João Pacheco de. Uma etnologia dos "índios misturados"? Situação colonial, territorialização e fluxos culturais In *Mana* 4(1), 1998.

Oliveira, Márcio Piñon de. Quando a fábrica cria o bairro: estratégias do capital industrial e produção do espaço metropolitano no Rio de Janeiro. *Scripta Nova* Revista Electrónica de Geografía y Ciencias Sociales. Universidad de Barcelona. Vol. X, núm. 218 (51), 1 de agosto de 2006.

Paiva, Carlos Henrique Assunção. Homem de ação, o sanitarista Noel Nutels levou serviço médico para os rincões do país e defendeu a causa indígena. Revista de História da Biblioteca Nacional, Rio de Janeiro, 24/1/2011. Acessível em http://www.revistadehistoria.com.br/secao/retrato/consultorioaoarlivre

Park, Robert E. (1979), "A cidade: sugestões para a investigação do comportamento humano no meio urbano", *in* VELHO, O.G. (org.), O *fenômeno urbano*, Rio de Janeiro, Zahar.

Passerini, Luisa. Mulheres, consumo e cultura de massas. In Duby, George e Perrot, Michelle (org). História das mulheres. O século XX. Ebradil, São Paulo, 1991.

Paula, Teresa Cristina Toledo de. Tecidos no museu: argumentos para uma história das práticas curatoriais no Brasil. Anais do Museu Paulista. São Paulo. v.14. n.2. p.253-298. jul.dez. 2006.

Pearce, Susan M. *Collecting reconsidered In Interpreting objects and collections. London and New York, Routledge, 2003.*

References

————. 1994. Objects as meaning; or narrating the past In Interpreting Objects and Collections. London: Routledge.

Pedrosa, Mario. O crítico e o diretor. *Jornal do Brasil*, Rio de Janeiro, 22 novembro, 1960. (FBN).

Pequeno, Fernanda. Lygia Pape e Hélio Oiticica: conversações e fricções poéticas. 1. ed. Rio de Janeiro: Apicuri, 2013. v. 1. 128p.

Perrec, George. A coleção particular. Cosac Naify, São Paulo, 2004.

Perrot, Michelle. História dos quartos. Paz e Terra, São Paulo, 2011.

Pollak, Michel. Memória e Identidade Social. *Estudos Históricos*, Rio de Janeiro, vol. 5, n. 10, 1992, p. 206 e lugar de memória

Price, Sally. Arte primitiva em centros civilizados. Rio de Janeiro, Editora UFRJ, 2000.

Queiroz, Andréa Cristina de Barros. A República de Ipanema da cidade maravilhosa. Anais do XV Encontro Regional de História da ANPUH-RIO, 2012.

————. Arauto da República de Ipanema. Revista de História. 27/3/2013. http://www.revistadehistoria.com.br/secao/artigos/arauto-da-republica-de-ipanema

Rainho, Maria do Carmo Teixeira. Moda e revolução nos anos 60. Editora Contra Capa, Rio de janeiro, 2014.

Ramos, Jair de Souza. Enredando Famílias: Estado e Família no Povoamento do Solo Nacional. Revista Campos, Rio de Janeiro, 5(2): 25-43, 2004.

Reinheimer, Patricia. Candido Portinari e Mário Pedrosa. Uma leitura antropológica do embate entre Figureção e abstração no Brasil. Garamond, Rio de Janeiro, 2014.

————. O Museu de Folclore Edison Carneiro e a Casa do Pontal: os discursos sobre o folclore e a arte popular. Cadernos de Campo (USP. 1991), v. 16, p. 31-44, 2007.

Renan, Ernest. O que é uma nação? Conferência realizada na Sorbonne, em 11 de março de 1882". Revista Aulas 02(Dossiê Subjetividades. Org. Adilton Luís Martins.): 30

Revel, Jacques (org.). "Microanálise e construção do social" In Jogos de Escala: a experiência da microanálise. Rio de Janeiro: Editora Fundação Getúlio Vargas, 1998.

Ribeiro, Berta G. Arte indígena, linguagem visual. Ensaios de opinião, v.7, Rio de Janeiro, 1978.

Ribeiro, Felipe Augusto dos Santos. A foice, o martelo e outras ferramentas de ação política: os trabalhadores rurais e têxteis de Magé/RJ (1956-1973). Tese de Doutorado apresentada ao Centro de Pesquisa e Documentação de História Contemporânea do Brasil CPDOC como requisito parcial para a obtenção do grau de Doutor em História, Política e Bens Culturais. Rio de Janeiro, 2015.

Richard, Lionel. Berlim, 1919-1933. A encarnação extrema da modernidade. Jorge Zahar Editor, Rio de Janeiro, 1993.

Rosales, Marta Vilar. As coisas da casa. Cultura material, migrações e memórias familiares. Imprensa de Ciências Sociais, Lisboa, 2015.

Sahlins, Marshal. Cultura na prática. Editora UFRJ, Rio de Janeiro, 2004.

Sant'Anna, Sabrina Marques Parracho. Construindo a memória do futuro. Uma análise da fundação do Museu de Arte Moderna do Rio de Janeiro. Editora FGV, Rio de Janeiro, 2011.

————. Presságios e projetos: o incêndio do MAM e os rumos da arte contemporânea. VIS Revista do Programa de Pós-graduação em Arte da UnB V.13 n 1/janeiro-junho de 2014 [2015] Brasília ISSN- 1518-5494

Santos, Boaventura Souza. Uma cartografia simbólica das representações sociais. Prolegômenos a uma concepção pós-moderna do direito. Revista Crítica de Ciências Sociais, n.24, Coimbra, março de 1988.

Santos, Heloisa Helena de Oliveira. Moda e Economia Criativa: agenciamentos em torno da produção de vestuário no Brasil. 38º Encontro Anual da ANPOCS 27 a 31 de Outubro, Caxambu/MG, 2014.

————. Mundos da moda: pensando o design de vestuárioa partir das teorias de Howard Becker. Anais do 8º Colóquio de Moda, Rio de Janeiro, 2012.

Sardelich, Maria Emilia. Obra e legado de augusto rodrigues para a educação brasileira. Anais do VI Congresso Brasileiro de História da Educação, Vitória, ES, 2011

Schapiro, Meyer. Nature of Abstract Art. Marxist Quarterly. Vol.1, janeiro/março 1937. p. 78-97. HTTP://cepa.newschool.edu/~quigleyt/vcs/schapiro-naa.pdf

Scheid, John e Svenbro, Jesper. O ofício de Zeus. Mito da tecelagem e do tecido no mundo greco-romano. Editora CMC, Porto Alegre, 2010.

Schwarcz, Lilian Moritz. Introdução. Sobre semelhanças e diferenças. In História da vida privada no Brasil. Novais, Fernando A. e Schwarcz, Lilian Moritz (orgs). Companhia das Letras, São Paulo, 2006.

Schwartz, Roberto. Nacional por subtração In *Que horas são? Ensaios.* SP, Cia das Letras, 1987.

Segalen, Martine. Mari et Femme dans la Société Paysanne. Paris, Flamarion, 1980. "Couple, Menage, Communauté", pp. 4-85.

Seyferth, Giralda. Identidade étnica numa comunidade teuto-brasileira do vale do Itajaí. Revista do Museu Paulista, nova série, volume XXIV, 1977.

————. A imigração alemã para o Brasil: Uma revisão bibliográfica *in BIB*, Rio de Janeiro, n.25, PP 3-55, 1988.

————. A invenção da raça e o poder discricionário dos estereótipos *in Anuário Antropológico*, 1993.

————. Identidade, território e pertencimento In *Psicologia e práticas sociais*, v.2, n.1, 1995.

————. Construindo a Nação: Hierarquias Raciais e o Papel do Racismo na Política de Imigração e Colonização". In Maio, Marcos Chor e Santos, Ricardo Ventura (orgs.) *Raça, Ciência e Sociedade.* Rio de Janeiro, FIOCRUZ/CCBB, 1996.

————. Assimilação dos imigrantes como questão nacional In *Mana*, volume 3, número 1, abril de 1997.

————. "*A Imigração alemã no Rio de Janeiro.* In: Gomes, Angela de Castro (org.): *Histórias de Imigrantes e de Imigração no Rio de Janeiro.* 7Letras, 2000, pp. 11-43.

————. A singularidade germânica e o nacionalismo brasileiro: ambigüidade e alotropia na idéia de nação In Bastos, Cristiana; Almeida, Miguel Vale de; Feldman-Bianco, Bela. (coord.) *Trânsitos coloniais:diálogos críticos luso-brasileiros.* Imprensa de Ciências Sociais, Lisboa, 2002.

————. Nacionalismo e imigração no pensamento de Gilberto Freyre In Kosminsky, E.V., Lépime, C. e Peixoto, F.A. (orgs) *Gilberto Freyre em quatro tempos.* São Paulo, EdUNESP, EDUSC, 2003.

Shanin, Teodor "Peasantry as a Political Factor". In: Shanin, T. (ed.) Peasants and Peasant Societies. Middlesex, Penguin Books, 1971, pp. 238-263.

Shapiro, Roberta. Que é artificação? *In: Sociedade e estado* vol. 22, n. 1, p. 135-151, 2007.

Silva, Fernanda Pequeno da. Lygia Pape e Hélio Oiticica: Conversações e Fricções Poéticas. Tese de doutorado defendida no PPGARTES/UERJ, 2007.

Simioni, Ana Paula. Dias, Elaine e Eleutério, Maria de Lourdes. Mulheres artistas: as pioneiras (1880 a 1930). Catálogo de exposição, 13 de junho a 25 de outubro de 2015. Pinacoteca do Estado de São Paulo, São Paulo, 2015. ISBN 978-85-8256-057-0.

————. Bordado e transgressão: questões de gênero na arte de Rosana Paulino e Rosana Palazyan. Revista Proa, n 02, vol.01, 2010. http://www.ifch.unicamp.br/proa

————. Regina Gomide Graz: modernismo, arte têxtil e relações de gênero no Brasil. Revista do IEB, n 45 p. 87-106 set 2007.

Simmel, Georg. *As grandes cidades e a vida do espírito In Mana.* vol.11 no.2 Rio de Janeiro Oct. 2005

————. O estrangeiro. In RBSE, Vol. 4, n 12, dezembro de 2005, p. 265-271.

Smith, Terry. ¿Qué es el arte contemporáneo? Siglo veintiuno editores, Buenos Aires, 2012.

Sohn, Anne-Marie. Entre duas guerras. Os papeis femininos em França e Inglaterra In Duby, George e Perrot, Michelle (org). História das mulheres. O século XX. Ebradil, São Paulo, 1991.

Souza, Gilda Melo e. o espírito das roupas. A moda no século dezenove. Companhia das Letras, 1987 [1950].

Souza, Vitor Galdino Alves de. Criador, Autor, Proprietário. Das imagens que somos à partilha do imaginário. Tese de doutorado defendida no Programa de Pós–graduação em Filosofia da UFRJ. 2018.

Spiegelman, Art. Maus. A história de um sobrevivente. São Paulo, editora Brasiliense, 1995.

Stallybrass, Peter. O casaco de Marx: roupas, memória, dor. Tradução de Tomaz Tadeu. 3. ed. Belo Horizonte: Autêntica Editora, 2008.

Stewart, Susan. 1994. Objects of desire. In Interpreting Objects and Collections. London: Routledge.

———. On longing. Narratives on miniature, the gigantic, the souvenir, the collection. Duke Hill Press, Durhan e London, 1993.

Stocking Jr., George W. *Afterward: a view from the center*, Ethnos 47: 172-86, 1982.

———. George Stocking, Presentism and Historicism Once Again: The History of British Anthropology as Intellectual and Personal History, *Journal of Victorian Culture*, 4, 2, (328), (1999).

Strohmeyer, Klaus. Harmonia aparente e crise latente In Richard, Lionel. Berlim, 1919-1933. A encarnação extrema da modernidade. Jorge Zahar Editor, Rio de Janeiro, 1993.

Stumpf, Lúcia Kluck. O indígena nas pinturas de Antônio Parreiras: uma leitura republicana. Comunicação apresentada na 29ª Reunião brasileira de antropologia. Natal-RN. 03 a 06 de Agosto de 2014.

Swann, Marjorie. 2001. *Curiosities and Texts. The Culture of Collecting in the Early Modern England.* USA: University of Pennsylvania Press ("Introduction").

Thébaut, Françoise. A Grande Guerra. O triunfo da divisão sexual. In Duby, George e Perrot, Michelle (org). História das mulheres. O século XX. Ebradil, São Paulo, 1991.

Thomas, Nicholas. *Possessions: Indigenous Art/Colonial Culture.* Thames and Hudson, New York, 1999.

Tiburi, Márcia. Feminismos em comum para todas, todes e todos. Editora Rosa dos Tempos, Rio de Janeiro, 2018.

Trizoli, Talita. CRÍTICA DE ARTE E FEMINISMO NO BRASIL DOS ANOS 60 E 70. Anais do V Seminário Nacional de Pesquisa em Arte e Cultura Visual Goiânia, GO: UFG, FAV, 2012

Trotsky, Leon. A Revolução de 1905 (prefácio à edição russa). 12 de janeiro de 1922. https://www.marxists.org/portugues/index.htm. Acessado em 3 de fevereiro de 2015.

Varajão, Alice. NHÁ BENTA 60 ANOS. A Nhá Benta celebra seus 60 anos. http://alicevarajao.blogspot.com.br/2010/07/nha-benta-60-anos.html. Acessado em 30 de janeiro de 2015

Velho, Gilberto. Projeto, emoção e orientação em sociedades complexas. In Um antropólogo na cidade. Ensaios de antropologia urbana. Editora Zahar, Rio de Janeiro, 2013.

———. *Projeto e metamorfose: antropologia das sociedades complexas.* 3.ed. Rio de Janeiro: Jorge Zahar Ed., 2003.

———. A Utopia Urbana: um estudo de antropologia social. Rio de Janeiro: Zahar, 1989.

———. Individualismo e cultura. Notas para uma antropologia da sociedade contemporânea. Rio de Janeiro: Zahar, 1987.

Vianna, Hermano, Kuschnir, Karina e Castro, Celso. Apresentação In Velho, Gilberto. Um antropólogo na cidade. Ensaios de antropologia urbana. Zahar, Rio de Janeiro, 2013.

Vilhena, Luís Rodolfo. *Projeto e Missão. O movimento folclórico brasileiro 1947-1964.* Ed. Fundação Getúlio Vargas, Rio de Janeiro, 1997.

Villas Bôas, Glaucia. (1992), *A vocação das ciências sociais (1945-1964): um estudo da sua produção em livro.* Tese de doutorado, São Paulo, USP.

———. Estética de ruptura: o concretismo brasileiro. VIS Revista do Programa de Pós-graduação em Arte da UnB V.13 n 1/janeiro-junho de 2014 [2015] Brasília ISSN- 1518-5494

Walle, Marianne. As berlinenses e seus combates. In Richard, Lionel. Berlim, 1919-1933. A encarnação extrema da modernidade. Jorge Zahar Editor, Rio de Janeiro, 1993.

Weiner, Annette e Schneider, Jane (orgs). Cloth and human experience. Smithsonian Series in Ethnographic Enquiry, Smithsonian Books, Washington, 1989.

Weiner, Annette B. Inalienable Possessions. The paradox of keeping-while-giving. Univesity of California Press, USA, 1992.

Woolf, Virginia. O valor do riso e outros ensaios: Virginia Woolf. Cosac e Naify, São Paulo, 2014.

————. Orlando. Companhia das Letras, São Paulo, 2014a.

Zolberg, Vera e Cherbo, Joni Maya. Introduction. In Outsider art. Contesting boundaries in contemporary culture. Cambridge University Press, Lodon, 1997.

Zweig, Stephan. O mundo insone In O mundo insone e outros ensaios. Zahar, Rio de Janeiro, 2013.

2. Ethnographic Sources

Aquino, Flávio. "Olly, tecidos 74". Leitura Dinâmica In (não tem referência ao jornal de onde foi retirado o recorte), 1974. MROW-G 48

Bandman, Guenter. "A pintura alemã através do século" In Revista DN 19 e 20 de fevereiro de 1961.

Bento, Antonio. "Vestido-objeto de Olly". Última Hora. 20 de agosto de 1969. MROW-G 35

Berkowitz, Mark. Coluna Artes Plásticas. Jornal do Brasil. 1974a. MROW-G 10

————. Coluna Artes Plásticas. Jornal do Brasil. Sábado, 28 de dezembro de 1974.

————. Manuscrito sem título. Setembro de 1969. MA-75

————. Obituário Olly Reinheimer. Reinheimer, setembro de 1986. MI-18

Brändle, Gerhard. "Antisemitismus in Pforzheim: 1920 - 1980". 1980. MROW-Li 04

————. "Die Jüdischen Mitbürger der Stadt Pforzheim". 1985. (MROW-Li 03)

————. "Jüdische Gotteshäuser in Pforzheim". 1990. MROW-Li 02

————. Judeus contra a Swastika: Desde a luta defensiva para resistir. Mimeo, s/d. MROW-G 103

Campofiorito, Quirino. "Cursos de Arte no M.AM". O Jornal. Rio de Janeiro, 02 de setembro de 1969.

————. "Tecidos e vestidos de Olly". O Jornal, 14 de agosto de 1969a. MROW-G 37

Casa & Decoração. Rio de Janeiro, Editora Vecchi, Ano IX, n. 53, outubro de 1979. MROW-G-82

Casa & Decoração. Rio de Janeiro, Editora Vecchi, Ano X, n. 66, Novembro de 1980. MROW-G 83

Casa Vogue. Rio de Janeiro, Março de 1976. MROW-G 90

Colônia, Regina Célia. "Olly Reinheimer, exemplo de aquário: dois e dois são cinco". Jornal de Ipanema. Janeiro de 1972. MROW-G 08

Correio da Manhã. 23 de fevereiro de 1969.

Correio da Manhã. Moda em cores de sonho. Correio da Manhã, Rio de Janeiro, 9 de abril de 1967. MROW-G-91

Correio de São Paulo. Revolucionada a indústria do rádio. Fala ao "Correio de São Paulo" o engenheiro Werner Hasenberg, pioneiro da electro-acústica e chefe da secção industrial da Philips do Brasil. São Paulo, 16 de junho de 1937.

Costa, Maria Heloisa Fénelon. A arte e o artista na sociedade Carajá. Fundação Nacional do Índio, Brasília, 1978.

DN. "Mãos que criam sonhos para vaidade da mulher". Revista DN, 5 e 6 de fevereiro de 1961. MROW-G-01

DOU. Diário Oficial da União, n 17437, 18 de agosto de 1937.

————. Diário Oficial do Estado de São Paulo, n 289, Ano 48, 39 de dezembro de 1938 e DO-20, do *Acervo Olly e Werner Reinheimer*.

Folha da Manhã, 1952

Folha de São Paulo. "Roupas para vestir e pendurar na parede". Caderno Nova Mulher, em comemoração ao ano internacional da mulher. Folha de São Paulo. 25 de junho de 1975. (MROW-G 16)

FUNARTE. OS PAPÉIS do papel. Rio de Janeiro, 1984. MR-OLi 102

Furtado, Celso. Dialética do desenvolvimento. Rio de Janeiro: Fundo de Cultura, 1964.

Giobbi, Cesar. "As roupastapeçariasquadrosfantasias. Para o corpo ou a parede". Jornal da Tarde, 23 de junho de 1975. MROW-G 47

Gorovitz, Mona. Moda e Consumo de Massa In Mirante das Artes, Etc. Maio & Junho 1967, N 3. Maio e junho de 1967. MROW-G 86

Guerra, Antonio. Mãos que criam sonhos para vaidade da mulher. Revista DN, Salvador, 5 e 6 de fevereiro, 1961. MROW-G 01

Habitat, n.7, 1952

Hartmann, Günther. Litjoko: puppen der Karaja, Brasilien. Berlin: Museum für Volkerkunde, 1973.

Hasenberg, Erika. I bauli. Book Sprint Editzioni, Itália, 2012.

Häzemer Dorf und Kultusvereins. Habitzheimer Geschichte(n). Publicação da Häzemer Dorf und Kultusvereins, 2010.

Interior e Decoração. Sem autor. "Simplicidade e bom-gôsto fazem casa de artista". Interior e Decoração. Rio de Janeiro, 1966. (MROW-G-80)

Jornal Diário de São Paulo. "Moda agora é no museu". 13 de dezembro de 1966. MROW-G 25

Jornal do Brasil. Sem autor. "Arte carajá é motivo para nova moda". 1 caderno, Jornal do Brasil. 6 de setembro de 1969a. Capa da Revista de Domingo. MROW-G 06

————. Sem autor. "O Brasil que Olly faz amar". Jornal do Brasil. 08 de setembro de 1969b. MROW-G-38

————. Sem autor. "Tecidos de Olly no MAM-RJ " Jornal do Brasil. Rio de Janeiro, 10 e 11 de agosto de 1969. MROW-G 64-A

————. Sem autor. "Que bons inventos nos levem às Índias". 22 de setembro de 1968. MROW-G 18

Jornal do Brasil, "Oli, teatro com nova roupa". Jornal do Brasil, Rio de Janeiro, 17 e 18 de março de 1968. MROW-G-03

Juliano, Mucia. "A arte colorida de Olly". Casa & Decoração. Outubro de 1981. MROW-G 84

Leite, Dante Moreira. O caráter nacional brasileiro: história de uma ideologia. Livraria Pioneira Editora, São Paulo, 1969.

Lispector, Clarice. O morto no mar da Urca In Onde Estivestes de Noite. Editora arte nova, rio de janeiro, 1974. MROW-G 79

MA-78. Manuscrito avulso. S.d. Acervo Olly e Werner Reinheimer

MAM-RJ. 10ª exposição de pinturas de crianças alunos de Ivan Serpa. Homenagem a Niomar Muniz Sodré. Museu de Arte Moderna do Rio de Janeiro. 1961.

MAM-RJ. Catálogo da 10ª exposição de pinturas de crianças alunos de Ivan Serpa. Homenagem a Niomar Muniz Sodré. Museu de Arte Moderna do Rio de Janeiro. 1961.

Maurício, Jayme. "Criações de Olly na Petite". Itinerário das Artes Plásticas. Correio da Manhã. p.2, 2o caderno. 20 de dezembro de 1966. MROW-G 92

————. "Tecidos de Olly conquistaram Salvador". Correio da Manhã. Rio de Janeiro, 25 de fevereiro de 1961. MROW-G 28

————. "Tecidos de Olly no museu". Itinerário das Artes Plásticas. Correio da Manhã, Rio de Janeiro, 22 de maio de 1960. (MROW-G 24)

Melo Neto, João Cabral de. Antologia poética. Editora do autor. 1960. (MR-Oli 529)

Morais, Frederico. "Olly Reinheimer: morte da artista múltipla". O Globo. 19 de agosto de 1986.

————. Olly: da roupa-tato às miniaturas tecidas. O Globo, 9 de maio de 1975. (MROW-G-12, MI-08).

————. Mimeo "Olly: da roupa-tato às miniaturas tecidas". MI-08/MROW 12

Moura, Elisabete de. "Formas e cores um encontro bordado em fantasia. Coluna Cidade-cobertura In (não tem referência ao jornal de que foi recortado). 30 de abril de 1975. MROW-G 17

MROW-G 61. Não tem capa e nem referência ao local da exposição, 1961.

MROW-G 58. Êxito em Lima. Nota de jornal não identificado. 1962.

O Dia. Sem autor. "Os vestidos-objetos de Olly". Caderno feminino. O Dia. Rio de Janeiro, 17 e 18 de agosto de 1969. p. 2. MROW-G 05

O Globo. Sem autor. "Olly no MAM-RJ ". O Globo. 9 de agosto de 1969.

O Globo. Sem autor. "Olly no MAM-RJ ". O Globo. 9 de agosto de 1969a. MROW-G 64-B

Olly. Manuscrito sem data (provavelmente 1985/6), MA-33.

Ostrower, Heinz. Carta encaminhada para Werner por Heinz Ostrower. 03 de outubro de 1990. CO-62

Pontual, Roberto. Dicionário das artes plásticas no Brasil. Editora Civilização, Rio de Janeiro. 1969. MROW-Li 08

Reinheimer, Werner. Carta de Werner para Patricia Reinheimer. 1o de março de 1992. CO-207

———. Carta de Werner para Betty White e Stephen Strauss. 18 de janeiro de 1988. CO-99

———. "Fidelidade", 1990 (?). MI-11

———. Geschichten und Anekdoten aus Brasilien. 1935 ging Werner Reinheimer in das Land der Samba-Rhythmen Pforzheimer Zeitung, 24 de dezembro de 1983. MI-14/ MROW-G 67

Rodriguez, Carlos. "Tejidos y tapices de Olly". Exprime, 25 de novembro de 1962. MROW-G-72

Valladares, Clarival do Prado. "Pintura ternura". Correio da Manhã. Rio de Janeiro, 26 de fevereiro de 1961. MROW-G 29

White, Betty. Correspondência por e-mail com Patricia Reinheimer, 27 de dezembro de 2006. CO-102-B

———. Carta de Werner para Betty e Steve. 18 de janeiro de 1988. CO-99

3. Testimonials/Interviews/Conversations

1. Abigail Pereira Nunes, 2014, 2015
2. Alaide Pereira Nunes, 1998
3. Aline e Sérgio Campos Melo, 1998, 2015
4. Anna Bella Geiger, 2015
5. Anna Letycia Quadros, 1998
6. Betty White e Stephen Strauss, 2015
7. Clementina Duarte, 2015
8. Hilda de Azevedo Soares, 2013
9. Duda Cavalcanti, 2014
10. Edith Weitzfelder, 1998
11. Erika Hasenberg, 1998, 1999, 2015
12. Fayga Ostrower, 1998
13. Franco Terranova, 1998
14. Franz Krajcberg, 1999
15. Frederico Morais, 1998, 2015
16. Geneviève Boghici, 2015
17. Geny Marcondes, 1998
18. Gerhardt Brändle, 2015
19. Heinz Pflug, 2015
20. Hetty Goldberg, 2015

21. Hilda Soares, 2014
22. Ira e Heinz S., 2015
23. Ivone Vieira Reinheimer, 1998, 2014, 2015
24. Jonas Bergamini, 2018
25. Liane Monteiro, 2014
26. Lídice Meireles, 2015
27. Lourdes e Rui Mello, 1998
28. Márcia Barroso do Amaral, 2015
29. Márcia Rodrigues, 2014
30. Maria Inês de Almeida, 1998
31. Maria Luiza Leão, 1998
32. Marília Rodrigues, 1998
33. Mela Pflug, 1998, 2015
34. Miriam Mamber, 1999
35. Nedra Westwater, 2015
36. Noemi e Carlos Acselrad, 2015
37. Noni Ostrower, 2018
38. Paola Terranova, 1998, 2017, 2018
39. René Renato Reinheimer, 1998, 2014, 2015
40. Roberto Padilha, 2014
41. Rudolf e Josefina Rothgieser, 1998
42. Sonia Guistino, 2013

4. Archive References

The project of which this text is a result has as one of its objectives, the organization of *Olly and Werner Reinheimer's Archive* of documents for later donation to an institution of cultural guarding and dissemination. Therefore, to clarify the documents from which the information was withdrawn is part of the proposal of disclosure and availability of this material for consultation and research.

The acronyms that refer to the Reference System of *Olly and Werner Reinheimer's Archive* are indicated in the ethnographic sources.

Reference system on *Olly and Werner Reinheimer's Archive*
CO - Correspondence
MI - Mimeo
MA - Manuscript
DFC - Financial and accounting documents
DE - Documents relating to education
DM - Health documents
DEV - Events and invitation documents
DO - Official documents
DCP - Personal Contact Documents

RE - Documents concerning culinary recipes
VIA - Travel Documents
IN - Manuscripts Concerning Purchases, Sales and Exchanges of Artistic Objects
PH - Photographs in paper
DIA - Slides
PAE - Artistic production, exhibitions
PAF - Tool folders
PAT - Folders referring to techniques
PACE - Documents for specific courses and studies
PACA - Folders on Artistic Creation
PAO - Artistic production, others
UNI - UNICEF cards or documents referring to them
PACT - Artistic production, ceramics, fabrics and textiles
CRB - Stamps
MROW-G - Reference material Olly and Werner, general
MR-OLi - Reference material, books, others
AUD - Transcript of Audio Interviews
TD - Fabric

Olly's Professional ChronologyArticles in books and periodicals
Courses taught
Courses taken
Individual or collective exhibitions and shows
Other miscellaneous

Year	Document	Activity/Bibliography	Observations
1952	DO-12	Olly already had a MAM membership #317	Olly appears in two photos of the Fridl Loos exhibition that year. Photo collection of MAM-Rio
1953	MROW-Li 08	II Salão de Arte Moderna do Rio de Janeiro II Modern Art Salon of Rio de Janeiro	
1954	MROW-Li 08	III Salão de Arte Moderna do Rio de Janeiro III Modern Art Salon of Rio de Janeiro	Ceramic acquisition award No DE-04-D mistakenly says it was in 1959
1955	DFC-04; DFC-11; MA-63	Olga had a ceramic workshop at # 248 Nascimento Silva Street. Authorization document for the transfer of the private and educational artistic ceramics workshop to this new address. This was the garage address of Geny Marcondes' house, where Geny also taught musical initiation classes	The transfer may refer to the atelier being first in her home
1956	DFC-04	She still had her ceramic workshop at # 248 Nascimento Silva Street	
1957	MA-25	Started painting fabrics	
1958	PAE-04; PAE-09; DE-04	(May 21st-June 4th) Exhibition and Prize at Norman Westwater Gallery of Contemporary Art	At Mobília Contemporânea
1959	DE-04	3 individual ceramic exhibitions, RJ	
	DE-04	Honorable mention for applied fine arts Punta del Este International Biennial	

	PAE-09; MROW-Li 08	Galeria Ambiente in São Paulo	
	MROW-G 19	Assembly of the play Tartufo, by Molière, directed by Sérgio Cardoso and represented by Cia Nydia Licia and Sérgio Cardoso, at Teatro Bela Vista, between 1959 and 1960	The play did not take place due to the separation of the director and the actress, but Olly did the costumes for the prologue characters
1960	PAE-09; PAE-04-B	MoMA-Rio de Janeiro	
	DO-14-C		Olga and Werner went to Germany this year to receive the definitive documentation of naturalization
1961	PAE-09	MoMA-Bahia opening of the exhibition Olly Fabrics, January 30th, Salvador	
	PAE-09; MROW-Li 08	II Annual Salon of Curitiba, in MoMA Curitiba	
	PAE-09; DEV-03	MoMA Belo Horizonte Exhibition of Artistic Crafts, Belo Horizonte	
Suponho 1961	MA-25	Bumba-meu-boi Exhibition	
1962	PAE-09	Exhibition of tapestries and fabrics at the Government Palace in Brasilia	
	DO-07; DO-08; PAE-09; PAE-13	Contemporary Art Gallery of Lima (at the Institute of Contemporary Art, sponsored by the Ministry of Foreign Affairs), Peru	(already had a telephone at this time DO-08 n° 54-665)
	PAE-09	Invited by Jack Lenor Larsen, of the Smithsonian Institute, as the only Brazilian representative to participate in an international textile exhibition that toured several museums in the USA	
	MROW-G 22	Assembly of the play Cinderela Tablado School of Theater, Olly's collaboration 1962	

1963	PAE-09; PAE-13-B; PAE-13-C	The Art Center, Lima, Peru	
	PAE-09	She taught fabric painting at the invitation of the National School of Fine Arts of Peru in Lima	
	DO-38; DO-18		Werner was naturalized Brazilian in February, Olly in March
1965	PAE-06, MA-18	In the First International Biennial of Applied Arts in Uruguay she won honorable mention for a drawing for fabric she called "evolution" which is a bean sprout coming out of the ground after forming two leaves. They look like two leaves coming out of the sun ", in the words of the artist MA-18, p28)	The drawing might be PACA-62
	CO-108	She was invited to exhibit at the National Institute of Fine Arts in Mexico	She traveled to Mexico this year and exhibited in Uruguay, but there is no mention anywhere she has exhibited in Mexico
	MA-50	Took a trip to Mexico City, Paris, London, Amsterdam, Milan, New York, Madrid, Lausanne	Olly lists people and places to visit
1966	PAE-09, MROW-G 92	Film and theater work, unspecified During the research, an Olly dress was found in the collection of L. C. Barreto. This producer released this year the film Father and the Girl (1966). Olly was very close to Ilo Krugli, but I found no references to what she might have done with him. It is possible (and even likely) that she contributed to his plays. The Franco-Brazilian production Arrastão, in which Duda Cavalcanti acted, showed 3 clothes produced by Olly	Document MI-03 is the Argument for a documentary by Elyseu Visconti Cavalleiro called Caboclinhos de Tapirapé, to be filmed in Recife in 1978

	MROW-G-25, MROW-G-26, MROW-G-7	Show organized at the Pinacoteca of the São Paulo Museum of Art, MASP, with 40 of Olly's clothes, all with motifs inspired by pre-Columbian ceramics and drawings	MASP was directed by Pietro Maria Bardi, who also edited the magazine Mirante das Artes etc.
	MROW-G 92, PAE-09	Exhibits in the Petite Galerie (in Olly's curriculum is dated 1967)	Owned by Franco Terranova
	MROW-G 33	Copy of newspaper clipping on Olly the wardrobe of the film Arrastão, with photo of Duda Cavalcanti	
	DO-35		Mina Reinheimer died
1967	PAE-09, MROW-G 86	Mention of Olly in the Magazine Mirante das Artes: "Fashion and Mass Consumption" Author: Mona Gorovitz In Mirante das artes etc. May and June 1967, p [41]	Edited by Pietro Maria Bardi, director of MASP
	PAE-09	Petite Galerie	Maybe 1966
	MROW-G 91	Mentions a show in the Teatro de Arena, but the date is not clear	
	MROW-G 91	Article about Olly in a newspaper: "A moda em cores de sonho" Correio da Manhã April, 9th 1967 p 6, 6o caderno, Caderno Feminino (feminine insert)	
		Donated works for an auction at Casa das Palmeiras, by Nise da Silveira	
	PAE-09	Towels made for the reception of the royal prince of Japan, commissioned by the Ministry of Foreign Affairs	
	PAE-09	Museum of Art of São Paulo MASP	
	MROW-G 03	Clothes for the play " Meia volta volver "by Oduvaldo Viana Filho, at theTeatro de bolso (Pocket Theater)	
	DE-04	MoMA-RJ	
1968	PAE-09; PAE-07	Gallery of the Copacabana Palace Hotel: along with: Márcio Mattar, Cleber Machado, Pedro Correia de Araújo and José Barbosa	
	MROW-G 04	Launches wood combs in various shapes. Jornal do Brasil, May 16th, 1968	

	MROW-G 18	Article "Que bons inventos nos levem às Índias". Revista de domingo, do Jornal do Brasil, September 22nd 1968	
	PAE-09	Gávea Golf Club International Song Festival	
	MROW-G 03	Costumes for the play Stanislaw Ponte Preta and the angry sex, by Max Frisch, with Neila Tavares and Adriana Prieto, directed by Wagner Melo	
	MROW-G 03	Clothing made for the musical spectacle by the Roberto de Regina's choir	
	PAE-09; DE-04-C	Shows in Rio de Janeiro	
1969	DE-04-D; MROW-Li-08	"Dictionary of Plastic Arts in Brazil "Author: Roberto Pontual	With dedication for the artist
	PAE-09	MoMA-RJ	
	PAE-09	Traveling exhibition Sweden, Finland, Denmark, the Netherlands and Germany sponsored by the Ministry of Foreign Affairs	
	MROW-G 30	Newspaper article about Olly "Olly no Museu: happening da nova moda" (Olly in the Museum: happening of the new fashion) Author: Edmundo Bittencourt, Paulo Bittencourt, Correio da Manhã	
	MROW-G 31	Column on Olly in the A Notícia newspaper. Author: Geni Marcondes	
	MROW-G 06	Article on Olly "Arte carajá é motivo para nova moda" (Carajá art is motive for new fashion) 1º caderno, Jornal do Brasil, September 6, 1969	
	MROW-G 34	Copy of newspaper clipping on Olly "Tecidos e vestidos de Olly" (Tissues and dresses of Olly) Author: Quirino Campofiorito. O Jornal, August 14, 1969	
	MROW-G 35	Copy of newspaper clipping on Olly Cópia de recorte de jornal sobre Olly "Vestido-objeto de Olly" (Dress-object by Olly) Autor: Antônio Bento, Última Hora, Augst 20th 1969	
	MROW-G 36	Olly newspaper clipping copy "Arte religiosa" (Religious art) Author: Frederico Morais, Diário de Notícias, August 27, 1969	

	MROW-G 37	Copy of newspaper clipping on Olly "Cursos de Arte no MAM" (Art Courses at MoMA). Author: Quirino Campofiorito, O Journal, September 2, 1969	
	MROW-G 38	Copy of newspaper clipping on Olly "O Brasil que Olly faz amar" (Brazil that Olly makes us love) September 8, 1969	
	MROW-G 39	Copy of newspaper clipping on Olly (image and comment)	
	MROW-G 60	Digital copy of newspaper article about Olly "Olly hoje no museu" (Olly today at the Museum) Author: Jayme Mauricio, Correio da Manhã, August 6th, 1969	
	MROW-G 64-A	Copy of newspaper article on Olly "Tecidos de Olly no MAM" (Olly's Fabrics in MoMA), Jornal do Brasil, August 10th and 11th, 1969.	
	MROW-G 64-B	Copy of newspaper article about Olly "Olly no MAM" (Olly at MoMA), O Globo, August 9th, 1969.	
	MROW-G 64-C	Excerpt with continuation of note in the Jornal do Brasil page, August 7th, 1969	
	MROW-G 70	"Fatos sôbre a relação URSS e a Romênia" (Facts about the USSR and Romania relations) Correio da Manhã newspaper, February 23rd, 1969	
	MR-OG 05	Women's Notebook of the O Dia Newspaper, August 17th and 18th, 1969	
	MROW-G 05	Article on Olly "Os vestidos-objetos de Olly" (Olly's objects-dresses), Caderno Feninino (female insert) on the O Dia Newspaper, August 17th and 18th 1969, p 2;	
	MROW-G 32	Copy of newspaper clipping on Olly "Vestido-objeto, objeto exportável" (Dress-object, exportable object), Jornal do Brasil, August 13th, 1969.	
	MROW-Li 08	"Dictionary of plastic arts in Brazil" Author: Roberto Pontual with dedication of the author to Olly, 1969	
	MR-OG 05	Caderno Feminino (Womens insert) of the O Dia newspaper, August 17th and 18th, 1969	Article in periodical
1970	PAE-09-A	Americas Maganize Nov-Dec	

	DEV-18;	Raised funds for earthquake victims in Peru	
	MROW-G 94	Note by Mr Walmir Ayala on the indication of the quality of the previous year's Olly exhibition	
1971	DFC-03; DFC-07	Studio on #261 Visconde de Pirajá Street, co01	
	DE-04-C	Show at the art galerie in the Copacabana Palace Hotel	
	DE-04-F; PAE-09-A; PAE-15	From that year on, she collaborated with architects and decorators. She did several works for the Hotel Porto do Sol in Guarapari, ES, City Bank of Rio and Bahia, Shell in the new Rio building, among others	
1971		Cruzeiro national and international June 30th	
1973	PAE-09	O rosto e a obra, Grupo B Galerie, Rio de Janeiro	
1973	DE 02	Member of the jury of the parades of group 1 of the samba schools of the carioca carnival	
1974	PAE-09-C	May, Brasília, Olly: Três anos de pesquisa: formas e cores em tecelagem (Olly: Three years of research: shapes and colors in weaving)	
1974	PAE-09-A; PAE-09-B; VIA-22	Novembre, Lume Galerie, São Paulo, Olly: Três anos de pesquisa: formas e cores em tecelagem. Visited the Caruaru Fair, Northeast of Brazil.	
1974	PAE-09-A	Veja	
1974	PAE-09-A	Manchete	
1974	PAE-09-A	Fatos & Fotos Flavio de Aquino	
1974	PAE-09-A	Visão	
1974	PAE-09-A	Jornal do Brasil: Summary of the Year, One of the Best Exhibitions, by Frederico de Moraes e Marc Berkowitz	
1975	DE-04-A; PAE-08	June, Opus Galerie, São Paulo, Olly: Formas e cores em tecelagem Vestidos e objetos (Olly: Shapes and colors in weaving. Dresses and objects)	PAE-01-C this or the other three of 1975
1975	PAE-12	Recife: Uma exposição de Olly e Clementina (An exhibition of Olly and Clementina)	Clementina Duarte, jewelry designer PAE-01-C from this one or the other three in 1975

1975	DE-04; PAE-09-C	Exhibition Cultural Foundation of Brasília	PAE-01-C it can be from this one or the other three from 1975
1975	DEV-02	Biennale Internationale d'art de Menton	PAE-01-C it can be from this one or the other three from 1975
1976	IN-30	She made decorations for the Hotel Porto do Sol, in Guarapari	
1978	PAO-07; UNI-01; UNI-02; UNI-03	Her grandchildren's drawings and hers were transformed into UNICEF Christmas card.	
1980	PAE-14	She launches at the Galeria Gravura Brasileira, at the Casino Atlântico, the book "A portion of sugar, two of love", by the publisher Antares, with texts by Henda da Rocha Freire and Olly's illustrations	
1980	MROW-G 93	Participates in the 1st Exhibition of Brazilian Mini-Textiles, in the Sala Cecília Meireles, June 2nd to 30th	
1981	DE-04-F; PAE-01; PAE-11-B	Galeria Centro Cultural Cândido Mendes Cores, formas, texturas (Colors, shapes, textures)	
1982	DFC-05	Member of the Brazilian Association of Professional Plastic Artists	
1982	PAE-11-A	October 23rd, opening of the Exhibition in the show room of the Forma Store, São Paulo	
1983	PAF-15; DO-19	She travels to Madrid, Holland, France, Germany, Italy. Takes her granddaughter Patricia who meets her cousins and aunt in Rome and Forte dei Marmi	
	PAE-11-E	Exhibition in Forma, Ipanema	I'm not sure of the date
1984	DO-19	Travel to Greece (First AVC)	
1984	PAO-08	She was producing handmade paper	
1984	DEV-05	Event O papel dos papéis (the role of papers)	

1985	PAE-05	November exhibition at Galeria Candido Mendes, with the donation of one of the works exposed to the gallery	Could not have happened. The contract was signed a year before. The artist may have suffered the second stroke between signing the contract and the date marked
1985	CO 21-A, B e C	Documents on the loan of works from Olly's collection to participate in the exhibition 'Neoconcretismo/1959-1961', 'Grupo Frente' and 'I National Exhibition of Abstract Art' at the BANERJ Art Gallery curated by Frederico Morais	'Aleluia', by Décio Vieira was loaned
1985	CO-111	"The engraving workshop at MoMA 1959/1984"	there is no confirmation of participation
1986	CO-109; CO-112	IV Michoacan Internacional del Textil em miniatura (IV Michoacan of International Miniature Textile) Argentina/Brazil/Mexico, material presented at the Casa de Cultura Michoacan and the Museo Carillo Gil, held in Mexico City in May 1986	
1986	DO016		Olga died on August 14
1986	MROW-Li-09	"6 Times of War: Hotel Internacional: Pensão Mauá" Exhibition Catalog Frederico Morais	Did not participate in the exhibition, but is quoted in the text
1990	MROW-Li-07	"Petite Galerie: a vision of Brazilian art: 1954-1988" Commemorative catalog	Did not participate in the exhibition,, but appears in a catalog photo
1992	DO-17		Werner died on October 23, 1992

1999	DEV-11; DEV-12	Cotidiano/Arte: O Consumo (Daily life/Art: The Consumption), Itaú Cultural, São Paulo, curatorship Adélia Borges	
No date			
	DE-04-B; DEV-10	Invited to the Franco-Brazilian party "Nuit de Parfum" in São Paulo with the participation of Pierre Cardin, where they were presented, and he acquired three pictures of the artist	
	DE-04-B	She taught a modeling course at the School of Art of Brazil	
	DE-04-B, MA-63	She taught a modeling course at the Instituto Pestalozzi	
	DE-04-B	She taught a modeling course at the Colégio de Crianças com Deficiências Auditivas (School of Children with Hearing Impairment)	
	DE-04-B	Request of ninety pieces from the President of the Council of the Institute of Cacao, for the Cocoa Festival in Itabuna Bahia	

Year	Document	Professor	Subject	Observations
1950?	MA-33 ou MA-18	Margareth Spencer	Ceramics	
1971?	PACE-04	Renina Katz	Color and shape	
1974	CO-97	ArtCenter	Photography	Photosessions? it may have been photo shoots, but it seems less likely because there are notes about photographs, as if they were classroom annotations
	PACE-06	Fayga Osgtrower	Composition	
	PACE-12-G	Milton Ribeiro	History and theory on graphic arts	
	PACE-18	Kazuko Abe	Dye-paint on fabric and wax basis	
		René Leblanc	Drawing	No proofing document
		Ivan Serpa	Painting	No proofing document
		Milton Golbring	Painting	No proofing document
		Zélia Salgado	Painting	No proofing document
		Santa Rosa	Painting	No proofing document
		Frank Schaefer	Painting	No proofing document
	MA-67	Hilda Schulenberg	Painting	
		Roberto Delamonica	Engraving	No proofing document
	PACE-03	Johnny Friedlander	Engraving